Coins and Archaeology

Coins and Archaeology

Lloyd R. Laing

SCHOCKEN BOOKS · NEW YORK

© 1969 by Lloyd R. Laing

Published in U.S.A. in 1970
by Schocken Books Inc.
67 Park Avenue, New York, N.Y. 10016

Library of Congress Catalog Card No. 75–97253

Printed in Great Britain

G.F.L.

Patri in Piam Memoriam Filius

Contents

List of Plates

Between pages 176 and 177

A*

Acknowledgements for Illustrations

The author would like to thank the following individuals and bodies for permission to reproduce illustrations in this book: The National Museum of Antiquities of Scotland for Plates 3, 4, 15, 16a, 16b, 25, 26 and 27; The Verulamium Excavation Committee and Verulamium Museum for Plates 1, 2a and 2b; The National Museum of Wales for Plate 14; Colchester and Essex Museum for Plate 13; The Guildhall Museum, London, for Plates 20 and 21, 22, 23; Professor W. F. Grimes and the Roman and Mediaeval London Research Committee for Plates 20 and 21; The Dorset Natural History and Archaeological Society for Plate 24; Le Cabinet des Médailles, Bibliothèque Nationale, Paris, for Plate 8e and g, Plates 9, 12a and b; The Glasgow University Court and the Hunterian Museum for Plate 5b, g–k, m; Plate 6d, e–k; Plate 8a–d, f, h–k; Plate 28a–b, d, k; Sir Mortimer Wheeler and the Honourable Society of Cymmrodorion for Figure 11; Professor Yigael Yadin, the Masada Archaeological Expedition for Plate 7. He would also like to thank the British Museum, Department of Coins and Medals, Scunthorpe Museum and the Dragonby Excavation Committee for supplying him with casts from which photographs were taken for Plates 10, 11, 18 and 19. Finally, he would like to thank Dr Anne S. Robertson of the Hunterian Museum for her help in obtaining photographs of coins in the Hunter Cabinet.

List of Figures

List of Maps

Introduction

The archaeologist's main source material is surviving material culture. Coins are one of the many different classes of surviving material culture, and accordingly it is not surprising to find that the techniques employed by the numismatist in working out a typological and chronological sequence for a particular issue of coins are broadly similar to those used by the archaeologist in making a similar typology of, let us say, bronze swords. In this sense numismatics may be said to be a branch of archaeology, though unlike the study of other groups of material culture such as pottery or bronze artefacts it is frequently studied independently of the other classes. Because numismatics is of sufficient complexity for it to be a subject in its own right it has undergone an unnatural divorce from its parent study. Coins have for so long been a study on their own that numismatists frequently fail to realize the importance of their work from the archaeologist's viewpoint, and similarly the archaeologist tends to regard the numismatist as a specialist in another field who can help him with his work.

This book has been written for the archaeologist, either professional or amateur, who wishes to learn more about the nature of numismatics and its application in archaeology. To some extent too it has been written for the numismatist who is unfamiliar with the work of the archaeologist, and who understands only imperfectly how he can help his colleagues in this field.

The first part is intended as an introduction to the aims, methods and principles of numismatics. The second part is a survey of their application in different fields of archaeology. In this part I have concentrated my attention mainly on Britain because in a work of this kind it is impossible to deal with Europe as a whole without the text degenerating into a series of unconnected anecdotes. An exception has been made in Chapters Six and Seven, where the field is broadened as an understanding of the British story is difficult without a fuller appreciation of the European background.

Acknowledgement for the illustrations is made elsewhere, but I should like here to record my debt to several people who gave help and encouragement and who have read parts or all of the manuscript in draft. Firstly I owe a special debt to Professor A. C. Thomas of Leicester University, who suggested that I should write this book and who read through the whole typescript. Dr Michael Grant also read the manuscript and offered valuable suggestions. Mr D. F. Allen very kindly read the draft of Chapters Six and Seven, and Dr Anne S. Robertson has offered advice on several points, in particular in connection with aspects of Roman coinage. My friend Mr Richard Reece of St George's School, Harpenden, read considerable portions of the book and is particularly to be thanked for his assistance with Chapter Five. Miss Mary Dyk discussed with me methods of cleaning and conserving coins, and Mr T. Borthwick of the Ministry of Public Building and Works in Edinburgh helped me by drawing many maps, for which I owe thanks. Finally I should like to mention Mr Timothy Clough of Norwich Castle Museum, who read the proofs and who has stimulated me with some ideas.

All views and errors are, of course, my own. In a work of this nature which covers such a wide ground it is inevitable that some sections will seem to the specialist to be superficial where I have not made a particular study of the subject. I might add that it is not intended to be a work for the specialist.

The text was written during the period August 1966 – December 1967, and except in a few instances does not take into consideration anything published subsequently.

Finally, I should like to record that the book was written on account of the pleasure that numismatics has given me in the last twelve years, and if I have been able to impart to my readers even a little of that pleasure I shall feel amply rewarded.

Edinburgh, The Feast of St Nicholas, 1967.   L.R.L.

Part 1

I Techniques of Coin Production

Coins were first struck by machinery in the Renaissance, following the invention of the first coining press by Bramante. Until that time, and indeed even afterwards in many parts of Europe, coins were produced entirely by hand.

To understand how the earliest coins were struck one must remember the origins of coinage itself. Coins were not the invention of one man, but rather a natural development from a type of money-barter in which precious metal was used as a universal unit of reckoning in trade transactions, the metal being weighed out to 'pay' for the commodity or commodities being purchased. Later, in order to avoid weighing the metal each time, small pieces of metal were used, each one stamped with the seal of the merchant to guarantee that it was of the weight specified. The process of coining, in early times, was very closely related to sealing, and indeed, as Sir George Macdonald so brilliantly demonstrated early this century, coin types at first were personal badges. The earliest coins were made quite simply by taking a lump of metal of the correct weight, laying it on an anvil with some projections to grip the metal, and stamping it with a punch, just as one would use a seal. This method is known as punch striking. A later development known as anvil striking entailed setting an engraved die in an anvil and striking a metal blank on it with a punch (Plate 5a).

Manufacture of Flans

The first operation, in coin production, is the preparation of the flan or blank piece of metal from which the coin is struck.

In the case of certain cities in Magna Graecia and Sicily, and also at some periods in Macedon, Athens, Corinth and Acarnania, we find that the flans were cast in the form of balls, in a two-piece mould. This resulted in a thin projection remaining round the flan where the metal had flowed into the crack where the two halves of the mould had joined. When coins were struck on such flans this line was generally inclined or was even vertical, in order to avoid having a thin, irregular line round the edge of the coin after it was struck. The result of this was that the coin had two projections opposite one another on the flan. This is shown in figure 1, and the effect can be seen in the coin illustrated (Plate 5d.).

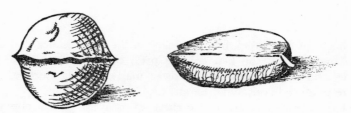

Fig. 1 Effect of striking a globular flan from a bivalve mould

Blanks themselves have survived from antiquity in a number of cases. They include a silver flan for a sixth century coin from Magna Graecia found in a hoard from Tarentum, a group of flans for bronze coins from Smyrna, and a number of flans for Celtic coins from Britain and Gaul. The British finds include examples from the Snettisham Hoard (Norfolk), from Colchester, Bagendon and Hengistbury Head.

The Greek flans suggest that they were generally cast in much the same size and shape as the coins that were struck from them, but slightly thicker to allow for 'spread' in striking. Very often they seem to have been cast in an open mould, with runners connecting the individual flans, which were then broken to separate them. This method was particularly common in the east Mediterranean in the late second and first centuries BC, and in the case of very small coins, such as the bronze lepta of the Hasmonaean Dynasty in Palestine, little care was taken to remove the runners. The moulds used for making the flans of these and the later Jewish bronze coins were slightly tapered towards the bottom, to facilitate the removal of the flans from the mould, with the result that the coins, when struck, have one broad flat face and another of lesser diameter, slightly curved at the edges. This bevelled edge is not the same as the bevel that appears on some large silver coins of the second century BC, notably the 'spread' tetradrachms of Ionia and Aeolis, which seem to be the result of hammering the edge of the flan before striking – possibly because the flans were coins of an earlier date (restruck) (Plate 5i.). Hammered edges also occur in a few rare cases in Greek coinage in order to make an irregular edge more even. It is mainly an East Greek phenomenon. Of the blanks from Smyrna, one was plano-convex, while another was cast in a cylindrical mould. The others were just dumps.

In Britain in the Iron Age blanks were made in clay moulds, and the nature and use of these is discussed in the appropriate section (see p. 183). The same method was employed in the continental Iron Age. Some of the coin flans from Bagendon seem to have been made by pouring out globules of metal on to a flat surface, without the use of any kind of mould. This is how the flans for early Greek coins may have been made. Roman coins in the third century AD in Gaul were made from flans cast in moulds, and they were probably of a similar type to those in use in the Iron Age.

Very occasionally flans seem to have been made by pouring molten silver into cold water. This was the case for some very small coins struck on the continent in the thirteenth century. The silver was probably poured through a sieve.

A few blanks were made by cutting pieces off a rod of metal. This is true of Romano-British minims from sites like Lydney (Gloucestershire), where in the casting of a rod 'piping' occurred which resulted in the flans having a hole in them, usually in the centre. Normally, when piping results from a casting it is in the upper part and is discarded, but due to the carelessness and economy of the Lydney moneyers the whole bar was used. The flans were cut off with a cold chisel. This technique was also used in Greece for small coins, and blanks made in this way have been found at Eretria. No less than forty-three blanks of this sort were also found in the remains of the mint at the Tauric Chersonese. These were for bronze coins. Apparently the rods were partly cut through, then the pieces snapped off. No doubt these flans were hammered flat before striking.

In the Middle Ages when the coins were very thin the flans were cut from hammered out sheets of metal, with shears. They were usually trimmed down to a circular shape, but sometimes they were left square since they were easier to cut that way and rounded by turning down the corners or by hammering out the straight sides to make them curved.

Cutting was also employed, though rarely, in Classical times. Indo-Greek coins which were rectangular, and early Indian 'punchmarked' coins which were polygonal, were undoubtedly cut from sheets of metal. Some coins of Chios and Cyprus have been struck on very irregular flans, and these were probably cut from sheet metal, as were the 'Siege Pieces' of Newark and elsewhere in England which were cut from ordinary silver plate at the time of the Civil War and which in a few cases still show the hallmark of the dish from which they were cut.

Frequently blanks were made out of old coins, hammered out and restruck. This was particularly common in Byzantine times, and Constans II (641–68) used coins which were restruck not only once but as often as three times. The shekels of the Second Jewish Revolt were made out of Syrian tetradrachms, while the smaller silver denomination was struck on Roman denarii.

In a few cases in the Roman Empire blanks were made out of flans with a central core of one metal and a rim of another. As this was used for medallions and sestertii only, it was presumably an aesthetic device. The 'tin' coinages of late seventeenth century England also had a metal plug, in this case to increase the value of the coin.

Dies

No fewer than thirty-eight Greek and Roman bronze dies have survived, together with eight iron. A considerable number of Medieval dies has also been preserved.

One die was found in Britain in 1930 at St Albans (Plates 2a; 2b.). This dates from the second half of the second century, and is made of 15 per cent tin bronze. It is a reverse die for a coin of Hadrian, with the legend ADVENTVS AVG and a type showing the emperor being greeted by Roma. A die of similar type has been found for striking Helvetian coins in Iron Age Switzerland.

A number of very early dies has been found in Egypt, including one of bronze for an Athenian tetradrachm of 430–322 BC. It is shaped like a pyramid with a rounded top, beneath which the four sides slope inwards with an offset just above the base to form a platform. As in the case of the St Albans die this is bevelled (Fig. 2).

Also from Egypt came another two Athenian dies, now lost, which were found in Sais in 1910, and two very curious lead dies, again for Athenian tetradrachms. These could not have been used for striking coins as they are too soft, and it has been suggested that they were made to bury with a dead moneyer, since strict laws forbade the original dies being buried in this way.

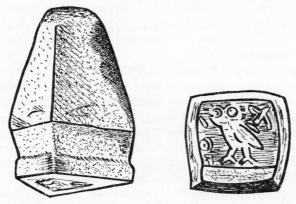

Fig. 2 Die from Egypt for striking Athenian tetradrachms, fifth century BC

A reverse die of Philip of Macedon also exists, in iron, consisting of a round bar tapering from the top, while a reverse die for Queen Berenice II of Egypt is simply a bronze cylinder with a projection on one side. This may have been for a hinge.

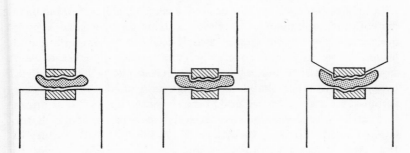

Fig. 3 Types of reverse dies

There are many dies for Celtic Gaulish coins, including one unusual one from Avenches, of bronze set in a cylindrical iron block. This is an obverse die, and the iron 'anvil' was to take the strain. Bronze obverse dies of Roman date exist, including one of Augustus, from a Roman camp at Moesia, which is also set in an iron block. Iron, or rather steel, dies of Tiberius, Caligula, Claudius and Constantius Chlorus are also known. There are many such dies from Gaul, and many were probably used by forgers. A coin of Caligula seems to have been struck with a cast-iron die. It is difficult to imagine how a cast die could give a good striking as the casting would blur the sharpness of the detail, but possibly details were engraved on the die afterwards. Iron dies seem to have been used in the later Roman Empire.

Dies were engraved, using punches and scorpers, rather than drilled with a bow drill, which was the customary tool used by the gem engraver. Another device for engraving dies was to employ a hub of another metal which had the type or part of the type required in relief engraved on it. This would be driven into the die when it was hot, leaving the impression, and the die could then be hardened. This was a useful method as it meant that when a die become worn it could be touched up by restamping.

Hubbing was certainly employed in the Roman Empire, and explains why the heads of emperors are always very well done and almost identical to one another on a wide range of coins. There is further evidence that hubs were used for portraits in the Empire because sometimes we find coins with the name of one emperor and the portait of another. This is a very rare occurrence, and is most common in the third century.

In the Middle Ages coin types and legends were made up entirely with hubs or punches, and the custom of engraving dies seems to have died out in Carolingian times (eighth to ninth centuries). As a result designs became much simpler and lettering more important and larger. Types and letters were both made with punches of very simple forms, which made lines, curves, crescents, pellets, annulets, triangles and other shapes both large and small. Wedges were favoured for making letters, and in the eleventh and twelfth centuries in France were used almost exclusively, as a result of which the letters tended to be very badly formed. In the thirteenth century in Italy some attempt was made to increase the range of punches to include heraldic devices such as a crown or a *fleur-de-lys*. During the Renaissance, with a revival of interest in ancient coins, we find engraving becoming common again from the fifteenth century.

In England in the time of Henry III about a dozen iron punches were used to engrave the die.

In the east we find a curious method employed for making dies. The Arabs made a lead pattern which they impressed on fine clay, which was then used for casting a die in bronze or iron.

The dies for Celtic coins often seem to have been made with punches, as in Medieval Europe.

Dies were frequently altered, and in a few cases we find that the whole of the edge of the die has been cut away to remove the legend and a ring of metal with a new legend put round the trimmed die.

Die Alignment

In very early times there was seldom any attempt to align dies so that the types lay in a special axis so that when the coin was turned over, it would display the reverse type the right way up. There is slight evidence to suggest that an occasional attempt to align dies was made before 480 BC but the custom did not become common before the second century BC.

Normally dies are aligned so that when the coin is turned round between the fingers both types will be seen to be upright. This is true of coins struck since 1887, but before that date the reverse was upside down so that in order to see both types the right way up the coin had to be rotated not with a horizontal movement but with a vertical one. In numismatic literature die axis is indicated with arrows, ↑ meaning that the reverse is upright when the obverse is upright, ↓ that the reverse is upside down, ↗ that it is at an angle of forty-five degrees and so on.

The first fixed dies appear in east Greece, in south-western Asia Minor, in the sixth century BC at places like Cnidos and Samos, and in the fifth century at Tyre and Sidon. Seleucid and Alexandrian coins seem to have been aligned with the reverse the right way up, and alignment appears more frequently as time progresses in the Roman Republic. Roman Imperial coins and medallions were usually aligned.

There were a number of ways in which alignment could be achieved. Firstly there could be some kind of projection or pin on the dies. This seems to have been rarely used. Secondly there could be some kind of toggle hinge. A third method is exemplified by a pair of dies for an aureus of Faustina II (146–75 AD). These were cut in steel and set in square sectioned bars, the top of which was hollowed to a depth of 2½ inches forming a socket into which the bottom die fitted. A similar arrangement seems to have been in use in Gaul in the second century BC, and was probably also employed in Anglo-Saxon England until about 875, when, rather strangely, moneyers reverted to the old freehand method of striking. Between 975 and 1017 this system seems to have been reintroduced, for when 640 coins of the period were studied for alignments they were all found to lie in one of four axes, corresponding with the four sides of the die.

In Medieval Europe fixed axes were very rare, though they do occur on some coins of Sicily and east Europe.

Pegging, as a means of fixing the dies, was a late invention, being first employed in the eighteenth century.

Methods of Coining

The earliest coins were oval or bullet shaped for the most part, with a type on one side only and the mark of a punch on the reverse. The punch, or in the case of the earliest coins, the punches, tended to present an oblong striking area, and as they did not come in contact with the whole area of the flan the coins so produced tended to be oval in shape or, where there were two punches used, even bean shaped (Plate 5a). Only when larger punches which covered nearly the whole of the reverse were introduced did coins assume a regular and circular shape.

The very early coins, although displaying two or even three incuse punchmarks on their reverses, were clearly struck by all the punches simultaneously, as the depressions are of equal depth showing that each punch had been driven into the softened metal with the same force. There are two possible explanations for this: either individual punches fastened together in some way were used, or a single punch was employed with two or three projections on the base. The latter is more probable, as there seems little purpose in using several punches unless it had been found easier to replace a small single punch when it became worn than a large oblong one. It is possible that the punches were connected with some form of trident.

The punches seem to have had a very irregular surface, and were probably produced by breaking off the end of a metal cast (if single punches were used this would be in the form of a square sectioned nail); as the fracture could not possibly be imitated it served as a convenient safeguard against forgery. The incuses left by the punches are often very deeply sunk into the metal, which suggests that the flans were struck red hot.

The obverse die was usually engraved in much higher relief than the reverse, due to the fact that the reverse had to take more strain as it received directly the weight of the hammer. From a simple punch mark the reverse was gradually elaborated. The first step seems to have been the introduction of a single square punch, though we also find an elaborate swastika punch in use in the sixth century in Corinth (Plate 6h). By about 550 we find reverse types being engraved on the punch, though on the coins they still appear as a type set in an incuse square (Plate 5c). Later a round punch became more common, and by the end of the sixth century BC coins usually had both obverse and reverse types.

The moneyer's equipment and the act of striking coins is shown on a number of ancient coins themselves. One of these is a denarius of Titus Carisius struck about 45 BC which shows on the reverse the pile, or anvil, with projections at the bottom for fixing it in the ground. It is slightly tapered towards the bottom. Above it is an object which is sometimes taken to be the reverse die, but is more probably the cap of Vulcan who was the patron god of moneyers in the Classical world, just as St Eligius was the patron saint of the moneyers in the Middle Ages. On either side of the anvil are tongs for lifting the coin after striking, and a small hammer (Plate 5j).

Another Roman Republican denarius, struck by Scribonius Libo about 71 BC, shows the Puteal in the Forum Romanum in Rome (Plate 5k). This was a structure shaped like a well head. On it is shown an anvil with curious feet like those on the coin of Carisius. Sometimes, instead of an anvil, we find tongs or a hammer.

A mint and a moneyer striking coins is shown on some late coins of Paestum (Poseidonia) in southern Italy, on some coins of the Balearic Islands and on an Imperial tessera from Vienna. Here the anvil is shaped like a truncated pyramid. In Pompeii there is a fresco in the House of the Vettii which shows cupids striking coins, though there is some dispute as to the interpretation of the scene, not a few scholars preferring to identify it as merely a goldsmith's shop.

There are three types of reverse die, all of which were used in the Greek world. The first was the punch or elaborated punch that produced an incuse reverse. The second type is what is known as a 'flat nosed' die, that is to say there is still a raised punch, with or without a type in the centre, but this is surrounded by a flat area which means that the whole of the flan receives the impact of the punch and the metal instead of welling up round the punch is flattened. A third type of reverse die is called 'bevelled' where the surface round the punch slopes upwards slightly instead of being flat and produces a dish-shaped reverse (see Fig. 3).

The incuse on the reverse seems to die out by the early fourth century BC though the reverses of most ancient coins show slight concavity. Occasionally, however, one finds a reverse with an incuse square even in Hlelenistic times. This was deliberate archaism, retained for aesthetic reasons. A good example can be seen in the very common hemidrachms of Argos struck in the second century BC (Plate 5e).

In Medieval numismatics the obverse die in its anvil setting is called the pile and the reverse or punch die is called the trussel. Large numbers of Medieval dies have survived, from Britain and elsewhere, and are fairly uniform in design. The trussel was a bar of metal about an inch in diameter and sufficiently long to hold in the hand (Plate 3). The obverse die was smaller and dumpier with a spike at the bottom which was used to set it in a wooden block. Trussel dies are usually splayed at one end from hammering. Due to the low relief striking was done by one man who held the reverse die in position with his left hand while he struck it with a hammer held in his right. There is an interesting twelfth century sculpture from the capital of a pillar at Saint-Georges de Boucherville in Normandy which shows a moneyer at work (Fig. 4).

Fig. 4 Romanesque sculpture showing a moneyer, from Saint-Georges de Boucherville, Normandy

Finally, before leaving the question of striking, mention may be made of composite dies. Sometimes we find that many obverse dies were set into the same anvil, and the flans were not laid precisely on one obverse before striking, so that they show parts of two obverses on the one side while the reverse is accurately centred.

Cast Coins

Some coins were produced entirely by casting. These include all the potin coins of Celtic Gaul and the Anhdra Empire of India, which were made of too debased an alloy to stand the shock of striking, and the large bronze coins of the Early Roman Republic. Normally the moulds were made by impressing an existing coin in clay, and using this to cast another coin. This resulted in a gradual reduction of size over a prolonged period, when each time a further cast was being used to make a mould, and also in a blurring of the type.

Considerable dispute has arisen over the method of production in the case of the south-eastern British speculum coinage. This issue will be brought up again elsewhere, but here it may be mentioned that the coins seem to have been produced by a type of *cire perdue* method in which a wax model of the coin was cased in clay, the wax melted and run out and the space left filled with molten metal. Another, less certain, possibility is that a wooden mould was used or that a wooden pattern was impressed in clay. Some of the coins display a curious grained effect that could be caused by a wooden mould or pattern (see p. 190).

At Hengistbury Head, in Dorset, one strange pewter coin seems to have been a pattern used in making the moulds for later pieces, and an Athenian lead pattern is also known, presumably used by a forger.

The coins of Celtic Gaul seem to have been cast very often in strips in a bivalve clay mould.

Serrated Coins

Some gold and silver Carthaginian coins struck during the Second Punic War have a notched or serrated edge cut after striking by two strokes of a chisel. The same feature can be noted on some slightly later Macedonian coins, on Seleucid coins of Syria of the second century BC and on many issues of Roman Republican denarii down to 69 BC (Plate 5h). In the case of the denarii the edge seems to have been filed to produce this effect.

Serrations must not be confused with striking cracks which appear on the edge of some coins which were struck cold and could not stand the strain of the pressure.

Silver Plated Coins

On some occasions of economic crisis, emergency issues of bronze coins coated with silver were struck, and these must not be mistaken for forgeries. A good example of this was the issue of 406 BC in Athens which was coined during the slump following the Peloponnesian War. Plated examples of almost all the issues of the Roman Republican denarii are known to exist, and numerous examples of plated early Imperial denarii as well. Whether these were official or the products of forgers has been a subject of great dispute.

In the third century AD many Roman coins were struck in base metal with a high silver content, and made to appear silver by a process of blanching. By this process the flan was heated over a charcoal fire in order to oxidize the copper on the surface, leaving a silver-rich layer underneath. The oxide coat was removed by immersion in a saline solution. The flan was then struck, and the process of striking helped to stabilize the silver.

Silver plating, *sensu stricto*, could have been carried out by one of three different methods. The simplest was to dip the coin in a wash of molten silver, the coin being first cleaned in a bath of borax or potash to make the silver adhere. The coin would then be struck, as the striking would harden the silver coat. Another method involved coating the coin in an amalgam of silver dissolved in mercury, and then heating it to evaporate the mercury. This method, popular with forgers in England in the seventeenth century and later, is very dangerous because mercury fumes are highly toxic. An electrolytic method that may have been used would entail immersing the coin in a bath of silver salt, in contact with a piece of base metal, usually iron.

Coins Produced by Unusual Methods, or of Eccentric Form

Sometimes one finds saucer shaped coins being struck. The earliest example of this is to be seen in the Rhine-Danube area in the first century BC where the Celts struck very characteristic *Regenbogenschüsselchen* or 'Little Rainbow Dishes'.

A similar feature can be noted on the scyphates of the later Byzantine Empire, first struck by Isaac Comnenus (1057–9). These have types on both sides, with a wide margin of metal all round. They were struck with a convex reverse die and concave obverse die; this device was probably to make the two dies grip the flan better (Plate 5l).

Due to the extreme thinness of the flans in the Middle Ages it not infrequently happened that the impression of one side came through to some extent on the other – on very many Medieval pennies for example the reverse cross is clearly discernible on the obverse. As a result, in the twelfth century in Germany and some neighbouring parts of north and east Europe, we find coins of extreme thinness with a type on one side only. These are called bracteates, and their large size enabled complex and often extremely artistic designs to be employed, using a technique of engraving comparable to that of the contemporary goldsmiths. They were probably struck on wood. The reverse shows the obverse design in intaglio, and they were made by a repoussé method of striking (Plate 5m).

Uniface coins sometimes occur which were struck by normal methods but with a punch which had a flat surface with no design.

Finally there is a very remarkable series of coins struck in Magna Graecia in the late sixth and early fifth century BC, at Sybaris, Poseidonia, Caulonia and Metapontum. These seem to have the obverse type in relief and on the reverse the same type in incuse (Plate 5g). At first sight they might be taken for pieces struck by a repoussé method like the bracteates, but in reality they were struck with two dies, the reverse die repeating in relief the type of the obverse, showing the whole type as viewed from the other side. These coins must not be confused with brockages, where one coin becomes wedged under another in striking, producing an incuse impression on the reverse of the obverse type, or on the obverse of the reverse type. This is common on Roman denarii and on English milled coins.

Roman Forgers' Methods

Forgery seems to have been fairly common in the Roman Empire, and we find that there were two important waves, the first in the time of the Severi and the second in the troubled years of the third century, notably between 274 and 286. The archaeological and historical implications of these outbreaks are discussed in another chapter, and we may reserve study of the forgers' mints for consideration in that context.

The methods of production are attested from a number of sites on the continent, notably Damery and Épernay (Marne), and from several finds in this country, the best known of which are the Lingwell Gate find of the early nineteenth century and the recent find from Whitchurch, Somerset.

It seems that the forgers made round pads of clay between which they pressed the coins that they wanted to imitate, then piled several pairs of moulds one on top of the other in the form of a *rouleau*. The edges of the pads usually cracked while taking impressions, and for this reason were trimmed with a knife – seemingly some kind of circular guide or counter was used to ensure regularity in the trimming. This was carried out while the moulds were still damp. About twelve moulds were made up into one pile. When the coins had been removed notches were cut to act as runnels for the molten metal. Two *rouleaux* of moulds were then set together, notch to notch, though occasionally we find three *rouleaux* being employed. The *rouleaux* were then encased in clay of similar fabric to the moulds themselves but tempered with straw to prevent it cracking in the initial filling of the moulds. The molten metal was then poured in, and up to forty coins could be cast at one time. Probably some of the moulds were reused. The method of manufacture is shown in Figure 5.

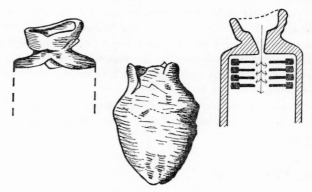

Fig. 5 Roman forger's equipment

The Introduction of Machinery

Little need be said about mechanical methods of coin production, as these were not introduced until the Renaissance. Machinery seems to have been first tried out for making Italian Renaissance medals, but the first person to use a press for coining was Bramante (1444–1514). Leonardo da Vinci devised a type of machine for stamping out coin blanks in 1514, and further developments in mechanical methods of coining were made while Benvenuto Cellini, the great Renaissance artist, was Master of the Mint in Rome in the early sixteenth century.

About the same time developments in mechanized coining were being made in Germany, and around 1550 there is a record that the French king sent an embassy to Augsburg to purchase from a goldsmith some secret apparatus for making coins of absolute regularity, both in weight and shape. With this new screw press France began issuing coins which were known as *monnaies du moulin* because the machinery was driven by a water mill. A refinement of this early milling was the introduction of collars to prevent the flan from spreading in striking, and these bore inscriptions (in relief) just as crowns and halfcrowns bore inscriptions in England in the time of Charles II. Good though these coins were, opposition was strong both from the moneyers who, finding themselves redundant, were unwilling to adopt new methods, and from the people of France, and milling was abandoned in 1585. Meanwhile, in 1560 Elizabeth I had invited a Frenchman, Eloy Mestrell, to set up a press in England, and between this year and 1571 milled sixpences, threepences and threefarthing pieces were struck alongside the old-fashioned hammered pieces. These coins were neater both in form and in design than the hammered pieces, the dies being of superior workmanship. They were as unpopular in England as they were in France (except with people like Shakespeare's Pistol who quite happily picked Master Slender's purse for them!) and milling was abandoned.

In France machinery was reintroduced between 1640 and 1645, and in England rolling mills were first introduced to the mint in 1628, to be followed by coining presses in 1662 which marked the start of milled coinage proper in Britain.

Further Reading

There is a considerable amount of literature concerned with coining methods, and a selection of useful articles will be found in the Bibliography. Particularly useful are the entries on Ancient and Medieval coining in Volume II of the *Oxford History of Technology*, (1956) and the relevant pages of R. F. Tylecote's *Metallurgy and Archaeology* (1962). Less accessible but worth reading is the chapter on 'Form, and Methods of Production' in Sir George Macdonald's *The Evolution of Coinage* (1916), though some of Macdonald's con-

B

clusions, such as those on the Ptolemaic indented coins, are now not universally held.

Among articles on the subject two will be found particularly useful, both in *Numismatic Chronicle*. The first is an article published by G. F. Hill on 'Ancient Methods of Coining' in *N.C.* 5th Ser. II (1922), 1–43, the other a more recent study by P. Balog entitled 'Notes on Ancient and Medieval Minting Technique' in *N.C.* 6th Ser. XV (1955), 195–202. This article is concerned with the manufacture of dies and the problems of pegged dies.

The standard work on dies is C. C. Vermeule's *Ancient Methods of Coining* (1954).

2 Chronology

There is a tendency among archaeologists to regard numismatic chronology as being as unalterable as the laws of the Medes and Persians. Probably this is because coins are usually assigned to a period with specific limits, giving the appearance of an historical date. The archaeologist, confronted with a date such as 196–146 BC immediately assumes that the coin with which he is concerned has been securely related to historical events, and could not possibly have been struck earlier or later than those years. In the case of Greek coins, this not necessarily so, and one finds quite frequently that a coin may be attributed to a particular chronological horizon purely because on stylistic grounds it seemed to be similar to another coin or coins which for various reasons had been attributed to the period between these dates. Although stylistic dating still forms the basis of Greek numismatic chronology, and indeed of the chronology of many later series as well, when applied too rigorously it can be very misleading. Even within seemingly well dated series there can be a wide margin in dating, and accordingly before studying coins the archaeologist or historian must be fully acquainted with the methods of dating used by numismatists.

The dating of Greek coins presents perhaps the biggest problem. Roman coins, on the whole, are more easily attributed, though the chronology of the coinage of the Roman Republic is fraught with difficulties, especially for the early period, as the first fairly reliable dates for Republican coins do not occur until the end of the second century BC. Imperial coins, however, can be closely dated, partly because of the short reigns of the emperors and partly because of the frequent weight reductions and coinage reforms. In the early Empire the Romans employed a system of magisterial dating which can often be used for assigning a coin to a particular year.

Medieval coins can usually be dated within a broad framework because they normally bear the monarch's name, but within the years of the individual reigns precise chronology is often uncertain.

Broadly speaking, there are three different types of numismatic dates. The first of these may be termed *absolute* or calendrical and applies to coins which bear the date, according to a certain era.

The majority of dates are *relative*; that is to say, they can be related to a sequence of coins, and from their position in the sequence they can be determined within a limited period. Such relative dates are of varying degrees of validity. Occasionally it is possible to date a coin in this way to a precise year, but at the opposite end of the scale it may only be possible to assign a date within a period of a century or even longer, in the absence of all external evidence.

The third category may be termed *dates by association*. This is rather a portmanteau category, and includes coins which make reference in their types or legends to historical events or personages, which in turn can be related to historical dates; coins which can be related obliquely to history because historical events would have dictated that they were struck within a certain period of time; and coins which have been dated on account of their association with other coins of known dates in hoards or with dated archaeological material in excavations.

Normally coins are dated not by one method alone, but by a number, all of which provide cross-checks with one another.

I Absolute Chronologies

(a) Ancient

We may begin by considering absolute or calendrical dates.

It is not often realized that some Greek coins actually bear dates in terms of one or another of the several eras employed in the ancient world. When one knows the year from which all subsequent dates were reckoned in a given area it becomes an easy matter to calculate the precise date at which a coin was struck. Unfortunately until the time of Alexander the Great systems of dating were not generally employed, and even then are mainly found in the east. There are five main systems of this nature, the Seleucid, the Asiatic, the Pompeian, the Caesarian and the Actian. Of these the Seleucid was the most important; it started in 312 BC after the defeat of Demetrius by Seleucus and Ptolemy at Gaza and the annexation of Babylonia by Seleucus. The civic year started on 31 October. Syrian coins in particular used this system, as did many other eastern coins. It became more prevalent however in the later second and first centuries BC.

The Asiatic era began in 134–3 BC, and was used for dating the cistophori of Ephesus. The Pompeian era started in 64 BC after the defeat of Tigranes by Pompey, when he reorganized Syria as a Roman province. In general 48 BC marks the start of the Caesarian era, after the defeat of Pompey the Great by Caesar at Pharsalus, though some cities reckoned it as beginning at other dates (Antioch, for example, calculated from 49 BC). The Actian era started in 31 BC when Octavian defeated Mark Antony at Actium.

In Imperial times many Greek coins were dated according to the year of the reign of the Roman emperor, a system particularly well documented by the coins struck at Alexandria, though it is to be found elsewhere (Plate 6b). In Judaea until the time of the First Jewish Revolt we find the small bronze lepta of the Procurators dated in this manner (Plate 6c).

The Ptolemaic coins of Egypt were normally dated according to the regnal year of the king (Plate 6a). Some, however, were dated from the time of Ptolemy I Soter (311 BC) and others from the time of the deification of Arsinöe II in 270 BC. Dating in Ptolemaic Egypt was not altogether a regular matter, and we find that both Arsinöe II and Ptolemy V began by striking undated coins before taking up the practice of dating.

Sometimes, on Greek and Greek Imperial coins, one finds that the date is preceded by the word $ETOY\Sigma$ (meaning 'of the Year') which in the case of Egyptian and Jewish coins is abbreviated to the character L derived from papyrus inscriptions, which is in fact a fragmentary form of the initial E. (Plate 6b.)

A particularly interesting system is that employed on the coins of the First and Second Jewish Revolts. Each of these series had dates calculated from the 'Deliverance of Zion' or the 'Redemption of Israel', a new sequence being employed for the Second Revolt, starting 132 AD (Plate 6d). A parallel to this can be seen in the way in which French coins were dated according to the 'Year of Liberty' in the years following the French Revolution.

Sometimes chronologies can be confusing because the same city sometimes used several different eras at different times. Antioch, the capital of the Seleucids, first dated its coins according to the Seleucid era as one might expect, then after 49 BC some coins were dated according to the Caesarian era. Until 40 BC coins can have dates calculated according to either system, but after 40 BC the

Seleucid dating falls out of use. In 31 BC the Caesarian dating is replaced by the Actian for a while, but Tiberius restored the Caesarian dating in the early first century AD. Gaius (Caligula) used his own regnal years on the coins struck there, while subsequent emperors used sometimes the Caesarian date, sometimes the regnal, and sometimes even gave the Greek equivalent of the year of their tribunician power.

Quite a number of Greek coins are dated according to important events in the history of the city-state which issued them. In a few cases we know what this event is and can date the coins accordingly, but more often such events have not been recorded in history and the dates given on these coins at the best only provide us with a relative chronology. The earliest of these local dating systems go back to the fifth century BC.

Local eras appear to have been commonly employed as a means of dating in the Imperial period. It is noteworthy that the custom of dating coins was a phenomenon mainly of the east Greek world.

Roman coins, strictly speaking, are not dated, insofar as they do not bear a year according to a particular era, although they can be dated accurately in the early Empire, since we know the years of the consulships and the year in which each emperor first held the power of the tribune. These systems will be discussed in a later section.

(b) Medieval

Byzantine coins were dated according to regnal years for only a short period – between AD 538 and the mid eighth century. Even then dates only appeared on bronze coins. Towards the end of the period regnal dates were infrequent even on bronze issues.

The idea of dating coins was essentially an eastern one. Just as most of the Greek dated coins were eastern, the short phase of dating in the Byzantine world was probably the result of eastern influence. In the east a regular dating system was established in the late seventh century by Caliph Abd el-Malik, who dated his coins according to what is now known as the Mohammedan era (AH), calculated from AD 622, the year of the Hegira. It is probably not accidental that the earliest dated coins in western Europe were struck in areas where there was strong Moorish influence.

In Spain there was a long history of Moslem influence, and it is not surprising that there we find dated coins at a very early period. Alphonso VIII of Castille (who married the daughter of Henry II of England) struck gold dinars after the Moorish fashion in order to trade with them. These were dated according to the 'Spanish era' which was supposed to commence in 38 BC with the capture of Spain by the Romans. Alphonso also struck some coins which are of great interest as they were intended for trade other than with the Moors. These have the date ERA MCCIIII, that is AD 1166. The Spanish era was used for calculating dates in south-west Europe until the late fourteenth century.

An interesting series of coins was struck by the Crusaders in Palestine. These also imitated Arab coins, as the Crusaders were forced to trade with the Arabs. The earliest were very blundered imitations, but later they improved. When the Papal legate who accompanied Louis IX on the Sixth Crusade saw that Christians in Acre and Tripoli were striking coins in the name of Mohammed and dating them in accordance with the Mohammedan era he was naturally horrified and called upon Innocent IV to threaten them with excommunication, which Innocent duly did. Shortly afterwards the penitent Crusaders at Acre issued bezants with the legend, 'There is only one God and He is the Father, the Son and the Holy Ghost. Struck at Acre in the year 1251 from the Incarnation of Our Lord and from our Regeneration. He it is Who saveth us and loveth us. God forbid that we should boast save in the cross of our Lord Jesus Christ in Whom is our salvation and our life'. Arabic lends itself to long legends, but even for a coin with Arabic legends this is quite a lengthy inscription!

The custom of dating coins in north-western Europe first became general in Germany in the fourteenth century, one of the earliest issues being struck in Aix and dated 1371. In Britain, coins were not dated until the time of James V of Scotland, who struck a dated 'Bonnet Piece' in 1540 (Plate 6e). England followed suit, first dating a coin in 1548 (this date appears on a shilling of Edward VI, struck at Durham House).

II Relative Chronology

If a coin does not actually bear a calendrical date, the date that is attributed to it is relative. Of this class of dates a small group are of an absolute character, as information is given on the coins from which an absolute date can be reckoned. This generally applies to coins which bear the names of magistrates who held office for one year only. Such a system of course is only valid for giving an absolute date when the date of a particular magistrate's office is known from other sources, or can be calculated by relating the coin to a sequence where the year of a previous or subsequent magistrate's tenure is known. The sequence of a series of coins can be established by studying die identities, as will be explained presently.

Sometimes, even when the magistracy is held over a period of several years by the same man, the date can be calculated if the coin indicates the year of office or annual sequence marks are employed for distinguishing the output of an individual year.

Greek Magisterial Dating

In the case of Greek coins the question of magisterial dating is complex. As early as the fifth century BC we find that in some of the east Greek cities like Abdera and Cyzicus a monetary magistrate was appointed each year, who put his badge on the coins struck under his authority. At Abdera (Thrace) the magistrate's badge appeared as a symbol in the obverse field, beside the Griffin which was the city badge. On the reverse of these coins his name was put round a quartered square, sometimes preceded by E (meaning 'under'). Later the quartered square was replaced by the magistrate's badge, leaving just the griffin on the obverse. It has been suggested that this magistrate was the chief priest of Apollo, the patron god of the city. Probably it was customary to date events from the year of office of these priests in Abdera, just as in Argos dating was according to the priestess of Hera. On two occasions it seems that the priest died while still in office, and as a result coins were struck in the name of the god himself. The badge employed for the god was his cult statue, and on one occasion the legend reads $E\Pi I\ KA\Lambda\Lambda IANAKTO\Sigma$ (under the Good Lord) and on another $E\Pi I\ A\Gamma O\Lambda\Lambda\Omega NO\Sigma$ (under Apollo).

Generally it is almost impossible to find out who these magistrates were from historical sources, or to establish a complete series with one or more fixed dates in it. Magistrates' names are fairly common on Greek coins, especially in the third and second centuries BC.

Some of the most common of all Greek coins, such as those of Argos in the period 220–146 BC (Plate 5e), the coins of the Dyrrachii (Illyria) in the period 229–100 BC, or the third century bronze coins of Erythrae (Ionia), have interesting sequences of magisterial names and symbols, but these cannot be related to a precise chronology.

Roman Republican Magisterial Dating

Fortunately in the Roman Republic, progress through the ranks of the offices of state (the *cursus honorum*) was regular, and certain offices were held at a certain age. A moneyer could not hold office before the age of twenty-seven, and a certain number of years had to elapse before he became a praetor or consul. Thus, if we know from historical sources when a particular man was praetor or consul we can calculate roughly how many years previously he was a moneyer, and the coins struck by him can then be dated. This is seldom very accurate, and there is often some difficulty in identifying the moneyer with a later consul or praetor. Some examples will make this clearer. C. Pulcher is known to have struck coins about 100 BC. Further, an inscription exists recording the fact that a C. Claudius Pulcher was consul in 92 BC, having been quaestor, triumvir of the mint, curule aedile in 99 BC and praetor in 95. From this information, assuming C. Claudius Pulcher and C. Pulcher were the same, the coin can be dated to about 98 BC.

Roman Imperial Coins

The classic case of magisterial dating is the tenure of the tribunician power by Roman emperors, from which the absolute date of early Imperial coins can be calculated. The tribunes in the Roman Republic were originally appointed to protect the rights of the plebs against the patricians, and their control was limited to the right of veto. In time their power increased, and though Sulla attempted to reduce it in the late Republic the tribunes were very strong. Pompey restored their rights, but they were again deprived of them by Caesar. Augustus, however, saw the tribunician power as an ideal office for exercising control, and in 23 BC had the power conferred on him for life, giving him the right to convene and disperse the Senate and the Popular Assembly at will, and to propose motions in the senate and assembly.

As it was the basis of his authority, he dated his reign according to the year of its tenure, which was renewed (nominally) every year. Until Antoninus Pius the renewal took place on the anniversary of its conferment, but in 147 the traditional date of 10 December was re-established for the renewal. This continued until the time of Septimius Severus (AD 193) who changed the date to 1 January. This was continued by the later emperors. On early Imperial coins the first year of tenure is indicated by the legend TR P (*Tribunicia Potestas*), the second by TR P II, and so on. Thus the precise date of a coin can be easily calculated. However, the custom of putting this on coins died out in the mid third century, Philip 1 (AD 244–9) being the last emperor to employ it regularly.

B*

For Roman Imperial coins there are other means of checking dates, though these are more complicated.

The tenure of the consulship is significant in this respect. In the Republic two consuls were elected each year and held the highest offices in the state. Under the emperors, however, although consuls were still appointed they held no power. The emperors frequently assumed the title, and this was usually stated on the coins. This office was not necessarily renewed each year. Some emperors, notably the Flavians, held it regularly (Vespasian was elected consul eight times in ten years), but most held it very irregularly. Hadrian held it three times in the first three years of his reign, but not thereafter, and a coin inscribed COS III struck under Hadrian could have been issued any time between AD 119 and 138.

Occasionally problems arise in the dating of Roman Imperial coins that cannot be solved by a study of a simple sequence. Commodus (AD 175–92) first held the power of the tribune late in AD 176 or early in 177, and it can be established that he held tribunician power early in that year. However he is TR P II the same year, and TR P III from 10 December 177. This can possibly be explained by the fact that in 177, because he had come into the office late in 176, he decided to put back the date of his 'election' to before 10 December 176, thus giving him an extra year of power.

Due to the fact that until the time of Severus the year of the tribunician power did not commence in January, there is usually some doubt as to whether a coin was struck at the end of one year or during the next. This can sometimes be solved by finding out when special titles which appear on the coin were bestowed; this was usually following some campaign, such as GERM(anicus), PARTH (icus), etc.

Die Links

Numismatists frequently use die links for establishing relative chronologies. A study of die links is based on the fact that dies are nearly always distinct from one another, differing slightly in small details. This is because in antiquity each die was made separately, and was not produced, as in the case of modern coins, by a mechanical means which rendered each one identical to the others.

The differences in dies for the same coin type may be of any description. The most distinctive, of course, are flaws in the die itself such as a crack or scratch which appears on the coin as a raised line. On the one hand it may be an irregularity in the alignment of the letters in the legend or a small error in engraving; or on the other it may be that one die has a different detail, such as the number of curls on a bust or an unusual shape of crown. The Dies which are distinct in this way are said to have separate *die identities*, or if the difference results in a variation in the type (due to the treatment of the hair, or the number of pearls to a necklace, etc.) as having separate *die varieties*. It is always possible to detect two ancient coins which have been struck from the same obverse or reverse die.

In antiquity many more reverse dies were required than obverse dies. The reason for this will become clear if we remember that the obverse die was set in an anvil, while the reverse die was a punch die, and bore the full brunt of the hammer in striking. The obverse dies too, were protected by the anvil in which they were embedded, while the reverse dies were engraved on the ends of narrow, rod-like punches, and often broke or cracked. Reverse dies were also more weakly engraved than the obverse, and wore out more rapidly.

This fact is very valuable in studying the sequence in which coins were struck. Thus, during the life of a single obverse die three reverse dies at least would have been used, before the obverse die was abandoned. This means that we can have a series of three coins, each struck from the same obverse dies but with reverses from three different dies. If we find two coins with the same obverse but different reverse die identities this means that between the striking of the first and the second coin the reverse die had to be renewed. By this method it is possible to build up a sequence of die identities, and thereby put the coins of a particular series into the correct order. This is perhaps best explained by the diagram, which shows how a sequence of die identities is arranged from two obverse die identities and six reverses (Figure 6).

Of course it is seldom possible to build up a complete sequence of die-links in this way for a given series of coins, due to the fact that there are many 'missing links'. We usually find that we can arrange five or six reverse dies then perhaps another group of five or six with a break between. But even such broken sequences can tell us a great deal about the coins that we could not learn if we studied merely a single example of each type.

Sequence Marks – *Poseidonia*

Occasionally we are aided in our studies of sequences by the fact that the dies bear sequence marks. This is of course not uncommon on modern coinage – Victorian coins, for example, often bore die numbers above the date – but it is much less common in antiquity. Among early Greek coins such a phenomenon occurs at both Thurium and Poseidonia in southern Italy. The importance of this was realised first in 1913 by E. J. Seltman, who studied the issues of Thurium.

The coins struck at Poseidonia belong to the period 430–410 BC and consist of silver staters which are marked with a series of letters from *alpha* to *iota*, of which about 150 varieties are recorded. The

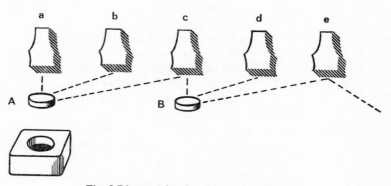

Fig. 6 Diagram showing the theory of die links

series is valuable as it stands out from the rest of the coinage of Poseidonia as a distinct group, and enables the numismatist to study the development of the style of the coins as well as coining procedure during the period. It would appear that the authorities responsible for the introduction of a series of sequence letters thought that it would be advantageous as a control system, and believed that the obverse and reverse dies would wear out simultaneously, though this in fact was not so.

The sequence starts with an obverse die and reverse die both with the letter *alpha*, then the same obverse die is used with a reverse die marked *beta*. Next we have the same *beta* reverse die with a new *beta* obverse die, while the next coin in the sequence uses the same obverse die (now badly corroded) with another reverse die marked *gamma*. There is a break in the sequence however when the *gamma* obverse die became worn, for it was replaced by a die without a letter, but with a scallop shell instead.

Later in the sequence after a stage at which scallops mark both obverse and reverse, the sequence of letters resumes with an obverse marked *epsilon* and a reverse marked *iota*. Now the letters appear in slightly different positions. The *iota* reverse die that is used is possibly an old survival put back into use, though it is not found linked with lettered dies in the sequence before the break. The break using a scallop shell can probably be interpreted as a period when a political move resulted in some magistrate using his personal badge (a scallop shell) to mark the dies instead of a sequence letter.

The date of the whole sequence must be before 390 BC when the Lucanians overthrew the city and renamed it Paestum, and on the grounds of style belongs to the last phase of the city's coinage, between 430 and 410.

Athenian 'New Style' Coinage

The most important series of coins with magistrates' names and symbols are those struck in Athens during the period 196–87 BC. These coins have long been of great interest to numismatists, as they provide an almost complete series with the names of hundreds of magistrates together with a sequence of control marks and letters which indicate in which month the coins were struck (Plate 6g).

Millions of silver tetradrachms were struck by the Athenian mint during the period 196–87 BC, not to mention tens of thousands of smaller denominations, of which about 7,000 coins have survived. These represent no less than 110 separate issues, each the product of a year's striking, with the exception of one issue which was connected with Mithradates of Pontus' occupation of the city. The substantial size of each year's output, and the fact that the coins were struck over most of the months of each year, shows that at least until 112 BC production was uninterrupted, though possibly thereafter there were occasional years in which coins were not struck.

The date for the start of the series is fixed by the Anthedon Hoard (found in 1935, in a village in Boeotia) which contained the earliest of the 'New Style' coins along with tetradrachms and octobols of Chalcis and Eretria. The coins in the hoard were all in almost mint condition, and as a result the date could be established fairly securely. The hoard seems to have been buried late in 192 BC as a result of an invasion scare in Euboea precipitated by the advance of Antiochus II. The earliest coins seem to only antedate the depositing of the hoard by a few years.

The terminal date of the series can be established as being 87 BC for a number of reasons. Firstly, it can be related to Sulla's occupation of the city in that year. Secondly, many of the names of the magistrates on the coins of the last period are those of men who played an important role in civic affairs just before the Sullan sack. Thirdly, there is hoard evidence from Crete where coins with countermarks can be related to Athenian issues in the same hoard.

Within these limits the coins can be carefully dovetailed by the study of die identities and sequences, by hoard evidence, by a study of style, and by trying to identify individual magistrates whose names appear on them. For the period 171–123 BC the sequence can be established with great certainty. Before and after that date hoard dating and die links are less satisfactory, and here a study of style is invaluable.

Fixed points in the sequence are given by historical references on the coins: in 152 BC an Egyptian device can be related to a celebration of the Ptolemaea, and about 132 BC the change in the character of the coinage and the sudden termination of two hoards from Delos with coins of 130 BC can be related to a period of slave revolts in Athens and uprisings in Delos and Laurium, the latter being the silver mines near Athens which supplied the city with this metal.

The coins bear no less than 634 names of magistrates, and fall into several distinct classes. First we have coins with two monograms, then coins with two abbreviated names, next coins with three names in full. Finally we have coins with two names in full. In the transitional stage between monograms and abbreviated names we find the two methods of marking coins used interchangeably.

The first magistrate seems to have chosen the symbol that was used on the coins in any given year, and these symbols were usually of a personal nature, though occasionally they were topical. The names appear on the reverses of the coins, in the field. The types are the traditional types of Athenian silver coinage – the head of Athene on the obverse and an owl on the reverse. On the New Style coins however the owl is shown standing on an amphora, and these amphorae have letters which indicate the month in which the coin was struck, during the main period of the coinage. An interesting feature of these month letters is the fact that occasionally one finds *nu*, the thirteenth letter in the alphabet. This was because there were periodically thirteen months in the Greek calendar in order to balance it with the lunar year. Eleven such intercalary years are attested by the coins, and twice in the second century BC we find two consecutive years in which a thirteenth month is attested by the coins: 171 and 170 BC in the first instance and 135 and 134 BC in the second.

In order to produce the coins, the mint kept between two and five anvils in constant use. In years when the output was relatively low we find that six to ten obverse dies were used, in a normal year's output about twice as many, and on occasions when a very large number of coins were being struck the mint went through as many as forty or fifty. Usually eight to twelve reverse dies were needed to every one obverse, and nine months is the longest recorded life of an obverse die while five is the record achieved by a reverse. At the end of a month if the die had not worn out the amphora letters were recut.

Because the New Style coins can be dated so closely they give us a great deal of valuable information about Athenian trade during the period. Between 196 and 162, for example, we find that they were being exported in large numbers to the Levant and further east, then suddenly this trade stops and in 162 BC the pattern changes to one of contact with the Balkans and Anatolia. This seems to have been prompted by the closing of the mines in Macedon. About the same time more coins were being exported to Crete and Delos. After 117 BC, however, the trade enjoyed by Athens dropped suddenly, and Athenian coins do not appear thereafter in the Balkans, Anatolia, or even northern and central Greece. After 112 there are no Athenian coins from Delos.

In some cases the symbols used by magistrates have shed light on the careers of these men. For example we learn from their symbols that Eurycleidas, who was magistrate in 154, was priest of Demos and the Graces, while Diokles of Kephisia, magistrate in 99, was priest of Asklepios and Hygieia.

Athenian 'Wappenmünzen'

A slightly different use of die identities can be seen if we consider the earlier coins struck at Athens. One series which is called the *Wappenmünzen* (heraldic coins) group, has obverse types which are quite unrelated, including an amphora, triskeles, beetle, astragalos and forepart of horse, as well as an owl, the last of which of course is familiar from later Athenian coins. The only reason at first sight for grouping these coins together is the fact that they are of similar fabric and weight. The reverse in each case is just a punchmark. At one time it was believed that these coins were struck in the Aegean islands, but in a classic study of Athenian coinage by Charles Seltman published in 1924 it was demonstrated that all the coins were struck in the same mint (Figure 7).

Fig. 7 'Wappenmünzen' stater of Athens

This conclusion was reached by establishing the die identities of the reverse punchmarks, for coins with an amphora as a type and coins with a triskeles shared the same reverse punch, while coins with a beetle, astragalos and with a forepart of a horse likewise shared the same reverse punch die (though not, it might be added, the same reverse as the amphora coins). A series of such links was built up, and from this Seltman was able to show the sequence of the striking of these coins, all of which could be attributed to Athens. By comparing the types with shield devices illustrated on Athenian vases he formulated the theory that they were the badges of Eupatrid families. The series as a whole could be linked to earlier and later coins – by a fortunate chance the earliest of this series has as a type a triskeles and shares a punch die with the last of the previous series, which Seltman (erroneously, as subsequent research has shown) called 'Solon amphora didrachms' (Figure 8). Although **no** die links

Fig. 8 Athenian 'amphora didrachm'

are available to connect the *Wappenmünzen* with the following series of coins, the first 'owls' struck under Hippias, there is a useful typological overlap which establishes a sequence. Although Seltman's absolute chronology has recently been modified, the earliest 'owls' being down-dated and the *Wappenmünzen* advanced to accord with the new date, his die links have not been questioned and are not likely to be.

The study of die links enabled Seltman to build up a complete picture of the sequence of coinage in Athens down to the Persian War, and the application of the same formulae elucidated many problems connected with the later Temple coinage of Olympia.

Sequence Marks – The Roman Republic

Turning from Greek coins to the Roman Republic, we find that here again die links and symbols are of great value in arranging coins in chronological order.

The earliest use of symbols on Roman Republican coins is in the period 222–214 BC, when we find a series of 'Romano-Campanian' didrachms with the types of Diana/Victory that bear on the reverse sequences of single or double Greek letters, (*alpha* to *omega* and *alpha alpha* to *omega omega*). There is no similar sequence of letters in the Republic, and the idea seems to have been derived from commemorative dekadrachms struck in the reigns of Ptolemy II and III in Egypt, probably as a result of an alliance between Roma and Egypt in 273 BC. The letters very possibly represent a system of dating, but problems here arise for a number of reasons.

First the whole sequence, if the letters denote years, would cover a span of forty-eight years, which seems too long for the issue, as most series of Roman Republican coins were short lived. Again, in the case of Ptolemaic coins, the numerals (not letters) employed indicated the regnal year or alternatively the year of the epoch. but in the Roman Republic there were no regnal years, and dating on coins in terms of AUC (*ab urbe condita:* the year of the foundation of the city in 753 BC) was never used. This, then, means that though we have a perfect sequence within the series we cannot date any coins in it, as there is a strong possibility that the sequence marks were not annual but related to the output of the mint.

From about 110 BC we find on Republican coins various letters, numerals and symbols which were employed to act as some kind of check on the output of the coinage. These are sometimes related to dies, but more often appear on several different dies. One of the occasions when symbols were used to mark dies was in the time of L. Calpurnius Piso, whose coins are among the commonest from the Roman Republic. Different sequence marks are to be found on the different dies used by him in the years 90–89 BC (Plate 6j). Where the sequence marks are numerals or letters they are easy to arrange in the correct order, but problems arise where symbols are employed.

There seem to have been six different systems of putting sequence marks on Republican coins, and these systems are related to one another chronologically, sometimes being derived from earlier systems. The first method employs variable letters or letters and symbols. The second employs a single letter with a dot which is placed in different positions beside the letter. The development of this employs the same system but on both obverse and reverse, while the fourth method employs a complex system with inverse alphabetical lettering on both obverse and reverse. Thus a coin with A on the obverse has X (the last letter of the Roman alphabet) on the reverse, while one with B on the obverse has V on the reverse, and so on. The last two classes employ a mixture of letters and symbols and letters and numerals on obverse and reverse respectively. Symbols, where they occur, usually relate to the moneyer, and are sometimes a pun on his name – what is termed a 'canting badge'.

One can date a coin approximately according to the complexity of the system of sequence marking that is employed, and use the sequence marks to arrange the coins within each series into chronological order, without of course being able to attribute calendrical dates to them.

Coins of Publius Crepusius

It is interesting to take one particular series of coins and consider how numismatists have made a study of the sequence marks on them. A good series to demonstrate this is that struck by Publius Crepusius, triumvir of the mint in 82–1 BC, at the time of the Civil War between Marius and Sulla (Plate 6i). This series of coins is the fourth biggest of the Roman Republic. It used three different kinds of sequence marks, a letter, a symbol and a number. This was the first series to use this type of sequence marking, the old system of employing letters and dots having fallen out of use during the Social War. The coinage follows the sequence marking systems employed by some moneyers in the early eighties, and subsequent systems were a development of Crepusius'.

The issue as a whole is divided into two, but throughout the whole series a numeral always appears on the reverse in the same position. The division into two series is based on the fact that one group has a Latin letter under the chin of Apollo, whose head appears on the obverse, while the rest have a Latin letter behind the head and a symbol below the chin.

Trying to work out the relationship of all three groups of symbols is rather like trying to crack a code, which indeed it is. The first task is to decide which of the two groups was the earlier. This question is fairly easily solved as the numbers on the reverses of the smaller series run from I to at least XXXVII, while those on the larger run on to DXXIII, using the same reverse dies as the smaller series until the numbers on these run out. From this it is possible to infer that the small group was planned first, then, due to a decision to expand the mint output, a more complex system of marking was brought into use.

The numbers in the small group make it possible to find the right order, following the reverses. But when this is done it is found that the obverse letters are in no way alphabetical, starting with O and going on to C, and so on. Early systematizers were completely beaten by this, and merely listed the coins in order according to the reverse numbers.

Subsequent work on the coins, however, shows that there is a definite pattern not in the obverse letters but in the obverse symbols. A statistical analysis of the coins has been undertaken, in order to find out how many reverse numerals were associated with one obverse symbol. The results, when expressed in terms of a graph, are extremely interesting, as they set the symbols in the correct order and also show how the mint seemed to have operated. There was a considerable overlap between the sequences of numbers controlled by consecutive symbols. The letters, on the other hand, do not relate to the numerical sequence. One of the interesting suggestions arising from this is that a 'die-box' technique was used, whereby the obverse dies with a given symbol were stored in a separate box and then were taken at random to be used with a current reverse die. The number of denarii that were struck from a given symbol controlled the length of time that the die was in use, the determining factor being not the life of the die but the amount of bullion allocated to it. Several dies with the same symbol were probably in use at the same time. The fact that there is an overlap in the numbers would suggest that the reverses to be used were similarly kept in a box and chosen at random. Most of the groups of symbols seem to have been associated with dies covering the whole alphabet, but one or two symbols cover a much smaller range, which suggests that the silver allocation ran out before many dies had been brought into use.

Mules

A mule is a coin which has an obverse die of one class with the reverse of another. Mules contribute to chronology in much the same way as die identities and sequence marks, and therefore need not be discussed at length here.

Style

Style is perhaps one of the major factors in arranging coins chronologically. In theory, this is very similar to the archaeologist's system of employing typology combined with art historical considerations. Greek coins are largely dated, in the first instance, on stylistic grounds. Stylistic considerations for the most part depend on study of variations in detail, for general art-historical considerations can do no more than suggest a very approximate date for the striking of a coin. In broad terms, too, within sequences of coins, one can see typological developments in the composition of types very much akin to the typological developments that archaeologists look for when arranging pottery types or metal types into a series. The rule which governs numismatists in this respect is the same as that which governs the archaeologist: the rule of evolution or devolution.

Oscar Montelius, the great Scandinavian prehistorian, once demonstrated the principle of typology by taking a series of railway carriages and showing how the earliest and most simple kind had been improved upon with the passage of time. Given a row of railway carriages, he pointed out, it is quite possible to arrange them so that the earliest comes first and the latest comes last, even if you are not an expert on them!

We can see a development for example in Roman Republican coin types – first we find coins with Dioscuri as reverse types, then someone has an idea of introducing a new but related type, Diana in a biga, and we find both being struck side by side for a while, until further chariot deities are added to the series and the Dioscuri fall from popularity. Gradually even more novel reverses are introduced, and after about 112 BC the reverses are no longer confined to figures in chariots at all but begin to show an ever-increasing variety.

Such distinctions are too crude to be of great value to the numismatist, who is more concerned with working out precise distinctions, but similar rules apply here. We may study two examples of how ornamental detail can be used as a basis of stylistic analysis of coins. The first concerns Roman Republican denarii again, the second English Medieval coinage.

Typology in Denarii

In the earliest period when the Roman denarius was being struck there is no way of distinguishing issues by moneyers, as no names appear on the pieces. The types are also very similar, with the head of Roma on the obverse and the Dioscuri on the reverse. The value of stylistic analysis in the case of these coins is important in the absence of other chronological indicators. The persistence as well as the morphology of stylistic details is important, almost in fact as important as the morphology itself. From a study of this one can first group coins together, then establish the chronological relationship between groups, then the rough order of issues within each group and finally the distinctive features of individual mints, for style is an excellent indicator of mint.

One of the most significant features of style in the early Republican denarii is the shape of the earring that Roma wears. One might think that such a small detail was merely a matter of personal taste

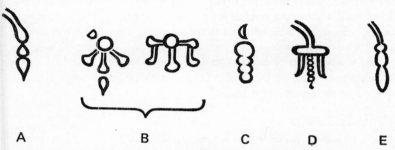

A   B   C   D   E

Fig. 9 Types of ear-ring worn by Roma on Early Republican denarii

of the die sinker, but this was not the case, and Roma periodically changed her earrings according to some deliberate policy of the mint – possibly as a control mark; we cannot now be sure. One version has triple pendants – a very popular kind that is frequently encountered on both Greek and Roman coins. A distinctive form of this appears on coins struck by the moneyers Saranus, Talna, Scribonius, Natta, Junius, and several others. All the moneyers who used this type of earring struck coins which are otherwise similar in style and fabric, and because of this can be taken as a distinct group. For various other stylistic considerations all their coins can be dated to the period 145–137 BC. Within the group stylistic details can arrange the issues in some kind of order. The moneyers' signatures given in a very abbreviated form (such as SAR, NAT, C SCR, etc.) are probably earlier than the coins on which the names are given in full or at greater length and which also give the moneyer's cognomen, such as Q MARC LIBO and so on. Similarly another determining factor is that early heads on these coins are smaller and in higher relief, while with the passage of time the engravers became more careless and the relief became shallower, the design more spread out over the field (Figure 9).

Three of the fifteen moneyers who use this kind of earring (Saranus, Talna and Scribonius) also use another type of single drop earring with a pearl and a pendant. This simple kind of earring was used by moneyers in the preceding period, and it suggests that Saranus and Talna began by following their predecessors with this early type of earring, then changed to the triple drop variety. Accordingly they must be the earliest of the series.

A stylistic feature too links the last of the moneyers of the series with the first of the next period. This monyer, Cupiennius, uses a very broad, low relief head and introduces a symbol on the obverse. The broad head and a symbol are used by Antestius, the first moneyer of the next series, who changes the style of earring to one resembling a tiny cluster of grapes.

The analysis can be carried on over a whole range of early denarii, which would otherwise be difficult to classify or date on the grounds of type or for historical reasons.

Edwardian Pence

At the opposite end of the scale we can consider how modern numismatists have classified the coins of Edward II, and ascribed dates to them.

The coins of the first three Edwards are at first sight almost identical, and certainly to the people who used them in the Middle Ages there was no immediate means of recognising whether a penny was struck by Edward I or Edward II. Numismatists however have studied the coins with great care, and used stylistic details not only to distinguish the coins of the different reigns but even different classes within each reign, which by an ingenious process of using ecclesiastical issues, notably those of Durham, have been equated with calendrical dates through historical associations.

The main stylistic feature of Edwardian pence is the crown on the full face bust of the king on the obverse. In the time of Edward I this began by having the last fleur trifoliate but later in the reign it became bifoliate. The bifoliate crown continued in use throughout the following two reigns. When a study of the crowns was made earlier this century, five different varieties were recognized for Edward II's coins, and these five species became the five main classes – class XI to XV of the general Edwardian sequence. But other features were seen to vary as well as the crowns – for example the shape of the king's face, the type of initial cross used to mark the start of the legend, and the forms of the letters (Plate 28i).

Medieval die sinkers used many punches for making up their dies, using one punch for the king's face, another for his crown, another for the wedge that was put on either side of the bust to indicate drapery, and individual punches were further used for each letter. But occasionally old punches were used and one finds a coin of one class or sub-class employing a form of letter in use in the previous class, or occasionally one finds muling, the reverse or obverse die of a previous class being coupled with a new die. From this it is possible to work out how the sequence of stylistic development has taken place, and to arrange the different classes in the correct order.

Overstrikes

An overstrike is a coin which instead of being melted down and cast into a new flan for striking has merely been restruck with new types. Overstrikes are of very great value in establishing relative chronology and would be used more frequently as a chronological indicator if it were not for their comparative rarity. Very often this process leaves traces of the original coin underneath the new types, which can be identified. Usually restrikes occur when a state acquires large numbers of coins of a neighbouring state whose issues are very plentiful and enjoy a wide circulation, and restrikes these due to a shortage of metal. Occasionally one comes across old coins struck in the same state being reused in this way, but this is less common.

The nature of an overstrike is such that it establishes without dispute that the coin which is overstruck is earlier than the new types stamped on top of it, though how much earlier of course it is not always possible to determine.

In the field of Roman Republican coinage overstrikes of bronze are of very great value in studying the earlier periods. In cases where they are overstruck on foreign coins the date of which can be determined precisely, we have a fixed date after which the Roman coins must have been struck. Again, some Roman Republican coins were restruck by foreign cities, and if the date of the restrike is known it follows that the Roman coin is earlier or at least contemporary. Where a whole series of Roman Republican bronze coins are overstruck by a foreign city this provides a valuable sequence. Sometimes we find that a Roman coin with a specific mint symbol or letter is regularly being struck on a coin or coins from a particular city or state. This can tell us where the Roman coin was struck, and in some cases has even led to the association of a symbol with a particular mint. Finally, where Roman coins are restruck on Roman coins we can learn not only about the sequence but follow a pattern of devaluation, if we find one value is being overstruck with another. This can lead to a greater understanding of mint practice, and the reasons behind overstriking.

If we consider one very important example we can judge the value of overstrikes in chronology. This is the case of a coin of Syracuse which was found to have been overstruck with one of the earliest Roman-Campanian bronze coins – a litra with the head of Minerva on the obverse and a horse's head on the reverse. Now if the date of the coin of Syracuse could be established, this would provide a date before which the earliest 'Romano-Campanian' coins could not have been struck. The coin of Syracuse, though without the name of a ruler, can be dated by overstrikes within its own series, and can be proved to have been issued between the end of the reign of Hiketas and the years following his expulsion from Syracuse and the first inscribed coins of Hiero II, i.e. between 282 and 278 BC.

Now there was one school of thought which maintained that the Romano-Campanian coins were being struck as early as 342 BC, while another was inclined to date the earliest issues to c. 269–8 BC. This coin shows that the first school at any rate must be wrong, for a coin of the fourth century BC could not be overstruck on one of the third. But if the date for the first Romano-Campanian coins was c. 270, it would not be surprising to find them overstruck on coins of about ten years earlier.

Countermarks

Into the category of overstrikes come countermarks. A countermark is a small stamp which is overstruck on a coin but which does not attempt to deface the whole of the coin. This punchmark is usually an incuse with a symbol or letters in it. They occur at all periods, from Hellenistic times until the nineteenth century, and served many different purposes. They occur particularly frequently on the coins of the early Roman Empire. Usually they are of less value as chronological determinants than overstrikes, though they can serve in this way, but they tell us much about the way coins circulated and about official mint policy.

One chronological value of both overstrikes and countermarks lies in the fact they can indicate how long coins were in circulation. Ptolemaic coins of the first few centuries BC were restruck in Cyprus in the second century AD by Antoninus Pius, and other Ptolemaic coins were restruck in the Roman Republic. A study of early Imperial countermarks further shows that these were sometimes countermarked after about 50 years of circulation, to show that they were still legal tender.

Epigraphy

This in itself is only of very approximate value in determining date, and is full of traps for the unwary. Broadly speaking, epigraphic dating is based on a study of the forms of letters used in legends, the formulae used for setting out titles and the way in which particular words are abbreviated, letters ligatured, and so on. Thus certain letter forms appear to be early, and others late. In the case of Greek coins, for example, one finds the form Ω for omega is earlier than the form ω, while alpha is rendered as ⅄ or A on early coins while on later ones takes the form *A* or Λ. Theta on early coins is sometimes represented as ⊕, while later this form is not used. We find sometimes deliberate archaism, with old forms of letters being used at a later date for traditional reasons. On some of the coins of Corinth struck in the third century BC we find an archaic letter, Koppa, ϙ, being used to indicate the mint (Plate 5f).

The same problem arises in the study of Roman Republican coins, where the forms Λ for A and V for L are archaic. Likewise with numerals we find the form ↓ is used for fifty at an early date, but is modified after 88 BC to become ⊥ and later still ⊥.

Some curious features of epigraphy seem to suggest an early date, but in fact have no relevance in terms of chronology. One finds that C is changed to K before A in some cases (e.g. Kalenus instead of Calenus), or XS used together (as in Maxsumus).

The changes that affected lettering on English Medieval coins cannot be discussed here in any length, but they have provided one of the main factors employed in their classification and dating. In the reign of Edward I, for example, we first find the early form of S employed, with two crescents and two wedges (S), but this is replaced in class 3F by another form with an egg-shaped centre (S). Other letters which frequently change their forms on Medieval English coins are N and E.

Leaving letters we may briefly consider epigraphy from the point of view of the formulae employed on the coins. In the case of Greek coins we find that the earliest coins usually employ a letter or group of letters to indicate the mint, but later magistrates' or tyrants' names are added. The title *basileus* (king) does not appear on a Greek coin before the death of Alexander.

The development of the titles employed on a coin can be a good indicator of date. This is especially so in the case of Parthian coinage where there is a tendency for the legend to become longer and more complicated with the passage of time. Thus Tiridates I used the legend *ΑΡΣΑΚΟΥ* (Arsaces was his father). Tiridates was succeeded by Arsaces II, who increased the legend to *ΒΑΣΙΛΕΩΣ ΑΡΣΑΚΟΥ*, [the coin of] King Arsaces. On his death in 191 BC the legends increase rapidly in length. By the time of Artabanus I (128–123 BC) we find the legend *ΒΑΣΙΛΕΩΣ ΜΕΓΑΛΟΥ ΑΡΣΑΚΟΥ ΦΙΛΑΔΕΛΦΟΥ ΦΙΛΕΛΛΗΝΟΣ*, [A coin of] the Great King Arsaces, Philadelphus and Philhellene. This epithet, 'Philhellene', literally, lover of things Greek, became a popular one from this date.

Mithradates III (57–54 BC) increased the legend even further, to *ΒΑΣΙΛΕΩΣ ΒΑΣΙΛΕΩΝ ΜΕΓΑΛΟΥ ΑΡΣΑΚΟΥ ΔΙΚΑΙΟΥ ΕΠΙΦΑΝΟΥΣ ΚΑΙ ΦΙΛΕΛΛΗΝΟΣ* [A coin of] the great king of kings Arsaces, the just, the noble and Philhellene.

Finally, in the time of Tiridates II (26 BC) we find the legend *ΒΑΣΙΛΕΩΣ ΒΑΣΙΛΕΩΝ ΑΡΣΑΚΟΥ ΕΥΕΡΓΕΤΟΥ ΑΥΤΟΚΡΑΤΟ(ΡΟΣ) ΦΙΛΟΡΩΜΑΙΟ(Υ) ΕΠΙΦΑΝΟΥΣ ΦΙΛΕΛΛΗΝΟΣ* (Of the King of Kings, Arsaces, the Benefactor, Emperor, Friend of the Romans, Noble and Philhellene.)

Greek coin legends can sometimes be equated with surviving stone inscriptions, and the two sources can be used as a cross reference for dating. A marble lion from Thebes in Boeotia now in the Thebes Museum was inscribed with the name *ΦΑΣΤΙΑΣ*, who seems to be the same man as *ΑΣΤ*(ias) who appears as a Boeotarch on Theban coins. Now some kind of chronology for both these inscriptions is possible, by a process of cross-referencing. The coins, on which the names of Boeotarchs, including Astias appear, stylistically date from the late fourth century. They disappear after 338 BC (the battle of Chaeronea) as after that date the legend on the coins was changed to *ΒΟΙΟΤΩΝ*. Subsequent research has identified Astias from the *Hellenica Oxyrhynchia* (papyri from the Oxyrhynchus in Egypt) and this has provided a more precise date for the coins and likewise for the inscription, which due to the treatment of the lion could be dated to the later, rather than the earlier, part of the period in which the coins were struck.

In Roman coinage there is also a changing pattern in the formulae employed in the legends, though because of the other chronological determinants it is not really required for dating Imperial coinage. Examples of this include the use of PF (Pius Felix), which does not appear on Roman coins before the time of Constantine I, or the title PM (Pontifex Maximus) which does not appear in the later third and fourth centuries.

Correlation of Types

Another useful method of dating coins is based on the fact that coin types employed in one city were imitated in others if they were sufficiently popular or if there was a connection between the two cities.

A classic example of this is the famous three-quarter facing head of Arethusa on the coins of Syracuse, engraved by Kimon *c.* 408 BC. This coin inspired a whole series of copies starting fairly early in the fourth century, and included the fine imitations struck at Larissa in Thessaly. By about 375 BC the type appears at Tarsus.

A good example of a coin which has been dated by the prototypes that it copied can be seen at Marseilles. Here we find at the beginning of the fourth century BC a series of 'heavy' drachms with the head of Arethusa on the obverse and a lion on the reverse. The obverse of this piece is clearly inspired by another coin of Syracuse engraved by Euainetos about 395 BC, and the reverse by a coin struck at Velia in Italy about the same time. It proves that this series of Massaliote coins must be later than *c.* 390 BC.

Similarly, some series of Celtic coins which are derived from Greek prototypes (such as those imitating the coins of Thasos or the coins of Carthage) can be roughly dated by establishing the date of the prototypes. Of course this method of dating through the association of types can only give an indication that the coin was struck after the date of the prototype, and gives no indication how long after, though the degree of its fidelity to the original is often a good indicator.

Metrology

Metrology is the study of the weights of coins. The pattern of debasement and inflation in most series of ancient coins makes it possible to work out a rough chronology for a given series based on the fluctuations in weight. The subject is a complex one, and more space will be devoted to considering the methods and objects of metrology in a later chapter. The best example of this is the aes coinage of the Roman Republic, which cannot be easily dated or classified by any other method.

Sequence Dating From Hoards

Sequence dating from hoards is perhaps the most important type of relative dating. It will be discussed again in some detail in the chapter on hoards. To show the way in which hoards contribute to our understanding of the dating of coins, we shall here look at three hoards which have altered the chronology of Republican denarii as it was set out by Theodore Mommsen.

The three earliest hoards of Republican silver coins are those from Masera (near Padua, discovered 1881), from Riccia (near Benevento, found in 1872) and S. Giovanni (near Fregellae, unearthed in 1892). These three hoards between them contained coins of almost every moneyer down to N. Fabius Pictor (119–110 BC).

All three hoards were buried about the same time, but the date of this was long in dispute – Mommsen suggested 125 BC, and another great scholar, Greuber, suggested 93 BC. A careful study of other hoards and the finds from these hoards themselves shows that the one date is too early, and the other too late.

The three hoards contain the entirety of a group of coins which on various grounds present a unity, and which are now known to numismatists as Series 20 of the Roman Republic. The last moneyer in this series is Pictor, who must be later than the other moneyers in the group because he was the first to experiment with sequence letters. This system seems to have been taken up almost immediately by other moneyers, and as their coins can be dated, the coins of Pictor can likewise be assigned to a few years previously. The three hoards, furthermore, do not contain any coins of C. Claudius Pulcher, who is known from historical sources to have held office as moneyer about 106 BC. Therefore the hoards are earlier than that. The coins of Pulcher first occur in the eighth of the series of Republican hoards. This leaves a group of hoards (IV–VII) belonging to the period between Pictor and Pulcher. In these hoards fourteen moneyers are represented. As moneyers had short terms of office, this means that between Hoard VIII and Hoard III a period of about fifty years had elapsed, and this dates Hoards I–III to about 110 BC. From this further equations can be worked out.

III Dating by Association

We may now turn to the last of our three categories of dating evidence.

Coin Types Referable to other Material

Sometimes coin types can be related to contemporary objects, buildings or works of art that can be dated and which by association can date the coins.

We have already seen that Athenian coin types in the sixth century BC can be related to the motifs on Attic Black and later Red

Fig. 10 Pegasos on a Protocorinthian vase

Figure vases. Other early Athenian coin types can be related to works of art from the point of view of treatment, and can be dated accordingly.

A similar example can be found in the earliest coinage of Corinth, which has as a type the winged horse Pegasos. Pegasos is frequently depicted on Corinthian pottery, but only at one period do we find him treated in exactly the same manner as on coins – during the Middle Protocorinthian period, about 650 BC. We can find a precise parallel for the earliest rendering on an aryballos or ointment flask now in the Boston Museum of Fine Art (Figure 10). Greek painted pottery can often be helpful in dating coins. The first Athenian coins show as a type a variety of storage vessel known as an amphora. The form of this amphora is distinctive, and can be identified as a 'Tyrrhenian' type, in use in Italy and Greece between 650 and 580 BC. They were made in Athens. Thus the coins with this type can be closely dated (see Figure 8).

Coins from Excavations

Coins can sometimes be dated by the context in which they are found. Usually, as will be shown in another chapter, the process is reversed, but there are one or two exceptions. The most famous example concerns the dating of the earliest coins known to us, the Lydian electrum pieces. The date of these is to a large extent dependent on the dating of the associated material from the great temple of Artemis at Ephesus, excavated as long ago as 1904–5 by D. G.

Hogarth and others, for the British Museum. Below the temple erected in the time of Croesus they found the remains of three others. No fewer than eighty-seven of the early electrum coins were recovered from the two earliest temples. Twenty came from between the slabs of the first building, five from beneath the foundations of the second. Clearly if the temples are contemporary with the finds from them, then here is some kind of date for the coins.

History tells us that Gyges who was king of Lydia in 685 BC was troubled by Cimmerian raids, and during the course of one in 652 they destroyed the temple of Ephesus. They were defeated by Ardys, Gyges' successor, who reigned until 635. For a long time it was believed that the ruins of the first temple discovered by Hogarth were those of the building destroyed by the Cimmerians in 652, and that the coins and other objects discovered with the debris of the temple were buried about that date or a few years later, in much the same way as the Athenians buried the broken statues and other remains on the Acropolis at Athens following the Persian devastation of the site in 480.

If this was the case the Lydian coins could be dated to possibly a generation or so earlier than the sack – i.e. in the earlier part of the seventh century BC.

Another school of thought attempts to date the coins even earlier, saying that they were a 'foundation deposit' made at the time of the building of the temple about 700 BC.

Developments in the dating of Greek objects, however, have led to a reassessment of the objects associated with the coins, and it is now fairly universally recognized that some of the objects must date from 600 BC or even slightly later, and that the early assessment of their date had been vitiated by a number of 'antiques' in the group.

The implications of this are very important, for it means that the date once 'fixed' for the earliest coins is no longer valid, and there is no certain evidence now that coins were being struck before 600 BC. This poses many problems and affects our thinking on the chronology of all the subsequent coinages, most notably the first coins struck at Aegina, a little island near Athens which is known to have been the first place in Europe to strike coins.

Prompted by the implications of this dating of the Artemisium, fresh study was undertaken of the earliest coins of Aegina which were traditionally dated, partly on literary evidence, to the time of Pheidon of Argos who reigned sometime before 620 BC. Careful study of hoard evidence would now suggest that the Aeginetan coins were not issued before 600 BC. A further argument against a Pheidonian coinage has been advanced on the grounds that his own state, Argolis, had no coinage of its own until late in the sixth century, not even using coins much before 550.

Numismatists are now working on the theory that all coins should be down-dated in the Archaic period (i.e. before 480 BC) and have advanced some quite convincing arguments in many cases. Although some of these new chronologies (including an attempt to down-date the *Wappenmünzen* referred to earlier in this chapter) are very tempting, they are by no means incontestable. However, this is perhaps a very good example of how one group of coins has affected thinking on a whole series.

Coins with Historical Types

Reference to historical events appear on Greek coins from the fifth century, but they are usually of an indirect nature and of little value for establishing dates since the historical significance is frequently read into the types once the approximate date has been determined by other methods.

The majority of Greek coins with direct historical type references date from the late Hellenistic period, when types are less expressions of formal art and more instruments of propaganda in the hands of individuals. A very early and typical 'historical' coin is a small gold piece struck at Syracuse at the time of the Carthaginian occupation of Sicily, about 400 BC. This has as a reverse Herakles strangling the Nemean Lion. The allusion to the Carthaginian occupation is at first obscure, until we remember that a lion frequently symbolized Africa. Slightly earlier, in another Sicilian city, Selinus, the usual reverse type of Apollo gave way to a winged Nike. This probably commemorated the defeat of the Athenians in the disastrous Sicilian Expedition of 413.

Turning to Roman Republican coins, we find a much wider range of historical types, especially in the later period. Before 135 BC such references are very few and as indirect as the Greek examples. Occasionally symbols may have an historical meaning. Victory flying over the Dioscuri on early denarii may symbolize the end of the Second Macedonian War, while Victory crowning Rome on other denarii may mark the end of the Punic Wars.

From 123 BC until about 70 BC references are more abundant, but still veiled. Now, however, the whole type may have an historical meaning. Coins commemorate the Gallic Wars, the Cimbrian Wars and the Jugurthine War. Others refer obliquely to Marius' campaign against the Cimbri and the Teutones. The great Social War between Marius and Sulla is well documented in the coin record, and the rebels struck coins including some with a type showing the bull of Italy trampling the she-wolf of Rome.

For the period 70–50 BC the allusions are still more abundant. An aureus shows the triumph of Pompey on his return from the east, with the head of Africa on the obverse. With the start of the Civil War between Pompey and Caesar the coin types become important as major instruments of propaganda, and from then until the end of the Principate of Augustus provide an invaluable chronological framework, always bearing in mind that a coin may not be absolutely contemporary with the event to which it refers.

Some of these references are of a very direct nature. One coin, perhaps the most famous of all those of the Republic, was struck by Brutus on the assassination of Caesar. On the obverse is the head of the conspirator, on the reverse is the Cap of Liberty between two daggers. The simple legend underneath removes any doubt as to the reference – it reads EID MAR (Plate 6k).

The coins of Octavian are particularly rich in allusion. On one coin, struck to commemorate the defeat of Antony and Cleopatra at Actium in 31 BC, there appears a winged Victory on a prow (Actium was a sea battle) with Octavian in a triumphal quadriga on the reverse. At a later date coins were struck with types which relate to the temple Octavian dedicated on the Palatine Hill to Apollo of Actium – the reverses not only depict Apollo but have the legends ACT or APOLLINI ACTIO to make it quite clear to which Apollo they refer (Plate 6l).

This topicality may at first appear strange to the modern reader. We seldom look at our coins, but in antiquity the situation was different, and it would be ridiculous to suppose that such thought and care was lavished on the engraving of dies if the results were not going to be noticed and appreciated. In antiquity, in the absence of newspapers and other mass communication media, coins were of great value for spreading news of what was happening outside the area in which they were circulating. Rulers soon realized that they could be used to promote propaganda and circulate official pronouncements of events, sometimes distorting the picture in the interests of politics.

In the Roman Empire the propaganda and allusions continue. The obverses bear the emperors' portraits, itself a piece of subtle propaganda, for the Romans, like contemporary Communists, fully appreciated the importance of making the citizens familiar with the features of their leader, whether it be Nero, Caesar or Mao T'se Tung. The reverses employed a complex language of personifications which today we sometimes have difficulty in understanding. This specialized shorthand must have been fully understood by the people who used the coins, even if some of the subtleties escape us today.

Our problem, however, is chronology, and the references to contemporary events on Roman Imperial coins are rarely of value in this respect, since the date of the coins can, as we have seen, be established by other methods. Occasionally when there is some doubt in which of two years a coin may have been struck, a reference to a campaign can sometimes clarify the question.

Coins Dated from Historical Connections

Quite a number of Greek coins can be roughly dated because they can be related in various ways to historical events. Obviously the foundation and destruction dates of cities provide useful *termini post et ante quem* in a number of cases. We may consider a few examples.

Between 476 and 475 BC the tyrant Hiero of Syracuse moved all the inhabitants of the cities of Catana and Naxos to Leontini. Catana was then repopulated and renamed Aetna. This was because he wanted to build up a reserve of allies near him in case Syracuse was threatened. After his death Aetna was attacked and the citizens driven out, to settle in a new Aetna on the slopes of the volcano with the same name. Hiero's Aetna became Catana once again. Coins are known with the types of the head of Selinus and a distinctive thunderbolt with the names of Aetna and Catana on them. As they are identical in treatment they must have been struck at the same city, and we can deduce that those with the name of Aetna must have been struck at Catana in the period 475–61 or earlier.

The city of Sybaris was destroyed in 510 BC; thus all coins of archaic style struck there must antedate this. It was refounded in 453 as New Sybaris, but in style the coins struck thereafter are quite different.

The Athenian colony of Amphipolis was not founded until 437 BC. The earliest coins of this city, however, must not be dated before 424, because until that year, when she was freed by the Spartan Brasidas, Athens forbade her to strike coins of her own.

A terminal date for the earliest coins of Chalcis, in Euboea, can be established at 506 BC when she became subject to Athens. Likewise

c

there is a break in the coinage of Aegina between 456 and 431 BC while she was under Athenian domination, though a few small denominations may have been issued. The coins that antedate 456 are distinguishable from those that postdate 431 in that the later series have a new type – a land tortoise instead of a turtle. This may be connected with Aegina's loss of sea power following the Athenian subjection.

Not infrequently coins can be related to history in other ways. Before 480 BC the sacred city of Delphi had only issued obols. Then suddenly, during the first quarter of the fifth century, there was a short-lived issue of large coins, didrachms and tridrachms. This is probably to be explained by the Greek victory over the Persians which resulted in many gifts of bullion to Delphic Apollo from grateful cities. These coins, therefore, can be dated to 479–8 BC. Their types have no reference, even indirect, to the victory.

References to Contemporary Coins in Ancient Writers

References to coins are rare in ancient writers, and when they do occur they are often of doubtful validity.

The earliest reference to an actual coin type appears in an epigram by the sixth century poet Simonides, written for the base of a statue of Artemis, in which mention is made of the goat type of contemporary Parian coins.

Such references, of course, are of no value for dating. Of much greater value is a reference in Aristotle to the coins of Rhegium in Sicily. He tells us that Anaxilas of Rhegium won a victory at Olympia with his mule car and imported hares to Sicily, following which he put a mule car and a hare on his coins.

Coins with these types are known, and as Anaxilas' victory at Olympia can be dated to 480 BC this gives us a date for the coins.

Aristotle is a fairly reliable source of information about coins. In his *Constitution of the Athenians* he tells us that under Solon the mina was increased from 70 to 100 drachms while the pre-Solonian coin in Athens was the didrachm. This can be related to the surviving coins, the old standard didrachm being the 'amphora didrachms' on the Pheidonian standard, while the new coins set the amphora on a shield and used a new standard.

Diodorus Siculus tells us how, following the defeat of the Carthaginians in 480 BC by Gelon, an indemnity of 200 talents was extracted from the Carthaginian leader. The Carthaginians too, we are told, presented Gelon's queen, Demarete, with a crown weighing a hundred gold talents. This she ordered to be melted down for coins which, on account of their weight, were known as fifty-litra pieces.

In the writings of the comic playwright Aristophanes there are numerous references to contemporary coins, and of particular value are the references to the plated emergency coins struck in Athens in 406 BC and current until 393. Occasionally Greek inscriptions have proved useful in dating coins.

References in Roman writers to coins are similar to the Greek. The early references in Plautus (particularly in the *Trinummus*) have been useful for dating purposes, and Pliny the Elder has given us a useful account of Republican coins which has likewise served in dating coins. Occasional references in Livy (for instance, to the introduction of the first silver coinage in 269) and other writers have occasionally provided clues to dating which have been substantiated by other means.

Further Reading

There is no comprehensive study of the different methods of dating coins, though for absolute chronologies the chapter on 'Dates, and Marks of Value' in Sir George Macdonald's *The Evolution of Coinage* (1916) will be found particularly useful.

The introduction to Barclay Head's monumental *Historia Numorum*, 2nd Ed. (1911, reprinted 1963), contains useful material on Greek magisterial dating and on dating according to art styles. Harold Mattingly's *Roman Coins* (2nd Ed. 1962) and the Rev. E. A. Sydenham's *Coinage of the Roman Republic* (1952) both contain good summaries of the methods employed in dating Roman Republican coins. The above books are fairly easily obtained, with the exception of Macdonald's work which is out of print.

Although it is only to be found in larger libraries in Britain Margaret Thompson's work on *The New Style Coinage of Athens* published in two volumes by the American Numismatic Society in 1961 is essential for anyone who wants to see contemporary numismatic *expertise* at its best – here every technique was employed by Dr Thompson to unravel this complex series with very impressive results.

For Roman Imperial coinage the methods of dating are outlined in Volume 1 of Mattingly and Sydenham's *Roman Imperial Coinage* (1923).

3 Hoards

Very few people, however sceptical they may be about the value of historical and archaeological studies, fail to be interested in the discovery of a large hoard of silver or gold coins. A hoard of coins is invested in an almost fairytale allure, and the word conjures up an image of a 'crock of gold' for many people who would not show the least interest in the discovery of a group of pots in a well or a pit. Probably the reason for this is that a hoard often means hundreds, sometimes even thousands, of pieces of gold or silver, and it is the idea of the chance discovery of wealth in a form that is quite calculable in terms of the twentieth century materialist's scale of values that attracts, not the antiquity of the coins or their importance in contributing to our knowledge of the past.

Nevertheless they are of utmost importance in this respect. It is through studying hoards that numismatists build up their framework of chronology and typology, and in another field the interpretation of a hoard or a group of hoards sheds a great deal of light on contemporary history.

'Hoarding is a habit', once wrote an eminent authority on Greek coin hoards. It is a habit, moreover, that is far from extinct. Often new issues of coins are put aside because of their novelty and their attractive appearance, and they return to circulation sometimes after the new issue has become familiar. When one is spending money one usually tries to spend the most worn coins rather than the shiny, newly minted pieces, or to hand over a dirty banknote and retain a crisp note that has not seen circulation since it left the bank. This is in a simple sense hoarding, and is of great significance as the principle governing the interpretation of coin hoards.

So significant a factor is it in a country's economy that the Commercial Advisor to Elizabeth I, Sir Thomas Gresham, formulated it as an economic principle, which we now know as Gresham's Law. This states, 'In every country where two kinds of legal money are in circulation, the bad money always drives out the good'. In essence, it means this: we prefer to spend bad coins than good provided the bad have the same purchasing power as the good. For this reason bad coins continue in circulation, and good coins seem to disappear. The French economist Gide in considering Gresham's Law explained the disappearance as having three causes: hoarding, payments abroad, and sales by weight.

This fact was recognized long before the time of Gresham, and an interesting sidelight on it is shed by a text from Aristophanes' *Frogs*, produced in 405 BC.

The public often has given us the appearance of treating our wisest and best citizens in the same way as it treats old and new coins. We do not use the latter at all except in our homes or abroad, though they are of purer metal and better to look at, the only ones that are well minted and circular; on the contrary we prefer to use bad copper pieces, struck and embossed in the very worst way.

(vv. 718–26.)

The circumstance which caused Gresham to make his Law was an attempt made to rectify the trouble caused by clipping, a prevalent crime in the Middle Ages when coins were 'hammered' and thin enough for this to be feasible. People used the silver that they clipped for their own purposes, and as a result a large number of underweight coins were in circulation. The new coinage intended to replace the old clipped coins only resulted in the bad coins seeming to be even more prevalent. In order to replace the old, the government was forced to have not one major recoinage, but several. From this particular example it is possible to extend the Law to say that whenever light coins are in circulation with heavy coins, whether the light coins are of better workmanship and standard than the heavier or not, we find that the light coins drive out the heavy.

The incidence of hoarding and the disappearance of good coins from circulation coincides, as one might expect, with prevalent economic crises or other events which result in a feeling of insecurity. One of the main problems of coins vanishing from circulation arises when, because of inflation, the value of the metal of coins exceeds the purchasing power of the denomination – for example, there is more than a pennyworth of bronze in our pennies at present, although our cupro-nickel coins are merely a token coinage; that is, the metal out of which they are struck is less than the face value of the denominations. Like banknotes, our 'silver' coins are merely tokens and are purely fiduciary. It was found necessary in the present century to replace silver coins first by base alloys and then by cupro-nickel, as the value of silver was greatly in excess of the face value of the coins struck from it, with the result that after the First World War when the bullion value of silver soared due to the shortage, people were keeping silver coins back and melting them down for the metal.

Hoarding still takes place where banking facilities are unsatisfactory or nonexistent, and even in some areas where there are adequate banks but where individuals do not trust them. Many people still keep their savings under the floorboards or in a crevice in the chimney because they like to think that the money is readily accessible whenever they want to use it. Hoards, however, are not often buried in the present age because there are better alternatives. In antiquity houses were simpler and the ground was the most secure place for money to be hidden.

Coins Favoured for Hoarding

At present there are no coins of high denominations which are likely to be hoarded, and people who do keep their savings at home tend to save paper money as this means that a large sum can be stored in a conveniently small space. The smaller the space savings take up the safer they will be. This has not always been the case, and in the days in the earlier part of the century when sovereigns and half sovereigns were in circulation these were hoarded. In France at the time of the French Revolution people did not hoard the paper assignats but preferred, not surprisingly, gold coins. Generally speaking in Savings Hoards (there are other types as will be seen presently but Savings Hoards are the most common) we find that people save first the best coins they can obtain (those likely to be the most readily redeemed at a future date), and secondly the highest denominations in order not to make the hoard too large to hide.

Relative Value of Coins

In antiquity hoards were usually buried in some kind of receptacle in the ground. It has already been stated that banks have reduced the incidence of hoarding in modern times, but there were very few banks in antiquity. That is not to say there were none – sometimes there were temple treasuries that served much the same kind of purpose, and there were individual bankers in the Greek and Roman world. The Romans were acquainted with the use of credit bills, and some business transactions were arranged through bankers without coins actually changing hands. For the most part, the care of money was in the hands of the individual. Due to the much higher purchasing power of coins in antiquity a few coins had a much greater value than they would have today – a juror's pay in fifth century Athens was an obol a day, an obol being a tiny coin about seven millimetres in diameter, several of which might be balanced on a shilling. A Greek soldier received for one month's service a single gold coin not much bigger than a sixpence. Augustus paid his legionaries nine aurei a year, an aureus being a gold coin about the size of a sixpence. In 1336 a pig cost a penny. In 1389 a cowherd was paid 6s. 8d. per annum.

Where Hoards Were Buried

It is interesting that hoards are usually found in places which are fairly remote from habitation sites. For example in the Roman town of Calleva (Silchester) which was extensively excavated in the late nineteenth century and again on a smaller scale in the 1950s we find that there are only four coin hoards recorded, although the number of single coins found is enormous. In the same way it is very rare to find hoards on military sites. When they are found on occupation sites they are usually very carefully concealed, being buried under the floor, in a pit, in a hypocaust or sometimes in a filled-up ditch. It is frequently the case that they were buried near some landmark, either natural or man made, in order to make them easy to find again. A prehistoric barrow was often chosen in Roman Britain as a suitable landmark, or a natural feature like a curiously-shaped rock. Sometimes they were carefully protected by stones or brickwork.

Hoards have been found in some very strange places – one was found buried in the crater of an extinct volcano, and another from Bologna was found buried under eight feet of sediment in a river during the construction of a bridge. Presumably the owner had been drowned while carrying his wealth across.

They can be found buried in almost anything. Usually pots were employed, but hollow stones, boxes, leather bags, cloth purses or similar containers were also used. When hoards are found without any evidence of a container it can be assumed that they were buried in some receptacle of perishable material, such as wood, cloth or leather. It is not uncommon to find other valuables which the owner wished to hide, associated with the hoard, usually jewellery or fine household plate. Sometimes one finds associated small objects which do not seem to have any value, and as these were probably of sentimental value to the owner it gives us an insight into the type of possession that people have treasured at different periods.

Types of Hoards

(a) Coins Collected

The collecting instinct is by no means a modern one, and there have been collectors at all periods of antiquity. There are instances of 'collecting' even in the Mesolithic period – at Thatcham in Berkshire a Palaeolithic implement was found on the Maglemosian settlement of the ninth millenium BC in a context which suggested that it had been brought there deliberately as a curiosity, and there is the well-known museum formed by the princess Bel-Shalti-Nannar at Ur in the sixth century BC. In Britain there are cases of hoards of a very peculiar nature containing coins which were not current at the time when the hoard was formed. One well-known but alas badly authenticated hoard of this sort was found at Bath in 1807 and comprised of 'small silver coins, Roman, Numidian and Cartha-ginian, none of a later date than the earlier Caesars'. Much more frequent are hoards in which the owner has carefully chosen the coins out of those in circulation. The best example of this is the Thorngrafton Hoard, found in the last century and consisting of three aurei and sixty denarii in a bronze purse. The interesting feature of the hoard was the fact that all the reverses were different, and the coins exactly filled the purse. This hoard was dated to the time of Hadrian.

Many Romano-British coin hoards contain very rare coins and a wide variety of types, suggesting that some collecting instinct was influencing the formation of them. One hoard dating from the time of Vespasian from Honley contained a rare silver coin of the Coritani with the CARTIVEL legend on it (once ascribed to Cartimandua of the Brigantes) and another hoard found in 1902 at Icklingham con-tained a unique coin of Flavia Maxima Helena struck in the early fourth century, the hoard being datable to the time of Honorius. (AD 393–423).

(b) Accumulations

Sometimes one finds an assemblage of coins which, strictly speaking, is not a hoard but is rather an accumulation. These are generally built up over a long period of time and were not usually the property of one individual. The most common case of this is the accumulation of coins thrown into a sacred well or spring as offerings. Visitors today still like to throw coins into fountains or 'wishing wells', perhaps the most famous instance of this being the custom of throwing coins into the Trevi Fountain in Rome.

These are of great interest in their own right, but they are more of value in studying the popularity of a particular well over a period of time than in serving as dating material for the numismatist or for providing him with a closed group for studying typology.

Perhaps the most famous accumulation is that from Carrawburgh on Hadrian's Wall. Carrawburgh was the Roman Procolitia, but is distinguished from other Wall forts by having a particularly active religious centre. There was a very fine temple of Mithras there and a well sacred to the nymph Coventina. From her well were recovered between 15,000 and 20,000 coins, of which 2,829 were of the reign of Antoninus Pius, when the well seems to have been most popular. The chronological range of the coins was very wide (the earliest being a Greek coin of Naples of the second century BC), and they extended through much of the Roman period. The well was discovered in 1876, and in addition to coins, pious soldiers had offered jewels, brooches and pots of different sorts. At Carrawburgh there seems to have been another water cult with a small shrine which has been called the Shrine of the Nymphs. Such water cults as these are essentially Celtic, and are fairly well attested from numerous places in Britain.

Into the category of accumulations also fall the contents of temple treasuries, which were the equivalents of banks. Needless to say seldom do such hoards come to light, although there were many such 'banks' in Classical times, such as the temple Treasury at Delos.

(c) Hoards of Coins lost in Catastrophes

Such hoards are collections of coins which the owner was unable to claim because he was prevented from doing so by some catastrophe. They are not hoards in the same sense as Savings Hoards or Merchants' Hoards because they were not buried on purpose in order to conceal them – concealment was accidental. The coins in such hoards may be the property of an individual but can just as easily be the

C*

property of a group. The best example of such a hoard is that from Boscoreale, on the slopes of Mount Vesuvius, which can be dated to AD 79. The hoard was found in a villa in 1895, and represented the valuables that were in the process of being collected for taking away when the owner was overcome by sulphur fumes. In one of the small rooms was a hoard of silverware, and near it was the body of the owner. The treasure included a small chest with over a thousand gold aurei, ranging in date from those of Augustus to pieces struck just before the date of the eruption. The coins of Augustus were more numerous than one might expect but all were worn. There are several other instances from Pompeii, Herculaneum and the vicinity. At Pompeii itself there are cases of citizens who collected up their money and took to flight, but were overcome before they could escape. One woman who lived on the corner of Mercury Street wasted too much time collecting her valuables while the rest of the household escaped, and was found with her money, her jewellery and her silver mirror. Nearer home we have a similar situation in Roman Wroxeter. Under a hypocaust of the public baths archaeologists found the skeleton of an old man clutching in his arms a bag of 132 coins. He had crawled into the hypocaust for safety at the time of a raid and had probably died of suffocation.

Another type of disaster which resulted in the accidental burial of coins was the sack of Rome by the Goths in AD 410. The Goths set fire to buildings in the Forum Romanum, and one of the buildings that was destroyed was the Basilica Aemilia. On the pavement of the nave coins can still be seen which fused together in the fire, having been part of the treasure stored in the building.

Wrecks also result in large numbers of coins being lost. One of the best recent examples is the Swedish ship *Vasa* which sank in Stockholm harbour in 1628, and which was recovered and refloated in 1961. There were four thousand coins on board, some of which were found in barrels and sea chests, others wrapped in cloth purses. The biggest collection from the ship came from a barrel on the upper gundeck, and another was found in a chest in the hold. Each of these hoards consisted of over nine hundred coins.

(d) Mercantile Hoards

Nearly all hoards belong to one of three classes, Mercantile Hoards, Bullion Hoards and Savings Hoards. Mercantile hoards are the property of a merchant, or at least represent the cash of somebody who was employed in selling commodities to the general public or collecting money from them to pay for taxes, special services, etc. Generally speaking, in these hoards the coins are of smaller denominations, being the coins in general circulation at the time at which an emergency resulted in the burial of the hoard. For this reason the coins may be quite worn, or may be of widely divergent conditions. Secondly, the time span covered by the coins is not likely to be as long as that covered by a Savings Hoard.

Mercantile Hoards are not very common. One interesting example from Egypt consisted almost entirely of small bronze pentadrachms, in varying conditions. This hoard puzzled numismatists for some time until it was realized that they represented the takings from a simple automatic machine which supplied ritual water at the door of a temple in Alexandria. The hoard was found near the door of a temple, and we have an interesting account of such machines in the writings of Heron, a third century BC Greek in Egypt who wrote a book about them, the *Automatopoetica*.

Egypt also provides us with another very curious example of a Mercantile Hoard. In Boston, Mass., there is an interesting Ptolemaic collecting box with coins of Ptolemy VI (181–156 BC). The box is of bronze, and was found near Memphis. On the lid there is an inscription which roughly means 'Get Healthy!' It has been suggested that it was used in the equivalent of a Health Service in Egypt in Ptolemaic times, whereby a syndicate subscribed and members could draw on the savings to pay doctors' fees. The box contained few coins.

Offering boxes are not unknown from the ancient world. Usually they were made of terracotta and shaped like temples or shrines. Frequently the deity was shown enthroned in relief on the inside. Examples are known from Ostia, Trier, St Germain and Priene and there was at Eleusis a large collecting box cut out of the living rock for pilgrims to the mysteries of Demeter to make their contributions.

Perhaps the most famous example of a Mercantile Hoard from Britain is the Dorchester Hoard, from Dorchester, Dorset. It was found in 1936 at 45 South Street, and consisted of 22,000 base silver antoniniani covering the period from Caracalla to Gallienus. (AD 200–60). The majority of the coins were of Philip I or Gordian III. The coins were buried in a bowl, a jug, and a metal box. It has been suggested, with some degree of probability, that the hoard represents the Imperial tax collection for the town of Durnovaria (Plate 24).

(e) Bullion Hoards

A bullion hoard is a hoard of coins collected not for the face value of the coins but for their metal content. These were normally hoards of coins which were intended for scrap-metal and would have been melted down had not some accident prevented it. Into this category usually fall Plunder Hoards, which are coins looted at a time of trouble by raiders or pirates. Generally speaking there is a tendency in Bullion Hoards for the coins to be fairly worn or battered, since good coins were not often melted down. As in Mercantile Hoards there is also a tendency for the coins to cover a shorter period of time, especially when the hoard is not that of a metal smith but rather of a raider.

Coins intended for the melting pot are usually recognizable because they are found along with other bullion, and this is often badly mutilated by being hammered down in order to make it easier to carry. This applies to Plunder Hoards too, which are often only distinguishable because the associated objects are not mutilated and include things which cannot be melted down to scrap metal. Sometimes a Scrap-metal Hoard and a Plunder Hoard may be one and the same.

Scrap-metal Hoards can occur at all periods, Plunder Hoards usually only at times of unrest. Thus we find a large number of coins associated with the hoards of Celtic metalwork from Snettisham, Norfolk, and these must have been intended as scrap metal. The hoards date from the end of the first century BC. Similarly there was a number of silver coins associated with the famous Traprain Law Hoard from Midlothian, which seems to have been looted by Irish pirates in the fifth century with the intention of breaking the silverwork of which it was comprised into scrap. Here again a large number of the vessels were distorted. The coins were fourth century Roman siliquae.

The period at which Plunder Hoards are most common is not surprisingly that of the Viking raids. It is not due to collectors that the Royal Museum at Stockholm has the best collection of Anglo-Saxon coins outside Britain.

(f) Savings Hoards

Of all types of hoards, by far the commonest is the Savings Hoard (see above, page 54). The coins tend to be of high denominations, in good condition and covering a wider range of dates than the coins in the other categories of hoards.

Dating Hoards

Occasionally, but very rarely, we know the circumstances in which a hoard was buried and the date at which the event took place. The hoards associated with the eruption of Vesuvius are a case in point. Sometimes, too, we can relate a hoard to a particular panic which resulted in widespread burial of hoards, which can date it to within a few years at least.

In Britain the Civil War resulted in numerous hoards being buried, and no doubt the most important of these, the Newark Hoard, which was found in 1961 and which consisted of ninety-seven gold coins, can be related to the siege of Newark in 1646. A more recent instance of an event resulting in hoards being buried was the 1798 Irish Rising to which a number of hoards can be related. At Killane in County Wexford 55 gold coins of George III were found in a farm outhouse beneath some cobbles.

Normally hoards are dated according to the point at which the hoard was closed, that is, to the date of the latest coin in the hoard. Sometimes, however, it is useful to consider the composition of the hoard as a whole to obtain a more precise dating for its burial. When the latest coins show little signs of wear and the coins taken as a whole provide a chronological sequence it is usually fairly safe to assume that the hoard was buried soon after the date of the latest coin. Here the condition of the latest coin may be a good indicator, and if it is worn, one must assume that the hoard was closed at a later date. Usually with such hoards there are breaks in the chronological sequence.

The date at which the hoard was closed, however, can give no accurate dating for when the hoard was first buried, for usually in the case of Savings Hoards the owner collected his money over a period of time, sometimes taking coins out to spend them and sometimes putting more coins in. Hoards seldom remained static. Here again the chronological sequence of the coins in the hoard as a whole is of great value, and if the coins present a continuous sequence then one can probably assume that the date of the last coins in the hoard is the date when the whole hoard was deposited.

In a case where a hoard has been built up over a period of years it is possible to arrive at a *terminus post quem* by assuming that the date from which the number of coins increases year by year and the amount of wear lessens is the date of the original deposition of the hoard. This is further verified if, after this date, the number of coins of each year (or reign) is steady or increases.

Another useful indicator for the date at which a hoard was buried is the vessel in which it was buried, or the objects associated with it, in the cases where there are such objects. Since pots, generally speaking, have a short life and the forms of vessels change very frequently, it is usually possible to date a pot fairly closely – this is particularly the case with Roman pottery, which in Britain can often be dated within a time span of a quarter of a century or less. Brooches, too, on account of changes of fashion can be dated closely and are not uncommonly associated with hoards, but here the date is less reliable since brooches had a long life, and could even be heirlooms.

When a hoard is dated by a numismatist the date given is always that at which the hoard was most probably buried, thus a hoard in which the latest coins are those of Constantine I would be 'dated' to the time of Constantine.

Although broadly speaking the rules used in dating coin hoards are relatively simple, there can be many complications. Hoards are seldom found in archaeological excavations, for the reason already mentioned – that hoards were buried away from settlement sites. Accordingly the entire hoard is not always recovered, some coins being missed by the finders or perhaps appropriated and sold before it is seen by a numismatist. Again there may be stray coins which have become associated with the hoard, either by accident or carelessness. If these are much later than the hoard they can be very misleading in trying to establish a *terminus post quem*. This is a particular hazard in the case of a hoard found, say, in the nineteenth century and not published but stored in a museum until it is noticed by a numismatist working with the museum collection. Nearly always the notes relating to such hoards are inadequate, and often coins have been added to the hoard because at a later date other coins were found in the same locality, and someone assumed that they were coins from the hoard that had been missed at the time of the discovery.

The Value of Hoards to the Numismatist

It has been said that archaeology stands on a foundation of potsherds, and it would be just as true to say that numismatics stands on a foundation of coin hoards. Coin hoards provide us with the framework of our classification of ancient coins, and frequently a single hoard has provided us with enough material to study a whole series of coins and classify it whereas before the discovery of the hoard the type of coin represented was extremely rare or even unique.

Until a huge hoard consisting almost entirely of coins of Henry II struck in the period 1158–80 was found at Tealby in 1805 this early issue (which is now called the 'Tealby Type') was almost unknown.

Apart from supplying the numismatist with new source material hoards are invaluable for other reasons. Once the date of burial is established it provides a date for all the coins in the hoard, as they cannot be later than the date at which the hoard was deposited. Admittedly there is always the problem of intrusive material, as has already been mentioned in discussing the problems of dating, but this is not a very frequent occurrence. In the case of hoards where we have a series of coins which were not accumulated over a very prolonged period of time we can gain invaluable information regarding how long different issues remained in circulation, and how far they travelled. There are problems relating to this, as a hoard cannot always give an accurate picture of the coins in circulation in a given area at a given time. There may be chance omissions or perhaps there has been a certain amount of artificial selection on the part of the owner. Certain types of coins are very seldom found in hoards, although they certainly enjoyed a fairly long and wide circulation. This is either because a period of peace resulted in fewer hoards being buried, or because the coins were of too low a denomination to be hoarded, or not good enough, following Gresham's Law. Thus we find that although we have an extensive series of hoards of silver denarii of the Roman Republic, there are practically no hoards recorded containing Republican aes.

Clearly the hoards that are of the greatest value for discovering which coins were in most general circulation are not the Savings Hoards but the much rarer Mercantile Hoards or Bullion Hoards, though the latter again tend to be unreliable.

When there is a whole series of hoards to study, a general picture emerges which is of great value. A series of hoards can provide us with sequence dating for coins, and indeed provide numismatists with the entire framework for dating coins at certain periods. This is particularly true of the dating of Roman Republican denarii from 123 BC on, when there is a long series of hoards which put the dating of denarii on a fairly sound footing. The method used in sequence dating is fairly simple, and is best explained by a purely theoretical example. Let us assume there are three hoards containing coins of a particular city, and that all three hoards can be dated because they contain coins of other cities which have been dated by other means. Perhaps the three hoards were buried at intervals of about forty years. If this is the case the coin types which are found in the second hoard, Perhaps the three hoards were buried at intervals of about forty years. which elapsed between the burial of the first and the second, and similarly the new types in the third hoard must have been struck in the period between the second and third hoard. Possibly a particular type was issued for a longer period than that which elapsed between two of the hoards or may only have been struck for the first time shortly before the second hoard was deposited. Here a greater series of hoards in which the overlap of certain types can be studied is valuable, and with a sufficient number of hoards the date and duration of output of a given type can be established.

Greuber outlined the whole study of Republican denarii on the basis of hoards in the introduction to the British Museum Catalogue of the coins of the Roman Republic. Nearly all the hoards on which the study is based come from Italy and, as one might expect, are connected with a series of disturbances – the Revolt of Fregellae in 126 BC, the Cimbrian War, the Social War, the Civil War between Marius and Sulla and the Revolt of Spartacus provide us with a valuable sequence down to about 70 BC. After that there is a lull in the hoards during the years of relative peace in Italy, but again there is a large number of hoards associated with the Civil War between Caesar and Pompey, and the hoards are very copious for the last years of the Roman Republic. The story provided by the Italian hoards is occasionally supplemented by hoards outside Italy – there are a number of hoards for the period around 100 BC in Spain, when there were revolts there.

The Value of Hoards to the Archaeologist and Historian

The value of hoards to the archaeologist and the historian lies in their interpretation and discovering the reasons why they were buried.

There are three reasons why hoards are buried: profit, safety or fear. In the first two cases it was only when the owner died suddenly that the hoard was left buried for future generations to find. In the case where a hoard was buried on account of fear there is more chance of something happening to prevent the owner digging it up again.

Accounts of emergencies which resulted in a widespread panic and the burial of hoards are recorded in literary sources at different periods. Appian gives us a very graphic account of how at the capture of Rhodes by Cassius in 42 BC the citizens buried their wealth. Cassius, realizing this gave orders for rewards to be given for information relating to hoards, and for those who concealed them to be put to death. As a result, the citizens unearthed their buried treasure from the ground, from wells, and even from graves.

A more recent account of a scare which resulted in hoards being buried is recorded by Samuel Pepys in June 1667, when people were terrified by reports of Dutch ships in the Thames. Pepys sent some of his money with his wife and father to a safer place in the country. Some, it seems, was buried in the garden, and in October of the same year he had great difficulty in finding it again.

... My father and I with a dark lantern, it being now night, went into the garden with my wife, and there went about our great work to dig up my gold. But Lord! what a tosse I was for some time in, that they could not justly tell me where it was; that I began heartily to sweat, and be angry, that they should not agree better on the place, and at last to fear that it was gone; but by and by, and by poking with a spit, we found it. . . .

Pepys' troubles were far from over, because the bags in which the gold coins were buried had rotted away. It seems that even after sieving the ground he was not able to recover all of them. As a postscript to this story it is interesting to record that about 1842 an iron pot was found in the grounds where Pepys' house had formerly stood, containing coins (mainly half-crowns) of Elizabeth, James I and Charles I. Possibly this pot was buried along with the bags of gold coins.

If we consider the Roman coin hoards from the British Isles we find that an interesting overall picture emerges. Although the 1,200 or more recorded hoards are spread out over the whole period of the Roman occupation we find that at certain times hoards are much more common, most notably in the reigns of Marcus Aurelius (AD 161–80), the Tetrici (AD 270–3), Carausius (AD 287–93), Constantine I (AD 306–37) and Honorius (AD 393–423). As occurrences of hoarding can frequently be related to historical disturbances it is fairly valid to assume that when there is a dense concentration of hoards at a given period and particularly in a given area, then in that area at that date there was some threat which brought about hoarding, even though it is not documented historically.

Sometimes, too, hoards give us insight into peculiar circumstances in localized areas regarding the circulation of coins which may be the reflection of historical circumstances.

Hoards are of great value to the economic historian, as the other main reason for hoarding, apart from fear, was economic fluctuations. The full significance of this has never been properly exploited by economic historians.

Hoards can also throw light on trade routes and patterns of commerce in antiquity. Thus, if the coins of a particular state travel to a number of other states and occur in hoards there, one can assume that the first state enjoyed some kind of constant relationship with the others, usually of a commercial nature, and in all probability the absorption of the coins of the first state by the others represents one side of a series of buying and selling transactions.

Treasure Trove

In Roman times Hadrian was responsible for a law which said that a man owned anything he found on his own land, but if he found treasure on another man's land he had to share it equally with the owner. This applied even to treasure found on property owned by the state. Later emperors, however, usually claimed a part of all treasure that was found. In Medieval times in England the king usually claimed all treasure found, though in cases where land had been granted in fief to others by the king they also received the right of claiming the treasure. Thus we find that Henry II granted to Ramsey Monastery, 'To receive sac and soc, thol and theam, forstal, blodwith, and the finding of treasure; and likwise all other privileges which belong to the king.'

The present laws relating to Treasure Trove in England and Wales are more complex, and dependent on two factors: first the metal of the treasure found and secondly the intention behind its concealment. The place where the hoard was buried is significant, and the original owner or heirs of the owner must be unknown or untraceable. The metals which come under Treasure Trove law are gold and silver, and their alloy electrum. Base metals may be the property of the finder or of the land-owner. It must be shown that concealment was deliberate with intent to recover the treasure at a later date, and if it is probable that a hoard was buried with no intent to recover it (offerings in a sacred well or grave-goods would fall into this category) then the hoard does not become Treasure Trove. The place of concealment was originally defined as 'hidden in the ground', following the old tradition of the right of the king to claim treasure from graves and barrows. In modern times, however, the scope has been increased and hoards hidden in holes in walls or in roofs have been claimed by the Crown.

When gold or silver coins, plate or bullion are found they must be reported to the police, and a Coroner's Inquest is held to decide whether they are Treasure Trove. If so, they become the property of the Crown; if not, they are awarded to the land-owner and not to the finder. In early Medieval times the penalty for not reporting Treasure Trove was death or mutilation but since 1348 the punishment has been merely a fine or imprisonment. Now finders of Treasure Trove are awarded an ex gratia (tax-free) payment equal to the current market value of the finds. The disposal of the finds is administered by the British Museum, acting for the Crown; they may be offered to another museum, which will have to raise the money for the ex gratia payment.

In the City of London, Treasure Trove belongs to the London Corporation, and similar rights are held by the Duchies of Lancaster and Cornwall. In Scotland the coins are taken by the Queen's Remembrancer and Treasurer for Scotland who can, after a certain period in which they are 'frozen', sell them. In Scotland the first choice goes to the Museum of Antiquities of Scotland.

In France the State claims everything found, but gives half its value to the finder. In Italy the State also claims all that is found, offering a very small reward. This results in far fewer finds being reported in these countries than in Britain.

Further Reading

Strangely, although numismatic literature is full of articles on single hoards or groups of hoards and their significance there are relatively few general studies discussing problems of interpretation.

The only book which considers general problems of hoard interpretation is J. G. Milne's *Greek and Roman Coins and the Study of History*, (1939) which is unfortunately out of print, but there are a number of articles which deal with the subject. Of these the most accessible is Dr Anne S. Robertson's article on 'Romano-British Coin Hoards', which was published in *Roman Coinage, Essays Presented to Harold*

Mattingly (1956), 262–85. Although as the title implies this study is chiefly concerned with Romano-British coin hoards, Dr Robertson draws some general conclusions which apply equally well to other areas and periods. Of greater importance is a classic study of S. P. Noe in *Numismatic Notes and Monographs* 1 (1920) entitled 'Coin Hoards'. This periodical is a publication of the American Numismatic Society. Noe compiled the *Inventory of Greek Coin Hoards* and had first hand knowledge of the problems of interpretation. This study formulates many useful rules which even experienced numismatists tend to forget. An early, but nevertheless useful, study by George Macdonald entitled 'Coin Finds and How to Interpret Them' was published in the *Proceedings of the Royal Philosophical Society of Glasgow* v (1902), 282 f. though this is often difficult to obtain.

Good examples of the uses of sequence dating from hoards can be found in H. Grueber's Introduction to *Coins of the Roman Republic in the British Museum*, three volumes, (1910), and in E. A. Sydenham's *The Coinage of the Roman Republic* (1952).

Mention may be made of a series of popular aticles by J. A. Mackay in *Coins and Medals* 1 (1964–5) entitled 'Treasure Trove'. These articles give abundant references to British coin hoards and their significance.

Finally, no suggestions for further reading are complete without mention of J. D. A. Thompson's *Inventory of British Coin Hoards, A.D. 600–1500* (1956) which is a masterly survey of all the hoards of the period found in Britain. An excellent introduction discusses their interpretation in the light of history.

4 Coins from Excavations

The archaeologist is primarily interested in coins not on account of their significance when stray finds are plotted on distribution maps or their types studied, but because they provide him with valuable chronological information in interpreting excavations. For this reason the first part of this chapter will be devoted to a consideration of the value of coins as dating material from archaeological strata.

Stratigraphy

Archaeological excavation is governed basically by the simple principle of sequence as revealed in the way in which material accumulates on a site, so that the earliest material is most deeply buried. The principle of stratigraphy, as this is called, was first outlined by a geologist, William Smith. In 1816 Smith published a book entitled *Strata Identified by Organized Fossils* in which he argued not only that one could date different fossils in relative terms by the sequence of beds in which they occurred, but also that these were deposited over a long period of time in an orderly manner. 'Strata' Smith's theory was not universally accepted, as many people refused to accept that strata or beds of rock could be laid down through normal natural causes, and preferred to think that the divisions between the layers were caused by catastrophes, as had been suggested by the French geologist Cuvier. In the years between 1830 and 1833 Charles Lyell propounded in his *Principles of Geology* the basic rules of stratigraphy – strata are laid down through natural agencies, and by studying the sequences and the fossils they contain it is possible to see a relative pattern of development.

The early geologists were convinced of the natural deposition of strata by observing fluviatile deposits in contemporary conditions, and indeed the principles governing archaeological and geological stratigraphy are broadly similar. Strata may be deposited on sites of human occupation through either natural or human agency, and the material culture which is contained in these strata is the equivalent of fossils in geological beds. The archaeologist is concerned with distinguishing the various deposits or strata and interpreting them. On a site that has been occupied intensively over a long period, a considerable quantity of material may accumulate on top of the original land surface. All the time, wind blows earth over a site and during periods of abandonment gradual revegetation of the area results in a layer of humus being deposited over the surface of existing deposits. On sandy sites, sand blows in to cover the vestiges with a layer of fine soil.

In theory this is fairly simple, but problems immediately arise because almost no site has a simple sequence of layers, each sealed off by the layer above and each extending over the whole area of the site. The first problem that one encounters lies in the excavating of features – ditches, pits and gulleys – which are dug either into the natural ground surface or into existing strata. Such features may be filled with only one deposit of material, but in the case of pits and ditches there are usually several layers, caused perhaps by different types of rubbish being tipped down into them or through silting up at various times when the partially filled-up feature has remained open. Such features, too, may be cut into by other features – pits may be cut into pits and ditches may be cut through already filled-in ditches. In the same way strata may not be evenly deposited over a site, due to a layer being eroded by weather action or having been removed intentionally as a result of levelling at some period before a phase of rebuilding. It is therefore quite possible to have a layer overlaid by a stratum of one period in one part of the site and with an entirely different stratum of another period elsewhere. One may also encounter two layers which are divided by a lens of different material, which in a small section might give the appearance of three layers. Such a feature might be caused by the dumping of rubbish in a small area during the period when a large deposit was being laid down.

Occasionally one is confronted with inverted stratigraphy, where the whole sequence is reversed, the earliest material being found at a higher level than the latest. This is best seen in the case of a large pit which has been left open and in which part of the side has collapsed as a huge block of earth, tipping over so that the whole mass is upside down. Inverted stratigraphy can also occur when material obtained from another, earlier, source is used to fill features or to raise the ground level for building.

The relative thickness of layers is no indication of age, and one may find a very thick layer deposited deliberately at one time to raise the ground level, or the accumulation of very many layers over a very short period indeed. This is particularly true of the filling of pits, where many layers of different lots of rubbish are tipped in during a brief period.

Just as it is possible to have numerous layers deposited over a short period of time, so is it possible to have one layer deposited over a very long period, usually when there is a phase of abandonment and the deposit is laid down by some natural agency. This is also true of deposits of the Palaeolithic, when the artifacts found at the top of a deposit may be very much later than those nearer the bottom, the difference amounting to millennia.

It is hoped this brief summary will give the reader some idea of the kinds of problems that arise during excavations in the interpretation of strata, and we may now turn to consider the significance of coins in the interpretation of the history of a site.

Coins and Stratigraphy

Broadly speaking it can be seen that coins which occur in a particular layer are of great value for dating that layer and the rest of the material in it, as they usually become incorporated at a period not very far removed from the date at which they were struck.

There are many cases, however, where this is not so. Archaeologists must always be on their guard against contaminating material in a layer, which can have become incorporated in it for a number of reasons. In soft soils coins can sink down from a higher level on account of their own weight. This is particularly so in the case of fine sandy soils and silts. For this reason coins which are found at the top of a layer are particularly suspect, as they could belong to the layer above. Similarly, worm action, mole action, or the activity of rabbits or rats can result in coins being either carried down from a higher level or sometimes brought up from a lower deposit. Secondly, coins which are in reality residuals may be present in the soil when it is laid down. This is the case when earth is dug to fill a feature– sometimes earth is dug out of an early layer in order to provide material to ram round a post in a post-hole or round a beam in a sleeper trench, and can also be brought from elsewhere to fill a pit, or even a ditch. A more frequent occurrence is the discovery of coins in the make-up of a Roman road – suitable materials for constructing roads were not always readily available and had to be brought from some distance, and occasionally the material came from an earlier site.

Duration of Circulation

Apart from intrusive material of this nature coins may be much older than the context in which they appear. To take a modern parallel a cursory glance through the coins that are still in circulation will show that there are some of Victoria's bronze coins of the 1860s in circulation – usually in a very worn condition certainly, although sometimes a coin which has been out of circulation for a time is put back, and accordingly is in much better condition than many more recent coins. This is the case in our own society where coins have been put in a jar or a drawer and later spent because of shortage of small change. This is particularly so in the case of collectors' coins or special issues that have been put aside as souvenirs. Wear does not always indicate the length of time a coin has been in circulation. In the case of ancient coins, some were in circulation for a very long time indeed. It is perhaps interesting to take an example. The most obvious cases of this are coins which on account of their good weight and metal became widely accepted and were used in areas outside those in which they were originally issued. A typical case can be seen in the Persian *sigloi* of the Achaemenids struck during the fifth and fourth centuries BC by Darius and his successors. These silver shekels, and the gold darics which bear identical types, were among the most famous of all pre-Roman coins, and even today on account of their quality enjoy a limited circulation in Eastern bazaars.

The popularity of a coin is not the only reason for its long circulation, and one frequently finds other ancient coins enjoying several centuries of use.

A single coin can provide only a *terminus post quem*, that is, the contents of the layer cannot be earlier than the date of the coin in it. Where there is more than one coin the inferences regarding date can be much more precise, and the whole group can be treated in much the same way as a small hoard, being governed by similar principles. Generally speaking, it is reasonable to infer that if a coin is in fine (F.) condition then it is not likely to have been in circulation for much more than twenty-five years. A coin in very worn condition is certainly more than a few years old and could be even fifty years to a century earlier than the context in which it appears. At certain periods coins have shorter lives than at others, as in the late Roman Empire, and when the archaeologist is dealing with these coins his inferences regarding dates can be more precise.

Archaeologists should distinguish between two types of wear. The first, which is due to prolonged circulation, produces a smooth appearance, and often the legends or parts of the edge are more worn than the centre of the field. Often such coins have a good patina. The second type of wear is due to abrasion, and such coins if studied carefully will show striations from rubbing against other coins in a sack or purse. Here the abrasion may be spread over any part of the field, though high relief is usually the most affected. Coins worn by abrasion may not have been in circulation very long.

To sum up, the basic rule which governs the interpretation of coin finds from a layer or site is that while the overall pattern is likely to present a true picture, the individual coin is not very reliable.

Coins and Segontium

Before turning to the question of the recording, cleaning and storage of coins from an excavation prior to detailed study some examples of the uses and abuses of coins in the interpretation of stratigraphy may be interesting.

An excavation which has now become famous because it was one of the first sites to be excavated and interpreted according to modern methods was that directed by Sir Mortimer Wheeler at the Roman fort of Segontium, in Caernarvon, between 1920 and 1923. This excavation employed techniques of detailed recording and observation of stratigraphy which had been pioneered by General Pitt Rivers at the end of the nineteenth century, but largely ignored by subsequent excavators.

The figure shows a section through the cellar in the sacellum, the small office in the praetorium or headquarters building of the fort where all the documents were kept along with other important valuables (Figure 11).

One hundred and fourteen coins were found in the cellar which was probably constructed in the early years of the third century and gradually filled up. Soon after it was constructed the original floor proved to be inadequate as a means of keeping out the damp, and it was covered with a layer of slates sealed with yellow cement. This was carried up the steps in order to prevent any moisture seeping up. On the original floor, which was in excellent condition (suggesting

SEGONTIVM: CELLAR IN SACELLVM. *SECTION AT S.E. END.*

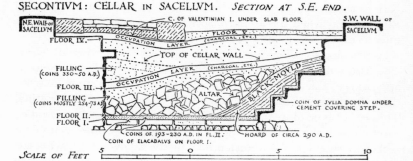

Fig. 11 Section through the Segontium sacellum cellar (After Wheeler, 1922)

that it had not been used for long, before it was sealed off by the slates) lay a denarius of Elagabalus in almost perfect condition (AD 218–22). This must have been lost before the cement was laid down.

Under one of the steps and covered by the cement was a denarius of Julia Domna, also in mint condition (she died in AD 217). Among the cement and slates of the second floor were denarii of Faustina the elder (d. 141), Septimius Severus (193–211), Elagabalus (218–22), Severus Alexander (222–35) and Julia Mamaea (d.235). They were all in good condition, except for the coin of Faustina. From this it was valid to deduce that the second floor was laid down around AD 225, or slightly later. It is very probable that, as damp would have been detected almost immediately, the floor was replaced soon after the cellar was built.

Over the steps had drifted a deposit of black natural soil, which covered a hoard of fifty-six coins ranging in date from Gallienus to Carausius (AD 253–93). There was only one coin of Carausius, in perfect condition. The hoard, which had been contained in a box, was deposited about AD 290. From this it was deduced that the cellar had lain open for a considerable time during which the earth had drifted in.

Above the earth was deliberately deposited filling material, including building rubbish which must have been littering the fort and a number of coins, ranging in date from Commodus (177–92) to a 'Constantinopolis' commemorative struck in the early fourth century. As nearly all the coins were of third century date it might have been thought that the filling took place *c.* 300 if it were not for this last coin, which lay near the bottom of the filling.

Above this again was a layer of burnt material containing nineteen coins, the earliest of which was a very worn sestertius, possibly of Nerva. Apart from five third century radiates, the rest were all fourth century. The latest was a coin of Constans of the mid fourth century.

Above this was more filling almost identical to the first, containing seven coins, all the decipherable examples being of mid fourth century date. On top of the filling was built a rough structure, under which lay a coin of Valentinian I (AD 364–75) which must have got there before the building was constructed.

Here, then, is an excellent case of the story of a building being documented by coins. Additional clues help to amplify the picture given by the coins. The two main phases of filling separated by the burnt layer could be of disparate date, as the coins in the lower were mainly third century. But as fragments of painted wall plaster were found in both lots of filling and the plaster was only a little more weathered in the upper, it would suggest that there was no great interval of time between them.

Treatment of Coin Finds

On an excavation it is usually the custom to treat coins in the same way as other small finds. 'Small finds' is a term used by archaeologists to describe any objects found in the course of excavation that do not come under the heading of pottery, slag, bone, charcoal, tile or shell.

When coins are found they should be bagged separately with their own finds label and then put back in the finds tray along with the other finds of pottery, etc., from the same context, until the recorder has time to give them a small finds number. The card should give the same information for the coin as for the finds from that context as a whole, namely the code letters for the site, the area or trench number (in the case of large scale excavations both may be needed) and the number of the layer from which the coin has come. It is customary, but not essential, to give a brief description of the layer, the date and the name of the finder. The last is needed in case some question arises regarding the precise circumstances in which the coin was found and the date relates it to the finds made on that particular day in cases where the excavation of a layer continues over a period of several days. Thus a code might read 'DR 68 Cutting 53, Site 1, Layer 3, (Lower Transitional, Dark brown soil), James McLaren, 18/7/68.' Usually it is customary to give a trench number in the form of a Roman numeral, and a layer number as an Arabic numeral.

In the case of coins it is sometimes found necessary to use a system of three-dimensional recording, where the depth is recorded from a datum line (not the ground surface, which is irregular, but a nylon thread fixed by nails a few inches from the surface along one side of the cutting, and levelled in with a spirit level). Its precise position is then recorded by triangulating from the sides of the cutting or from pegs at the intersection of cuttings which have been surveyed on a master plan. This is generally a better method than using the sides of the cutting from which to record, as they invariably have a slight batter or alternately are undercut. Subsequent erosion too during the course of the excavation can greatly distort actual measurements. Three-dimensional recording is normally employed when such finds are rare and there is likely to be some dispute about the precise position at a later date.

The recorder on an excavation is responsible for giving each find a small finds number, and cataloguing it in the small finds index. As a numerical reference may cause confusion it is often wise to employ an alphabetical system for small finds recording, using a double letter. Thus the first find will be given the index AA, the second AB and so on until AZ, when one goes on to BA. Bad writing is always a hazard, and certain letters are better omitted completely, particularly I and V.

Usually the site-supervisors (or, in the case of a small excavation, the director) keep a site-book, in which a description of the layers, features, etc., is given as they are excavated together with sketch sections and plans. In this site-book notes are made regarding various problems that arise and other relevant material of importance when the final report is being prepared. It is important that all small finds, particularly coins, should be listed at the end of an entry describing a layer or feature, as this facilitates finding them rapidly when a particular layer is being considered.

At the end of the day the coins, along with the other small finds, should be separated from the rest of the finds and stored together. Most small finds can be stored in polythene 'Mini-grip' bags, which are ideal for the purpose as they enable the finds to be seen without having to open the bag, and the bags have press-seals which keep the contents airtight and waterproof. This is an important consideration for during the day finds lie in the finds tray and if it rains paper bags become soggy and useless. Mini-grip bags can be obtained in various sizes and can be stored in boxes. Many coin dealers stock them now as coin collectors have in recent years realized the convenience of storing their coins in polybags, a cheaper and handier method than in coin cabinets. On a large excavation it is usually a good plan to order them to size from the maker, but on a small site they can be bought from coin dealers, complete with a storage box specially designed to contain them. These boxes hold one hundred bags.

As soon as possible the director (or whoever is responsible for making the preliminary examination of the coins) should make a detailed identification, and this should be recorded in the coin index. The information that should be recorded must include the name of the emperor, monarch or issuing authority, the denomination preceded by the metal (A/ for gold, Æ for silver, Æ for bronze or copper, Bil. for billon and P. for potin) or where the denomination is not known the diameter of the coin should be given in millimetres.

If the obverse legend and type is the monarch's portrait and titles a description can be omitted. The reverse type and legend should be given, however, and where parts of the legend are missing these should be enclosed in square brackets.

The mint name should also be listed, together with the mint mark. In the case of Roman coins where there is part of the mint mark in the field and part in the exergue it should be given thus: $\frac{S/F}{ARLP}$. This means that the letter S is to be found to the left of the type and the letter F to the right of it. The letters ARLP are those which appear in the exergue, and indicate the coin was struck in the first mint shop at Arles.

Of primary importance is the date, and this should be given as precisely as possible.

Last of all should come the condition and reference to a catalogue, where one is available.

The condition should be given according to the standard grading employed by numismatists. The terms 'Mint', 'Very Good', 'Good', 'Worn', 'Very Worn', 'Corroded' or 'Illegible' should be avoided as these can have any meaning at all and only give a vague idea of the actual condition of the coin. The system used by numismatists is shown in the following table:

E.F.   Extremely Fine. This is a coin which shows no signs of wear but which may have scratches or similar minor flaws.

V.F.   This means the coin is only showing signs of wear on the areas of highest relief, but looks as if it is almost uncirculated. The best coins from an excavation are usually V.F. (Very Fine).

good F.   This means the highest relief is rubbed, or the coin is scratched, but the types still show most of the detail.

F.   Fine. This means the coin is quite worn except for the areas of low relief which may be almost unrubbed. Except where they do not appear on the coin because of badly centred striking or a misshaped flan or weak striking, all the letters, symbols, etc. should be visible.

fair.   The usual condition for early Roman Imperial coins. (Late Imperial are nearly always good F. or V.F.) This means the coin is quite worn, but the types and legends are still recognizable and legible.

M.   Mediocre. This is used to describe a coin that is very badly damaged but on which the types are just recognizable.

poor.   This covers all other grades of very worn coins. A poor coin may be just recognizable due to some feature (such as a silhouette) being visible, but may be completely unrecognizable.

In cases where the obverse condition differs from the reverse the obverse condition should be given first, and should be separated from the reverse condition by a line, thus: V.F./good F.

Peculiarities such as when a coin is pierced or tooled should be noted along with the condition.

The archaeologist may complain that he does not have sufficient knowledge of coins to record all this information, and for that reason calls in a numismatist to prepare the final report on the coins. Many archaeologists seem to have quite an unnatural fear of coins and do not realize that a few hours of studying photographs would probably make them sufficiently familiar with the portraits of Roman emperors and the denominations to make it possible for them to look up the coins in a simple catalogue. Fortunately such a catalogue exists, and is both inexpensive and easy to carry. This is David Sear's *Roman Coins and Their Values* (1964). This contains an excellent series of plates from which the archaeologist can familiarize himself with the portraits on Roman Imperial coins, and lists most of the main types of coins that one is likely to find on an excavation of a Roman site.

in Britain. It also includes useful introductory material on denominations and mints.

As the archaeologist is not likely to encounter modern British coins in an excavation (and if he does they are easily identifiable) the only other coins which are likely to turn up are ancient British and medieval British. Even on Iron Age sites ancient British coins are rarely, if ever, found, and so unless the site is known to yield Celtic coins the archaeologist need not trouble about them. If he does require to look them up there is an excellent series of plates in R. P. Mack's *Coinage of Ancient Britain* (1964). For Medieval English coins another copiously illustrated catalogue will usually suffice. This is the *Standard Catalogue of British Coins* I, of which new editions are published regularly. This incidentally covers the main types of ancient British coinage as well as all subsequent English coins. Unfortunately there is no longer a standard catalogue which includes Scotland and Ireland, the last edition of the *Standard Catalogue* to do this being that published in 1960.

It is well known that late third and fourth century coins are far commoner than any others on any Romano-British site, and therefore the standard work on fourth century bronze coinage, *Late Roman Bronze Coinage* by Carson, Hill and Kent (1960) is invaluable. With the aid of this the archaeologist can give a complete identification of any fourth century coin he may find. The work is not without its faults, for clarity has suffered due to brevity and the complex tables and abbreviations make it difficult to use until constant consultation makes the reader familiar with the writers' shorthand.

In the case of early Imperial coins the precise dating (using Tribunician and Consular years) is often difficult without tables or without consulting a larger work than Sear's catalogue (such as *Roman Imperial Coinage*). This can be left to the numismatist to do when he prepares the final report. The date given can be that of the emperor.

These notes on the preparation of the preliminary report may be concluded with a specimen entry from a coin register.

Small Finds No.

BX   *Constans.* Æ 4. (15 mm.) AD 341–6. Rev. 'Victoriae DD Augg Q NN'. Two Victories with wreaths. Trier mint, mm. $\frac{D}{TRP}$ *L.R.B.C.* 148–50 Good F.
(DR.66, Cutting 53, Site 1. Area over FN 245, dirty sand. Found 12/7/66, Helen Waterhouse.)

Cleaning coins

Sooner or later the question of whether coins should be cleaned after they have been unearthed is bound to arise, and on this issue *quot homines, tot sententiae*. The question is one which is of unfailing interest to coin collectors, and numismatic periodicals are filled with articles on different methods of treating coins and with disputes between those who believe coins should not be cleaned and those who think that they should.

It is of great importance for the archaeologist to distinguish between coins which are patinated and those which have active corrosion products. In the case of patinated coins there is no need for any drastic treatment beyond brushing with a stiff brush to remove the surplus earth. A patina is stable, and the coin is not undergoing any chemical change. A patina is a stable layer of inactive corrosion products which protects the metal underneath from the chemical action of the soil, of water or of the atmosphere. It is frequently dark green in the case of bronze coins, but it may be black, dark brown or yellow. Patina, strictly speaking, only occurs on copper coins or copper alloys like bronze, orichalcum or brass. A true patina does not obscure the details on the coin and any attempt at stripping it off is unwise. An imperfect patina on the other hand (one which has patches of active corrosion) should not be left untreated, and the archaeologist must decide on the nature of treatment which is best for the coin.

Active corrosion will spread sooner or later and if left unchecked very probably will completely change the metal into corrosion products in the end. In treating coins the archaeologist must first decide whether he wants them to look attractive for exhibition, or whether he wants the maximum amount of information possible. He must also decide whether the coin is suitable for cleaning, for it not infrequently occurs that there is little or none of the original metal left, and any attempt at cleaning would result in the destruction of the coin. It sometimes happens that the details of the coin can be seen in the form of corrosion products which have retained the shape of the original metal which they replace. In such cases cleaning will only remove such features and instead of a recognizable type which he had before, the archaeologist will be faced with a pitted and featureless piece of metal. Broadly speaking the best plan is to brush all the coins at the time of their discovery and endeavour to identify them without treatment. Coins with a stable patina should not be treated, and coins with only very small spots of localized corrosion should first be treated without using chemical methods. Chemical cleaning should only be used in cases where the coin is affected by extensive active corrosion which will do further damage if left unchecked. If it seems fairly certain that there is a good core of metal the coin should be stripped. In the case of copper or bronze coins this frequently leaves the coin with an ugly raw metallic appearance which does not always enhance them for display. It might be remembered however that this is how the coins were meant to look, and that a green or other surface is unnatural, even though it is admired by some collectors.

Because of the wide range of alloys that were used for coins in antiquity and the widely divergent conditions in which they were buried it is not surprising that there are many different types of corrosion products. The nature of these and the degree to which coins are affected are the result of the action of salts and organic acids in the soil which produce a complex electro-chemical process. The degree of aeration in the soil, the extent to which the soil water is flowing and the temperature of the soil all affect the rate of corrosion. The change of environment when the coin is removed from the soil usually speeds up corrosion, as stable conditions in the earth tend to keep the coin stable.

Before submitting coins to any form of chemical cleaning process it is useful to treat them simply by trying to chip off the corrosion products by a careful use of a dental probe or in the case of more stubborn accretions a 'Vibro-tool'. This is operated on the principle of the pneumatic drill, but is powered by electricity, which causes a needle set in its head to vibrate at an adjustable speed. It is particularly useful for removing accretions such as sand, pebbles, etc., which have adhered to the coin during the process of corrosion. Great care must be exercised lest the coin be damaged in the process. It is, however, the best method for making legends clearer.

Gold

This seldom needs any treatment further than washing in soap and water. Sometimes gold coins may be found to have an organic deposit and this may be removed by soaking in methylated spirit or some such solvent for about quarter of an hour, the process being repeated after brushing if the result is not satisfactory. Some gold coins may have lime deposit (white and powdery) and this can be removed in 5% hydrochloric acid. Gold alloys should be treated for

D

the corrosion products of the alloying metal – silver – gold alloys for example may have a silver chloride deposit (dirty white) which can be removed by soaking in dilute ammonia.

Silver

In the case of pure silver the main corrosion product is silver chloride, which can be removed by treating with dilute ammonia (10 per cent solution). Frequently silver coins may show a 'tarnish', either gold or black, which is silver sulphide caused by sulphur fumes. This can be removed by wrapping the coins in 'tinfoil' (actually aluminium foil) and immersing them in a 25 per cent solution of hot sodium carbonate (i.e. washing soda). This is the equivalent of treating them in an electro-chemical cell.

Coins of silver which have copper alloy and show various copper corrosion products can be treated in an electrolytic tank. This can be made quite easily if one has either a battery or a transformer, but frequently neither of these is easily obtained on an excavation. If either can be obtained, the coin should be suspended in a 2½ per cent caustic soda solution in a glass vessel by a copper wire which is attached to the negative pole of the battery. The positive pole is wired to a piece of graphite which is also immersed in the solution.

Copper and Copper Alloys

These present the greatest problem to the archaeologist. Organic deposits can be removed in the same way as they can be removed from gold or silver.

The salts which do most damage to bronze and copper coins are soluble chlorides. These can either be removed from the coin or stabilized. The removal of chlorides can involve the stripping of the patina (which is a stable layer) or can be effected without damaging it, using mechanical methods like a glass bristle brush.

The usual stripping agent is Alkaline glycerol (120 gms. sodium hydroxide to 40 mls. glycerine to 1,000 mls. distilled water). 'Calgon' (sodium hexametaphosphate), which is sold as a commercial water softener, will also strip off corrosion layers – the process is slow, but has the advantage of being easily controlled, and can be used for removing lime deposits on top of a patina. Acids are sometimes used for stripping, such as 5 per cent citric acid or 30 per cent formic acid but these must be free of atmospheric oxygen or else the metal will be etched and there is the additional hazard that metallic copper may be redeposited on the coin's surface. Chlorides can also be removed by soaking the coin over an extended period in sodium sesquicarbonate (1:1 by molecular weight of sodium carbonate and sodium bicarbonate). This maintains the patina intact and in fact tends to build up the patina by depositing equal quantities of azurite and malachite. This however is a slow process, and takes from nine months to five years to complete.

After the initial stripping cuprous oxide, which is a red layer, must be removed, or else the oxide will be reduced to the metal if the coin is subsequently treated in an electrolytic tank, and, in effect, plate the coin with copper.

The next stage in the stripping process is the removal of chlorides in the electrolytic tank, which takes about two weeks, and a final process of intensive washing to remove remaining chlorides.

It is often more practicable to stabilize chlorides, though this is less permanent. The simplest method is by keeping the coin in a low and controlled relative humidity (under 50%). By preventing moisture reaching the chlorides they are prevented from going into solution and are more or less stable.

A new method of stabilizing bronzes involves impregnating them with the chemical benzotriazole. Essentially the object is placed in a solution of this chemical (3 per cent by weight in industrial methylated spirits) and put under vacuum until no more bubbles come from the object, after which it is kept under vacuum for another hour. The coin is then tested in a humidity chamber (or in the field in a plastic bag with damp cotton wool which is sealed and left in a warm place) for twenty-four hours. If it remains stable it may be lacquered. By this method coins however have to be periodically re-treated.

In the case of small coins with only small spots of corrosion these can be removed mechanically and silver oxide carried in methanol put into the cleared spots. This should not be done in bright sunlight as the oxide might be reduced and silver metal redeposited on the surface. This is an expensive method, and is usually only used when the coin is likely to be an important display piece.

Problems inevitably arise in the case of coins which have been silver washed, such as some of the third century antoniniani. It is almost impossible to retain the silver coating in any chemical treatment, and the archaeologist must decide whether he wants to clean the coin or preserve the silver wash. If the coin needs cleaning he should make a note in the appropriate entry of the coin register 'Showed silver wash before cleaning'. Benzotriazole treatment is probably the best for such coins.

After any kind of chemical treatment the coins should be very carefully washed and dried, and this should be first effected by putting them in a shallow dish in a sink and letting the water flow over them from the tap. The coins should then be boiled in distilled water and allowed to cool, the process being repeated between three and five times. To make sure they are dry they should be slowly heated in fine sawdust.

The coins should then be left for a few weeks for observation to see if any subsequent corrosion is taking place, in which case they will need further treatment. The need for careful washing and drying cannot be stressed enough, as salts can remain in crevices and crystallize, exerting great pressure (as does all active corrosion) and causing the coin to disintegrate. Traces of acid can attack a coin in a similar way.

As the coins are not required for private collectors, when it is certain that corrosion has been halted it is a good plan for them to be coated to prevent further attack from moisture or salts in the atmosphere.

The simplest method of coating is to wax the coins with paraffin wax or beeswax, both of which are easily removed. For a more permanent coating a thin covering of amyl-acetate in which some celluloid has been dissolved is very effective, so is the stand-by of the archaeological conservation room, P.V.A. (polyvinyl acetate). Bedacryl or the product 'Ercalane' can also be used, as can 'Incralac' in a suitable thinner, such as acetone or toluene.

For waxing (and also for drying) a vacuum desiccator can be used, in the first instance the coins being laid in a tray of wax, in the second on gauze above a tray of silica gel.

Preparation of the Report

We must now turn to the question of how the final report on the coins should be prepared. If the site has only yielded one or two coins these can be simply be described, and if the archaeologist who is preparing the report is sufficiently competent to locate the precise types in catalogues there is no need to call upon a numismatist to prepare the coin section of the report.

Some archaeologists in the past have called upon a numismatist to prepare a report on two or three coins which they could quite easily have looked up themselves, merely because they think that the excavation report looks more competent if appended to it are a whole series of ancillary reports by various authorities in the appropriate fields. This is merely wasting the numismatist's time. It is important to invite a numismatist to prepare the report when a large number of coins are involved that can be used for statistical and comparative study, or when unpublished varieties of coins occur. In Britain it is usually advisable to consult a numismatist concerning the finds of Celtic coins or concerning the occurrence of unusual coins such as an Arabic dirhem or some Venetian soldini from a medieval town site, for example, or whenever the archaeologist cannot identify the types precisely.

The archaeologist must never make the mistake of only publishing the coins which were of value to him in the dating and interpretation of the site. In referring to them in the context of the report it is not enough to say 'associated with this group of pottery was a "Genio Pop.Rom." of Constantine I in worn condition'. Where a reference is made to a coin in the text its number in the list of coins in the appropriate section of the report should be given, and the relevant reference should read, e.g. 'associated with this group of pottery was a coin of Constantine I (no. 45, see p. 124) in fair condition'. This enables the precise coin to be identified. It is of little use to anyone to know that there were two silver and five aes of Vespasian from a particular site.

When submitting coins to a numismatist for his report it is important to furnish him with information regarding the circumstances of discovery of each coin, namely the context and associated material. To receive a coin in an envelope marked 'Area III, Layer 9' will mean nothing to him, but it is of value if he is told that the coin was 'associated with pottery dated to AD 125–60 at the bottom of a well', as this can give him information regarding the length of time the coin had been in circulation. Archaeologists seem to think that the numismatist wishes to work in a vacuum unrelated to the sequence of the site, being only interested in the coins as coins.

Ideally, every coin should be photographed and described in full. In reality this is impossible, for the costs of production are too high where there are several hundred coins (as there are from an excavation of a major Roman site spread out over a number of seasons) when even a reasonably detailed list of all the coins is not feasible. Fortunately the fact that reference can be made in most cases to Mattingly and Sydenham's *Roman Imperial Coinage* means that in the case of Roman Imperial coins it is possible to refer to a coin by the number in which the precise variety is catalogued in this work, saving several lines of description. Unfortunately *R.I.C.* is not complete, and only covers without a break the period up till AD 337 (Volumes I–VII). The period from AD 324 is covered to a large extent by *Late Roman Bronze Coinage*, though part of the period is dealt with in Volume IX by Pearce. The other missing volumes are, however, in the process of being written and some, it is hoped, will be out in the very near future. For English coins reference can now be made in a similar way to the two volumes of *English Hammered Coinage* by J. J. North for the period up to 1660, and thereafter to H. A. Seaby's *English Silver Coinage* II. Coins which cannot be located precisely by reference to one of these works must be described in full, and preferably illustrated with a photograph. It is always a good plan to give a brief description of the reverse type, even when a catalogue number is available, as it is not always convenient to the reader to look up the standard works. In any case – and this is a great disadvantage for anyone preparing such a report – many of the volumes of *R.I.C.* are not often available in libraries, though it was reprinted in 1963.

Reference is still sometimes made to Henri Cohen's *Description Historique des Monnaies Frappées sous l'Empire Romain*, which was published in eight volumes between 1880 and 1892. Cohen's work was an outstanding achievement for his period – he went round all the main cabinets of Europe cataloguing the coins – but is now very out of date and unreliable.

One class of coins which should always be illustrated with photographs is that of barbarous imitations, as these cannot be described adequately and there is no catalogue for them. These, in Britain, comprise the barbarous imitations of the coins of Claudius I that were issued just after the conquest to remedy a deficiency of official aes, the 'barbarous radiates' (copies of the coins of the Gallic emperors, particularly the Tetrici) of the third century, and the barbarous Fel. Temp. Rep. imitations of the fourth century. Only when archaeologists realize the importance of publishing these fully can there be any satisfactory method of classifying them.

Interpretation

It is not enough merely to catalogue the coins. If the report is to be of value there must be some attempt to analyse the finds and to relate the story told by the coins to the history of the site as a whole and to related sites. This is where most reports are deficient, for though they are adequate in cataloguing the coins they seldom attempt to draw any conclusions from them.

The first useful conclusion that can be drawn relates to the chronology of the site as a whole. Here the same conclusion regarding the date of the earliest occupation can be drawn from the general pattern of the coins as can be drawn in interpreting hoards – namely the date at which the coins rise in number per reign and either increase in number as the years pass or remain constant is the date at which the occupation commenced. Naturally there will be some earlier coins which were brought to the site by the first settlers, but these will tend to be worn and probably will be relatively rare, whereas the coins after the date of the first settlement will be commoner and generally speaking in better condition. Similarly the overall subsequent pattern will to some extent reflect the pattern of occupation – for periods of abandonment or sparse occupation the coin finds will be few and for periods of intense occupation the coin finds will be more abundant. As in all such cases, this is more apparent in theory than in practice, and there is often difficulty in distinguishing periods of slight occupation unless there are vast numbers of coins and the periods were prolonged – a decade or even quarter of a century will not necessarily greatly alter the general pattern where the coin finds are few, for the people who reoccupy the site again after the lull will possibly bring coins with them that were in circulation during the lull. Just as the coins give an idea of the date of the earliest occupation, they also give an idea of when the occupation ended. One advantage of this as a means of studying the history of the site lies in the fact that unstratified coins and coins picked up as surface finds in the years before the excavation are equally valid as evidence as those found stratified.

One other hazard to be borne in mind in making such a study is the fact that at certain periods and in certain areas coins seem to have been much rarer or hardly used at all, and here there may be only a few coins even in times of intense occupation. Such a fact is of great interest to the numismatist, and here it is important to compare the coin evidence with the evidence from the site as a whole.

Relative percentages of coins at different periods are best shown in the form of a graph or a histogram. The following histograms show the relative rarity of coins and pottery at different periods at Chichester, and it can be seen that the pattern is remarkably similar. (Figure 12.) This sheds a great deal of light on the history of the town in general, and it might be stressed that relatively little of the material was properly stratified in archaeological excavation. The problem of fluctuation in population density at different periods in Roman towns is one which is coming more and more to the fore in Britain, and one on which the coin evidence can and does shed considerable light.

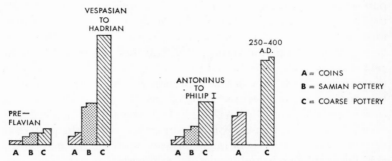

Fig. 12 Histogram of relative percentages of coins and pottery in Roman Chichester

Recently numismatists have evolved a new system for studying the coin patterns from individual sites and from regions. This method is an extension of that developed by Dr Alison Ravetz for studying the coinage of fourth century Britain, and discussed at greater length in Part II (p. 245–7). The method involves dividing up the whole period of the Roman Empire into twenty divisions, as shown in the table below:

I	27 BC–AD 14	XI	211–38
II	AD 14–41	XII	238–60
III	41–54	XIII	260–95
IV	54–68	XIV	295–317
V	68–96	XV	317–30
VI	96–117	XVI	330–46
VII	117–138	XVII	346–64
VIII	138–161	XVIII	364–78
IX	161–180	XIX	378–88
X	180–211	XX	388–402

This method was first employed by Richard Reece in his report on the coins for B. Cunliffe (Ed.), *Fifth Report on the Excavations at Richborough*, (1968), in making a study of the 57,000 Roman coins from that site. The main difficulty of course in extending Ravetz' method is that it was devised to study only the fourth century copper coins from Britain, and when one is dealing with gold, silver and copper over such a long period and is taking into consideration various calculations regarding inflation in order to study coin loss on a site the possibility of error is quite considerable. In the case of Richborough, in order to reduce all the denominations to one histogram silver and gold coins were expressed in terms of their copper equivalents, the basic unit of reckoning being the smallest denomination, the quadrans. This presupposes that the loss of one silver coin is equal to the loss of, for example, a hundred copper coins. In the case of Richborough this proved fairly reliable since every coin (or almost every coin) was recovered, due to the total excavation of the site, even though it involved presupposing a basic relationship between metals. The 'Richborough Method' then seems to be reasonably sound when studying the variations in prosperity of a 'closed' site, and can be used with equal success for a hoard where one can be confident that all the coins have been recovered. The method however is very limited, and another technique has to be evolved to study 'open' sites and museum collections. A system has been evolved for this by Reece in a study of Roman coins in museums in southern France, but cannot be discussed at length here. It is outlined in his 'Roman Coinage in Southern France', *N.C.* 7th Ser., vii (1968), 91–131, and to this interested readers are referred.

Further Reading

Excavation technique can only really be understood through practical experience in the field, and every site poses its own problems so that there are almost as many methods as there are sites.

A few good books have been written on excavation technique, of which perhaps the best is Sir Mortimer Wheeler's *Archaeology from the Earth* (1954). This book discusses the recording and treatment of coins and simple conservation. One caution, however – Wheeler was considering excavation technique and management from the point of view of large scale operations, and the book is therefore more a manual of how to run a Near Eastern site than the average small British dig with a dozen or so volunteers. A book which is oriented more towards the British approach to field archaeology is R. J. C. Atkinson's *Field Archaeology* (1953), which covers a wide variety of topics in little space. More recent is Graham Webster's *Practical Archaeology* (1963) which is very good for its coverage of small excavations and has very useful illustrations. For stratigraphy and its

D*

geological origins one should consult E. Pyddoke's *Stratigraphy for the Archaeologist* (1961), a work which perhaps promises more than it actually discusses.

On the subject of conservation one book is indispensable – *The Conservation of Antiquities and Works of Art* by H. J. Plenderleith (1956). For a more detailed study of methods of cleaning coins a series of articles in *Seaby's Coin and Medal Bulletin* (1961), January–July, by I. M. Allen and A. Wootton entitled 'Notes on the Cleaning and Preservation of Ancient Coins' will be found the best source.

Finally, for those wishing to study the coin story at Segontium in greater detail, the source is Sir Mortimer Wheeler's 'Segontium and the Roman Occupation of Wales', *Y Cymmrodor* XXXIII (1923)

5 Coins and the Scientist

Archaeometry is a word which describes the accurate measurement of early data, often through the application of the techniques of the physicist and the chemist.

In spite of the close connection that should exist between the archaeologist and the physicist and chemist, until the last decade or so archaeology remained apart from the scientific revolution of the twentieth century. This is not to say that archaeology was not making rapid advances in its aims and techniques, for it is the twentieth century that has witnessed the growth of the subject from a dilettante's weekend diversion to a precise discipline whose real exponents are professionals. But until recently it was self-contained, and the archaeologist, if he were at all competent, could feel reasonably confident that he could analyse all his evidence himself, except perhaps when he called to his aid a zoologist to report on the bones from his site. It is true that already the chemist was helping him to clean and preserve his finds, but although this was of service to the general public who might want to look at the finds in a museum, except in a few cases (such as Sutton Hoo) it did not greatly alter the conclusions of the excavation report.

Fortunately this independence is no longer maintained, and archaeologists and scientists now collaborate to their mutual advantage. Perhaps each does not derive maximum benefit from the work of the other due to a limited understanding of the respective disciplines, but nevertheless archaeology is undergoing a revolution as a result, and the scientist too is benefiting from the partnership – he is learning, for example, more about the behaviour of the magnetic field of the earth in the past as he aids the archaeologist with data derived from magnetic dating. But it is perhaps important to emphasize that scientific developments will never obviate the need for archaeologists and their techniques, and the evidence derived from science must take its place along with all the other categories of evidence that the archaeologist uses in his work.

We have been concerned here with archaeology, and the reader may wonder to what extent this applies to numismatics. One of the important developments in the field of archaeometry has concerned metallurgy, and the work of the metallurgist is of equal value whether it is being employed in analysing a sword blade or in examining coins.

The Examination of Metals

The scientist can help the numismatist either by analysing the metal of coins by one of a number of methods which are outlined below, or by examining the structure of the metal. In the first instance the information that can be derived is of value in determining the origins of the metals employed in making the coins, in constructing a typology where a series of coins is periodically debased, or even in the determination of the authenticity of a particular piece. In the second instance the conclusions illuminate the methods employed in striking or casting the coin in question. There are of course many problems involved in drawing such conclusions – it is often extremely difficult to pin-point the origins of metals by the detection of trace elements in them, and frequently the conclusions are negative rather than positive, the analyst being able to tell us that the metal for a particular coin was not derived from a given area rather than vice versa.

The basic problem in analysing coins is that frequently it is important for the specimen to suffer no damage, and usually in conventional analysis the sample is totally destroyed during the investigation. Again, the condition of the coin may pose several problems to the analyst – coins which are badly corroded cannot be satisfactorily examined by means of X-ray fluorescence, and some silver and gold coins, due to a phenomenon known as 'silver enrichment' may look as if they are in perfect condition while the interior structure may be entirely different from the exterior. In order, too, to make a satisfactory analysis the analyst must know the particular problems which the numismatist wants him to solve. The analysis of one or two coins of a particular class is not always reliable, and in order to reduce the sampling error and to extend statistical spread a large number of coins should be examined. As non-destructive analysis is always to be favoured in examining coins, we need only consider the physical methods of quantitative analysis here.

Three modern methods all involve exciting the metal in some way and then observing the results. These methods are known as Neutron Activation Analysis, Emission Spectrometry, and X-ray Fluorescence Spectrography. In each, some part of the atoms of each metal is excited, and in this excited state the different metals produce different results. By examining these results which will show the sum total of the metals present in the coin, the constituents can be sorted out.

Neutron Activation Analysis

This involves bombarding the coin with a stream of subatomic particles called neutrons. The nuclei of each kind of atom absorb different numbers of neutrons and usually become radioactive, that is they give off alpha and beta particles and gamma rays. The atoms give off these radiations because they have become unsettled by the neutrons, and giving off the particles and rays makes them stable again and no longer radioactive. This process could be watched on the level of alpha, beta or gamma radiations, but in practice the last is the most reliable and needs least equipment. Since only a few atoms in the coin become radioactive the excitement soon dies down and the coin is safe to handle or replace unharmed in a collection.

As a general method of analysis this has a drawback in that gamma rays from different metals tend to interfere with each other, so that a complex mixture of metals gives a picture which is impossible to sort out. Fortunately coins are usually made of fairly simple alloys and the method has had great success when applied to the problem of their composition. A more serious disadvantage of this method is that it needs a good source of neutrons. These can either come from an atomic pile, or, at one step removed, from a mobile source. Atomic piles usually have no time to deal with minor projects such as these, and charge considerable sums when they do. A mobile source is not only expensive in itself but in all the equipment needed to house and handle it.

The two main advantages of the method are that it leaves the coin completely unharmed and it gives an accurate picture of the whole of the coin, not just its surface.

Spectrometry

While Neutron Activation analysis depends on exciting the nucleus of the metal atom, both methods of spectrography depend on observing the result when the electrons in the atom are excited. In the case of Emission Spectrometry the exciting is done by heating up a small sample of the metal until it gives a clear light. This is often achieved by putting the sample on one side of a carbon electric arc, and thus the sample is completely destroyed. The method cannot be used for any coin of individual importance, but is excellent for fairly common coins. It has been used successfully to determine the trace impurities in Euboean silver, and would probably be useful for late Roman coinage.

The second method of spectrometry can be described before the actual methods of detection, since these are similar in both cases. X-ray Fluorescence is almost a self-explanatory term. If a metal is excited by a good stream of X-rays its surface will fluoresce or glow gently. Unfortunately the weakness of the method lies in the fact that it can only be used to study surface layers. It is useful, however, for studying the process of surface enrichment, or blanching, if a complete section through the coin can be examined, but it is a method with severe limitations.

Having excited the metal by heat or by X-rays to produce a light of its own, this light has to be examined because different metals will lend their own particular colours to the total. This means that the light has to be split up, and the easiest way is through a quartz prism. A spectrum or band of colours is produced, just as sunlight is diffracted by broken glass, or electric light by a cut-glass chandelier. Sunlight or electric light produce a full band of colours, red, orange, yellow, green, blue, indigo, violet, but a sodium (yellow) street lamp would only give yellow light. If the sodium light is examined through a microscope it does not even cover the area where yellow should be, only two thin lines. A mercury vapour lamp with its greenish light put through a spectrometer just as above, would show a small number of green, blue and red lines. Thus the light from any excited mixture of metals is easily analysed.

Metals can be seen to be present or absent by their lines. If the amount of metal is to be measured, then the relative brightness of the lines must be measured by a carefully standardized microdensitometer. The standards change with the materials in use so new standards have to be worked out for each new material analysed.

Density Determination

For the examination of gold coins a simple procedure can be used for testing their fineness – that of density determination, the discovery of Archimedes. As the density of gold is 19·3 and the usual metals alloyed with it, copper and silver, have densities of 8·9 and 10·5, the error in determining the gold content is slight, no more than about one per cent, when the alloying metal is known. When the alloy is unknown but the gold content is above 95 per cent the margin of error is more likely to be about 2 per cent. This method has been used by Caley for examining fifty gold coins, mainly Roman Imperial, and from this he was able to demonstrate that the majority have a very high degree of purity, more than 95 per cent.

Metallography

Metallography is the study of metals in order to understand their structure and that of the corrosion that forms on them. This examination may be carried out in one of two ways – either by macrography, when the piece of metal is studied when magnified about ten times, or micrography, where the magnification may be even as much as 2,000 times the diameter of the piece of metal. In order to examine the crystalline structure of the metal it is customary to polish the specimen before etching it with some chemical reagent. Then it is studied in light which is directly reflected from its surface. When the metal is cold-worked the grains of which it is composed become elongated, and numerous straight lines appear crossing them. These are called slip-bands. When the metal is reheated this structure is not affected until what is known as the 'temperature of recrystallization' is reached, when new crystals are formed which do not show either elongation or slip-bands. They can be distinguished because they form broad bands caused by the twinning of the crystals. If the metal is cold-worked again the grains become distorted again, but the previous evidence is not destroyed because they retain their twinning though these twin boundaries are now bent. The significance of this is obvious, for by studying the character of the crystals, information can be gained about the methods employed in the production of the coins.

The Application of the Techniques

We may now consider how some of the techniques described above have helped the numismatist in his work. It is important to stress that the older methods of inorganic chemical analysis are still applied to the analysis of coins in cases where the destruction of the coin is of little importance – for example Richard Reece recently examined a series of Roman silver coins of the late fourth century, and was able to demonstrate that the fineness of the silver remained fairly constant during the period under consideration, though either tin or copper was added, or had not been removed in the refining.

Using Neutron Activation Analysis Dr Colin Kraay of the Ashmolean has studied a series of early Greek silver coins, with very interesting results. When he studied the 'owl' coinages of Athens of the period 500–480 BC he found the silver had a low percentage of gold and copper, but that an earlier coin series of Athens (the so called *wappenmünzen*), showed no real uniformity and had a high gold and copper content.

This would suggest that in the earlier period the Athenians were either using irregular surface deposits of silver from the Laurion area, or some external source for their metal – Kraay suggests that Macedon and Thrace, which fell to the Persians at the end of the sixth century, are likely places of origin. After 500 the source for the metal would seem to be the deep Laurion mines.

Neutron Activation has also been applied with some success to the detection of forgeries. Ancient forgeries are often difficult to recognize, as the forgers used on some occasions identical dies to those used by the mint which issued the original coins. This problem is particularly difficult in the case of plated coins, some of which are official mint products (like the emergency issue of 406 BC in Athens to which Aristophanes alludes in *The Frogs*). Fourteen doubtful coins were tested in this way and one, a fifth century stater of Terina, was proved to be a forgery.

An analysis of 56 early electrum coins also gave interesting results. In Ionia and later in Lydia, electrum was used for the earliest coinage, as this was found as a natural alloy in the rivers of western Anatolia. Electrum continued in use as a coinage metal in Asia Minor until the fourth century BC, and it was hoped that by analysing the coins it would be possible to tell when the natural alloy (electrum is a mixture of gold and silver) ceased to be struck and a deliberate alloy used instead. The results showed that the earliest issues of Ionia, minted at various uncertain cities, had a 45 per cent variation in the alloy, suggesting they were not struck from native electrum. The analysis also suggested that although at about 400 BC Phocaea and Lesbos had entered a treaty which regulated the amount of metal in electrum, the coins of Lesbos used far less gold.

	Au.	Ag.	Cu.
Late Phocaean electrum	47	41	9
Late Lesbian electrum	43·6	49	7·4

It could also be seen that in the late Phocaean coins there was a marked drop in gold content from 56 per cent to 49 per cent.

So far these examples have been drawn from Greek coinage. But the uses of analysis are not merely confined to this series but apply equally to Roman coins, where they are of particular value in studying late Imperial coins at a period when monetary reforms and inflation are of the greatest importance in the study of economic history. In order to study fourth century copper coins, 122 pieces representing the main issues during the period under consideration were subjected to Neutron Activation Analysis. The results showed that until AD 364 most issues contained small amounts of silver, but after that date, when there was apparently a supply of good silver coins (see p. 245), the state no longer attempted to issue bronze coins with low silver content as 'silvered' or 'billon' coinage, and the coins were frankly bronze. Up to 364, too, in cases where the small bronze coins were being issued at the same time as the silver it seems probable that they were not intended for circulation as 'silvered' coins. Moreover the results of the analysis showed that there was a decline in the silver content of the coins between 330 and 346, and that the reform of 346 was short-lived, although it is probable that Julian returned to the good silver standard of the earlier reforms. Different mints seem to have followed different policies.

The historical and archaeological significance of these conclusions cannot be overestimated. It can now be seen that a coin's purchasing power depended not only on its size and weight but also on its silver content. This sheds much light on the composition of hoards and why particular issues were hoarded; now hoards of different dates may be compared by studying not the numbers of coins in them but their purchasing power in terms of silver content.

Dr C. H. V. Sutherland made a comparable study for the silver content of Diocletian's early post-Reform copper coinage. From this study he was able to prove that the follis was intended to be a five-denarius piece, the 'radiate' as a two-denarius piece and the laureate as a *denarius communis*. The follis contained on an average about 3·78 per cent silver after the reform (perhaps diminishing down to *c*. AD 296) and after the reform there was one per cent more silver than before – a considerable increase considering the number of coins struck.

Examination of coins by metallographic and other methods is of value in determining methods of coin production. When a dupondius of Hadrian was examined it proved to have been made from a blank which had been cast and struck cold. Reference has already been made to the Dorchester Hoard, coins from which were studied in order to determine by similar means the method of fabrication. In this particular case it was found that the coins had been struck after casting either while they were still hot, or in the cold state, the blanks not being reheated after cooling as a prelude to striking. These coins were 'blanched', that is, dipped in a saline solution to remove the copper impurities on the surface of the metal and thus reveal the silver-rich layer beneath. This device was frequently used in the third century to give a silvery appearance to coins of low silver content and was also carried out in Medieval England, where pieces were cut from a square sectioned bar which had been cast, and the flans forged from this. At Lydney, the Romano-British temple site in Gloucestershire, blanks were made for the tiny barbarous imitations of Roman coins that were used in the late Roman period. Here they had been made by cutting off pieces from a cast round copper alloy bar, with a cold chisel. These well-rounded pieces had been flattened before striking. Some of these coins had holes in them, as a result of piping in the casting of the bar. Normally this defect was only present in the top part of the bar and cut off, but material was scarce and striking careless.

A die of Hadrian was found at St Albans, with the reverse type of Hadrian being greeted by Roma, with the legend ADVENTVS AVG. (see p. 6), (datable to AD 134–8). The face of this die had a hardness of only 150 Brinell, which is not suitable for coining metals harder than gold or silver in a cold state, and if coins were indeed struck cold then bronze, copper and orichalcum coins must have been struck with steel dies (a steel die of Faustina used for striking aurei is known). Vermeule has made a study of Greek dies, and he points out that there are 38 known Greek and Roman bronze dies, but only eight iron. However it must be remembered that iron corrodes much more easily than bronze.

Mathematics and Metrology

We may now turn from the value of different methods of analysis of the metal content of coins to consider another way in which the 'scientist' can help the numismatist, this time in the field of mathematics, and with particular reference to metrology.

One of the most important aspects of numismatics is metrology – the study of the weight systems employed at various periods in different series of coins. The study of metrology is a complex one, and essential to a full understanding of ancient coinage. The study of the weights of coins is in the first instance of value in detecting forgeries, for frequently forgeries, either ancient or modern, though close to the original coin in appearance, are not of the correct weight. Secondly, metrology is of value in determining the origins of particular series of coins.

Metrology is important in other fields, too, especially that of dating. Due to progressive debasement, reduction of weight, etc., over a period of time, it is possible to arrange a series of coins in chronological sequence without having to pay attention to typology in the first instance, and this is often a valuable check on other dating systems or sequence arrangements based on typology, hoard sequences, etc. In some cases dating can only be arrived at by a study of metrology, perhaps the best instance being in the field of Roman Republican bronze coins which do not occur in hoards and which cannot be dated on stylistic grounds. Here it has been possible to relate changes in weight to economic factors, which in turn can be related to historical events, thus providing the coins with a reasonably sound dating. This of course works both ways, and in a dated series changes in weight can reflect economic crises, inflation, and so on, giving a valuable indicator of contemporary history. A careful study of the French sou has shown that it began as the Roman gold solidus, and it has been possible to study the devaluation of the coin over a long period, with very interesting results for the economic historian.

A study of standards can show why certain coins enjoyed a very wide and prolonged circulation, and why others were of limited duration. It can shed light on metal resources and similar problems which confront the numismatist.

The uses of metrology have been recognized by numismatists since the eighteenth century, and indeed comparative study of weight systems in use among the ancient Greeks had a very important place in the studies of the late nineteenth century. At times the importance of metrology has been overstressed, and has prompted so much wild theorizing that there has been a tendency in recent times to record the weight of individual coins and leave it to someone else to interpret them. In the field of archaeology, it may be recalled, weights and measures have been avoided as a respectable study for a very long time, made infamous by the studies of early antiquaries. Nevertheless, properly applied the conclusions can be quite valid in the study of weight systems.

The Homogeneous Random Process

A major development in the study of metrology was made in the late 1930s with the evolution of the theory known as the homogeneous random process. This method of studying data can be applied to many fields of natural phenomena, e.g. the diffusion of molecules of one substance among the molecules of another or even the fluctuations of the Stock Exchange.

One of the basic problems of numismatic metrology had been the fact that there was always some loss of weight through wear or corrosion. Similarly in antiquity absolute uniformity of weight was not possible due to the nature of ancient balances, and accordingly coins could have been either a little over or a little under the standard weight when struck. It was therefore important to devise some system of calculating the mean difference in the weight of coins due to one or a combination of factors, and of arriving at a correct weight through the study of a selection of similar coins. This is where the Homogeneous Random Process became important.

The method for taking these factors into consideration was first outlined by Hemmy in 1938, and elaborated by him in subsequent years. A series of three graphs show the result when this theory is applied to a group of coins in circulation. The first of these graphs shows the 'Gaussian Curve' of the weights of a group of newly minted coins – coins that are very much above or below the accepted weight have been of course rejected by what is known as the 'legal remedy' (Figure 13).

When the coins have been in circulation for some time the curve of the weight distribution is still regular, but has changed from a high and narrow shape to one in which wear has caused the curve to flatten, the middle of it moving to the right, indicating that the average weight of the coins has decreased.

With the passage of time the curve becomes flatter and moves further to the right. The flattening of the curve takes place more rapidly than the movement to the right, because the standard deviation from the correct weight becomes much greater, but the movement to the right is an even and slow process as the average loss of weight is standard for each equal unit of time.

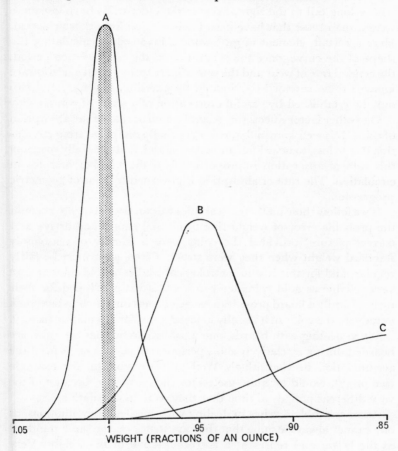

Fig. 13 Graphs showing coin wear

Eventually, as the third graph shows, the mean weight has declined to such an extent and the variation in weight increased to such an extent that only half the distribution falls into the limits of our chart of acceptable variation.

This regular change in the pattern of course is only valid when we are considering a series of coins which were struck at the same time and which were of the same weight, more or less, when they first went into circulation. But the numismatist is not often dealing with coins which were put into circulation in the same year, and accordingly the weight distribution through wear would be assymetrical with a long tail to the right, because the older coins have lost more weight than those that have been in circulation for a shorter period. Here a certain element of guesswork is involved in calculating the shape of the curve, once the proportion of the coins of each period, the general rate of wear and the rate of increase in weight variation are known; these cannot be estimated by guessing, however, and can only be established by careful observation of a series of coins.

One other factor affects the general pattern: that of the absorption of coins. It is well known that coins gradually disappear from circulation due to loss, to hoarding, and other causes, and generally speaking this rate of absorption is proportional to the number of coins in circulation. The rate of absorption is governed by that of geometric progression.

If we follow these mathematical rules we can then take into account the probable error of weight due to normal causes and arrive at a correct picture, provided the coins were originally of reasonably standard weight when they were struck. Circulation must be fairly regular, and for this reason metrological studies of gold coins are not very reliable as gold coins tend to be hoarded or clipped for their metal. Ideally a hoard provides a range of coins on which to base such a study, as the coins in it usually enjoyed a similar circulation history.

When dealing with hoards, one must be careful that the coins are hoarded during a relatively short period of time. The coins from the accumulation in Coventina's Well at Carrawburgh, for example (see p. 57), would be quite useless for such a survey, because of the very different periods of time that they were in circulation.

Another problem arises in dealing with smaller denominations, as one cannot always assume that they are struck on the same standard as the larger and represent a correct fraction of the weight. Very often they seem to be underweight, and the ratios may be quite divergent. The so-called tetrobol of Philip II of Macedon should be a sixth of a stater, but is actually in the ratio of 1: 5.5. Again, the smaller denominations, being thinner, lose more metal proportionately.

The Results of Metrological Studies

We may here briefly consider some of the results that have been reached using the method described above to remedy error in weight measurement.

Hemmy studied a series of Persian and Greek weight standards using this method and arrived at some interesting conclusions. He was able to demonstrate that in Aegina the standard of the stater was constant throughout the whole period of its minting at 12.57 gm. This was either related to the Egyptian beqa as Flinders Petrie had asserted some time previously, or alternatively might have been derived from the Babylonian standard. If it originated in Egypt the question of how the Egyptian standard reached Greece arises. The standard itself was one of the oldest of those used in Egypt, which by the late period (1200–650 BC) had degenerated, and we find at that time two beqa standards in use, but the one disappears to occur again at the Greek trading port of Naucratis, which rose to importance in 565 BC after Defennah ceased to be a Greek port. The fact that it appears at this Greek port might suggest that it was reintroduced to Egypt from Greece. It does not appear to have been used at Defennah, the earlier port. It might be pointed out that although Ionians, Dorians and Aeolians seem to have been the main elements in Naucratis, we are told by Herodotus that the Aeginetans had built a sanctuary there. It must be remembered that at this period Greece was engaged in active trade with all her east Mediterranean neighbours, and was absorbing a very varied cultural background from them.

Similar studies of the coins of Athens, Macedon, Abdera, Lydia and Persia were able to trace the origins of the standards and the pattern of their development, and it was possible to show that throughout the period of the history of Abdera there was a continual decrease in the weight of the coins, probably as a result of inflation. In the case of Athens it could be demonstrated that the standard remained constant until the time of the 'New Style' coinage, but was at its best during the period 527–430 BC, as one might expect – the period before the Peloponnesian War.

In the field of Roman coinage it was possible to demonstrate by this method that the value of the Roman pound in terms of gold remained constant from the early Republic until the end of the second century AD, except for the period of the Romano-Campanian coinages when it was slightly higher. This same situation, with a different standard, was seen reflected in the silver and copper coinages of the Romano-Campanian series. This was probably the result of contact with Greek standards, and as the Romano-Campanian coinage was intended primarily for trade with the Greek colonies of southern Italy it is not surprising that we find a deliberate adjustment of the Roman pound so that eighty Roman pounds equalled the Attic talent.

We may consider another more complex problem on which the statistical analysis of weights has shed a great deal of light. This concerns the dating and study of two hoards of Indian coins which were very cleverly interpreted by D. D. Kosambi using statistical methods.

The first hoard was found in 1924 in Taxila in Pakistan, one of the most famous cities of early India. It consisted of some 1,510 silver coins of Indian origin in a bronze jar, and the date of the deposit could be fixed by a relatively unworn coin of Alexander the Great (who invaded India in 327 BC) and a mint condition coin of one of his successors, Philip Arrhidaeus. For this reason it was possible to date the hoard to 317 BC, the date of the assassination of Arrhidaeus. Thus it was possible to establish that the Indian coins in the hoard must have been in circulation about that date. Nothing more could be said about them. The obverses, in keeping with many early Indian coins, had five punch marks which only varied slightly from coin to coin. The reverses, however, showed a complex series of punchmarks, with great diversity. The problem which was posed by these coins was that of establishing some kind of sequence.

The date of the hoard showed that it was before the time of the Mauryan Empire which was founded in 312 BC, and the only kingdom before that date which was sufficiently powerful to strike its own coins was the Magadha. A study of the coins found in the area of this kingdom and its sphere of influence showed that the coins that circulated there were in fact similar to those from the hoard. From the Magadhan royal coinage it became possible to understand the sequence of marks on the obverses of the coins – the first four punches indicated the king, the fifth the issuing authority, often a crown prince. Where the fifth mark moved into the fourth place, it indicated that the issuing authority had become king. This useful sequence made grouping of the coins possible within a broad framework. In theory it should have been possible, using these sequences alone, to build up a chronological framework, but because there is no reliable history for the period, and one king is called by several names, this could not be done.

The punchmarks on the reverses were of much greater value. A series of coins all with the same combination of obverse punches could show a blank reverse or one with twenty or more different punches. Careful study showed that the more punches there were on the reverse, the lower was the average weight of the coins. This was because the reverse stamps were like the bankers' stamps that frequently appear on the coins of the Achaemenid Empire, and were intended to show that the particular banker through whose hands they had passed had tested them for fineness and weight and had passed them, punching them to show this had been done. It could further be shown that this checking was done at regular intervals, possibly every twelve years, and this proved that the sequence of coins must have started about 500 BC.

Both obverse and reverse sequence marks were then considered in making a metrological survey of the coins. Some 95 per cent of the coins were found to conform to the stone weights found in the excavations of Mohenjo-daro, the Indus civilization site which dated back to the third millennium BC. Similar weights were found at the other great Indus site, Harappa. This showed that, in spite of the fact the civilization had been lost, the old weight system survived down to the time of the Mauryan Empire.

The weight curve of the coins in the Taxila hoard had a definite tail to the right, and in addition the number of coins, when compared with the number of reverse marks, follows the theoretical absorption curve. The general pattern showed that 70 per cent of the coins survived after each checking period, and this indicates the economy of Taxila was stable for more than two hundred years. (This is proved by the regularity of circulation as shown by the curves of weight loss and absorption). It further showed that Taxila had a well established trade throughout the period, indicated by the Magadhian coins which must have come as payment for exports from Taxila.

Further Reading

As one might expect, although in recent years numerous articles have been published in journals on aspects of the application of scientific methods to the study of coins, the majority of these have been extremely technical and usually confined to reporting on individual experiments. Summaries of the methods employed have appeared, however, in four less specialist books all published since 1960. Of these perhaps the most useful is M. J. Aitken's *Physics and Archaeology* (1961) which was published in New York, though Dr

Aitken is a British scientist. This explains the methods used in examining coins without destroying them. Dr R. F. Tylecote of Newcastle gives good accounts of modern methods of examining coins in *Metallurgy in Archaeology* (1962). This book has excellent references to important articles. Two articles in *The Scientist and Archaeology* edited by E. Pyddoke (1963) may also be found useful, though not directly concerned with coins. The first, 'Analysis and Microscopic Study of Metals' by R. M. Organ discusses metallography, while the second, on 'Physical Methods of Chemical Analysis' by E. T. Hall, discusses non-destructive ways of examining metals by Neutron Activation analysis and other methods. The fourth book to consult is L. Biek's *Archaeology and the Microscope* (1963) which, though less exhaustive than the other books referred to from the numismatist's viewpoint, still gives information not readily obtained elsewhere.

Metrology is not discussed adequately in any recent book, and the majority of articles on the subject have appeared in technical journals which are difficult to obtain. One which is particularly valuable by D. D. Kosambi appeared in *Scientific American* (1965), 102–11 and was entitled 'Scientific Numismatics.' This article summarizes statistical methods of studying coins and makes Hemmy's method intelligible to the layman.

Part II

6 Classical Coins and the Prehistorian

The cultural traditions of modern Europe are diverse in their origins and distinct in their overall character. But whenever we seriously contemplate the nature of western European civilization as we know it and its origins, we can see that this distinctive character is a feature not merely of our own era but of Medieval Europe.

Over the shoulder of the nuclear physicist breathe the ghosts of Galileo and Copernicus, and behind Beckett and Joyce stands Dante. Western society as we know it is the result of the consolidation of the diverse and chaotic traditions of early Medieval Europe, forged in the Classical revival of the Renaissance. For the origins of European character it is tempting to turn to the Classical world of Greece and Rome, and to look to the ancient philosophers, inventors, artists and writers as the fathers of all that is essentially European in it.

Yet this offers only a half truth. To some extent Romania and Romanitas only veneered western Europe with an overlay of Mediterranean culture – beyond the Roman *limes* European society was not greatly affected by the ideas of Rome, and even within the Empire itself there flowed the undercurrent of European barbarism that was to come to the fore during the fifth to the tenth centuries, the formative years of Medieval civilization. We would be dishonest with ourselves if we did not recognize in our society something of the heritage of the barbarian Europe of prehistory. The germs of Medieval polity were present in pre-Roman times, and indeed prehistorians frequently claim that Europe had assumed its character by the commencement of the second millennium BC.

In the next two chapters we are concerned with Barbarian Europe and its relationship with the Classical world, as reflected in its coinage.

Coinage is a relatively modern and sophisticated invention and accordingly, for much of prehistory, the numismatist can contribute little to a study of human societies. When coins were first struck in

Asia Minor probably at the end of the seventh century BC Europe was just passing into the Early Iron Age, and by the time coins were being struck by the Celts their culture was at its zenith. Accordingly, although Classical coins can contribute to a study of the European Iron Age as early as the sixth century BC, it is only for a very short period that the Celts were striking coins for themselves. Yet for this period their importance in prehistoric studies is far from negligible and for this reason is worthy of special consideration in any study of coins and archaeology.

Two classes of coins, then, provide us with our evidence, the Classical and the Celtic. In this chapter we shall consider the former, and in the next the latter.

Early Iron Age – Hallstatt[1]

To the Greeks there were two main groups of barbarians, the Cimmerians in the east and the Celts in the west. The term 'Celt' as now used is a linguistic one, and it is not easy to trace how early Celtic was being spoken in the west. It seems probable that the Late Bronze Age 'Urnfield' peoples of central Europe were in fact Celtic speaking, and brought Celtic to Spain in the eighth century BC. Some have argued, on the grounds of cultural continuity in the European Bronze Age, that the first Celtic speakers were the peoples who brought the wheel and the rite of single grave burial to Europe from the Caucasus at the end of the third millennium BC. The problem is a complex one, but we may be fairly sure that by the late eighth century BC a form of Celtic was being spoken in Europe.[2]

At this date the impact of immigrants from the Steppes together with internal developments resulted in the birth of the Hallstatt culture, named after a famous site near Salzburg. The term 'Hallstatt' is used by prehistorians to cover both the Late Bronze Age Urnfield cultures and the Hallstatt Iron Age. *A* and *B* phases of Hallstatt are, strictly speaking, Bronze Age. The full Iron Age began about 700 BC with Hallstatt *C*. The knowledge of iron, which was first apparent in Hallstatt *B*, was probably introduced by people from the steppe lands to the north of the Black Sea.

The Hallstatt cultures were at first very restricted in their distribution, being concentrated in central Europe, but by Hallstatt *D* (the sixth century BC) there was an extension of the culture to the south of France, where we find characteristic burials with accompanying four-wheeled waggons.

Greek Colonies in the West[3]

From barbarian Europe we may look back for a moment to the Greeks and their period of colonization in the seventh century BC.

Towards the end of the eighth century BC some Greeks, probably Euboeans from Pithekoussai and Kume, established contacts with southern France, which at this time was still technologically in the Bronze Age. At places like St Marcel, Hyères and possibly Marseilles, early pottery of Greek origin dating from the last years of the eighth and early seventh centuries has been found.

About 600 BC Greek colonists from Phocaea in Ionia founded the city of Massalia (Marseilles) and during the sixth century the city grew, developing a vigorous trade. Other Greek cities, such as Ensérune, sprang up, and the barbarian inhabitants of southern France welcomed the refinements which the Greeks introduced, most notably the vine. Sites like Mt Garou show us that native pottery was supplemented with Greek, Etruscan and Phoenician imports.

The Auriol Hoard[4]

Towards the end of the sixth century the first phase of Massaliote trade was at its height, and to this period the earliest coins of Massalia can be attributed.

These are the coins found in a very important hoard at Auriol, near Marseilles, in 1867, consisting of about 2,130 uninscribed silver coins of small denomination. Similar coins have been found at Volterra in Etruria, at Rosa, Ampurias and Morella in Spain, and at St Rémy de Provence in France (Figure 14).

The coins fall into two main classes: those with animal foreparts (protomes) as types, and those with a facing or profile human or mythological head. These coins are of the greatest importance in the study of the early economic history of Gaul.

The mint is not easy to determine. Although the weights vary they appear to be struck on the Ionian standard, and some of the coins are apparently of Phocaean origin. Coins of Aegina and Velia also appear in the hoard, suggesting that some at least are imported. One group is of high standard of workmanship and has types which relate to Ionian cities. The remainder are crude and have no parallels in East Greece. These, therefore, are assigned to Massalia on both stylistic and metallic grounds, since they are silver rather than electrum.

Here, then, is sound evidence that at the period of the hoard Marseilles was very prosperous indeed. She was striking her own coins, and was using others that were imported from the Mediterranean world. She had some kind of trading contacts with Italy and Spain, and, as will be demonstrated, with the Hallstatt world.

Fig. 14 Two coins from the Auriol Hoard

Stylistically the coins can be dated to the period 550–500 BC, but a more accurate date can be arrived at by other means. In the late sixth century the main powers in the Mediterranean were Carthage, Etruria and the Greeks. In 540 BC at the battle of Alalia off the coast of Italy the Phocaean Greeks were defeated by the combined forces of Carthage and Etruria. At this time Phocaea also fell.

Evidence for Sixth Century Massaliote Trade[5]

This route was connected with a trade in iron with the Hallstatt people of Germany, and there is ample evidence for this. At the Heuneburg, a fort in south-west Germany, we find Greek building techniques with brick bastions like those at Gela, and fragments of Attic Black Figure pottery.

In the west of France we find a similar state of affairs, as exemplified by the famous Vix waggon burial. Here a Celtic princess was buried with a huge bronze krater (mixing bowl), Greek painted pottery, bronzes and native objects such as a fine gold torc. The grave could be dated to c. 500 BC and the krater must be regarded as some

kind of diplomatic present in return for trading rights. At the nearby
fort of Mont Lassois further finds of Greek pottery were made.

Thus coins and archaeological evidence combine to bear witness
to a trade not attested by historical sources.

La Tène[6]

About 480 the prosperity of Marseilles must have declined, and the
trade with the north ended. This decline seems to be contemporary
with a change in the centre of Celtic activity from Germany to the
Champagne and slightly later to the Marne region of France. This
shift coincides with the start of the La Tène phase of the Iron Age.

The earliest La Tène culture seems to have developed in the middle
Rhine (but it is named after a site called the 'Shallows' on Lake
Neuchâtel), and at first is only represented in the archaeological record
Tène burials is a change from four-wheeled to two-wheeled vehicles,
by a group of aristocratic graves. The characteristic feature of La
either a chariot or a cart. This of course means that at the beginning
of La Tène there was also a change in tactics of warfare, with the
introduction of the chariot, probably ultimately derived from Etruria.
The second characteristic of La Tène is the development of Celtic
art, which is perhaps the greatest achievement of prehistoric Europe.

In a series of these chariot burials from the Marne and the Middle
Rhine dating from the fifth century we find once again imports,
notably Greek pottery of the period 450–420 BC. Such Greek pottery
(Attic Red Figure) comes from graves at Somme-Bionne, Klein
Aspergle and elsewhere. There are also some Etruscan imports from
these graves, suggesting that the Alpine passes were more important
as trade routes than the overland route from Marseilles and the
Rhône. These imports continue to appear until the end of the fifth
century.

During this period, as one might expect, the coinage of Massalia
was not very copious. Until the middle of the century she issued a
very limited coinage of obols, and these were replaced by a further
coinage of small denominations which continued to be struck until
the end of the century.

Massaliote 'Heavy' Drachms[7]

At the end of the fifth century a series of obols were struck with the
obverse type of Apollo and the reverse of a wheel. The earliest of

E

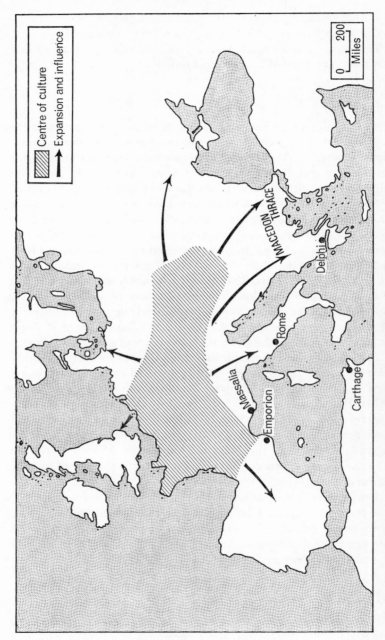

1. Extent of La Tène culture Province (After Powell, 1958)

these are of excellent work, and are signed by Magna Graecian artists (Figure 15.). They seem to be accompanied by the first issue of drachms on the Phocaean standard, with Artemis on the obverse and a lion on the reverse. The former copied the famous head of Arethusa by Euainetos which appeared on the silver coins of Syracuse *c.* 395 BC while the latter was possibly modelled on a type used at Velia about the same time. A date of *c.* 390 BC would therefore seem reasonable for these drachms.

  Fig. 15 Massaliote obol, late fifth century BC

The issue has been associated by Rolland with a curious story told by Justinus about Catumandus, a Celtic chief who is supposed to have led an attack on Marseilles about this time, but who dreamed of Athene and made peace with the Massaliotes in order to worship at her temple in the city.

The story at face value is mythical, but on analogy might suggest that the Massaliotes were attacked by the Celts about this time and forced to pay a ransom. Thus the coinage might be explained as 'ransom money'.

If not, it could possibly be explained in the light of another event that took place about the same time. Brennus sacked Rome in 390 BC and demanded a considerable ransom (his own weight in gold). On this occasion we are told Marseilles emptied her coffers to help Rome, laying the foundations of a long alliance between the two cities.[8]

Massaliote 'Light' Tetrobols and Obols[9]

Massalia did not long suffer Celtic oppression, and by the end of the fourth century BC was issuing a copious coinage and rebuilding her old commercial power.

In the last years of the fourth century BC the old 'heavy drachm' weight standard was abandoned in favour of a lighter Athenian one. This was used for a coinage of 'light' obols and tetrobols (often wrongly called drachms). The types were similar to the old, though stylistically later, and the sequence of dies can be established by a study of the magistrates' symbols that appear on the reverses (Plate 8d; Figure 16).

The earliest are in good style, but by the end of the third century are increasingly barbarous. The output of these coins was considerable – the Paris Collection has 812 examples, probably the only coins surviving out of 18,000 struck.[10]

There is good literary evidence for the importance of Massalia at this period. Strabo tells us that the defensive powers of Marseilles

Fig. 16 Massaliote 'Light' tetrobol, late fourth-early third century BC

were equal to those of Rhodes, Cyzicus or Carthage. Polybius tells us of its significance in the Second Punic War, and he and Livy both record that Rome made a great effort to protect her and her ally Saguntum from the Carthaginians.

About 200 BC Marseilles began her output of token bronze coins, and these continued until the fall of the city to Julius Caesar in 49 BC.

The Tin Trade with Britain

There is no reason, archaeological or numismatic, to suggest that the tin trade between Marseilles and Britain alluded to by later Classical writers commenced before the time of Pytheas who, we are told by Diodorus, visited these islands towards the end of the fourth century BC.

The main output of the new 'light' tetrobols in Marseilles began shortly after his voyage of discovery, and might conceivably coincide with the start of a new phase of trading.

About this time, c. 300 BC, we find Italian pottery and lamps spreading up the Rhône valley for the first time, suggesting the start of a new period of commerce. The tin trade may have started then, or more probably slightly later. There is reason to believe that Massalia's greatest prosperity dates from the years following 250 BC. About then Emporiae, the sub-colony of Massalia, began striking coins. Marseilles also began issuing a token bronze coinage soon after this date, and later certain groups of Celts began issuing their own coins imitating the Massaliote. The period 250–200 BC seems to have been one of great commercial prosperity for Marseilles and her colonies.[11]

Over two hundred Greek coins have been found in the British Isles. One interesting group of these, from Dorset, all come from a nineteenth century collection formed by a local parson, and for various reasons cannot be regarded as reliable evidence.[12] Another group, which is also unreliable, was found at Exeter.[13] Apart from these two collections we are left with a large number of scattered finds, very few of which come from archaeological contexts. Recently, however, one coin of Ptolemy v (204–181 BC) was found in Winchester, stratified with Iron Age 'Second B' pottery, in a context datable to the first century BC.[14] Other Greek coins have been found in contexts which might point to their being Iron Age losses – such as a coin from the Caburn, Sussex (an Iron Age hillfort),[15] another from Poole, Dorset[16] (also an Iron Age hillfort), or yet others from Selsey,[17] Carn Brea[18] or Dragonby,[19] all known Iron Age sites.

Leaving aside the question of Roman and modern losses, which some at least of the coins must be, we may be fairly certain that a percentage came to Britain in the last two centuries BC. The appearance of these coins at this date could be explained in the light of the tin trade, and the period at which they appear in Britain coincides with the postulated date of the trade from Massaliote and other coin evidence. Presumably the coins were brought as trinkets in the same way that Roman sestertii were traded to the Germans or pendants were made out of imitation coins of Tiberius at Kondapur, Hyderabad.

Apart from coins and two finds of Greek vases which seem to be authentic from Reading[20] and Teignmouth,[21] the majority of finds of Greek objects from Britain are probably modern losses or hoaxes.[22]

The texts which describe the tin trade from Marseilles refer to the tin being collected at Ictis, and there has been much dispute as to where this was. The distribution pattern of the coins shows a marked concentration in the south-east, especially in the neighbourhood of the Thames mouth and the Isle of Wight. It is perhaps not altogether wise to speculate on this, but it is tempting to follow current thinking among both French and British prehistorians and identify the Isle of Wight as Ictis. The other main contender is St Michael's Mount in Cornwall, but strangely neither coins nor Greek pottery have turned up to any great extent in Cornwall. If indeed it was Cornish tin that was traded, which seems likely, it is probable that the trade was by way of middlemen (Map 2).

The trade seems to have come to an end about 60 BC with the destruction of Corbilo, and certainly had ended by Caesar's capture

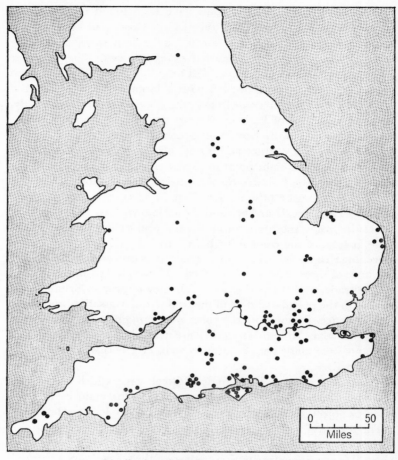

2.   Distribution of Greek coins in the British Isles

of Marseilles in 49. Strabo visited the city and made no mention of the trade, which he probably would have done were it still flourishing.

Greek Coins in France

In France the distribution of Greek coins is particularly interesting, and has been used to study the phases of Greek trade with the barbarian hinterland. As in Britain, finds are usually strays, but there are a few hoards, chiefly in the south.

In these hoards it is not uncommon to find Celtic coins associated with the Greek, as at Tourdan, where a tetrobol of Histiaea (Euboea) was associated with both Massaliote and Celtic coins. At St Bernard, coins of Histiaea, Carthage and Tarentum were found associated. It is odd that coins of Histiaea are so common in these French hoards – in 1881 no less than thirty were found in a small hoard at Nice.[23]

The general sequence of currency in the Greek colonies of southern France is well demonstrated at Glanum in the Rhône valley.[24] The town was founded about 200 BC and the first occupants were upper class residents who built Greek-plan town houses.

The majority of the early coins are Massaliote, suggesting strong influence from there. Compared with 21 silver and 228 bronze coins of Marseilles the other Greek coins are few – five from Minorca and one from Syria. There are six Celtic coins from the Rhône valley and 29 other Celtic bronze pieces. Roman influence in the later days of the first century BC is reflected in the discovery of nine denarii, three quinarii and thirteen bronzes.[25]

The Paul Hoard

A few finds of Celtic coins in Britain may possibly be connected with the tin trade. Coins of the Namnetes, a tribe which centred on the Loire valley round Nantes, occasionally turn up in Hampshire. These date from the end of the second century BC.[26] They also circulated well into the first century BC or early years AD and have sometimes been associated with coins of Augustus and Tiberius.

It has been suggested that two coin hoards from Cornwall may also be related. The first is the Paul Hoard, found near Penzance.[27] This consisted of forty-three copies of Massaliote tetrobols of 'Milan' and 'Scorpion' types, struck in the Milan and Ticino river area. With the exception of one from eastern France the finds of these coins are all concentrated in the southern foothills of the Alps and the Po valley (Map 3).

One eminent authority has suggested that the hoard was traded to Britain along the trade route from Marseilles, but this theory is open to question since no coins of this type have ever been found within a wide range of Marseilles. Probably we should see them as coming to Britain by way of the Alps and Germany. In Etruscan times this route brought to central Europe a series of bronzes which are associated with Hallstatt graves. There is some evidence to suggest that this route had an extension to Britain, and again in the first

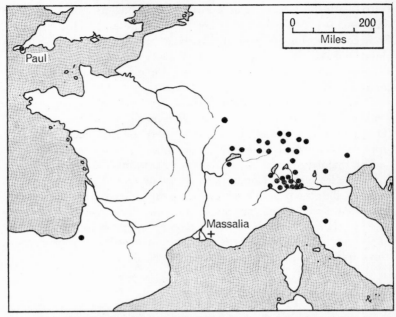

3. Distribution of coins of 'Paul Hoard' type (after Allen, 1961)

century BC Roman bronzes travelled to these shores the same way. The coins from the Paul Hoard were of the Insubres and Cenomani, who seem to have been among the tribes which organized the trade in Roman times with other Celts beyond the frontiers of Roman control.

A second hoard has been found at Penzance itself, consisting of one Belgic coin and a series of copies of bronze coins of Massalia, struck on the Swiss-French border. Here again the coins, though imitating Massaliote issues, are not found in the neighbourhood of Marseilles, and are much more likely to have come to Britain through Gallia Belgica.[28]

Other imitations of Massaliote coins have been found at Pevensey and Cirencester.

Greek Coins with Types Relating to the Celts[29]

Greek coins sometimes have types which relate to the Celts. Of these perhaps the most interesting are those struck to commemorate Greek victories over the Celts, who invaded Greece in the third century BC. In 279 BC they laid waste Macedon, and small bands under Brennus (a different Brennus from the chief who sacked Rome) and Acichorus invaded Thrace and Thessaly. They were defeated by the Athenians at Thermopylae, but turned their attention on Delphi, which they looted. Eventually they were defeated by the Phocaeans and Aetolians.

A tetradrachm of the Aetolian League has on the reverse the figure of Aetolia seated on a pile of Celtic and Macedonian shields, with a Celtic trumpet (carnyx) at her feet. The coin must date from about 279 BC and is important archaeologically in a study of shield and carnyx types, about which more will be said in the next chapter. Sometimes the Celtic shield is inscribed A for Acichorus. The figure of Aetolia was modelled on a statue set up at Delphi.[30]

In 277 BC the Celts also suffered defeat at the hands of Antigonus Gonatas of Macedon, and his tetradrachms have as an obverse type a Macedonian shield with the head of Pan in the centre, referring to the panic he instilled in the Celts. Some of his bronze coins (often wrongly ascribed to Doson) have on the reverse Pan setting up a trophy.

Classical Prototypes for Celtic Coins – Macedon (Eastern Series)

Greek coins were the prototypes for several series of Celtic coins. The Celts probably realized the need for coins when they first traded with the Greeks and Romans and when they came into direct contact with the Classical world through their incursions into Italy and Greece. Celts served as mercenaries in the Greek armies – Antigonus Gonatas had Celtic mercenaries – and it would seem that the Celts also served in the Roman legions from an early date. They would have received their pay in the form of coins. By the third century BC the Celts had built up a sufficiently strong internal economy to produce a surplus, with the result that there was an increase of trade and the need for coinage.

The first coins to be struck by the Celts were modelled on coins which entered the barbarian world by way of Thessaly and Macedon. Within a century local coinage had developed within several different areas, modelled on Classical prototypes. The earliest were direct imitations, these being followed by cruder copies from which stemmed regional developments, some coins acquiring local legends. Certain basic types had a long life, even a century or more. The

E*

evolution of coin types was at first slow, but later gained momentum.[31]

Celtic coins and die groups are confined to small areas, and it must be assumed that they were not tribal issues but those of individuals.

The earliest Celtic coins were imitations of tetradrachms of Philip of Macedon, with the head of Zeus on the obverse and a horseman on the reverse (Plate 8a; 8b). These appear, not long after the prototypes, in Serbia and Bosnia then spread into south-west Rumania and east and north into Transylvania and Hungary. Later copies were made of heavy tetradrachms of Alexander and Philip III. Later still, after 146 BC, the staters of Thasos, an island off Thrace at the head of the Aegean, were imitated further north by the tribes living near the Black Sea.

Apart from these copies of silver tetradrachms among the eastern Celts we can distinguish another major series of imitations of Macedonian coins. This series is modelled on the gold stater of Alexander the Great, and enjoys essentially an eastern distribution at the same time as the gold staters imitating those of Philip of Macedon were circulating in the western Celtic world. The two series are more or less contemporary during the third and second century, but the western series outlasts the eastern by almost a century (Figure 17).

Fig. 17 Celtic gold stater, imitating one of Alexander III of Macedon

The earliest of these imitations are accurate copies of the gold stater of Alexander, and are close to the original weight. The copies seem to have travelled up through Moravia and along the Elbe, and we find fractional denominations being struck alongside them. They occasionally turn up in oppida, such as Staré Hradisko in Moravia, or in hoards, especially in Bohemia.[32] Strays are found even in Austria and Hungary. By the first century BC we find very stylized versions at Ingoldstadt and later round Lake Constance.[33]

The types of Alexander's stater, with a helmeted head of Athene on the obverse and a winged Nike on the reverse give way to modified types based on the silver staters of Philip V (220–179 BC), with Athene Alkis on the reverse instead of Nike. These copies begin probably in the second quarter of the second century. They are associated again with oppida, most notably Stradoniče in Bohemia.[34]

From the Alkis series stems another, struck by the Boii and well studied by Karel Castelin. The Boii, having caused the Romans and Etruscans a great deal of trouble, were overthrown at the end of the third or beginning of the second century and left their settlements in northern Italy to migrate to the middle Danube and possibly

Fig. 18 Very late Central European 'Mussel' stater, with BIATEC legend

Bohemia. Historical sources attest the presence of the Boii in Bohemia prior to 113 BC when they repulsed the Cimbri. The Boii, it would appear, are responsible for imitations of the Alkis series known as the 'mussel' staters, the mussel type being the ultimate breakdown of the head of Athene. These continue until the third quarter of the first century BC[35] (Figure 18).

At this point we shall leave the eastern series of gold coins, to return to it again in a later section.

Celtic Imitations of Greek Coins – Macedon (Western Series)

The second stream of imitations of the coins of Macedon are all derived from the gold stater of Philip II, with the head of Apollo on the obverse and a charioteer on the reverse. This, the second main gold stream of Celtic Europe, is encountered in Gaul and Britain (Plate 8c).

Its origins have been hotly contested and there are, in fact, three schools of thought which suggest how these gold staters came to be imitated.

The first, and most generally accepted now, is that the copies of the *philippeioi*, as they are called, came by way of the Danube and through Switzerland. Hoards of staters of Philip have been found in Rumania (at Anadol and Maraşesti) at the start of the route. The presumed prototypes must antedate the Alexander gold imitations referred to in the previous section, and as we know that the Boii found the Alexander-type coins being used when they reached Bohemia in the third century BC, we can assume that the prototypes for the Gaulish *philippeioi* must be earlier than this. There are certainly some very good early copies of Philip's staters from Lake Neuchâtel, all fractional denominations.[36]

The second theory was advanced at the beginning of this century by Adrien Blanchet, who maintained that the staters of Philip came by way of Massalia up the Rhône to northern France.[37] There are many objections, however, against this theory – staters of Philip are extremely rare in France; in fact there have been only two authenticated finds, and there is very little evidence to suggest that they were used commonly in Marseilles. The majority of the *philippeioi* were struck for trade with the east.

In 1933 G. C. Brooke in two papers suggested another origin for the Celtic copies of the *philippeioi*. He suggested that between 194 and 167 BC the Romans, having defeated Philip V, the Galatians and Antiochus III of Syria, brought back to the capital numerous gold staters of Philip as booty, and exacted yet more as indemnities from Greek states. In 121 the Averni and Allobroges were defeated by Fabius Maximus, and a league was formed consisting of these two tribes together with the Aedui and Sequani. They formed a Roman protectorate and became familiar with the gold coins, which Dr Brooke believed were widely circulating in the Roman world. He suggested, therefore, that the first copies were made by the Averni at the end of the second century BC and from there the custom spread in all directions in France and Switzerland.[38]

There are, however, many sound arguments against this theory, attractive though it is. It vitiates the chronology of the *philippeioi*-type coins, condensing the period of spread into a very short time range which is difficult to accept. Secondly, it misinterprets many texts in the Classical writers as meaning that the *philippeioi* were actually circulating in the Roman world, whereas the Romans used the word 'philippus' for gold coins, just as sovereigns were called 'napoleons' in the last century, or in contemporary English slang we speak of 'half a dollar' meaning a halfcrown.

It is most unlikely that the gold staters of Philip were circulating long after they were struck – hoard evidence from Greece shows that the *philippeioi* disappeared from circulation early in the third century. There is only one hoard after 280 in which they occur – the Buccheri hoard in Sicily, *c.* 134 BC, where two staters of Philip were found along with many silver coins.[39]

At any rate, we can be sure that the copies of the gold staters of Philip reached central Gaul at a fairly early date, and spread outwards from there. The earliest series of copies have often been associated with the Averni, but this is probably fallacious.

The first generation of copies were close to the originals, though the legends are blundered and they exaggerate the mint symbols. In the second generation of copies many deliberate peculiarities developed, and we find pseudo pattern legends. The two horses of the chariot on the reverse become one in these second generation coins. Smaller denominations, the half and quarter stater, become common, and the stater itself is sometimes absent. One coin acquires a mysterious legend in Greek – the Celts seem to have used Greek letters at first, but later adopted the Latin. There is a sword inscribed *KOPICIOC* from Port, Bienne, Switzerland, in Greek letters, though later inscriptions from the La Tène world are in Latin letters.

These second generation copies spread to influence the coinages of Armorica and Gallia Belgica, and to the Manche, Picardy and Meuse, while yet another group was centred on northern Switzerland.

A date in the 'philippus' coinage is provided by a hoard from Tayac in central France, which included second generation copies. This hoard can be related to the events surrounding the incursions of the Cimbri and Teutones into the Celtic world at the end of the second century BC, before they were finally repulsed by the Romans in 101 by the combined forces of Marius and Catulus. The hoard probably dates from c. 108, just before they met their first setback at Roman hands in 107. It is of great importance as the hoard contained examples of some of the earliest coins of Gallia Belgica, Allen's Gallo-Belgic A series, which are also found in Britain.[40]

From this time the various series of philippus-derived coinages can be considered in terms of tribes and local issues, and the sequence can be established by numerous hoards and site finds, in the latter case the most important being from Alesia, Vercingetorix's oppidum. To these coinages we shall also return in a later section.

Imitations of Coins of Massalia

Celtic coins can be studied in terms of the belts of metal standards.[41] So far we have been concerned only with the gold belt – the coins struck in central Europe, Switzerland, north and central France and Britain in the first instance were on the gold standard, which did not seem to depend on the availability of the metal. In southern France and east Europe silver was the metal chiefly used for coins. In Spain, apart from the Romano-Iberian issues of cities like Osca, the standard seems to have been bronze.[42] This division of Europe into provinces is valid until the first century BC but thereafter breaks down.

As one might expect the coins of Massalia provided prototypes for the Celts. The earliest Massaliote imitations were those struck in the southern foothills of the Alps and the Po valley, of which later variant types appeared in the Paul Hoard. In this region the Celts had first settled around 400 BC coming in from east France, southern Germany and Switzerland. The prospect of plunder tempted them down into Italy on numerous raids – the sack of Rome in 390 was the outcome of one of the earliest. For a while the Celts occupied extensive territories in what was Cisalpine Gaul (north of Italy), but in 225 BC Roman forces penetrated the area occupied by the Boii, and as we have seen annexed the whole region occupied by them and the Insubres. About 190, more territory passed into Roman hands and the Celts were forced back to the Alpine foothills. Here they remained until in 82 the whole of Cisalpine Gaul became a Roman province and the extent of their power was further diminished. Throughout the period they had been in contact with the Romans, and it is not surprising that they adopted coinage not long after it came into vogue in Rome. The coins that were imitated were the tetrobols of Massalia, and though the Capitol Hoard shows they were being struck as early as 200 BC they continued in use down to the time of Augustus and Tiberius, occurring in graves of that date.[43]

The later bronze coins of Massalia with Apollo on the obverse and a bull on the reverse were also imitated, mainly in the south, as one might expect, but some penetrating even to central Europe. Bronze coins with the Massaliote bull have turned up at Mont Beauvray and Stradoniče.[44]

The complex series of potin coins of central and east Gaul struck between the head waters of the Seine and Rhine are also derived from the Massaliote prototype. An offshoot of these are the enigmatic British 'tin' (speculum) coins of the Thames valley, Kent and Sussex. These were in use until a late date both on the Continent and Britain, as German and British excavations have proved. Some have turned up in a Claudian context in Lullingstone villa in Kent. They probably began in the mid first century BC[45] (Plate 10b).

Among the tribes which issued bronze imitations of Massaliote coins were the Tricorii and Samnagenses, both near Marseilles.

Imitations of the coins of Rhoda and Emporiae[46]

Rhoda was a colony of Rhodes, in Hispania Citerior, at the foot of the Pyrenees. It struck from about 250 BC a series of drachms with Persephone on the obverse and a rose on the reverse (Figure 19).

Fig. 19 Silver tetrobol of Rhoda, after 250 BC

These were imitated in Gallia Aquitania, where the cross of the full-bloom rose became the main feature of the reverse. Copying began fairly early, and at first was of high standard. The Rhoda types however were taken up by the warlike Volcae Tectosages, who first put decorative motifs in the angles of the reverse cross, later symbols and letters. The main symbol used was an axe. The coins spread up to Switzerland and ultimately Czechoslovakia, where they have turned up at Stradoniče (Plate 8g; Figure 20).

Fig. 20 Silver coin of the 'Volcae Tectosages' ultimately derived from the coins of Rhoda

Emporiae, a Phocaean colony which grew up as an offshoot from Massalia, was founded in the early fourth century BC. It became one of the main ports of the west Mediterranean, replacing Rhoda which stood not very far away. The coins that were imitated by the Celts were drachms with Persephone on the obverse and Pegasos on the reverse. The imitations began later and persisted longer than those of the coins of Rhoda.

Roman Coins and the Celts: Early Imitations[47]

Until the time of Caesar, Roman coins did not circulate very extensively in the Celtic world. Nevertheless, in certain areas it would seem that they enjoyed a limited circulation, and we find several series of Celtic coins modelled on Roman denarii.

These, as one might expect, are chiefly to be found in southern

Gaul, particularly Gallia Narbonensis, where prolonged contact with the Romans resulted in a veneer of 'Romanitas' among certain tribes.

Among the earliest copies were these found in Gallia Cisalpina, along the east bank of the Rhône. Here, at a date not far removed from that of the prototypes, we find a series of coins modelled on the Romano-Campanian didrachms of the period 241–222 BC. Romano-Campanian didrachms, too, were perhaps partly influential in the Celtic modifications of the Alexander gold staters in east-central Europe.[48]

Alongside these silver coins of Romano-Campanian origin we find others derived from the issues of Carthage of the third to second century BC. It may be remembered that coins of Carthage were common at Marseilles and its neighbourhood. Some coins inspired by Carthaginian models are later found even in central Europe.[49]

Later in the Rhône valley area we find a series of small silver coins imitating Roman Republican denarii, with Roma on the obverse and a horseman on the reverse, derived from the Dioscuri type. These have quite a wide distribution, and occur for example in Switzerland in territory of the Allobroges where the horseman on the reverse has degenerated into a hippocamp-like figure (Plate 8e).

This area was that in which the Roman campaigns of Fabius Maximus took place. These campaigns were followed by the formation of a League of Tribes, and accordingly Roman influence was very strong. The Allobroges were among the first to submit to the Romans at the time of the conquest.

Roman Coins in Iron Age Britain[50]

It is interesting to study the pattern of the circulation of Roman coins in Britain before the Roman conquest. This is well demonstrated by two important hoards, the Weston Longville Hoard (Norfolk) and the Almondbury Hoard (Yorkshire). In both these hoards Roman Republican denarii were found associated with native British, and in the latter hoard the Roman denarii predominate. It is not very easy to date them, as they both come from areas not affected by the general pattern of Romanization in the Augustan and Tiberian periods, and accordingly may be as late as the time of the conquest. Nevertheless they are essentially pre-conquest native hoards.

In the south the increasing Romanization just before the conquest probably resulted in a larger number of Republican and even Imperial coins being put into circulation. In a hoard from Ayott

St Lawrence, Herts., (one of the key areas), two hundred coins were found. Of those examined a large percentage were Republican with a number of Augustus and a couple of Tiberius. In Yorkshire the Lightcliffe Hoard contained thirty Roman coins, all bar three (of Augustus and Gaius) Republican, together with four local Coritanian coins. There are other finds – at Baldock, Herts., a coin of Cunobelin was found with one of Augustus and at Savernake, Wiltshire, a denarius of Tiberius was found with a coin of Epaticcus. More recently a hoard was found at Lakenheath in 1959 consisting of two coins of Cunobelin, one of Antedrigus, 396 of the Iceni and 63 of the late Republic.[51]

There are few finds of Republican denarii from excavated Iron Age sites, but they do occasionally turn up. One, for example, was found in the Iron Age fort of Salmonsbury in Gloucestershire.

The occurrence of a pendant made out of a coin of Augustus at Lexden, Essex, in a chieftain's tomb, is again evidence that Roman coins were finding their way across the Channel, though the fact that the coin was made into a pendant would suggest they were not in universal circulation[52] (Plate 13).

The fact that after the Conquest Republican coins remained in circulation renders invalid as evidence the thirty or so stray finds of Republican denarii from the British Isles. Republican aes never never seem to have been in use, only the denarii, and after the Conquest these retained their former popularity.

Romanization in native British coinage

The effect of Romanization on coinage is well attested in the pre-conquest period by a series issued by the Trinovantes, the Catuvellauni and the Atrebates.

During the last thirty years before the conquest we see the effect in south-east England of Roman influence. It can be seen in the fine imports from chieftain's graves, which are particularly concentrated in Essex, Hertfordshire and Cambridge. Here leaders were buried in splendour with Roman bronze and silver cups, bronze ornaments and amphorae, probably of Falernian, and imported Italian and Gallo-Belgic pottery. The pottery also found its way into the homes of lesser mortals in the areas of the Belgic kingdoms. Some fine pottery, imported from the continent, even found its way to Lincolnshire and Yorkshire.[53]

This was part of a 'softening up' policy employed by the Romans, who seemed pleased to encourage the Romanization of Britain.[54] Coins issued by these Belgic dynasties reflect the increasing Romanization, beginning with those struck by Tasciovanus of the Catuvellauni (*c.* 10 BC) and Tincommius of the Atrebates (*c.* 5 BC) (See for examples Plate 10f; 11a).

The Roman style reaches its peak just before the conquest with the coins of Cunobelin. Classical motifs are frequently used, though they are not merely blind copies but essentially Celtic interpretations of the Classical concepts. The coins of Tasciovanus with the head of Augustus on the obverse and Pegasus on the reverse might quite easily be taken for a product of a provincial Roman mint. The head of Augustus on this coin, incidentally, lends further support to the theory that denarii of the emperor were circulating quite widely in Britain at this time, to familiarize people with his portrait. At Silchester coins of Eppillus show the same features – a silver quarter stater has on the obverse a bird which would not be out of place on a Roman standard[55] (Plate 10h).

The coins struck in Gaul at the time of the campaigns of Caesar show a similar tendency to Romanization in their types.

Roman Coins in Central Europe

We left our account of Celtic coinage in central Europe with the Alkis series and the 'mussel' staters. These fall into many different groups. An associated series are the *Regenbogenschüsselchen* (little rainbow dishes) which are found throughout Bavaria, but which also occur in a belt stretching from Bohemia to eastern France. These are curious cup-shaped coins. They take their name from the way peasants used to believe that they were found at the end of the rainbow, and their curious cup-shape was due to the fact that they were 'the tears of the rainbow'. Some of these are blank on one side. They turn up frequently in hoards and in oppida, such as Manching or Stradoniče.[56]

Later on, silver coins came increasingly into circulation and are well represented in oppida. Roman coins penetrated even into Czechoslovakia in the first century BC and we find various series of coins modelled on them, starting with some large silver pieces struck 70–60 BC in the Bratislava region with the legend BIATEC. The obverse type is two jugate heads and the reverse usually a mounted figure or an animal, with a legend in Roman lettering, often BIATEC, but later with other personal names (Plate 8f).

These Biatec coins are found in Slovakia, Austria and Pannonia. Associated with one hoard from Bratislava itself was a gold 'mussel' stater, and one type of mussel stater actually has the legend BIATEC[57] (see Figure 18).

This is interesting, as it suggests that the Boii shifted their settlement from Bohemia to Slovakia-Pannonia – the occurrence of large numbers of hoards of these coins possibly relates to the hostilities between the Boii and the Dacians about 60 BC.

Towards the end of the first century BC coinage seems to have declined in this area as elsewhere in Europe, and only round Budapest were coins still issued by the Eravisci, who modelled them on Roman denarii of the mid first century BC.

During the first few centuries AD Roman coins penetrated into central Europe and beyond, and it is enlightening to study these finds. They turn up in Czechoslovakia, Poland, Denmark, Germany and even in Russia and Sweden.

In Czechoslovakia there are over two hundred and fifty hoards of up to a thousand Roman coins. These were not currency but were regarded as 'wealth' and were accumulated through trade with Roman merchants.[58]

Roman Coins in Free Germany[59]

Turning to Free Germany, we find that thousands of Roman coins of all metals passed across the Rhine and the Danube. They occur as single finds and in hoards, and turn up on settlements, in graves or from peat bogs.

It is not easy to determine whether any circulated. Probably in most cases they served as bullion in barter transactions, just as Roman coins were used in India. This is corroborated by the fact that Roman aes are relatively rare, whereas gold and silver coin finds are common, especially the latter. Copper and gold appear to a greater extent in fourth century finds. Tacitus tells us that 'The Germans nearest us value gold and silver for their use in trade', and also says that 'the people of the interior employ barter'. This would imply that on the frontiers coins circulated as coins but not beyond it.

Denarii Seratii in Germany[60]

We have already seen that in Britain Republican denarii were very popular, at the expense of later silver coins. The same phenomenon is to be noted in Germany, and Tacitus tells us that the Germans liked coins that were old and familiar, especially the denarii seratii with a biga on the reverse, struck in the late second century BC (see also Plate 8h for a variant).

Another reason, apart from pure conservatism, why these denarii were favoured was possibly the debasement under Nero in AD 63 which meant that the Germans, like the Indians, lost faith in the good metal of the Imperial denarius. Outside the Empire the quality of the metal was what mattered, not the fact that the Roman government stated the debased coins were as good as the issues of pure silver.

In the same way following the debasement of Septimius Severus a preference was shown in coins struck before his reign.

Gold Coins in Free Germany[61]

Gold coins are relatively rare. One of the earliest groups found are coins of Augustus and are concentrated between the Ems and the Weser. These can probably be associated, not with trade, but with an historical event – the Varus disaster. In AD 9 three legions under Varus were completely defeated and destroyed by the forces of Arminius. This, one of the greatest disasters in Roman history, terminated the series of campaigns inaugurated by Augustus to expand Roman interest towards the Elbe. The coins probably represent part of the loot taken from the Roman soldiers by the followers of Arminius (Map 4).

After this date gold coins are rare. There are only two small hoards of aurei of first century date from Germany, though there is one other from Bohemia. No hoards of gold date from the second century, and to this period few stray finds can be attributed. These are mostly of coins made into ornaments. Third century gold appears to have been buried in the fourth century. During the fourth and continuing into the fifth century there was an influx of gold across the frontier, and gold hoards become particularly common in east Germany. This was largely on account of the start of the Migrations, especially those of the Goths and Huns. To some extent too it was the result of barbarians from beyond the frontiers serving in the Roman army then returning to their own lands with Roman money. This certainly accounts for the increase of Roman gold in Poland.[62]

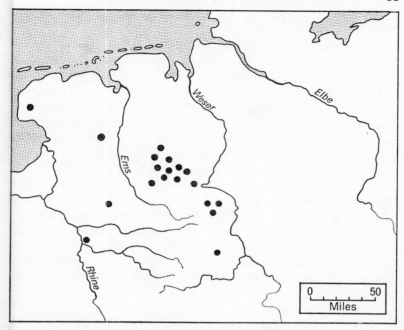

4. Augustan gold coins between the Rhine and the Elbe (after Wheeler, 1954)

Trade too was being established between the Baltic and the Byzantine world, and a route extended from Scandinavia to the Black Sea.

Hoards in Germany[63]

Hoards seem to be associated with historical phenomena, as one might expect. The large number dating to the late second century are probably the result of troubles caused by the Marcomannic War, begun by Marcus Aurelius in 167. The fact that hoards ending with Aurelius occur as far afield as Schleswig-Holstein or even Sweden shows the extent to which the effects of the war were felt.

Hoards from the Vistula region of both Marcus Aurelius and Commodus may relate to another event – the earliest movements of the Goths out of Scandinavia. Possibly some of the third century hoards may similarly relate to the migrations of the Burgundians and Vandals.

Coins in Graves – Germanic Burial Customs[64]

A very striking example of the application of numismatics in prehistory can be seen in a study made of the occurrence of Roman
coins (mainly sestertii) in graves in east Prussia. Most of the graves
containing coins have been found north-east of the Gulf of Danzig,
extending to the old Poland-Russia border. Some graves have the
coins as ornaments (which explains why sestertii were favoured on
account of their large size and gold-like metal), but others had coins
in the mouths of the dead – the equivalent of Charon's fee for his
ferry across the Styx. They are particularly common in the late second
century. The same custom of putting coins in the mouth, essentially
Classical, also occurred at an earlier date in the Celtic World.

If the distribution of the coin-graves is compared with the
distribution of graves with Roman bronze vessels we find a striking
phenomenon – the distribution of graves with coins begins where
that of bronze vessels ends, the two groups being complementary.
Thus the distribution reflects difference in trade rather than in burial
customs (Map 5).

Scandinavia and Russia

Roman coins have also been found in what is now Russia, in the
Chernyakovo region. Here we have open settlements which were
occupied by the forerunners of the east Slavs, centred round Kiev.
The sites are distinguished by numerous finds of Roman coins and
objects which include glass vessels, fibulae, amphorae and Samian
pottery. In all there are no less than 90 hoards and 799 single finds
from the area, all of which seem to have been acquired as a result
of a very lively trade with the Roman Empire.[65]

In Sweden the presence of large numbers of Roman coins – there
are about 7,000 denarii from the south, mainly Gottland – was the
result of an early Baltic trade. One hoard consisted of 1,500 coins of
different emperors.[66]

In Denmark there is a very interesting series of bog deposits which
include coins.[67] In Scandinavia, even in the Neolithic TRB culture,
votive offerings were made in meres which in the passage of time
have turned to peat.[68] The custom continued until the Iron Age
when it was a feature of other parts of barbarian Europe. Votive
deposits, for example occur at Carlingswark in Scotland,[69] Llyn
Cerrig Bach in Anglesey,[70] Hjortspring in Denmark and Duchcov

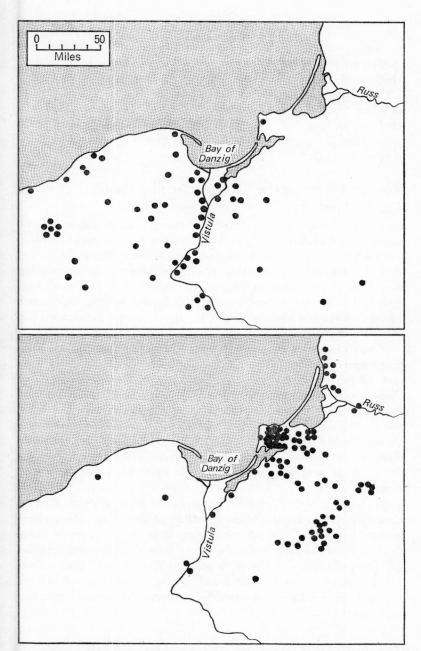

5. Comparative Distribution of Graves with Roman Bronze Vessels and Graves with Roman Coins near the Bay of Danzig (After Wheeler, 1954)

in Czechoslovakia.[71] There is also a votive deposit from the lake which gave its name to La Tène and a famous deposit at Toulouse, which Strabo tells us was looted by the Romans in 106 BC.

The votive deposits of the early centuries AD in Denmark are therefore more or less a continuity of the Celtic custom. There is a whole series, and they can be dated from the coins associated with them. Most belong to the late third and fourth centuries, the time of greatest unrest.

Roman Coins in the Caucasus – The Eastern Trade Route[72]

Large numbers of coins of Augustus have been found in Soviet Armenia and eastern Georgia. The presence of these coins in what was ancient Armenia need not surprise us, since Rome constantly vied with Parthia to control this area. Eastern Georgia is rather more surprising, until we remember that in this area lay the client kingdom of Iberia (not to be confused with Spain) which, though not advanced materially or culturally, lay in a strategic position on the eastern trade route.

It was along this route that Chinese silk travelled, having been exchanged for precious stones by middlemen in Sinkiang and Afghanistan. From here it travelled to the Caspian, north by way of the Kura river through the Caucasus to the Black Sea and Trebizond. The route was a circuitous one to avoid the Parthians, who hated the trade carried on between Rome and China. It was in order to keep Iberia free for this traffic that money was poured into the little kingdom. The coins, not surprisingly, were widely imitated beyond the frontiers, and even within the Principate itself they were also copied.

At the other end of the trade route, in the Mekong delta, excavations have been carried out on a settlement known as Oc-eo. Here, apart from native elements and imports from India, were found Roman gems and two gold coins, one of Antoninus Pius and another of Marcus Aurelius. A few coins and a reference in the Han Annals to an embassy from Marcus Aurelius and further trade involving coins of gold and silver is the evidence from the terminal point of the trade route.

Roman Coins in India[73]

Augustan silver is found in considerable quantities in southern

India, particularly the denarii of 'Two Caesars' type. Slightly later these are augmented by large numbers of Tiberian issues. Twenty of the twenty-nine coin finds from southern India are hoards. These hoards, which never contain bronze coins, sometimes consist of hundreds or even thousands of coins. The gold, however, are always cut or mutilated, though few silver coins have so far been found thus treated (Map 6).

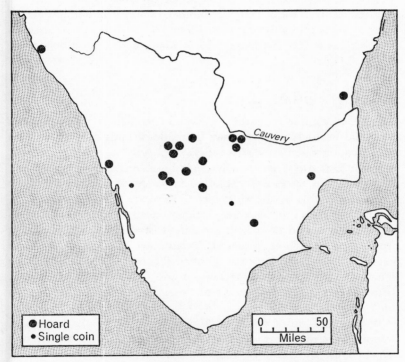

6.   Roman coins in southern India, first century AD (after Wheeler, 1954)

Pliny said that India every year absorbed fifty million sesterces, and this meant coins rather than wares to that value. The coins, however, never circulated, but served as bullion. The natives relied on their weight and quality, and the fact that they were already of established weight meant that they could be easily measured out in exchanges. This explains the absence of copper and why they are nearly all of Augustus and Tiberius – Nero debased the denarius in 63 and shook the faith of the Indians in Roman integrity.

It would appear that in India the Kushana Empire reserved the right to restrike Roman aurei with new types, but made sure that outside their territory all Roman gold was defaced for bullion use only, giving them the monopoly of gold coinage. The Kushana did not restrike silver, so the need to deface denarii did not arise.

In return for the coins the Romans probably received pepper and beryls, which are mined in the area in which the coins turn up, and were greatly prized by Roman ladies for eardrops.

From central India come a number of terracotta imitations of Roman coins probably originally gilded. The most important series of these come from Kondapur, Hyderabad, and imitate denarii or aurei of Tiberius.

Roman Coins in Africa[74]

Finally, to complete this brief survey of Roman coins beyond the Imperial frontiers mention may be made of finds of Roman coins in Africa, outside the province itself.

From East Africa ivory, rhinoceros horn, tortoise shell, palm oil, cinnamon and slaves were exported to Rome, if we can believe the account given us by the author of the *Periplus of the Erythraean Sea*. Evidence for this trade is largely lacking, except for a series of Roman coins found at Port Durnford, 250 miles east of Mombasa, extending from one coin each of Nero and Trajan down to coins of the fourth century. By far the greatest number (79 out of 85) were of the fourth century – Constantine I and II and Constans. Further south, between the Sudan and the Cape, a complete hoard is reputed to have been discovered.

A thousand miles south of Algiers where the Sahara ends in mountains, a small fort was excavated between the First and Second World War. In one of the rooms a skeleton was discovered with a remarkable array of grave goods. Among these were fragments of Roman glass and a coin of Constantine the Great. In another room of the fort was a Roman lamp. The burial was of a lady, and local tradition said that the monument was built for a lady called Tin Hinnan who rode out of the desert with a lady-in-waiting and some slaves, on a white camel, and who was later to found the line of Taureg nobility. Whether the lady found in the fort was Tin Hinnan or not will never be known, but the coin at least dates the mysterious fort in the limbo between Rome and Timbuctoo.

Celts on Roman Coins

Turning to Roman coin types, we find that there are some interesting illustrations of Celts and references to Celts on Republican denarii. As one might expect, the coins of Caesar are not without allusion to his Gallic War,and one coin in particular is of special interest since it depicts a Celtic prisoner seated beneath a trophy. The Celt is shown naked except for a belt and a torc. The trophy, though of typical native type, also included a characteristic Celtic shield of long type, similar to those that have survived from antiquity like the Witham shield or the Fayum wooden shield. It also shows a carnyx. The coin was struck about 50 BC.

The coins struck by the moneyer Hostilius Sarsena are also interesting, since they have types which relate to the Celts. They were struck *c*. 48 BC. One shows the head of a Celt, sometimes taken to be Vercingetorix, with a beard and moustache and stiff, lime-washed hair. In reality it is a personification of Gaul. Behind the head is a Celtic shield. The reverse shows a warrior and his charioteer in a Celtic chariot drawn by two horses. The warrior holds a spear and a shield (Plate 8i). A similar warrior in a less realistic scene (without a charioteer) appears on an earlier denarius of Lucius Cosconius struck in 188 BC at the time of the founding of Narbo. It may represent Bituitos of the Averni (Plate 8h). Here the warrior also holds a carnyx, and is naked. The chariot is less accurately depicted. The same type is used by a series of moneyers, of the Aurelia, Porcia, Pomponia and Publicia *gentes*, but all renderings are very schematic.[75] Another coin of Sarsena shows the head of Gallia on the obverse with a carnyx behind, and Diana with a stag on the reverse. The latter is a statue, and possibly the coin relates to the capture of Massalia by Caesar.

The depiction of the chariot on these Roman coins can be paralleled with the depiction of a Celtic chariot on a coin of the Remi described in the next chapter, struck about the time of Caesar's campaigns. It is usually thought that Caesar was very surprised to encounter chariots in Britain as he had not seen any in Gaul, where it was believed they had fallen out of use by the first century BC. This would not seem to be accurate, and a text from Strabo would suggest that chariots were still in use in some districts (Plate 9e).

At a slightly later date we find the head of Gallia appearing on a denarius struck during the Civil War of AD 69–70. The types on the coin are intended to be symbolic of nationalism. On the obverse

Gallia is shown wearing a torc, with a trumpet (this time not a boar's head carnyx) behind her head. The reverse shows clasped hands, ears of corn and the Celtic boar symbol.[76]

An interesting denarius of Augustus from an eastern mint, probably in Asia Minor, has a building on the reverse which has been taken to be a Romano-Celtic temple, though why one should appear on this coin is a matter of conjecture. It has a tall central shrine or cella, with a window over the door, and a colonnade with a pent roof. The architrave has the inscription IMP CAESAR, with a winged Victory and two warriors on the pediment. Possibly the coin refers to Caesar's campaigns. This type of temple was common in Britain and in the Seine valley round Rouen, and later in the Moselle valley round Trier. They also occur as far south as Lyons. They seem to have been a Celtic architectural development under Roman influence[77] (Plate 8k).

Another coin with a very interesting reverse is a denarius of Albinus Bruti f. (son of Brutus) struck in 49–8 BC, and again connected with Caesar's Gallic War. Here the type is two carnyxes in the form of a saltire with a Celtic shield above and another below. The one is oval like the others we have encountered, but the second is circular with radii like the spokes of a wheel. The obverse shows the head of Mars[78] (Plate 8j).

Imperial coins, for the most part, are of little value for shedding light on the peoples beyond the frontier with whom the Romans waged their wars. On the coins of Domitian we sometimes find depicted a German prisoner or a symbolic figure of the Rhine with a broken spear – neither give us any fresh light on the appearance of the Germans, for both are conventional. As one might expect, some coins of Marcus Aurelius have reverses which allude to the Marcomannic War. These show a pile of arms, presumably looted from the Germans, but again the rendering is conventional.

Further Reading

Mention will not be made here of works on Celtic coins since a discussion of these appears at the end of the next chapter. For the background of Iron Age Europe the reader should consult first the relevant chapters of Stuart Piggott's *Ancient Europe* (1965) and Piggott and Grahame Clark's *Prehistoric Societies* (1965). The former is perhaps one of the finest general surveys of European prehistory to be published and has copious illustrations and a first-rate bibliography. The second work covers a wider field than Europe, is not well illustrated and tends to suffer from compression, but is still useful. For the Celts two books may be cited, the first T. G. E. Powell's *The Celts* (1958) which, though extremely good for certain aspects of Celtic culture such as religion, tends to ignore basic archaeology and concentrate on history. The plates, however, are excellent, and the book has useful information on coins – Mr Powell is one of the few British prehistorians who is really conversant with European Celtic coinage. Of greater value is Jan Filip's *Celtic Civilization and its Heritage* (1962) which is a remarkable work of synthesis and has a valuable section on coinage based on material rarely obtainable in Britain. It tends to concentrate on the Celts in Czech lands (the author is Czechoslovakian) and is sometimes erroneous when dealing with Britain or Gaul.

The story of Greek colonies in France is well summarized in John Boardman's *The Greeks Overseas*, a Penguin book published in 1964. Finds of Greek coins in Britain were discussed by J. G. Milne in *Finds of Greek Coins from the British Isles* (1948), a work which was vitiated by his acceptance of the Rackett collection from Dorset and which advances theories no longer generally accepted. The problem is further discussed in the light of more recent findings by the present writer in 'A Greek Tin Trade with Cornwall?' in *Cornish Archaeology* 7 (1968). The historical evidence is well summarized in Hugh Hencken's *Archaeology of Cornwall and Scilly* (1932).

Roman coins beyond the *limes* are discussed with further references in Sir Mortimer Wheeler's *Rome Beyond the Imperial Frontiers* (1954), and in Michael Grant's *Roman History from Coins* (1958).

NOTES

1 For a general discussion of the archaeological background see Piggott, 1965; Clark & Piggott, 1965; Powell, 1958; Filip, 1962.
2 Linguistic problems discussed in Hencken, 1945, and briefly in Piggott, 1965. Continuity of culture in Bronze Age Europe discussed in Gimbutas, 1965.
3 Boardman, 1964; Villard, 1960.
4 Original account in Babelon, 1902–32, further discussed in Blanchet, 1905; Blanchet & Dieudonné, 1913. A reappraisal in Villard, 1960.

5 General discussion of these finds is given in the sources quoted in n.1 above. For Vix see also Joffroy, 1954.

6 Sources as in n.1. The original account of La Tène in Vouga 1923 and Déchelette, 1927. Chariot burials discussed in Joffroy & Bretz-Mahler, 1959.

7 Discussion of Massaliote coinage in Blanchet, 1905; Blanchet & Dieudonné, 1913; Villard, 1960. The earliest obols and drachms are also discussed in Déchelette, 1911. The heavy drachms are dealt with in Rolland, 1935, and Laing, 1966b. The general problems of early Greek coins in southern France and Spain and their imitations has been dealt with fairly exhaustively in many works, recent useful discussions being Rolland, 1949 and Rolland, 1961.

8 Laing, 1966b.

9 Sources as in note 7, and Rolland, 1936.

10 Villard, 1960; see also Muret & Chailbouillet, 1889.

11 General discussion of Massaliote trade in de Navarro, 1928; Cary, 1924. Coin evidence in Blanchet, 1913; Bonnet, 1937; Laing, 1966b; Laing, 1969 'A Greek Tin Trade with Cornwall?' *Cornish Archaeology* 7 (1969) 15-23, gives a full discussion of the tin trade evidence.

12 Originally published in Milne, 1948. Reconsideration in Laing, 1969, see n. 11 above.

13 Haverfield & Macdonald, 1907; Goodchild, 1937. Original list in Shortt, 1841. See also Fox, 1964.

14 Cunliffe, 1965.

15 Curwen, E. C., *Archaeology of Sussex* (1954).

16 Milne, 1948.

17 Curwen, as n.15 above.

18 Hencken, 1932.

19 May, 1966.

20 Boon, 1954.

21 Fox, 1956.

22 General list in Harden, 1952.

23 Hoards listed *passim* in Noe, 1937.

24 Discussed briefly in Reece, 1967.

25 Reece, 1967.

26 Allen, 1961a.

27 Allen, 1961b.

28 Allen, 1961d.

29 Powell, 1958, comments on plates.

30 Head, 1959.

31 The main early discussion on the origins of Celtic coinage is to be found in Forrer, 1908. The coins of the Celts in east Europe are

discussed in Pink, 1936, 1939; Pick, 1898 and Pick and Regling, 1910. For the spread to central Europe Blanchet, 1902. Castelin, 1962 for the dating of these. Pink 1960 summarizes the latest thought on this area, and a short, not very adequate discussion of origins appears in La Baume, 1960. The best discussion of the theory of an eastern origin of Celtic coinage in Christ, 1957, which has a useful bibliography.

32 Useful summary from Czech viewpoint is Filip, 1962, not however universally accepted.

33 Filip, 1962.

34 Castelin, 1956.

35 Castelin & Kellner, 1963. An earlier account of Boian coinage is given in Paulsen, 1933.

36 Advanced by Milne, 1940 – convenient summary as it is in English. More recently the view has been supported by Christ, in Christ, 1957. The Danube route for the origins of the Western 'philippeioi' is also favoured by Allen, 1961b.

37 Blanchet, 1905.

38 Brooke, 1933; Brooke, 1933a.

39 Noe, 1937; Milne, 1940.

40 Allen, 1961b.

41 Milne, 1940.

42 Heiss, 1870; Hill, 1931.

43 See Allen, 1961a for useful summary.

44 Blanchet, 1905; Blanchet, 1951.

45 Allen, 1961b; Mack, 1964.

46 For prototypes see Hill, 1931. For Celtic derivatives Blanchet, Blanchet & Dieudonné, 1905; 1913. See also de Gaudan, 1954.

47 As n.46 above.

48 Blanchet, 1951; Lengyel, 1954.

49 Blanchet, 1951.

50 Main sources are Sutherland, 1937; Laing, 1966a. Hoards with Republican coins in Allen, 1961b, and Mack, 1964

51 Briscoe, 1964.

52 Laver, 1927.

53 Stead, 1967.

54 Stevens, 1951.

55 Main sources for Roman influence in style are Fox, 1958 and Toynbee, 1964. Also mentioned briefly in Allen, 1944, Mack, 1964, Allen, 1962, and Grant, 1958.

56 Castelin & Kellner, 1963.

57 Ondrovich, 1958, with English summary. Also Filip, 1962 (briefly) and Neustupny, 1961.

58 Neustupny, 1961.

59 Wheeler, 1954.
60 Wheeler, 1954.
61 Wheeler, 1954.
62 Jazdzewski, 1964.
63 Bolin, 1930; Eggers, 1951; Eggers, 1955.
64 As n.63 above and Wheeler, 1954.
65 Mongait, 1961.
66 Stenberger, 1963.
67 Klindt-Jensen, 1958.
68 Klindt-Jensen, 1958; Wheeler, 1954.
69 Piggott, 1953.
70 Fox, 1946.
71 Filip, 1962 for this and the foregoing. Also Piggott, 1955, *passim*.
72 Grant, 1958.
73 Wheeler, 1954.
74 Mattingly, 1935; Wheeler 1954.
75 Piggott, 1952. 'Celtic Chariots on Roman Coins', *Ant.* xxvi, 87–8.
76 Powell, 1958.
77 Powell, 1958.
78 Powell, 1958.

7   Celtic Coins and the Prehistorian

In our study of the contribution of Classical coins to prehistory we have traced briefly the origins and spread of Celtic coinage in Europe. In this chapter we must now consider further the complex coinages of prehistoric Europe. As with Classical coins their value is twofold. Their types provide information about aspects of Celtic life and belief, and their distribution patterns provide clues in tracing cultural contacts.

The Problems of Studying Celtic Coin Iconography[1]

There are upwards of 12,000 different Celtic coins in the Bibliothèque Nationale in Paris, and some 500 different coin types represented in the British Museum collection of Celtic British coins.

The problem of interpretation is a difficult one. Some Celtic types are direct copies of Classical prototypes, while others may be modelled on Classical designs but have been interpreted in the light of Celtic thought. Some Celtic coins too may show Classical influence either in detail (such as the use of a Greek type of earring on an otherwise purely Celtic head) or in style, while the subject matter is purely Celtic. The dividing line between the Celtic and the Classical is often narrow, and therefore unless a coin has types which are quite without Classical prototype one must always bear in mind the possiblity of Classical influence. One wonders often what interpretation the Celts made of the coin types derived from the *philippeioi* – in the Celtic mind did the portrait of Apollo represent some local deity and the charioteer a character from Celtic lore? To suggest that the Celts just regarded them as meaningless designs is ridiculous; their popularity as types must have meant they had a significance in the Celtic mind in their own right.

In the same way there are many types of probably Celtic inspiration which we now cannot interpret in the light of our knowledge of

F

Celtic religion, but which may nevertheless have a religious significance. Figures which we study in order to gain insight into Celtic
armour may not have been merely figures but war gods or heroes.
Probably much of Celtic coin iconography has a broadly 'religious'
connotation.

This brings us to the question of the nature of Celtic religion.
The sources from which our present knowledge of Celtic religion has
been built up are diverse and at the best usually secondary. We have
the evidence of Classical writers like Posidonius or Caesar, whose
accounts were coloured to some extent by an interpretation in terms
of the Classical pantheon,[2] and we have the Celtic literary traditions
of the Irish and to a lesser extent Welsh stories, which though set
down by monks in the Early Middle Ages embody much earlier oral
traditions which were often preserved basically unaltered for centuries until they were set down in writing, strange though this may
seem. Yet even in their original form they were the traditions of a
late and insular flowering of the Celtic world – the Irish sources
such as the Ulster Cycle may possibly reflect Ireland of the second
century AD – and obviously, although certain ideas may be basic, in
details the beliefs of second century Ireland would have differed
from those of central France of the third century BC.[3]

In addition to the important literary sources we also have Gallo-
Roman and Romano-British art and to a lesser extent pre-Roman
La Tène art in Britain and Gaul. Romanization in both Britain and
Gaul to some extent was a veneer, and beneath the surface native
Celtic traditions lingered on, sometimes embodied in Roman cults.

From all these sources a general picture of Celtic life and belief can
be built up, which in its broadest terms is probably fairly accurate.
Using our other sources as guidance we can make certain broad
interpretations of Celtic coin types which are in all probability
valid.

It is important to remember that the Celts did not have an
organized religion but were rather concerned with magic, and had
local deities as opposed to an organized pantheon such as existed
in the Classical world. Celtic religion, too, was eclectic. Unlike the
Greek and Roman gods the functions of individual deities were not
clearly defined, and one god might have many aspects. The nearest
parallel to this in the Classical world was the way in which one deity
could be patron of a number of different aspects of life. The Celts
carried this much further, or perhaps one should say not so far, since
they did not regard their gods and goddesses as being specialists but

rather as being supernatural magicians. For this reason they found it quite possible not only to equate one tribal deity with another (a very useful fact when two tribes amalgamated or formed an alliance) but to identify the Celtic deities with the Classical. Similarly too Caesar said that Mercury was the greatest of the Celtic gods, and that Apollo, Mars, Jupiter and Minerva were also worshipped. In the same way in Roman Britain the native deity Sul was associated with Minerva at Bath, where we find a temple dedicated to Sul-Minerva.[4]

With these cautions in mind we can begin to classify some of the wide diversity of Celtic coin types.

The Head in Celtic Iconography[5]

The Celts seem to have venerated the head as a symbol of divinity. They seem to have regarded it as having a life of its own, separate from the body. The head was a symbol in all spheres of life, and the cult has an origin deeply rooted in European prehistory. There is abundant evidence in Classical writers for Celtic head-hunting, and indeed also of the veneration of heads. In Celtic literature, too, references to heads, head-hunting and the veneration of heads are plentiful. In the *Tàin Bò Cúalnge* an Irish Epic, we are told how the hero Cú Chulainn, while still a boy, proves his heroism by taking the head of an enemy and fixing it to his chariot, and another story from the *Tàin* tells how Cet, one of the Connaught heroes, says that, 'It is a custom among you Ulstermen that every youth who takes arms among you makes us the goal of his hockey playing'. In the same story Conall Cernach, one of the heroes, says to Cet, 'Since I took spear in my hand I have not been without killing a Connaught man every single day and without destructive fire every single night, and I have never slept without the head of a Connaught man under my knee.' In other stories there are references to talking heads, the most famous of course being that of Bran, who was beheaded by his companions when mortally wounded but whose head remained a delightful companion for them on their travels, presiding over a feast, the Assembly of the Wondrous Head. Other tales tell of singing heads, including one which was placed on a pillar at a feast, and prophetic heads, one of which was kept on a rafter in a hall but bounced down to make its utterances.[6] Classical sources tell how the Celts kept heads in chests and regarded them as valued possessions.[7]

In the archaeological record also there is abundant evidence for the cult of the head. At Roquepertuse and Entremont in southern France

Tribes shown thus: *SENONES*
Sites shown thus: ● La Tène

7.   Celtic Gaul at the time of Caesar's campaigns, s

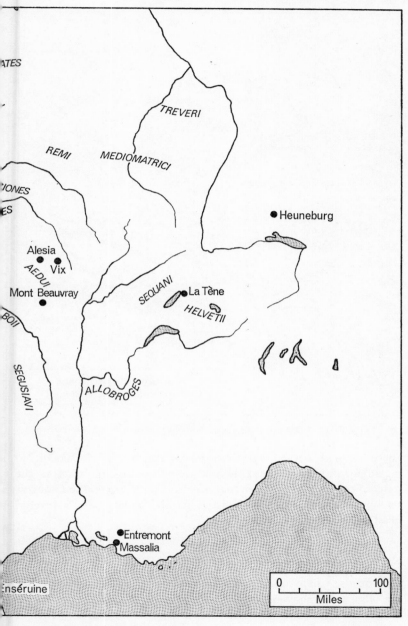

ATES

TREVERI

REMI   MEDIOMATRICI

IONES

ES

Heuneburg

Alesia
AEDUI   Vix
Mont Beauvray

SEQUANI   La Tène

HELVETII

BOII

SEGUSIAVI

ALLOBROGES

Entremont
Massalia

nséruine

0   100
Miles

ition of tribes and places mentioned in the text.

8.   Celtic tribes in Britain on the eve of the Roman conquest (after Rivet, 1958)

there are both carved representations of severed heads and niches on monuments which actually held human skulls. Skulls adorn the gates of oppida, from l'Impernal near Cahors to Bredon in Gloucestershire.[8] Later, in both Gaulish and British iconography, the severed head plays a major role.

Appearance of Heads on Celtic Coins[9]

The heads, which usually form the obverse type of Celtic coins, are often clean shaven, except in a few cases in east Europe where they are modelled on the head of Zeus from the tetradrachms of Philip of Macedon.

There are a few bearded heads not inspired by Classical models, usually of a short, stubbly nature, and these turn up in all parts of the Celtic world. A bearded head appears, for example, on a coin of the Abrincatui,[10] and on coins of the Remi[11] and Ambiani[12] (Plate 9l). Beards are more common in Britain, where they appear not infrequently in areas where Romanizing influence was most strongly felt. One cannot but wonder whether most of the bearded heads on Celtic coins owe something to Jupiter (Plate 8b). Moustaches are also surprisingly rare, in view of the traditional image of the Celt with his long 'Zappa' moustaches. They do occasionally appear, most notably on a fine coin of the Carnutes,[13] another Armorican tribe, which has a head very similar in style to the famous Mšecké Žehrovice head from Bohemia. (Plate 9a; Figure 21).

Fig. 21 The Mšecke Žehrovice head

Coins of the Carnutes show another feature common to many heads on Celtic coins – tattoos.[14] Sometimes these may be shown as a group of pellets, sometimes as a symbol reminiscent of a 'thunderbolt' (this appears on coins of Armorica),[15] sometimes as a wavy line. Tattoos are particularly common in Armorica, though they occasionally appear in other parts of the Celtic world – one appears, for example, on a coin of the Sequani.[16] The custom of tattooing was widespread in the barbarian world – a Scythian tomb at Pazyryk has preserved in Altai snow a totally tattooed barbarian body –

and literary references inform us that it was a widespread practice amongst the Celts[17] (Figure 22).

Hairstyles show a remarkable diversity, suggesting that it was not always backward swept and starched into spikes – Cú Chulainn's,

Fig. 22 Coin of the 'Aulerci Eburovices' showing tattooed face

Fig. 23 The Pfalzfeld pillar

we are told, 'bristled all over his head like branches of a red-thorn thrust into a gap in a great hedge'. On the contrary, it is usually wavy or curly (possibly the outcome of the torsive nature of La Tène art), and may sometimes be tied in a bun or a pigtail, as on some coins of Cunobelin.[18] Variations in style again may be due to some extent to Classical influence (Plate 11d). A curious series of coins show heads with radiant manes – possibly the result of starching, more possibly to give the effect of radiance.[19] The most important series of these can be seen in Armorica (Plate 9h).

The coins of Armorican Gaul, too, show other very distinctive features in their obverse types. Some have a boar or hippocamp in or just above the hair, which is difficult to interpret.[20] (Plate 12a). Such symbols also appear on the reverses of Armorican coins. The boar had an important cult value among the Celts – more will be said of this presently – and boars are not infrequently associated with severed heads in Gallo-Roman iconography.

Celtic coin obverses are never portraits. At one time it was believed that the head of a clean shaven young man that appeared on coins of Vercingetorix actually represented this formidable opponent of Caesar, but a recent study has shown that in reality the head is merely a generalized type derived from a Classical Apollo[21] (Plate 12b).

Horned heads appear sometimes on coins, especially in Britain, where they are derived from the Classical Jupiter Ammon. The ram was associated in Celtic iconography with war gods, and therefore this particular representation of a Classical deity no doubt appealed to the Celtic mind. It is found particularly on the coins struck at Colchester, where the Belgic war god Camulos was venerated.[22] Horned deities abound in Celtic iconography.

Severed Heads

Severed heads appear on Celtic coins, sometimes as smaller heads associated with larger, sometimes as frontal facing masks (Figure 24), sometimes as heads carried by figures (Plate 9h). An interesting coin of Cunobelin has as a reverse type a figure wearing only an apron and holding a severed head and a sceptre. Behind him is what appears to be a flaming altar. It is possible that this refers to human sacrifice[23] (Plate 11f). Facing severed heads appear in sculpture (Figure 23).

It has been suggested in another context that full face heads in Celtic iconography represent divine heads, profiles those of heroes.[24] Although this might be substantiated by some objects such as the Marlborough vat,[25] the Gundestrup cauldron depicts gods both in profile and frontally,[26] and this also appears to be the case with coins. One can hardly imagine that the head that appears on many Armorican coins with smaller heads attached to it by chains is intended to represent anyone other than a god, and presumably the whole type should be interpreted as a central power drawing upon others, in this case lesser deities.[27] The type is without good parallel in Gallo-Roman iconography (Plate 12a).

F*

Severed heads appear frequently as coin types – there is a particularly frightening series on the coins of the Ambiani, in one case associated with a snake.[28] A severed head on a coin of the Leuci appears with a boar above it.[29] Some facing heads on coins from southern France are probably inspired by Classical Medusa heads or antefixes,[30] while yet others from eastern Europe are derived from

Fig. 24 Coin of the 'Boii' showing facing mask

Fig. 25 Coin of Cunobelin with facing head

Greek coins struck at Larissa in Thessaly.[31] Small heads frequently appear as symbols in the field, most notably on the reverses of some of the coins of the Lemovices.[32]

One interesting coin, struck by the Aedui and bearing the legend DUBNOREIX, shows a naked warrior with a scabbard on a belt carrying a carnyx and boar standard in one hand and a severed head in the other[33].

Facing Medusa-like masks appear frequently on British coins, and recur in Romano-British art, as on the pediment of the temple of Sul-Minerva at Bath[34] or from other monuments at Chester and Caerleon. The similarity between the head of Medusa and the Celtic severed head was happily sufficiently close to make an equation possible. Such heads are a feature of the coinages of Tincommius[35] and Cunobelin, in the latter case assuming masculine attributes like the head of Sul-Minerva[36] (Figure 25).

Multiple Heads[37]

The number three was of great importance to the Celts, and Irish literature refers to three deities born simultaneously and sharing the same name but having different attributes. Similarly there are abundant references to deities which are grouped in threes. The traditional Welsh lore is embodied in a series of triadic statements. Thus it is not surprising to find three-faced heads in keeping with Celtic iconography. The phenomenon can be noted in the Romano-British Tres Matres cult, known from sculptures at Cirencester and elsewhere, and three-headed sculptures, though relatively rare in Britain, are occasionally found, as in the case of one from Sutherland or another from Corleck, Cavan, in Ireland. Triads are frequent in Irish lore, such as the Three Macha, and even the Dagda sometimes is a triad. A strange three-headed creature was Ellen Trechend, who came out of a cave in Cruachain and devastated all Ireland.

The most famous triple deity to appear on a Celtic coin is that which is depicted on the obverse of a bronze coin of the Remi, the tribe which occupied the area round Rheims[38] (Plate 9e). This three-faced deity seems to have served as an equivalent of Mercury in the Classical period. A triad of a slightly different sort showing the complete figures rather than the heads occurs on another coin from the territory of the Remi.[39]

Janiform heads occur frequently, sometimes bearded but usually clean shaven. They occur for example on coins of the Mediomatrices, in one case in what appears to be a torc[40] (Plate 9d). The janiform figure seems to be of Etruscan origin, and spread from the Rhône northwards. It is represented in the Celtic world on a number of statues, including the famous one at Holzgerlingen. In Britain janiform heads appear on coins of Cunobelin.[41] The Celts had a strong belief in the power of twins, and there are a few sculptured janiform heads from Britain.

Rather more common than janiform heads are conjoined heads. These appear in both Britain and Gaul – a double head appears on a coin of Tasciovanus[42] (Plate 11a), and double heads appear on some of the BIATEC staters from Czechoslovakia referred to in a previous chapter[43] (Plate 8f).

Torcs

Very often the heads, where a neck is shown, have torcs. Torcs, too, are very frequently depicted either as a type or as part of a type, not infrequently being held by some figure.

The torc was a penannular neck ring, usually with expanded terminals. They were made of gold or bronze, occasionally silver. The name implies that they were made of twisted metal but this seems to have been the exception rather than the rule, though the most famous example from Britain, the electrum Snettisham torc, is in fact made in this way.[44] They first seem to have come into vogue in the mid-fifth century BC and were thereafter worn by all freemen. They were possibly inherited, as a symbol of the headship of the family or tribe, and certainly had a ritual significance (Plate 9m).

On coins they usually are depicted as plain rings with globular terminals. A torc is the main reverse type of a small silver coin of Verica, now in the Ashmolean [45] (Figure 26), and is shown worn on a head that appears on a coin of the Caletes.[46] Another of similar type appears on a coin of the Suessones.[47]

 Fig. 26 Coin of Verica, showing a torc as a main type

Fig. 27 Cernunnos from the Gundestrup Cauldron

Torcs are shown held by figures on coins of the continental Catuvellauni – one particularly interesting coin shows a walking figure with a torc in one hand and a snake in the other[48]. Another shows a squatting figure very reminiscent of the figure of Cernunnos on the Gundestrup cauldron (Figure 27), though Cernunnos is horned and these figures are without horns.[49] The snake, it has been suggested, is a spear (or perhaps a moon symbol) and the torc a sun symbol[50] (Plate 9m). Some torcs appear to be very similar to those from the Waldalgesheim grave, with buffer terminals, others more like the Snettisham torc with ring terminals.

Occasionally busts are shown with necklaces, again possibly derived from Classical prototypes.

Figure Types

Single human figures, with the exception of warriors, are relatively rare in Celtic coin iconography. Very often, however, where they do occur they are recognizably deities.

An interesting series showing Roman influence appears on late coins of the Carnutes. One, obviously modelled on a Roman Victory, is a winged female holding a shield and a Celtic carnyx.[51] Presumably she represents some winged war goddess – war goddesses were frequently ornithomorphic, such as the Morrigan of Irish literature or the Badb Catha, the Raven of Battle, whom we shall meet again presently, and who was in fact one of the aspects of the Morrigan. Similar winged female figures are quite common in Celtic coin art, but not as common as winged males.

A naked winged male figure appears on another coin of the Carnutes, holding a sceptre in one hand and a remarkable pole or pillar in the other with a forked top, while he also clutches a snake. In front of him is an eagle.[52] It is possible that this figure could relate to a cult which associated a native Mercury with trees – an interesting relief from Trier shows a woodcutter god with a tree and egrets. Yet another coin in this series of the Carnutes shows a goddess in Roman attire leaning on a pillar and holding a snake of 'beads'.[53] One of the series shows a running male winged figure carrying a peculiar object which resembles two balls joined by a cord.[54] Further coins of the Carnutes show two pugilistic figures, sometimes holding swords, sometimes torcs in the unoccupied fists.[55]

Little running figures with pigtails on coins of the Namnetes may represent Sucellos, the 'Good Striker' since they carry hammers.[56] Sucellos is a figure rather like the Irish Dagda who sometimes is shown on British coins beating a dish (symbolizing a cauldron), as in the case of some coins of Cunobelin[57] (Plate 11d).

Sometimes one finds a figure very like the Dagda leaning on a huge club or carrying a club. In the stories connected with him in Ireland he is represented as a grotesque figure with a club that is sometimes so heavy that he has to drag it round on wheels. The Dagda, like Sucellos, was associated with the attribute of a cauldron, which to the Celts was an important symbol of abundance. One Irish character, Gobniu, used it for brewing the beer of immortality. The Celts cooked their food in a huge communal cauldron. One is depicted on a coin of the Unelles suspended from chains, and is almost identical to Late Bronze Age and Early Iron Age cauldrons from British and Continental finds.[58]

Coins of the Veliocasses show running figures carrying torcs or wheels,[59] while figures on coins of the Continental Catuvellauni

Fig. 28 Coin of the Silvanectes showing a man being eaten by a monster

carry torcs or snakes. Wheels are important sacred symbols, and have a long tradition in European prehistory, being associated with sun discs. A bearded god holds a wheel on the Gundestrup cauldron, and the well-known god Taranis, the 'Thunderer', is associated with the wheel symbol. Serpent lore is abundant in Celtic literature, the serpent being one of the most important cult animals.

A very interesting bronze coin in Marseilles museum, with Classical influence, depicts on the reverse an ithyphallic horned god with outstretched arms, very reminiscent of the Cerne Giant.[60] Presumably he owes his origin to some Hercules cult – Hercules, who in Gaul was associated rather strangely with Ogmios, the god of poetry, was popular among the Celts. The fact however that the figure is horned might point to him being connected with the horned war god or Mars equivalent.

A curious deity with double fish tail like Classical nereid representations appears on a coin of the Ambiani.[61]

A macabre series of coins struck by the Aulerci Eburovices show what appears to be a fight between a man (sometimes winged) and a winged griffin.[62] Seemingly the contest ended in triumph for the griffin. On a coin of the Silvanectes a monster is eating a man. Possibly this is symbolic of death, and was a theme which recurs in La Tène art, its most famous manifestation being in the sculpture of a monster eating a man, from Noves (see also Figure 28).

Coins, both British and Gaulish, show figures wearing a sort of tunic or kilt, and women wearing long robes akin to the Classical stola. Some figures wear cloaks.[63]

Warriors on Celtic Coins

We find copious illustrations of warfare on Celtic coins, which is hardly surprising in view of the heroic nature of Celtic society. How often these figures represent war gods and how often humans is of course impossible to tell.

Warriors are usually shown with various attributes. On a coin of Dubnorix we find one holding a boar standard, a carnyx and a severed head[64] and on another coin of the Pictones we find a similar figure with a shield instead of a severed head and the legend VIIPOTAL[65] (Plate 9e). Another coin of the same tribe shows a warrior with a double axe. Both these coins show the warriors fully armed, with chain mail. There is evidence from other sources that the Celts wore mail on occasions, namely sculptures and surviving fragments. There were some fragments of scale mail from a native chieftain's grave at Stanfordbury in Bedfordshire,[66] and chain mail appears on sculpture from southern France. The figures on these coins have Celtic helmets of bowl type, and similar representations of bowl-type helmets appear on many coins. The 'centaurs' on Armorican staters frequently have bowl helmets, and a curious coin from Pannonia shows a 'Harpy' with a helmet[67] (Plate 9n).

Sometimes the helmets are decorated with crests, and on one unusual coin of the Remi a helmet actually has horns, reminiscent of the horned helmet from Waterloo Bridge. The Celts frequently adorned their helmets with bizarre crests, in one case from east Europe with a Roman eagle with jointed wings. Some helmets are shown with cheekpieces.

The other main type of Celtic helmet, of conical form, also appears on coins, though much less frequently. One figure is shown with a helmet or hat akin to the Phrygian cap that in Roman times was an attribute of Mithras. Many helmets are derived from that of Roma on early Republican denarii, and of course such representations are of little value. Other renderings show not only cheekpieces but a vizor, as in the case of one coin of Cunobelin. This, too, one assumes, is derived from Roman models.[68] Some amazing helmets appear on coins of the Boii, in one case decorated with baubles and a curious lys-like ornament.[69]

As one might expect, in view of Classical authors' statements that the Celts fought naked, the majority of representations of warriors are of naked figures, one interesting rendering appearing on a coin of the Germani showing a warrior brandishing a sword and holding a shield of oval shape with curious bosses.[70]

Warriors are frequently depicted mounted, in fact more often on horseback than on foot, again possibly due to the influence of Roman denarii. They are shown carrying swords, javelins, shields, carnyxes, and boar or sometimes eagle standards. A few have what appear

Fig. 29 Coin of the 'Unelli' showing on the reverse an anthropomorphic sword and figure with torc

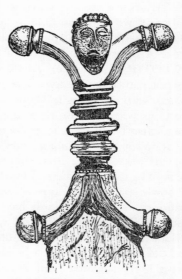

Fig. 30 Hilt of an anthropomorphic sword from Grimston, Yorks

to be slings, and one a barbed spear which makes one think of Cú Chulainn's spear, the Gae Bolg.

An archer appears on a coin of the Ambiani,[71] and an arrow is shown between the legs of a figure on another coin.[72] This is particularly interesting since fighting among the Celts, according to literary and archaeological sources, was with sword, spear and sling, the bow and arrow disappearing to a large extent in warfare after the early third millenium, to reappear with the barbarian invaders from the Steppe in the Dark Ages.

A series of British coins gives us a good idea about horse trappings and horsemanship. A fine coin of Verica shows a saddle cloth with four girths and straps passing from the corners of the saddle cloth through rings on the shoulders and haunches, from which are suspended decorative bands. The horse's mane is braided.[73] The coins also show us that the warriors could guide their horses without using reins.

A type of short sword with anthropomorphic hilt is frequently shown on Gaulish coins and indeed forms the main reverse type on a coin of the Parisii. It is also used as a symbol in the field of a coin of the Unelles.[74] This type of sword came into fashion about the end of the fifth century BC and later types were in use even in the first century BC[75] (Plate 9j; Figure 29; Figure 30).

The normal La Tène sword, however, was a long one of iron, and this is frequently depicted on coins. A short sword is shown on some British coins. These warriors carrying short swords appear on coins of Tasciovanus and Cunobelin, and are shown naked with round shields.[76] Very many warriors depicted carry either a carnyx or a boar standard.[77]

A few representations show warriors performing 'feats' of the sort described by the Irish myths. Celtic warfare, which favoured display and combats between champions rather than whole armies, often involved exhibitions of such feats with swords, spears, etc. The description that Caesar gives us of warriors in Britain running out along the chariot pole to stand on the yoke was just such a feat. The *Tàin* tells how Cú Chulainn performed 'the thunder feat of one hundred, the thunder feat of two hundred' and so on while in his scythed chariot. Some Gaulish coins show figures running out on to the yoke of a chariot, and others, small figures leaping on horseback.

The Carnyx

Reference has frequently been made to the Celtic carnyx, a trumpet with a long mouthpiece and head in the shape of a boar's head or that of a dragon. This very characteristic object is commonly represented on Celtic coins, both British and Continental. The carnyx itself is known from a number of finds of fragmentary examples, the most famous of which was found at Deskford, Banffshire and is now in the National Museum of Antiquities of Scotland [78](Plate 16).

Two types of carnyxes are shown on British coins, the one on coins of Tasciovanus, the other on issues of Eppillus (Plates 10g, 11g). The latter type can be paralleled from an altar at Nîmes.[79] The most common type is that shown on coins of Tasciovanus, though this differs from the Deskford carnyx, which is more akin to those shown

Fig. 31 Figure of a Celtic warrior – sculpture from Mondragon

Fig. 32 The Euffineix Figure

being blown by figures on the Gundestrup cauldron or carried by figures on Gaulish coins.

On British coins the carnyx is shown carried by a rider, not being blown but brandished (Plate 10g). From this it may be inferred that it was used as a kind of standard. One Gaulish coin shows a carnyx with a standard attached.

The Celtic Chariot

We have already encountered Celtic chariots depicted on Roman

Republican denarii. Although chariots appear frequently on Celtic coins, they are usually schematic and derived from the chariot of the *philippeioi*.

One undoubtedly Celtic chariot appears on a bronze coin of the Remi[80] (Plate 9e), and is similar to the one which was reconstructed from the votive find from Llyn Cerrig Bach in Anglesey[81] (Plate 14). The body seems to have been a small platform, about four feet square, with a chariot pole about eighteen feet long. It had semi-circular wickerwork sides, but no front or back. This enabled the warrior to run out along the chariot pole in the manner described above.

Animals – Naturalistic

Representations of animals abound on Celtic coins. As one might expect, those most frequently depicted are the animals which were associated with cults – the boar, the swan, the raven, the owl, the eagle, the crane, the bull, the wolf, the stag and the horse together with fishes and serpents.

Of these the most important cult animal was the boar, which appears associated with numerous other symbols such as the human head, the wheel, the raven and the tree. It was a symbol of war and of the sacred ritual of hospitality, and was frequently the object of metamorphosis. Helmets frequently had boar crests, and a boar standard was carried into battle. Boar joints frequently occur in Celtic graves. A coin of the Baiocasses shows a human head with stylized horns, surmounted by a boar. A coin of the Veliocasses shows a man holding a boar, and other coins of the Veliocasses show boars in conjunction with other symbols.[82] Coins of the Ambiani show boars associated with wheel, fish, horse and oxhead symbols,[83] while yet other coins show a boar with a raven on its back.[84] In Britain a coin of Cunobelin shows a boar beneath a tree,[85] and a boar is introduced as a coin type by the Coritani for the prototype silver coins[86] (Plate 11j; Figure 32).

Bulls appear not infrequently, sometimes with boar or other symbols, in one case bound with a 'saddle cloth' or fillet (on a coin of the Petrocorii),[87] in another with an eagle on its back (on a coin of the Carnutes).[88]

The stag, the companion of the antlered god Cernunnos, was associated with a cult of Bronze Age origin. It is relatively rare on Celtic coins but a stag's head appears as a main type on a coin of the Boii[89] (Figure 33).

A common feature of Celtic belief involved the zoomorphism of many of their deities. This was based not so much on the idea of animal worship but more on the concept that deities had no fixed form. One of the figures in Irish legend is Badb Catha, the Raven of Battle, a fierce goddess who changed into a raven to gloat over

 Fig. 33 Stag on a coin of the 'Aeduan derivative' type

bloodshed. A raven-like figure appears on the back of a horse on many coins from all parts of the Celtic world, in one case on the back of a man-headed horse on a coin of the Coriosolites.[90] On a fine coin of the Baiocasses an eagle-like bird similarly rides on a horse beneath which a strange scorpion-like figure crouches[91] (Plate 9g).

In Gallo-Roman times a very widespread cult was associated with the horse-goddess, Epona, and she seems to have been popular in earlier times as well. Representations of horses are frequent on Celtic coins, usually mares, and though many are derived from the *philippeioi*, this is not always the case, Sometimes, especially in Armorica, the horse has become a centaur with human head.

Birds appear frequently on coins; in one case a bird is shown attacking a serpent, in another attacking a smaller bird.[92]

Animals – Mythical

Many strange beasts take their place alongside more familiar creatures on Celtic coins. One very strange coin with an obverse modelled on a Massaliote tetrobol has on the reverse a creature that looks like an owl with a face on its body, or alternately a man with a beard whose hair is made of feathers and who has no body.[93] The owl was a minor cult bird in the Celtic world (Figure 34.).

Griffins are frequently depicted; in one case on a coin from Pannonia it has a bird's head and wings, a bull's forepart and a horse's rear finished off with satanic tail. The whole creature is not a little reminiscent of a Romanesque Satan[94] (Figure 35). These griffins and winged horses seem to be a popular feature of the Celtic otherworld bestiary, and appear on the Gundestrup cauldron (Figure 36). Literary sources tell us that they were brightly coloured, and that races were held in the hereafter employing them.

Other Pannonian coins show more fantastic beasts, including a

'Harpy',[95] a cow with a winged female forepart[96] and a very mysterious maned creature.[97] Sea horses are fairly common, and appear on the Gundestrup cauldron as well as on coins. It is true in fact to say that there is nothing from Gundestrup that cannot be paralleled from Celtic coin iconography.[98] One strange coin has a cock with a human face on its breast.[99]

Fig. 34 Coin derived from the Massaliote tetrobols with a mythical beast on the reverse

Fig. 35 Central European Celtic coin with mythical beast as a type

There is a series of coins with serpents, some with horned ram's heads and some with heads at each end. On a series of Boian coins there is a curious serpent with animal head which attempts to bite its tail – this motif, known as a *Rolltier* seems to be derived (like many other mysterious beast designs) from the Scythian world[100] (Figure 37).

Fig. 36 Griffin from the Gundestrup Cauldron

Fig. 37 Central European Celtic coin with 'Rolltier' motif

Pillar Cults

In the Celtic world sanctuaries sometimes occur associated with columns and posts. These seem to have an ancestry going back to Urnfield times, and a famous Hallstatt example was excavated at the Goloring, near Koblenz.[101] Although we have no precise parallels in Britain there do occur pits with stakes, and in Ireland stone pillars have been found of Iron Age date. At Libeniče in Czechoslovakia there was a sanctuary with two posts and associated torcs. Posts with attachments sometimes figure on Celtic coins. One, of Tasciovanus, shows a priest-like figure stretching out to a post surmounted by a crescent. Behind the throne is another post with what look like branches, possibly a tree[102] (Plate 11b). A coin of Verica shows a post with a bowl and two projections like cornucopiae[103] (Plate 10i).

An odd coin of the Segusiavi shows a naked figure standing beside a column, while a smaller, draped, figure stands beside him. As this shows Classical influence it is possibly a representation of a Classical statue group and not connected with Celtic belief.[104]

Trees, with animals standing in front of them, are common in coin iconography[105] (Plate 9k). Altars, usually with flames, appear as symbols on some Armorican coins, and also appear on British coins. A few coins show what looks like a temple pediment decorated with an eagle.[106]

Domestic Utensils

Celtic coins are of little value in depicting objects in household use. We occasionally find different sorts of vessels shown, but seldom are they identifiable. An exception to this are amphorae, or wine storage jars. These are not native objects but Roman, imported into the Celtic world. They are shown on many coins, especially on those of Vercingetorix, and here the representation is so accurate that the precise type can be recognized[107] (Plate 12b). They are spindle shaped amphorae of the type known to continental archaeologists as Dressel Class 1, in Britain as Camulodunum Form 181. These amphorae were the products of the Falernian area of Italy. Two such amphorae of pre-Caesarian date have been found in the area in which the coins circulated[108] (Figure 38).

A coin of the Ambiani shows a peculiar vessel very like a pedestal urn, the characteristic pot of the Belgae both in Britain and on the Continent[109] (Plate 9l). Although it is not easy to identify the type due to the stereotyping of the die engraver, it would seem quite in keeping with the series of vessels from, say, La Poterie in the Ardennes[110] (Figure 39). Bowls appear on British and Continental coins but they are not easy to identify. One, shown being worked by the smith (Sucellos?) already alluded to, looks very like the imported silver bowls from the chieftain's grave at Welwyn, Hertfordshire.

These are vessels of Augustan Italian work[111] (Plate 11d). A patera rather like a Gallo-Belgic *Terra Nigra* platter is shown on a coin of Cunobelin, being held by a seated figure.[112] The coin of Verica with the post already referred to depicts a bowl with two handles which probably is metal.

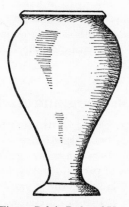

Fig. 39 Belgic Pedestal Urn from La Poterie, Ardennes

Fig.   38   Camulodunum Type 181 amphora

Miscellaneous

Finally mention may be made of a few miscellaneous but nevertheless interesting types.

Ships are very rare, the only certain example being on a coin of the Unelli with animal heads at prow and stern, just like later Viking longships. It seems to be decorated with spirals, and has a mast[113] (Plate 9j).

A few coins show strange concepts such as heads with animals seeming to walk in one ear and out of the other.

It is important to remember, however, in studying Celtic coins that the types and symbols are not necessarily related, nor are they ordered with any sense of being anchored in space. In order to understand the various parts of the types it is necessary to turn the coin round and study it from different angles. Similarly there is seldom any connection between obverse and reverse, though one coin of Cunobelin shows a hunter setting out on the obverse with a bow and a dog and returning with a stag on the reverse!

Many puzzling symbols appear on Celtic coins that are difficult to interpret – symbols on the coins of many Armorican tribes seem to be tribal badges – the Redones, for example, marked their coins with a wheel, while the Coriosolites marked them sometimes with a boar and sometimes with a horse. It has recently been suggested that the whole of Celtic numismatic iconography is pervaded with sun symbols, moon symbols and magic numbers, but this is extremely hard to believe. Sun symbols, wheels, crescent moons and stars do, however, appear.[114]

Gaulish Coins and Archaeology

Although Celtic coins have long been recognized as an important branch of Iron Age studies on account of their artistic merit (the first book on the subject was published in 1865), their value to other branches of prehistoric studies has only recently been fully realized. Adrien Blanchet, the great French numismatist, who is known for his standard work on Celtic coins published at the beginning of the century, was one of the first to consider coinage in the broader context of prehistoric archaeology. Since the last war, and particularly since the publication of Blanchet's *Réflexions sur les monnaies Gauloises* in 1951, shortly before his death,[115] advances have been considerable, led on the Continent by J. B. Colbert de Beaulieu and Karel Castelin and in Britain by D. F. Allen.

The main hazard in studying Celtic coins from an archaeological standpoint lies in the wide diversity of their types, which cannot be adequately classified typologically to provide a sound chronological framework, since they do not always follow the normal rules of numismatic typology.

Problems also arise due to the peculiarities of local series, for, broadly speaking, Celtic coins were struck by chieftains and local centres (usually oppida) rather than tribes. There is a tendency to attribute coins to tribes for the sake of convenience, but this custom is unwise since the tribes as we know them are those of Caesar, and due to the migrations and other movements of groups of Celts we cannot make reliable inferences about the precise boundaries of tribal territory before 58 BC. Thus, when a coin is attributed to the Allobroges all it means is that the majority of the coins of that type have been found in the area occupied by the Allobroges in the time of Caesar.

In making local studies we must remember that many factors regulated the development of types, the most important of which was geographical. Gaul in the first and second century BC was more densely wooded than it is now, and was also considerably wetter, with many areas of marsh and bog which provided both a protection to local groups and a hindrance to communication. Yet here lies one of the most important contributions of Celtic coins to prehistory, for their distribution shows clearly the character of commerce in individual areas, the trade routes, the areas traded with and the strength of the occupants of the region.

This information is not as clearly attested by any other class of material culture, since coins tend to spread over a wide area. In Britain, for example, similar pottery was used by all the 'Belgic' tribes of the late pre-Roman Iron Age, but the coins of each tribe are quite distinctive. The tribal history of Britain before the Roman conquest has largely been reconstructed, sketchy though it is, from numismatic evidence.

Coin Types as Evidence of Trade

The dispersal of various types of coins constitutes the best indicator of trade and trade routes, but information on this subject can sometimes be garnered from coin types themselves. We have already considered the Classical prototypes behind various series of Celtic coins, and the way in which they spread as increasingly barbarous imitations. Occasionally we find a single distinct type being imitated with no evidence of intervening intermediaries, and from this it must be assumed that there must have been some trade which brought the prototypes into the area. This is the case with certain issues in central Gaul imitating Carthaginian coins.

Another, more curious example, can be seen in the coins found in east-central Gaul with an obverse type reminiscent of that used on coins of Neapolis Campaniae, not the more usual head of Massaliote prototypes. They are struck too in gold, while most Massaliote-derived coins are silver. Blanchet has argued, with some justice, that at the end of the third century BC there was an attempt at Marseilles to introduce a gold coinage for international trade, the incentive possibly being the *philippeioi*. He has suggested that it was a limited coinage which met with no success, but which travelled into the hinterland by way of the Rhône and Saône.[116]

League Coins[117]

Tribal leagues in Gaul are fairly well attested historically and figure prominently in the writings of Caesar. Divitiacus of the Suessiones, we are told, wanted to hold sway over both Brittany and Gallia Belgica. Certain coins from the Channel Islands and Gallia Belgica seem closely related, and this could arise from such an alliance.

In the Rhône valley a large series of coins bears witness to another league, that of the Rhône valley tribes against Ariovistus and the Helvetii. These, which are modelled on Roman denarii and which have legends like DURNAC and AUSC have a helmeted head on the obverse and a horseman with a lance on the reverse (Plate 8e). Ariovistus was a German chief called upon by the Sequani to defeat the Aedui, and claimed as his reward some of the territory of the Sequani, staying on with the intention of founding a German kingdom in Gaul. He allied with the Romans, and it was the advance of Ariovistus together with the expanison of the Helvetii from their homeland in Switzerland that precipitated Caesar's Gallic campaigns.

Coins of the Carnutes, Veneti, Veliocasses, Ambiani, Silvanectes, Suessiones, Bellovaci, Remi, Senones, Sequani, Bituriges, Lemovices, and Santones circulated in the region occupied by the Parisii – in the Paris basin. This suggests that the Parisii had a political, and, more especially economic importance in Gaul. There may have been some kind of Common Market existing among the tribes. The Parisii themselves struck a very varied gold coinage, as is attested by the finds from hoards at Charenton, Puteaux and elsewhere.

On the Continent there seems to have been a much more open market than in Britain, where coins are generally very limited in their distribution – at Colchester out of some 222 Iron Age coins, all but two or three (of the Iceni and Coritani) were local issues.[118] Continental oppida, however, usually yield coins of several tribes – issues of the Aedui, Sequani, Segusiavi and Marseilles all turned up in the fort at Essalois in northern France.[119]

Vercingetorix

The coins of Vercingetorix have always attracted attention in the past, especially those with the chief's name and what has sometimes been taken to be his portrait. In reality, as Colbert de Beaulieu has recently shown, this is merely another derivative from the head of Apollo on Classical coins, with a good typological sequence of development behind it[120] (Plate 12b). What is particularly interesting about the coins of Vercingetorix, apart from the legend which ascribes them to Caesar's most famous opponent, is the fact that they include a series of bronze coins which have only been found at Alesia and the neighbourhood. An assemblage of no less than six hundred came from the ditch at Alesia itself.

Although it has been argued quite convincingly that these coins are probably a Roman deposit, the Romans having acquired them from the Celts whom they were besieging, this does not detract from the fact that the siege of Alesia by Caesar resulted in an emergency bronze coinage.[121]

Channel Island and Armorican Hoards[122]

Still on the subject of Caesar's campaigns, an interesting story is told by the coins found in numerous large hoards in the Channel Islands and Armorica. In the winter of 57–56 there was an uprising in Brittany prompted by the Veneti, who knew of Caesar's intended invasion of Britain and were afraid that it might terminate their trading relations with their British counterparts. There are over fifty hoards in north-west France and the Channel Islands which date from this period, mostly of coins of the Coriosolites, the tribe occupying the Channel Islands. These hoards fall into two main groups, the first being very homogeneous, with few coins other than those of the Coriosolites (such as the La Maquanderie Hoard), the second group being very mixed and including British coins (like the Little Caesarea Hoard or the Le Catillon Hoard).

Colbert de Beaulieu has carefully studied the die identities of the coins of the Coriosolites and has been able to show that the hoards dated before 58 BC are homogeneous, as might be expected, since the circulation was limited to tribal areas (Plate 10j).

The Venetian uprising was met with a counter-attack from Caesar, who destroyed their fleet and that of their allies in a sea battle off Morbihan. A scatter of Venetian coins in the territory of neighbouring tribes to the north and north-east marks the flight of the refugees.

Their allies tended to concentrate their defences in large forts with timber laced ramparts – the *Murus Gallicus* of Caesar – abandoning smaller settlements. Caesar's legate Quintus Sabinus turned his attention to Venetian allies, and defeated them in another sea battle off the Channel Islands.

Refugees from Brittany had taken shelter (from the Romans) in the Channel Islands and this scare resulted in large numbers of hoards of La Maquanderie type being buried. Native resistance, however, was not yet dead, and an alliance of various Celtic tribes was formed against Caesar. This protracted trouble resulted in a further wave of hoarding in the Channel Islands, the hoards now becoming heterogeneous.

Hoards continued to be buried in Jersey for some time after the events of 56, no doubt associated with the revolts that we are told recurred in the years down to 51 BC. Some hoards are even later, post-Caesarian, for Roman coins of 39 and 32 BC occur in two Jersey finds.

These hoards are extremely important for students of Celtic coinage on both sides of the Channel, especially the finds from Le Catillon and Little Caesarea, to which we shall return.

Coins for Dating Oppida[123]

Occasionally coins can be used for dating the phases of occupation in oppida, a particularly good example being afforded by the oppidum at Pommiers which has produced about 2,600 coins. Of these about 1,900 have been studied by Dr Colbert de Beaulieu, who has been able to demonstrate that the site was abundantly occupied during the last years of Gaulish independence and more especially during the time of the war against Caesar, that is 70–51 BC. Thereafter occupation declined, but continued to some extent until the time of Augustus. From the time of Tiberius until the third century AD there was sporadic occupation or visitation. Against this story told by the coin finds the history of the oppidum can be set in its perspective.

The history of Bibracte (Mont Beauvray) and Essalois can likewise be traced through the coin evidence. At Essalois the coin evidence shows that the tribe who occupied the fort, the Segusiavi, had trade contacts with Marseilles and the neighbouring tribes, coins of the Aedui and the League against Ariovistus being particularly common. These links between the Segusiavi and the Aedui continued even after the time of Caesar, down to 15 BC when the fort seems to have been abandoned. Evidence for this takes the form of coins with the legend GERMANVS INDVTILLI L, which are the latest repre-sented. These coins fortunately can be closely dated – they did not turn up in the Alesia battlefield deposits (52 BC) nor in the Hussigny-Godbrange hoard which contained a good cross-section of the currency of Belgic Gaul of the period 33–31 BC.

The story is repeated at Mont Beauvray, where the coin sequence shows that the most active period of occupation was the second half of the first century BC. The most common coins present were of GERMANVS INDVTILLI L type and the colonial bronzes of Nîmes, struck after 36 BC.[124] Coin evidence further shows that the oppidum was abandoned c. 5 BC when the population seems to have been moved to the new Roman city of Augustodunum.

Celtic coins have provided valuable dating evidence for the period of construction and occupation of a number of oppida. They have corroborated the theory that some *Murus Gallicus* forts were built as a defence against Caesar – at Huelgoat, Gaulish coins were found in the occupation layers of the fort which would suggest the time of Caesar, and in the occupation layer at Petit Celland a hoard of coins of c. 56 BC was found.[125]

Iron Age Britain

The British Iron Age has been divided by Professor C. F. C. Hawkes into three cultural phases, known as A, B, and C. The Iron Age A cultures came into being as a result of immigration and contact with the Hallstatt World; in the Iron Age B cultures, the effects of similar connections with the La Tène world can be seen; Iron Age C is derived from the culture of Belgic Gaul. In terms of date the earliest Hallstatt influenced cultures begin c. 550 BC in England (though Hallstatt contacts with Britain go back further, to the seventh century BC), and the first phase of the British Iron Age lasts until c. 350 BC. Period II lasts until c. 150, and Period III until the Roman Conquest. Throughout the Iron Age, although the cultures are derived ulti-mately from the Continental, the native traditions of the Bronze Age to some extent survived, and the British Iron Age cultures are distinctly insular. The A, B and C divisions are not chronological, and in some areas A cultures were never ousted by B or C, while B and C cultures can be found existing systadially in neighbouring areas. One can also find hybrid cultures, such as Trent Valley AB. Within the broad framework archaeologists have divided Britain up into

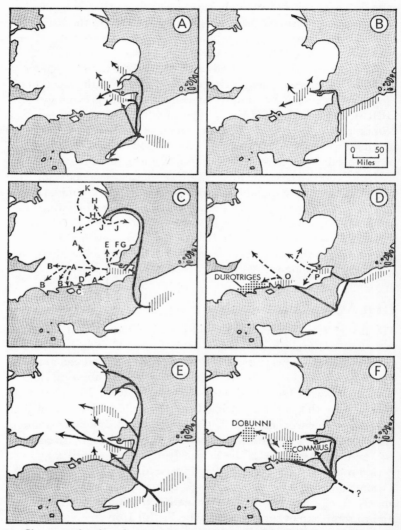

9. Six maps showing the progress of main Gallo-Belgic coinages, A–F, from Gaul to Britain. Hatched areas show concentration of finds, small letters and stippled areas distribution of British derivatives (after Allen, 1961)

regions, and have recognized a variety of separate cultures, with names like 'Western First A' or 'South-Eastern B'.[126]

Currency Bars[127]

There are no coins in Period I or even Period II of the British Iron Age, the introduction of coins coming early in Period III.

Even in Period III coins were not used universally among the Iron Age peoples of southern Britain, and the B cultures in certain areas seem to have used currency bars in the earlier first century BC as a medium of trade and for amassing wealth. Money barter was by no means a new phenomenon in prehistoric Europe – the Early Bronze Age Unetiče culture of central Europe used 'ingot torcs' and *rippenbarren* probably as a type of currency, and in the Atlantic Late Bronze Age it appears that very small bronze axes were also used in this way in Brittany.

The British currency bars are of three types, those shaped like swords, those shaped like spits, and those like ploughshares, though it is not certain whether the last two types were used as currency.

The use of sword-shaped bars, of fairly uniform weight, was very widespread. With a centre in the area of the 'Durotriges' their usage stretched east and north, into the area that was later the territory of the Dobunni, and into the north-east Midlands. The distribution of hoards suggests a trade route. There seems to have been little interchange between the regions in which sword-shaped bars and spit-shaped bars occur –the latter appear mainly in an area on either side of the Severn.

Only at Hod Hill in Dorset have bars and coins been found in any kind of association, but unfortunately the coins from the site are generally too late or too unusual to be of value in establishing a relationship between the two.

Belgic Invasions of Britain

G. C. Brooke's theory of the spread of the *philippeioi* was outlined in the previous chapter, where it was seen that Brooke believed the first copies to have been made by the Averni in the second century BC. From this he deduced by a series of chronological links that the first Gallo-Belgic coins were not struck until *c.* 75 BC, and to this period was attributed the first settlement of Belgic or Iron Age C people in Britain.

D. F. Allen has however recently shown that Brooke's theory was in fact wrong, and that the Gallo-Belgic A coins, the first to reach Britain, were being struck in the late second century BC. He has also argued that there were no fewer than six influxes of coins from the Continent, which he has named Gallo-Belgic A–F.[128]

This new dating and sequence solved many problems for pre-historians, who had felt that Iron Age C had been telescoped into too short a time, but at first seemed also to pose some new ones, since the six influxes could not be readily equated with similar influxes of typically 'Iron Age C' cultural attributes from the areas of Belgic Gaul from which the coins came.

Caesar, in his *Gallic War* mentions that the tribes that settled in the 'maritime part' of Britain came from 'Belgium', for long taken by archaeologists to mean Belgic Gaul in general, but which Professor Hawkes has recently pointed out was Caesar's term for a parti-cularly 'Belgic' area of Belgic Gaul, to the south of modern Belgium.[129]

Now a study of Mr Allen's six coin waves and their continental origins shows us quite clearly that the only two waves that could have been responsible for the settlement to which Caesar alludes are the A and B Gallo-Belgic series, both of which came from what has now been defined as 'Belgium'. They are not, it is true, associated with a contemporary influx of characteristic 'Belgic' material culture, but one would not expect it, since at this early date 'Belgium' was not Belgic in the accepted archaeological sense. A careful reconsideration of the finds of La Tène II origin in the areas in Britain in which Gallo-Belgic A and B coins are found has shown that such finds are known, even though they are few in number.[130]

Gallo-Belgic A-C[131]

The Gallo-Belgic A coins seem to have come from the Somme Valley, and their users settled in Kent and the lower Thames with some infiltration into Essex and the Home Counties (Plate 10a.).

Soon afterwards there was a second influx, marked by Gallo-Belgic B coins, coming from somewhere to the north of the region occupied by the users of the Gallo-Belgic A issues. These settlers passed through Kent into areas south and west of those occupied by the users of Gallo-Belgic A coins. The dies from which the Gallo-Belgic B staters were struck were obliterated by chisel cuts or alternatively were engraved to look as though they had been defaced

Belgic coin flan mould from Bluehouse Hill, St Albans

2 Bronze die of Hadrian for the reverse of an aureus or a denarius;
(a) general view (b) the striking surface showing Roma greeting the emperor

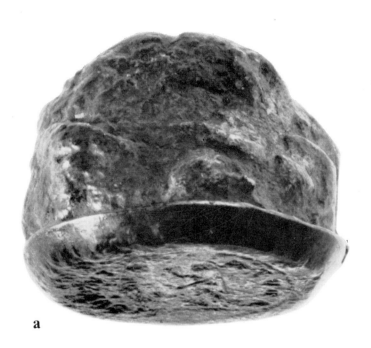

a

b

3 Trussel or reverse die of David II of Scotland (1329–71)
4 Sterling (penny) of David II's First Coinage, struck before 1357 (enlarged)

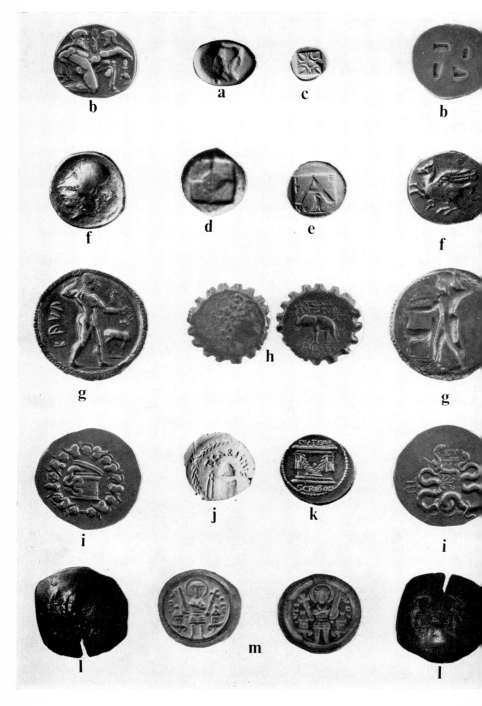

a

b

c

a

d

e

d

g

f

g

h

i

h

j

k

l

7 A hoard of shekels being unearthed at Masada in Israel

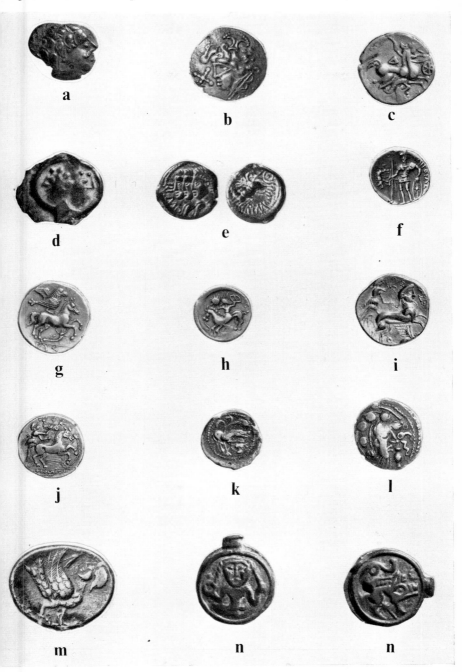

a

b

c

d

e

f

g

h

i

j

k

l

m

n

n

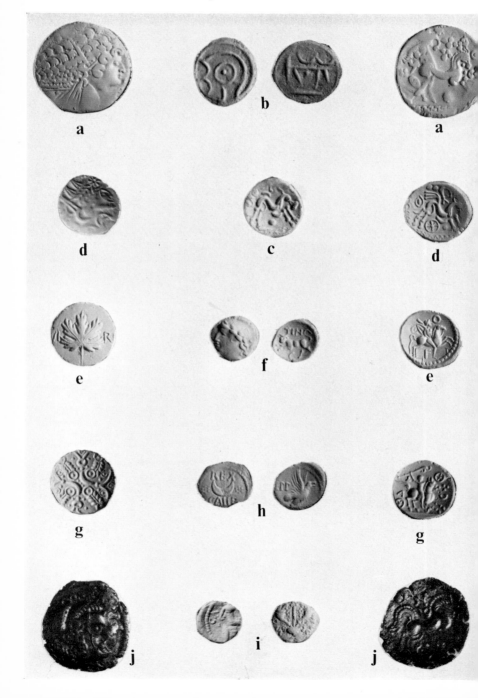

a

b

a

d

c

d

e

f

e

g

h

g

j

i

j

12 (a) obverse of an early gold stater of the Veneti (actual size 20mm)
(b) gold coin of Vercingetorix (actual size 19mm)

a

b

14 Reconstruction model of the Llyn Cerrig Bach chariot

15 Gold ring-headed terminal of a torc from Shaw Hill, Peeblesshire, with two bullet shaped coins

16 The bronze Deskford carnyx or boar-headed trumpet

17 Bronze buffer ended torc from Kelton, Kirkcudbright, first century BC

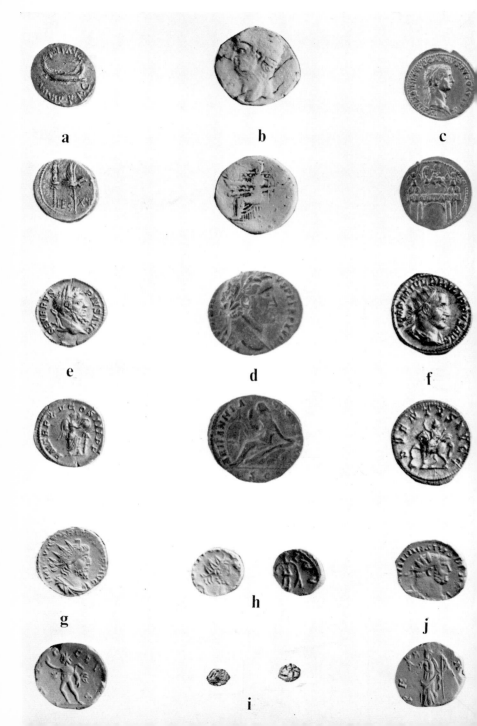

a

b

c

e

d

f

g

h

j

i

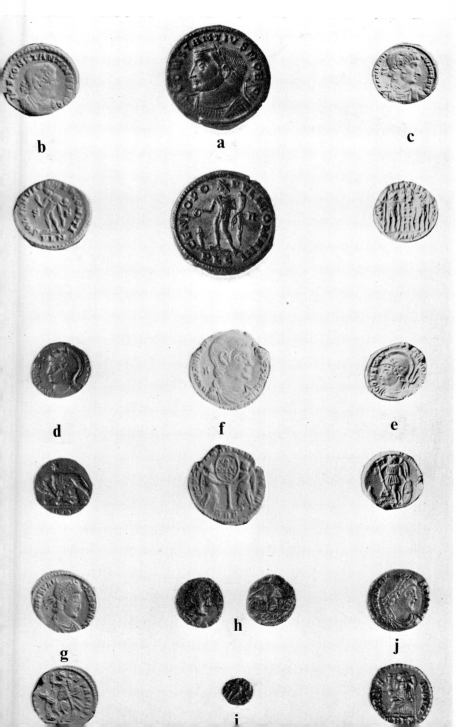

20 Hoard of 'barbarous radiates' found at Newgate Street, London, before cleaning

21 A selection of the Newgate Hoard coins after cleaning

22 Coin of Trajan found in the mast step of a Roman boat at Blackfriars, London

23 Electrotype copy of a gold medallion of Constantius Chlorus found at Beaurains, near Arras, in 1922

a

b

25 The Skaill Hoard, Orkney; a selection of silver ornaments and Saxon and Arab coins from a late tenth century Viking hoard of plunder

26 Sixteenth century money box, or Pirlie Pig, from Perth, with two of the coins found in it
27 Brooches and ornaments associated with the coins in the Canonbie (Dumfriesshire) Hoard *c.* 1295

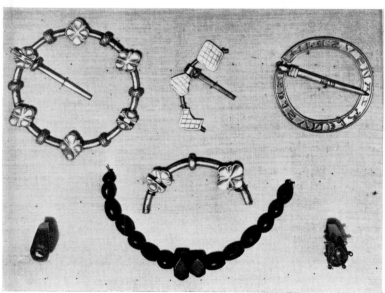

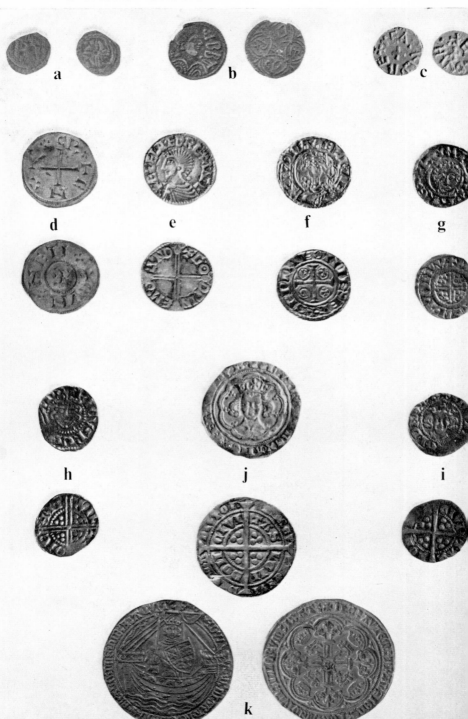

by a chisel (Figure 40). This probably indicates that the group of people who struck them were showing their independence from their parent tribe, though no coins from undamaged dies are known either in Britain or on the Continent.

Fig. 40 Gallo-Belgic B stater

To the period of the Gallo-Belgic B coins belongs a remarkable hoard found at Shaw Hill (Kirkcurd) in Peeblesshire, consisting of gold bullet-like coins of a type found in the Soissons-Rheims area and with Germanic antecedents (Plate 15.). There are no parallels for the hoard either in Scotland or England, unless a find of gold 'bullets' from Dunnichen in Angus (now lost) represented a similar hoard. They are associated with three gold torc terminals, reminiscent of those from Snettisham.[132]

The third wave, Gallo-Belgic C, came again from the Somme area. In its homeland the coinage started *c.* 95 BC and continued until *c.* 65. In Britain the first C coins probably arrived *c.* 90 BC (Figure 41).

Fig.41 Gallo-Belgic C stater

The influx represents no large scale migration – the coins are few and fairly widely scattered, but as Professor Hawkes has pointed out the leader must have been a man of great prestige since it was this series of coins that was first copied in Britain. He has argued quite reasonably that this leader must have been Diviciacus of the Suessiones, who according to an account preserved in Caesar was in his day the most powerful king in Gaul and whose rule extended over several tribes – seemingly he even had influence in Kent where he would have found Belgic peoples already living.[133]

Gallo-Belgic D-F[134]

Gallo-Belgic D is represented by the appearance of quarter staters in Britain, originating outside Caesar's 'Belgium'. They are known here

G

from their British copies which are distributed along the coast from Kent to Hengistbury Head, where they circulated along with foreign coins from Armorica until replaced by Gallo-Belgic E. We know from hoard evidence that Gallo-Belgic D was contemporary with British B, *c.* 75 BC.

Gallo-Belgic E was the largest of all the invasions (Plate 10c.). The coins are widespread in Gaul and Britain, and are gold uniface staters. In Britain they are found in three main areas – in the Sussex coastal plain, in a zone from north Essex to the south-east Midlands (where earlier coins are rare), and thirdly in Kent. The three zones are quite separate. They start in Gaul just before Caesar, and continue until after the time of his campaigns. This migration may in part be associated with Caesar's wars, but not entirely, as the relationship of the coins with Gallo-Belgic D indicates.

The final wave, Gallo-Belgic F, followed Caesar's victory in Gaul in 52 BC and is not well represented in Britain by the Gaulish originals but is better documented by the British versions, the British Q or 'triple tailed horse' series (Plate 10d).

Although the archaeological evidence for these coin waves is not yet adequate to associate particular elements in the British Iron Age C or Belgic culture with particular movements, we can see in the period between Gallo-Belgic A–B and F the gradual building up and appearance in Britain of the cultural traits, such as cremation burial and characteristic pottery – pedestal urns, bead-rim bowls, tazzas and cordoned bowls. Gallo-Belgic C may be associated with the appearance in Kent of 'Fécamp' type fort works, and by this time the Belgae were in a state of transition from La Tène II to La Tène III.[135] Possibly at this period Kent was beginning to adopt La Tène III models in pottery. Dr Ann Birchall, who has studied the pottery sequence both in Britain and on the Continent, starts her sequence in Britain with an 'Earliest' phase, which might possibly have its origins in Gallo-Belgic C. It is followed, in the sequence from the cremation cemeteries of Swarling and Aylesford, by a distinct 'Early' phase, dating back before 50 BC and which can certainly cover the movements associated with the refugees from Caesar's campaigns and the earlier Gallo-Belgic E migrations.[136]

British Derivatives of Gallo-Belgic Coins

At the time of the Gallo-Belgic C invasion we find the first native British coinages. These are called British A and are found in Hampshire and Sussex, to the west of Gallo-Belgic C (Figure 42). Almost immediately afterwards a British B series was struck in Wiltshire and Dorset, with similar origins. This series can be dated to about 75 BC from the Le Catillon Hoard, in which a worn British B coin was found. As the hoard was buried at the time of Caesar's campaigns in the Channel Islands, the coin must have been struck at least as early as 70 BC and therefore British A, from which the B coins were derived, must be earlier still – this in turn provides an earlier date for the prototype, Gallo-Belgic C.[137]

Fig. 42 British A stater

In the west and East Anglia the A and B coinages are followed by other imitations, British C–F. Further north, where Gallo-Belgic C seems to have been more influential, we find other series of British imitations derived from them, including the prototypes for the coins of the Coritani. These are known as the British H to K series, and probably represent direct contact with the Continent, by way of the Humber in the first stage – some of the British H coins are so close to late Gallo-Belgic C coins they may in fact have been struck not in Britain at all but in the Somme Valley. British H and I in the east Midlands may represent two groups that are later fused into one, the historical Coritani. Slightly later than the 'Coritanian Prototype Gold' are early prototype silver coins, with a boar on the obverse and horse on the reverse. There seems to be no Continental model for these coins, and they represent an indigenous development, though boar-and-horse bronze coins are known in Gaul. The later inscribed coins of the Coritani have double names like ESUP–ASU, AUN–AST, VOLISIOS–DUMNOCOVEROS, which Derek Allen has suggested might indicate a dual magistracy.[138]

The Gallo-Belgic D–F influxes gave rise to further series of copies in Britain, British L–P.

The last coin wave, Gallo-Belgic F, gave rise as we have seen to a series of British imitations of 'triple-tailed horse' type, stemming from British Q.

British Q has a distribution from the south coast to the valley of the middle Thames. Here the invasion, for that is what the coins represent, forked, one branch extending to the Cotswolds and providing the prototypes for the coins of the Dobunni, the other turning back on itself and appearing as a new inscribed coinage in Berkshire, Hampshire and Sussex, bearing the name of Commius. This Commius can be none other than the infamous Commius Atrebas, the chieftain that Caesar often employed to further his purposes and who later fled to Britain to settle at what was to become Silchester.

In the following period we see the first coinages of the historical Celtic tribes. Silver and bronze coins appear in Britain for the first time, and the emergence of the Catuvellauni was characterized by a distinctive coinage which replaced the old E. This coinage is too late to be associated with Cassivellaunus, the opponent of Caesar, and probably belongs to the period of anarchy following the break-up of his kingdom.

This period of confusion in Belgic Britain was followed by a more orderly one, lasting until the Claudian invasion. During these years gold, silver and bronze coins with inscriptions were struck by individual chiefs and tribes, and for this period the coin evidence is of particular value since we can draw upon a combination of historical and numismatic evidence to reconstruct the great days of the Belgic dynasties.[139]

Tasciovanus[140]

We do not know what coins were struck by Cassivellaunus, the chief of the Catuvellauni who opposed Caesar. He may have used Gallo-Belgic E or British L, though the latter are probably too late. The earliest inscribed coins of the Catuvellauni were those of Tasciovanus, who is otherwise unknown to history, but who must have reigned c. 20 BC – AD 10. His coins are descended from the preceding gold coinage of the Catuvellauni, the 'Whaddon Chase' (British L) series. He was probably the grandson of Cassivellaunus. One early coin of Tasciovanus bears the mint mark of Colchester, which was in the territory of the Trinovantes, and which suggests that contrary to Caesar's terms with the Catuvellauni he had begun expanding his territory to the east. This particular stater is rare, and it is suggested that the expansion was initiated by Tasciovanus on the defeat of a Roman force on the Rhine in 17 BC. He probably withdrew in the following year, when Augustus himself came to Gaul. In the following period the Catuvellauni continued to expand under his leadership, from Northampton to the Thames, and possibly even had territory in Kent. Although Tasciovanus was not above using Roman imports and employing Roman-style coin types, some of his coins use the title RIGONVS, the Celtic equivalent of the Roman REX, suggesting a policy of anti-Roman feeling.

Tasciovanus struck the first coins to bear the mint mark of St Albans, VER (for Verulamium), and he should probably be associated with the earliest occupation of the St Albans area.

There is evidence for two Belgic mints near St Albans. The evidence for the first, and earlier, takes the form of a number of fragments of coin flan moulds and sherds of native and imported pottery, found underneath the earliest Roman defences.[141] The absence of imported Gallo-Belgic wares like Terra Nigra, Terra Rubra or Butt-beakers and the presence of Roman amphorae suggests a date before c. AD 5–10, and the mint should therefore be ascribed to Tasiovanus. The second mint seems to have been located on Bluehouse Hill, where further excavations revealed two pits filled with Belgic pottery and coin moulds, the former including Terra Nigra. Here an almost complete mould was found (Plate 1), while one of the mould fragments contained a bronze pellet.[142] It is unlikely that this second mint was in operation under Epaticcus, on the eve of the Roman conquest, as has been suggested. The main reason against this is the distribution of the coins of Epaticcus, which are found essentially south and west of St Albans, and whatever his status his territory did not centre on Verulamium, but rather somewhere to the south-west. The second reason why Epaticcus is an unlikely contender is one of date – there is good reason to believe that he did not outlive his brother Cunobelin (or adoptive brother, for both style themselves 'Son of Tasciovanus'). Tasciovanus appears to have had many sons or adopted sons: apart from Cunobelin and Epaticcus we can infer a third, Adminius, from history, and from coins can probably infer others, notably Sego(nax?) and Andocommius.[143] The former's name appears on a late issue of Tasciovanus, and the latter struck coins imitating those of Tasciovanus, probably late on in his reign (c. AD 5–15). Other coins still of Tasciovanus bear the names Ruas and Dias, which may however not be personal names but titles.[144] It has been suggested that before the end of his reign Tasciovanus allowed his sons to build kingdoms on the edge of his territory, Epaticcus among the Atrebates, Andocommius on the western borders of the kingdom, Cunobelin in the east and Segonax at St Albans, possibly as heir-apparent. On the death of Tasciovanus Cunobelin began expanding from the east, and at an early date took over Verulamium. The second mint should therefore be attributed either to Segonax, who on stylistic grounds we know coined there, or to Cunobelin, who also appears to have coined there as well as at his capital of Colchester. The coins of St Albans bear the title 'Son of Tasciovanus' those of Colchester the mint name of Camulodunum. The difference in legends has been taken to imply that Cunobelin ruled at Verulamium by force, not by right, but used a legend to indicate his authority. If the mint was that of Segonax, the destruction could be explained in terms of Cunobelin's activity, though it is just as probable that the mint belonged to Cunobelin, and indeed as further evidence a fragment of a coin mould was found with a coin of Cunobelin in 1960 near the Colchester Gate.

Coin Moulds

Fragmentary coin moulds are known from numerous other sites in the British Isles, as can be seen from the distribution map. (Map 10.)

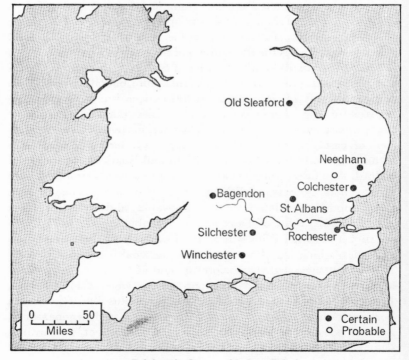

10.   Belgic coin flan moulds from Britain

What is particularly interesting about these is that although they have been found at major sites like Bagendon,[145] Colchester, St Albans and Silchester,[146] they have also turned up at lesser sites, such as Needham in Norfolk, which is a minor Roman village site occupied in the first two centuries AD.[147] The mint at Colchester was Cunobelin's. Moulds have also been found at Old Sleaford, in Lincolnshire,[148] in a Belgic timber building at Rochester, possibly here connected with a subsidiary mint of Eppillus,[149] and at Winchester. This last find, when taken in consideration with other Belgic material from the city, makes one wonder whether the Iron Age capital was not moved from St Catherine's Hill some time before the Roman conquest.[150]

How these moulds were used has long puzzled numismatists, but recent experiments conducted by R. F. Tylecote of the Department of Metallurgy in Newcastle University on the Old Sleaford moulds has shed some light on the method employed in casting coin blanks from them.[151]

It would now seem that instead of the metal being poured into the moulds directly it was in fact melted down in them by a jet of flame directed into the top of the compartment. The metal bullets so produced would then be softened and struck.[152]

One of the interesting facets of the problem arises from a spectographic analysis of the moulds from Silchester which, in the example studied, produced evidence of having contained metals which do not occur as an alloy in any of the coins known to have been struck at Calleva.[153]

As yet much remains to be discovered about the nature of Belgic mints, and this no doubt will shed much light on the general problems of economics in Iron Age Britain, once it is understood. It is quite clear that the moulds were not always used for making flans, and sometimes blanks were made by merely pouring a measured amount of metal on to a smooth surface and allowing it to harden.

The only flan found at Bagendon could never have been cast in a mould and must have been made in this way, as were the flans from Hengistbury Head and Selsey. On the other hand, of the three flans found at Colchester one was of the correct weight and size for a coin of Cunobelin and was in fact found along with four coins of that chief on the floor of a hut. Another fitted the Colchester moulds perfectly.

At Bagendon, apart from the moulds, there was ample evidence for the mint, including a metal working furnace and water carrying ditches. Crucible fragments were also found. At Colchester in association with the moulds was a similar assortment of crucible fragments, burnt clay, metal working refuse, fuel, etc., and here, as at St Albans, pits had been dug especially to bury the moulds. St Albans also had associated crucible fragments.

There is a find from Bagendon of an anvil and some battered pieces of bronze which it has been suggested, rather imaginatively, were coin dies. These seem to be very small for dies, and are much too badly damaged to reveal any evidence of ever having borne types.[154]

The Harlow Temple[155]

A Romano-British temple at Harlow, Essex, seems to have had an Iron Age predecessor. From the Belgic layer into which the foundations of the Roman temple were cut, and mixed with some Roman material as rubbish survivals, a very large number of Celtic coins were found. In the excavations of 1962–4 no less than 43 coins were recovered, and since then further finds have brought the number up to 205 coins, a remarkable number for a small site. It must be assumed that they were offerings, and indeed most of them are in mint condition. This series of coins presents an interesting story about the political history of the area in the late pre-Roman Iron Age.

The earliest coins from the site are two Gallo-Belgic E coins and eleven British uninscribed. A link with the Atrebates is suggested by British QC quarter staters, but the link was short-lived and in place of it is a new link with the Catuvellauni, suggested by British L coins. The next group of coins represented are 33 bronze coins of Tasciovanus, which are followed in turn by a great number of coins of Cunobelin together with a number of coins of other tribes struck in the same period. The latter include issues of the Durotriges and Coritani, suggesting that pilgrims were visiting the temple from outlying parts of the country. The majority of the coins of Cunobelin are of the Verulamium mint, outnumbering those of Colchester 3:1. From this it can be inferred that Harlow lay in the area administered from St Albans rather than Colchester, which is reasonable when it is remembered that St Albans is only 20 miles away, while Colchester is 35. After the Conquest coins continued to be buried for about 30 years, but the coin series ends with Vespasian (69–79), when the Roman temple was finally built.

Derivative Coinages of British Q Origin – Atrebates[156]

A study of the coinage of the Dobunni sheds a great deal of light on the history of the tribe as a whole. As it is a particularly good example of the way Celtic coins can contribute to archaeology it is perhaps not out of place if rather more space is devoted to the subject here.

To understand the history of the Dobunni we must return to the British 'Q' coins with the triple tailed horse reverse mentioned earlier in the chapter. These coins, as we have seen, started soon after the mid first century BC and continued in use until around 25 BC in their homeland in Sussex, Hampshire and Surrey. They are followed by similar coins bearing the name of Commius, which in turn are followed by further derivative coins with the name of Tincommius.

Soon after his accession Tincommius began striking coins with 'Romanizing' types which seem to be roughly contemporary with the similarly 'Romanizing' coins of Tasciovanus (Plate 10f.). They can be dated to soon after 15 BC since one of his coins is modelled on a denarius of Augustus struck at Lugdunum (Lyons) about that date. This Romanizing phase in the coinage may be associated with the new policy of Augustus of trying to win a diplomatic victory in Britain – Horace in one of his Odes of this date includes the Britons among the admirers of Augustus, though Cassius Dio had written in 27 BC, when Augustus was planning a British invasion, that the people of Britain would not 'come to terms'.

The important fact which emerges at this juncture is that the Romanizing coins of Tincommius, and indeed those of Eppillus and Verica, who followed him and who struck coins at Silchester, are almost entirely confined in distribution to Sussex, Hampshire and Surrey, few penetrating Berkshire, Wiltshire and the territory of the Dobunni beyond.

British 'Q' Derivatives – Dobunni[157]

About the time of the 'Romanizing' coins of the Atrebates the Dobunni were striking coins in the Cotswolds derived from the 'triple tailed horse' series. They seem to have come from Wiltshire, and appeared in the area about the last quarter of the first century BC (Plate 11i). Here they imposed their culture, which was essentially Belgic, upon the native Iron Age peoples of earlier 'B' stock.

Their coins are closely related to the triple tailed horse issues of the Atrebates struck before Tincommius' Romanizing coins, and for this reason it seems probable that the Dobunni were an offshoot of the Atrebates and had broken away from the parent group before 25 BC when they were still using triple tailed horse coins. It is probable that they were established as an entity by Commius himself at the end of his reign, as a result of his expansion to the edge of the Cotswolds, though they could have been another group who made a pact with the Atrebates when they arrived at the edge of Atrebatic territory and adopted coin types from them.

The distribution of the earliest gold staters of the Dobunni would seem to indicate that they first centred on south Gloucestershire. In south-east Gloucestershire (where Bagendon and another important site, Salmonsbury, are located) there is no evidence for early Dobunnic occupation. Soon, however, they expanded into the part of Somerset which adjoins south Gloucestershire. Here, at Camerton, were found four coins, slightly later than the earliest issues of the Dobunni but still uninscribed. These date from the end of the first century BC.

During the first quarter of the first century AD there was further Dobunnic expansion in Gloucestershire, when the capital of Bagendon was founded, and in north Somerset.

Early Inscribed Dobunnic Coins[158]

The Dobunni did not adopt the Romanizing style of the Atrebates, and we can assume that this was a part of a deliberate policy of showing their disapproval of the tribes who must have seemed traitors to them because they had adopted ideas from the Roman enemy. They continued to strike triple tailed horse coins, but now bearing the names of chiefs.

The earliest of these inscribed coins, with the names Anted, Eisu, Catti and Comux, have a distribution which demonstrates the expansion of the Dobunni into Worcestershire and more of Somerset. Archaeologically this is attested at the fort of Worlebury at Weston-super-Mare and at Bredon in Worcestershire, where there is good evidence that the inhabitants were massacred by invading Belgic people.

Catuvellauni and Dobunni[159]

Although the Catuvellauni adopted Roman-style coins and imported Roman pottery and other material from Gallia Belgica they did not share the Atrebatic liking for Rome and only saw the Empire as a useful trading contact.

When the Catuvellauni and Dobunni were more or less adjacent to one another in their spheres of influence and were both hostile to the Roman-admiring kingdoms of the southern Belgae, it is not surprising that we find evidence of some kind of alliance. It can be seen in the similarity of the defences of Bagendon to those of Wheat-hampstead and Prae Wood, and can also be seen in the way in which Bagendon imported Roman and Gallo-Belgic pottery from Col-chester.

The evidence of imported pottery from Bagendon shows that after AD 20–25 the flow of imports, and presumably the link between the Dobunni and the Catuvellauni, increased, and this is confirmed by the find of a coin of Epaticcus from Bagendon itself.

The coin evidence shows us, however, that the Dobunni remained politically independent of the Catuvellauni in the thirties of the first century AD when the coins of Antedrigus and Eisu were being struck. Similarly, the coins of Cunobelin, at all periods throughout his reign, barely entered Dobunnic territory. This would not have been the case if they had been a client kingdom.

Disunity Among the Dobunni[160]

Soon after the death of Cunobelin (c. AD 41) there is good evidence that there was disunity among the Dobunni. We find a series of coins with the names of Comux, Inam, Catti, Corio and Bodvoc. The coin of Inam is unique and tells us little, and those of Commux very rare, hardly providing a distribution pattern. But those of Catti were current in the west or south of the territory, and when we con-sider the coins of Corio and Bodvoc we find the former in the western part of the realm (south Gloucester and north Somerset) while those of Bodvoc occur in the east and north-east of Gloucester and Oxford.

Possibly on the death of Cunobelin his sons tried to assert over-lordship in the lands of the Dobunni, and as a reaction against this, the kingdom spilt up. It may be that the remoter part, where the coins of Catti are found, resisted the Catuvellauni, while Commux was a client ruler. Cassius Dio tells us that the Dobunni were in subjection under the sons of Cunobelin, and also tells us that one part surrendered to the Romans at the time of the invasion. Possibly it was because they wanted to see the Catuvellauni overthrown; we cannot be sure. The coins of Corio and Bodvoc complete the tale – the coins of Corio possibly stand for the last phase of Dobunnic resistance and independence, while those of Bodvoc, showing Romanizing influences in their style, represent the rule of a client king under the Romans.

Maiden Castle and the Durotrigan Problem[161]

There are two magical dates in British Iron Age studies, the first is 75 BC (which, we have seen, was associated with the Belgic Invasions), the second is 56 BC. The latter of course has Caesarian connotations, and has been connected by archaeologists to many phenomena in Britain which in the past were believed to be associated with the destruction of the Venetian fleet and the events which followed it. Archaeologists have tried to explain three movements entering Britain about the middle of the first century BC in terms of the panic following the destruction of the fleet – the first being the appearance of a peculiar type of pottery in the Bristol Channel area known as 'Bristol Channel B' or 'Duck Stamped Ware'. Now the Bristol Channel 'B' people, if not the first to exploit the iron of the Forest of Dean, at least expanded the industry, and are associated with the iron currency bars which turn up on 'Bristol Channel B' sites. As Caesar tells us that currency bars were in use in Britain when he visited it, this points to the Bristol Channel 'B' people being well established before 56.[162]

The second group of people associated with 56 BC are those who brought what has been loosely called 'South Eastern B' pottery to Britain. Recent work has shown that what was grouped together as 'South Eastern B' is in fact a much more complex phenomenon not merely confined to the south-east (pottery of this type has turned up at Dragonby in Lincolnshire) and with origins other than in Brittany.

That leaves us with only one intrusive culture to consider, the Durotrigan of Dorset.[163] The important site in this connection is Maiden Castle, the most impressive hillfort in Britain, excavated by Sir Mortimer Wheeler in 1934–8.[164] At Maiden Castle, after two phases of Iron Age 'A' we have a first phase of Iron Age 'B' which Wheeler suggested began in 56 BC. This was followed by a second phase of Iron Age 'B' which lasted, Wheeler believed, until about AD 25 when the site was taken over by Belgic people.

No coins were associated with the Iron Age 'B' culture at Maiden Castle, and no coins of the Durotrigan type have been found in any Iron Age 'B' context in Britain, only in Iron Age 'C' (i.e. Belgic) or Roman levels. Thus we can assume that the Belgic peoples introduced coins. However, if Wheeler was correct in his chronology this would mean that the Durotriges began coining at a very late date, after 25 BC. Until the discovery of the Le Catillon Hoard we had no date for Durotrigan coinage, but in that hoard, which we have seen was deposited before 50 BC, there were silver Durotrigan coins.[165] The coin-using period at Maiden Castle must now be pushed back from AD 25 to the time of Caesar or before, and Wheeler's 'B' culture must in turn be pushed back from 56 BC to the beginning of the first century BC or even earlier.

The coins in the Le Catillon hoard were not the earliest of the Durotrigan series, behind them lie gold prototypes which must go back well before 50 BC. The origin of the Durotrigan silver coins may have been in a movement of British 'A' under pressure from Gallo-Belgic 'E' about the time of the Gallic Wars.

The implications of this in archaeology are too complex to discuss in full here – other cultures dated from Maiden Castle, such as the famous Lake Village culture (South Western Third B) of Glastonbury have had to be reassessed.

Numismatic Evidence for Continental Trade[166]

There is, as one might expect, quite a number of finds of Continental Celtic coins in Britain, and this would substantiate Caesar's statement that trade was conducted between the Britons and the Gauls. A large number of these coins (apart from the important Armorican series mentioned below) are of bronze, and there are concentrations in Kent (especially round Canterbury and Richborough) and in the territories of the Catuvellauni, Trinovantes and Atrebates. There are particularly large numbers from the vicinity of Silchester, Braughing and Sandy.

Evidence that there was a trade route connecting the Loire with Hampshire is attested by the distribution pattern of gold coins of the Namnetes, who were centred in the Loire valley round Nantes. These have turned up at Hengistbury and Swindon.

Base silver Armorican coins of the Coriosolites are relatively common all along the south coast, and have been found even as far afield as Scotland, Yorkshire or Durham. Other tribes more rarely represented among the south coast finds are the Baiocasses, the Redones, the Unelli and the Osismii. Probably the Coriosolites were responsible for much of the Channel trade, which conflicts with Strabo's assertion that the Veneti were the greatest traders. Venetian coins are relatively rare in Britain, though one, of very thin silver, turned up at Hengistbury Head.

The transition from gold to silver among the Durotriges was possibly prompted by Armorican influence and by the availability of silver from the Mendip mines. The Durotriges were not greatly influenced by Armorican coins in their choice of types, which were essentially Belgic in derivation, though their culture seems affected by other elements.

The latest coins represented are those of Germanus Indutili type, which have turned up at Colchester and Silchester in contexts probably dating from the end of the first century BC.[167]

Papyrus in Iron Age Britain?[168]

Recently an interesting study was published of the technique of manufacturing the early 'speculum' coins (often called the 'tin' coins) which seem to have a long life in Britain, from the beginning of the first century BC to Claudian times (Lullingstone), and the origins of which are still rather mysterious as they do not seem to relate to any known tribe, but which possibly represent some invasion from the head waters of the Seine, of people who settled along the Thames valley.

Sir John Evans, who originally studied these coins, suggested that they had been cast in wooden moulds and drew attention to the striations on the surface of the coins which he took to be the impressions of the grain of the wood. In order to test his theories he made specimen casts, and seemed satisfied with the conclusions.

Recently, however, it has been suggested that the technique of manufacture was more complex, and entailed using a piece of papyrus on which the design was piped in clay using an *en barbotine* technique, this papyrus strip being used as a matrix for clay moulds, in order to produce the correct alignment. If this is so, it would mean that papyrus was being imported from the east Mediterranean – it has been suggested that the Celts used it for keeping accounts, since the Druids relied mainly on oral traditions and did not commit their ideas to writing. But the problems that this theory poses are very complex, not least in connection with the route whereby the papyrus was traded; it was certainly not that of the tin trade which was too early for many of the coins. Presumably it would have been through Gallic intermediaries. With this puzzle we shall conclude this coin survey of prehistory.

Further Reading

There is no book in English on Continental Celtic coins and no general modern book in any language except la Baume's *Keltische Münzen* (1960) which is a mere 58 pages long and is of necessity very sketchy, though the illustrations are good. Lengyel's *L'art gaulois dans les médailles* (1954) is rather wider in its scope than the title implies, and has splendid plates of enlargements of coins in the Bibliothèque Nationale. These are printed on loose cards. Unfortunately very few copies were printed and it is difficult to obtain. Of the earlier books mention must be made of the two standard texts on Gaulish and Central European Celtic coins respectively, Blanchet's *Traité des monnaies gauloises* (1905) and Forrer's *Keltische Numismatik* (1908), which though out of date in detail are still sound in broad outline: a new edition of Forrer with a second supplementary volume edited by Karel Castelin is forthcoming. (Vol. I reprinted 1969).

Turning to British coins the standard text is R. P. Mack's *Coinage of Ancient Britain*, the second edition of which appeared in 1964. This book has excellent plates and is a useful all-round study, though Commander Mack perhaps could have done more to set the coinage in its archaeological perspective and the work lacks the depth of Derek Allen's. The latter's 'Origins of Coinage in Britain, a Reappraisal' in Frere, Ed. *Problems of the Iron Age in Southern Britain* (1961) is a masterpiece of modern numismatic method, and discusses, as the title implies, the Gallo-Belgic coinages and their British derivatives. The same volume (which was the proceedings of a conference held by the Council for British Archaeology) contains other useful material, notably Frere's comments on the Maiden Castle coin question. For the rest, the interested reader must turn to Allen's other papers listed in the bibliography. One word of warning, however, to those unfamiliar with numismatics – most of these papers are very technical and demand a certain familiarity with numismatic method.

For those interested in the background of Celtic life Professor Kenneth Jackson's *Oldest Irish Tradition, a Window on the Early Iron Age* (1964) will be found invaluable, while the value of coins in this respect is well demonstrated in Allen's paper in *Proceedings of the Prehistoric Society* for 1958, listed in the bibliography.

For illustrations of Celtic coins, continental and British, the interested reader ought to turn to de la Tour's *Atlas des monnaies gauloises* (1898), recently reprinted by Spink. This is a book consisting of nothing but fine engravings of coins.

Finally mention must be made of an article on the origins of Celtic coinage, which has a very useful bibliography listing key papers by region. This is Karl Christ's 'Ergebnisse und Probleme der Keltischen Numismatik und Geldgeschichte (Bericht 1935–55)' in *Historia* **6** (1957), 215–53.

NOTES

1 Celtic religion discussed in Powell, 1958; Filip, 1962; Ross, 1967; Chadwick & Dillon, 1967.
2 Classical sources for the Celts in Tierney, 1960 and Tierney, 1964. This gives a good impression of the tendency by the Classical writers to 'Classicize' the Celts.
3 Jackson, 1961.
4 Useful discussion of Romano-Celtic religion in Britain in Ross, 1967.
5 Account in Ross, 1959a and Ross 1967.
6 Jackson, 1961.
7 Tierney, 1960.
8 Summary with references in Piggott, 1965.
9 Lambrechts, 1954; Sjoenstedt-Jonval, 1936 for coin evidence. Also mentioned briefly in Ross, 1967.
10 de la Tour 6813.
11 de la Tour 8094.
12 de la Tour 8577.
13 de la Tour 5994.
14 de la Tour 5951.
15 de la Tour, J. 15.
16 de la Tour 5318.
17 Wainwright, 1955.
18 Mack, 238.
19 An example on a coin of the Suessiones: de la Tour 7729.
20 de la Tour 6826 (boar); de la Tour 6830 (hippocamp) – both on coins of the Veneti.
21 Colbert de Beaulieu, 1963.
22 Mack 251 and 253.

23 Mack 260 and 260a. Discussed in Allen, 1958.
24 Ross, 1967.
25 Fox, 1958.
26 Gundestrup in Klindt-Jensen, 1961a and 1961b; numismatic comparisons in Moberg, 1952.
27 Most notable on coins of the Veneti – see de la Tour 6826–8 etc. The coinage of the Veneti is discussed in Colbert de Beaulieu, 1953b – they were previously attributed to the Aulerci Cenomani. For chain symbolism see Ross, 1959b.
28 de la Tour 8405.
29 de la Tour 9180.
30 For example on coins of the Segusiavi – de la Tour 4633. Possibly also derived from facing heads on Greek coins, such as those of Syracuse or Rhodes.
31 Such as de la Tour 9692–6.
32 de la Tour 4555 or 4551.
33 de la Tour 5044.
34 Discussed in Toynbee 1964 and more briefly in Toynbee, 1962.
35 Mack 97.
36 Mack 223.
37 Sources as n.1. above and Ross, 1959a.
38 de la Tour 8040.
39 de la Tour 8030.
40 Muret & Chaibouillet 8106.
41 Mack 252.
42 Mack 167.
43 de la Tour 10170.
44 Fox, 1958.
45 Mack 132.
46 de la Tour 7177.
47 de la Tour 7704.
48 de la Tour 8124.
49 de la Tour 8145.
50 Koenig 1966. An interesting but improbable suggestion. This paper is not regarded as valid by many numismatists.
51 de la Tour 6398.
52 de la Tour 6388.
53 de la Tour 6396.
54 de la Tour 6385.
55 de la Tour 6400–6.
56 de la Tour 6721–2.
57 Mack 248, discussed in Allen, 1958.
58 de la Tour 6391.
59 de la Tour 7283, etc.

60 de la Tour 1969.
61 de la Tour 8472.
62 de la Tour 7046, 7064, etc.
63 British examples discussed in Allen, 1958.
64 de la Tour 5044 (Aedui).
65 de la Tour 4484.
66 Stead, 1967.
67 de la Tour 10159.
68 Discussed in Allen, 1958.
69 de la Tour 9911.
70 de la Tour 9375.
71 de la Tour 8426.
72 de la Tour 9018 (Leuci).
73 Allen, 1958.
74 de la Tour 1927, etc. It is used as a rev. type on de la Tour 6943.
75 Piggott, 1950.
76 Discussed in Allen, 1958.
77 British examples in Allen, 1958.
78 Piggott, 1959.
79 Discussed in Allen, 1958.
80 de la Tour 8040.
81 Fox, 1946.
82 de la Tour 7300 (man holding boar standard); de la Tour 7328 (horse and boar standard); de la Tour 7333–52, boar as reverse type.
83 e.g. de la Tour 8529 (horse and boar); 8449 (boar and ox head).
84 de la Tour 7608 (Meldi).
85 Mack 220.
86 Mack 410.
87 de la Tour 4349.
88 de la Tour 5958.
89 *Revue Numismatique*, 1863, V. 22.
90 de la Tour 6582.
91 de la Tour 6950.
92 On coins of the Veliocasses, for example, de la Tour 7596.
93 de la Tour 2177.
94 de la Tour 10144.
95 de la Tour 10159.
96 de la Tour 10141.
97 de la Tour 10162.
98 See references cited in n.26 above.
99 Other strange beasts include a human headed boar (de la Tour 4305) and 'ostrich' (de la Tour 3952).
100 de la Tour 9421.

101 Decker & Scollar discuss them generally in Decker & Scollar, 1962.
102 Allen, 1958.
103 Allen, 1958.
104 de la Tour 4622.
105 e.g. de la Tour 6309; de la Tour 4316.
106 de la Tour 7100.
107 For a series of illustrations see Colbert de Beaulieu, 1963.
108 Discussed in Callender, 1965 and Uenze, 1958. See also Hawkes & Hull, 1947, for Camulodunum examples.
109 de la Tour 8153.
110 Birchall, 1965.
111 Stead, 1967 for comparisons. Mack 248.
112 Allen, 1958. Terra Nigra type series in Hawkes & Hull, 1947.
113 de la Tour 6927.
114 Koenig, 1966.
115 Blanchet, 1951.
116 Blanchet, 1951.
117 Blanchet, 1951.
118 Hawkes and Hull, 1947. (Discussion of the coins by D. F. Allen.)
119 Wheeler and Richardson, 1957.
120 Colbert de Beaulieu, 1963; Colbert de Beaulieu, 1962a.
121 Colbert de Beaulieu, 1964; Colbert de Beaulieu, 1955a.
122 Literature on Armorican and Channel Islands coinage is extensive, the most convenient summary in English being Colbert de Beaulieu, 1958. For the coins of the Veneti see Colbert de Beaulieu, 1953b. Useful summary appears in Giot, 1960, with a complete bibliography to date. For the Coriosolites see Colbert de Beaulieu, 1951.
123 Colbert de Beaulieu 1955a, 1964; Wheeler and Richardson, 1957; Déchelette, 1927.
124 Todd, 1965.
125 Wheeler and Richardson, 1957.
126 Hawkes in Frere, 1961, outlined classification.
127 Allen, 1967.
128 Allen, 1961b.
129 Hawkes, 1968.
130 Hawkes, 1968.
131 Allen, 1961b; Mack, 1964. Useful summary in Allen, 1962.
132 Stevenson, 1967.
133 Hawkes, 1968.
134 Sources as in n.131 above.
135 Hawkes, 1968.

136 Birchall, 1964, 1965. Original study of the Belgae in Hawkes and Dunning, 1930.
137 Outlined by Allen in his summary of the significance of le Catillon in 1961b; also Colbert de Beaulieu 1958.
138 Allen, 1963.
139 Allen, 1944; Mack, 1964; also Allen 1962 for summary.
140 Allen, 1944; Mack, 1964.
141 Frere, 1957.
142 Frere, 1958.
143 I differ here from the more usually accepted view that Andocommius was the chief of some lesser tribe to the west of the Catuvellauni, possibly a client.
144 Mack, 1964. But see also Anon, 1968.
145 Clifford, 1961.
146 For St Albans Frere 1957, 1958 above; for Colchester Hawkes and Hull, 1947; for Silchester Boon, 1958. General summary in Laing, 1961.
147 Frere, 1941.
148 Allen, 1963 – summary in Laing, 1961.
149 Anon, 1962.
150 Biddle, 1966.
151 Tylecote 1961.
152 Tylecote, 1961; Tylecote, 1962a.
153 Boon, 1958.
154 Clifford, 1961.
155 Allen, 1964; Anon, 1968.
156 Clifford, 1961.
157 Clifford, 1961.
158 Clifford, 1961.
159 Clifford, 1961.
160 Clifford, 1961.
161 Original chronology in Wheeler, 1943. Reassessment in Frere, 1961.
162 See discussion of currency bars, p. 175 above.
163 See also Brailsford, 1958 for this culture.
164 Wheeler, 1943.
165 Allen, 1961b, Appendix III.
166 Allen, 1961b, passim.
167 Todd, 1965.
168 Wild, 1966. Original discussion in Evans, 1864.

8 Coins and the Archaeology of Roman Britain

In no field of archaeology are coins of greater value than in that of the Roman provinces. Coins trace quite clearly the process of Romanization and its extent, the vicissitudes of Roman trade beyond the Imperial frontiers, and even the fortunes of individual sites. In studying Imperial history too, their types, frequently instruments of propaganda, record campaigns and official policy.

Britain is a good subject for study; being a frontier province it reflects perhaps more clearly the changing pattern of currency and the way it is affected by external history than do provinces nearer the heart of the Empire.

The Claudian Invasion

With the Claudian invasion of AD 43 we can see a change in the pattern of currency in the British Isles.

Our main historical sources for the invasion are Tacitus and Cassius Dio, who tell us that four legions were employed for the conquest, the Second, the Ninth, the Fourteenth and the Twentieth. They were aided by auxiliaries, and set sail in three forces, under the general command of Aulus Plautius. Although it is probable that the whole force landed at one point it is possible that a division of the invading army into three was made to provide a main attacking force and a decoy, with a third detachment to link up with the Roman allies to land perhaps at Bosham in Chichester Harbour. Archaeological and numismatic evidence strongly favours the view that the invaders used Richborough as a base camp.[1] Here, following a phase of Iron Age occupation, we find an early military base with associated Claudian coins, pottery and military equipment. The defences of this first fort at Richborough were of a temporary nature, and were later replaced by more permanent timber buildings when it became a supply base.[2]

The landing seems to have been unopposed, but Plautius' army met the British forces probably just above Rochester. Coins provide possible corroboration for this, for in 1958 at Bredgar on the North Downs a hoard of thirty-four gold coins was discovered, the latest of which were four of Claudius struck between AD 41 and 42. The hoard can be interpreted as the savings of one of the soldiers who died in the battle and who had buried his money for safety before the engagement.[3]

The leaders of the British resistance were Togodumnus and Caratacus, who had come into power on the death of Cunobelin. The former had taken over Essex and Hertfordshire, the latter annexed territory on the middle Thames, Hampshire and Surrey. Togodumnus was killed in the first campaign, and Caratacus fled west, taking shelter among the Silures of south Wales. The way was now clear for the Romans to advance on Colchester. At this juncture Claudius himself joined Plautius in Britain, and took a part in the campaign.

The Romans found a useful ally in the person of Cogidubnus, whose territory, that of the Regnenses (which take their name from his title of *rex*) was carved out of the former land of the Atrebates. Cogidubnus, whose home may have been the palace discovered at Fishbourne, near Chichester, was the successor to Verica, who had fled just before the conquest as a petitioner to Rome. No coins of Cogidubnus are known, though two inscribed CRAB may have been struck by him (could the legend mean Cogidubnus Rex Atrebatum Britannorum as has been suggested?)[4] and have been found at Hod Hill and Portsmouth.

Other leaders, too, seemed eager to ally themselves with the Roman invaders; Prasutagus of the Iceni and Cartimandua of the Brigantes were two of these, while Boduocus of the Dobunni (who struck the last of the Dobunnic inscribed coins, those with the legend BODVOC) may have been a third.

Prasutagus was the predecessor of Boudicca, and we know he died in 60. The date of his accession is uncertain, and no coins struck in his name are known. A hoard of coins found at Lakenheath in Suffolk in 1960 included one inscribed SVBIDASTO with a head which had a Roman prototype.[5] The hoard included coins of Claudius, and this suggests that Prasutagus had a predecessor who ruled after the conquest, perhaps until *c.* 47, when Prasutagus succeeded him and entered into closer relations with the Romans.

To commemorate the success of the British invasion Claudius struck a series of coins, both aurei and denarii, at the Rome mint in the years 46–7. These coins have as a reverse type a triumphal arch inscribed DE BRITANN(is), surmounted by an equestrian statue between two trophies[6] (Plate 18c).

The Arch of Claudius was finally dedicated in Rome in 52, and stood on the Via Lata, which led from the Forum Romanum to join the great North Road to Gaul and, ultimately, Britain. Another arch stood at Boulogne, from where the offensive had first been mounted. The coins represent the Rome arch, of which now only a part of the dedicatory inscription remains. The coins, which continued to be struck until 51, the year before the dedication, help us to reconstruct the arch, which judging by the equestrian statue shown on the coins was modelled on the Arch of Drusus.[7]

A few more coins of Claudius relate to Britain. These are rather surprisingly silver didrachms struck at Caesarea in Cappadocia in 46 and which have as a reverse type Claudius in a triumphal quadriga, with the legend DE BRITANNIS in exergue.[8]

Coinage and Currency in Claudian Britain[9]

If we study a series of hoards which end with coins of Claudius, we find that silver coins of his reign are rare, but there is the sudden appearance of a large number of Claudian aes. This group of hoards in which the coins are entirely Roman, occur chiefly in the south-east, with the exception of two from Oxfordshire and one from Somerset. The Claudian coins are chiefly asses or dupondii.

An explanation for this phenomenon can be found in the dearth of small change in Britain at the time of the conquest, for although in the south-east some small bronze coins had been struck before the conquest on the Roman model (notably by the Catuvellauni and Trinovantes), elsewhere in Britain the natives had to rely on a system of barter when they wished to trade in commodities of low value. For this reason Britain absorbed all the Roman aes that it could acquire.

The story is perhaps even more clearly reflected in the native hoards of the same period. One hoard from Santon Downham (Suffolk) consisted of 30 coins of the Iceni along with two Claudian aes. In another native hoard from Nunney (Somerset) we find that out of 249 coins there are 232 British silver along with 3 Republican denarii, a denarius of Caligula and 4 Roman aes, two of which were native imitations of Claudian coins.

Broadly speaking, then, in the period immediately following the

11. Roman Britain

conquest we find that Roman bronze coinage is added to the native gold and silver currencies, and Republican silver, which had been popular before the conquest, fell into disfavour in the south. This was also possibly because there was a considerable influx of base silver legionary denarii of Mark Antony, which had a very long life in Britain. These coins were so poor in quality that following Gresham's Law they drove the good Republican silver coins out of circulation[10] (Plate 18a).

With the debasement of the silver coinage in the time of Nero there was a marked increase in the amount of Roman silver in circulation, and a diminishing of the native silver currency.

Native Imitations of Claudian Coins[11]

The great popularity of the newly imported Claudian aes resulted in a shortage of the official mint products and a period of production of local imitations in Britain. This phenomenon is of course not an unusual one in the history of coins, for a similar shortage of small change resulted in the issue of tradesmen's tokens in mid seventeenth century England, and again in the later eighteenth century. When authority does not meet the demands of the people the latter not infrequently take the law into their own hands and produce a supply themselves.

Apart from a few silver denarii, the majority of these forgeries, as one might expect, were of bronze. Although most of these finds lie in the south-east, namely the initial area of conquest, surprisingly they are also found further afield, in the north and south-west.

There seem to have been four classes of the copies, starting with very good imitations. These occur mainly in the centres of Roman military control, and quite probably were semi-official and intended to supplement the pay for the military. Good copies are particularly common at York, Richborough, Gloucester and even Wroxeter. Slightly poorer examples appear on civil sites like Silchester or Dorchester. The second grade of copies are probably the result of secondary imitation in tribal centres once the best copies became fairly widely absorbed into the currency. The third class are very blundered, and are copies of copies, or made in backward areas. The last class, which is rare, rather strangely has the types in mirror fashion, presumably because an impression of an existing coin was taken to make a die (Plate 18b).

These coins all seem to be more or less contemporary with the official issues, though one finds survivals as late as AD 150 – there were no less than 13 in the 'Southants' Hoard. An occasional residual has been known in contexts as late as the third century.

The extent to which these copies circulated can be seen if we study the earliest coins from Sea Mills (Abonae), near Bristol. Here seven denarii of the period Republic-Augustus are followed by an as of Agrippa (struck under Tiberius), eight official Claudian aes and no fewer than eighty-six copies.[12]

Colchester[13]

The Belgic capital of Colchester lay to the north-west of what became the Roman *colonia* of Camulodunum, on a site that is now known as Sheepen. At Sheepen we have a sequence of occupation covering the period AD 10 to 65. Mention has been made in a previous chapter of the pre-conquest coinages of Cunobelin's capital, and they need not be further considered here.

After the conquest, occupation of the Belgic capital continued until the time of the rebellion of Boudicca. Due to the rich native currency struck at Camulodunum before the conquest there was little need for imported Roman Republican coins there or, for that matter, the denarii of the earlier Caesars.

If one studies the general picture of pre-Neronian currency from Sheepen one finds an interesting picture which can be compared favourably with some of the Claudian forts of the German *limes*, such as Hofheim, where, incidentally, copies of Claudian aes were similarly common. The important fact to notice is the fairly large percentage of pre-Claudian coins that must have been imported to the site just after the conquest. The following chart shows this clearly:

Republican coins	33	6·9 per cent of total.
Pre-Claudian Imperial	156	32·5 per cent of total.
Claudian	290	60·6 per cent of total.

In comparison with other Claudian sites, 40 per cent pre-Claudian coins is not excessive, and it seems unlikely that many of these reached Sheepen before the conquest. Of the 33 Republican denarii, less than 7 were of the Mark Antony legionary type. The aes of Augustus are all worn, though the silver coins of his reign are in fairly good condition. Tiberian silver coins, as opposed to the Claudian, are relatively common, and from these finds and the finds of Tiberian silver elsewhere it seems apparent that they, rather than Claudian silver, were in fairly general circulation just after the conquest.

The Claudian aes are very important for the light they shed on the types most commonly in circulation after the conquest, and upon the the British imitations, which are well represented at Sheepen. Stylistically it seems probable that a large number of the copies were in fact made at Colchester itself. A study of which coins were copied shows that those favoured are the earliest of Claudius' reign, struck in 41. Now this would point to the imitations being first struck in the earliest months after the conquest as an official method of supplying the Romans with cash. They cannot be regarded as native products since the natives would not have become sufficiently familiar with the prototypes in the space of a few months to start imitating them. The later coins of Claudius, struck in 42–45/49, came to Sheepen too late to be imitated.

The Romans founded their colonia at Colchester not long after the conquest, but it was not extensively occupied until about 49. By that date Claudian aes were predominant everywhere, being used extensively till 64, and they usually turn up worn on the site. From the colonia come relatively few pre-Claudian coins, but not less than 239 of his reign.

The story of the sack of Sheepen by Boudicca is clearly reflected in the pattern of the coinage. The aes coins of Nero circulated on a wide scale in Britain, but at Sheepen are very rare. The site was sacked by Boudicca in AD 61, and the presence of 8 coins of Nero, struck in 64, reflects that following the sack there was a short period of 'tidying up' on the site, before it was abandoned entirely in favour of the colonia. Of these eight, four were found near a temple which was built in Flavian times, and are probably to be associated with it. In contrast with the rarity of Neronian coins at Sheepen we have no fewer than 128 coins of Nero from the colonia itself. A few coins, extending down to AD 360 or slightly later, suggest occasional occupation – possibly it became an artisan quarter – but the great days of Cunobelin's Camulodunum were over.

The Conquest–Second Phase[14]

The period from 43–7 was the phase in which Plautius advanced to occupy the whole of the area which lies roughly to the east of a line drawn from the Humber to Exeter. In 47 Ostorius Scapula subjected the Iceni and East Anglia, and then turned his attention to the

Marches and Wales. The process of the subjection of Wales was interrupted by the revolt of Boudicca, and the army had to be withdrawn from the west to put down the rebellion. The revolt delayed the process of Romanization, and a long period of consolidation followed.

In studying the Claudian advance of 43–7 coins are of great value for determining the origins of the occupation of individual sites. The plan of occupation as envisaged by Plautius was probably that of a triple advance into the interior of Britain. The first of these campaigns was concerned with the south-west and was under the command of Vespasian, who later became Roman emperor. This attack was primarily focussed on the area of strong British resistance in Dorset and Somerset, extending into Devon as far as Exeter. The second advance proposed by Plautius was a drive along what was later Watling Street into the Midlands. The third and last line of attack was concentrated on the north, as far as Lincoln and the Humber. Following on these campaigns roads and forts had to be constructed to open up the country and hold it against insurrection.

The first campaign of Vespasian was completed by the end of 43, though the Midland and northern campaigns took a little longer.

Vespasian in Wessex

Vespasian found himself up against strong resistance in Wessex, where the natives had constructed massive hillforts for defence. The focal point of the opposition lay in the territory of the Durotriges, a tribe who owed little to the culture of the Belgae and whose origins are puzzling. Their pottery owes its inspiration to several sources, certainly in part continental, and their coins likewise have a Gallic origin. Their great capital was the oppidum of Maiden Castle, near Dorchester, which fell to Vespasian after a massacre of the natives.[15] We are told that Vespasian captured in all twenty hillforts, but which these were is difficult to determine, with the exception of Maiden Castle, Hod Hill,[16] Ham Hill and Spettisbury Rings. Of the Roman forts established by Vespasian again archaeological evidence is scanty, but coins as well as pottery give us some kind of clue. The coins from Chichester, which has recently produced evidence of a Claudian fort, begin in the Claudian period.[17] The coin sequences from Camerton,[18] Dorchester[19] and Ilchester[20] likewise begin at this date, though evidence for Claudian military occupation is still lacking.

Exeter is particularly interesting in this connection, as the coin sequence here begins in the Claudian period and is well attested as running into Flavian times, when there is a marked drop in the percentages of the coins of each emperor.[21] It has been argued that this together with Claudian samian and a small section of military ditch is evidence for an early military occupation there – for a similar sequence can be observed in the coins from Wroxeter – although there is no proof in the form of military equipment from the excavations in the city. It is perhaps fair to add that the theory of a military origin for Exeter has recently been attacked,[22] though why a civil settlement should have been founded there on the edge of the frontier without a military precursor is difficult to determine, unless because of its importance as a trading port. Sea Mills, to which reference has already been made, was founded at this time to operate a ferry across the Bristol Channel.

The Midlands and North

For the Midland and northern campaigns coin evidence is rather less helpful, though together with pottery, coins help to date the origins of certain sites. Castle Hill (Margidunum) in Nottinghamshire seems to have had a Claudian fort preceding the later settlement,[23] and occupation at Ancaster, Lincolnshire, seems, on the weight of site finds as well as on the evidence of an early ditch, to go back to a military centre of Claudian date which preceded the later civil settlement.[24] The coin finds from Leicester (Jewry Wall Site) present a long sequence covering the whole of the Roman occupation, and begin with coins of the Republic, Tiberius and Claudius.[25]

Elsewhere there is evidence of Claudian military bases preceding civil sites. This is so in the case of Worcester,[26] and also in the case of Mancetter, where a Claudian hoard with a large number of good copies was found near an early ditch.[27]

Finally, to round up the survey of civil sites with Claudian military predecessors, mention may be made of Cirencester, where a good sequence of coins suggests a Claudian foundation, a theory which seems to be verified by the military equipment and soldiers' tombstones from the town.[28]

With the exception of the Claudian aes Roman coins were not rapidly absorbed by the native population of Britain, and indeed the general picture of the currency in the Claudian forts does not present an even pattern, suggesting that in spite of the considerable numbers of coins imported to Britain the rate of absorption was slow and uneven. Early native sites produce few coins, and one must depend on hoards of native origin for an indication of the extent to which Roman currency was used in the first decades following the conquest. This picture is made clearer by a study of coin finds from early civil sites such as Great Chesterford,[29] Silchester,[30] St Albans[31] or Caistor St Edmunds.[32]

The Revolt of Boudicca[33]

The story of the revolt of Boudicca, that fiery queen of the Iceni, is one of the most romantic in Romano-British history, though in fact the story is one of a particularly savage rebellion being put down with comparable savagery.

Boudicca's sack of London, St Albans and Colchester is well attested in the archaeological record. In London it is characterized by a layer of burnt debris, including large amounts of daub and burnt samian pottery of the period Claudius–Nero. This layer is encountered on both sides of the Walbrook, but especially on the east side, to the south of Cornhill.[34] Associated with the burnt level of the Boudiccan sack was a coin hoard, presumably buried by a frightened citizen when the news first reached the city.[35]

In Colchester a similar story is told by the coin finds. The burnt levels associated with Boudicca's sack at North Street, Colchester, included a number of burnt coins, notably a denarius of Tiberius and one coin of Cunobelin, as well as coins of Claudius.[36]

In any event it seems that rebuilding went ahead in the three towns fairly rapidly – an inscription shows that Verulamium was rebuilt by 79, and there is good reason to suppose that London and Colchester rose from their ashes almost as rapidly.

Early Campaigns in Wales[37]

Originally it seems to have been the plan of Claudius to leave the conquest of Wales until a later stage. After a phase of rapid conquest to the east of the Fosse Way in the years 43–7 and the departure of Plautius, there seemed little point in annexing the hilly and hostile territory of Wales, which offered little profit and would be difficult to hold. His successor, Ostorius Scapula, arrived however to find the land behind Plautius' *limes* the scene of trouble, stirred up among the Silures of south Wales and the Ordovices of the north by Caratacus.

There was a raid into allied territory – either that of the Dobunni or the Cornovii – but Scapula drove the raiders back, then, having secured his rear with a campaign of consolidation in East Anglia, prepared to drive a wedge between the tribes of Wales and those of the Pennines by overcoming the territory of the Deceangli of Flint. However disturbances broke out in Brigantia – Cartimandua probably had difficulty in controlling the whole of her territory – and Scapula abandoned the campaign to turn his forces against the Silures, leaving an escape route which Caractacus was to follow in 51 when he sought refuge with the Brigantes. During his campaign against Caractacus and the Silures a fortress was built at Gloucester in 49, which became the base of the Twentieth Legion.

Following the defeat of Caractacus in 51 a legionary detachment was left behind to build forts in the territory of the Silures. The sites of these forts are uncertain, but numismatic evidence suggests that one was at Usk where, apart from a samian bowl datable to the period 50–60, a series of Claudian imitation coins was found.[38] After this date there is a good coin sequence from the site, suggesting continued occupation, though another fort at Llandovery seems to have been abandoned for a period after the first Scapulan occupation.

Connected with the early campaigns in South Wales and the Marches was a system of naval patrols in the Bristol Channel. Two signal stations have been discovered on the north coast of Devon presumably connected with these, at Old Burrow and Martinhoe. Old Burrow has yielded in excavations coins of Tiberius and Claudius along with a military entrenching tool, while Martinhoe has produced coins of Nero. Both probably continued in use until a later period.[39]

In AD 61 Suetonius Paulinus carried on the work of the annexation of Wales, concentrating on the main trouble spot, Anglesey. The operation was again interrupted by a rebellion, that of Boudicca, and his troops were withdrawn to deal with it.

Agricola had already campaigned in Wales and no doubt the experience was of value to him when in turn he led the war against the north Welsh tribes in the summer of AD 78. Agricola turned his attention on the Ordovices, who had just destroyed a cavalry detachment which had been sent out from Chester or Wroxeter to forage. He then pressed on and, using Chester as a base, proceeded to complete the subjugation of north Wales, setting up a series of forts and roads to connect them. The key fort was Segontium, now Caernarvon, where the coin sequence begins about this date.

Segontium was excavated by Sir Mortimer Wheeler in 1921–3 and was particularly rich in coin finds.[40] The sequence is illuminating as the earliest coins (up to Vespasian) give us a good idea of the composition of the currency in the first decades after the conquest.

The sequence runs:

Republican	3
Augustus	1
Tiberius	1
Nero	2
Vitellius	2
Vespasian	20

It is interesting to note that the earliest Republican coin was dated to the period 88–6 BC. Apart from Segontium other important forts were founded at Caerhun (Canovium), Bryn y Gefeiliau, Caer Gai, Tomen y Mur and Llystyn.[41]

The evidence for Chester being the legionary base for Agricola's North Welsh campaign is the discovery of water pipes with imperial titles, the name of Agricola, and the date 79. Further dating evidence comes from building rubbish below a barrack in the Flavian fort which incorporated slightly worn coins struck in 72 and 73.[42]

The conquest of south Wales was the work of Julius Frontinus, Agricola's predecessor, who began by occupying the fertile sea plain of Glamorgan, in the territory of the Silures. Just as Segontium and Chester was to hold north Wales, in the south another series of forts, headed by the legionary fortress of Caerleon (Isca), maintained control. Forts were built at river mouths, and the Usk valley provided an important arterial route. About 75 a town was founded at Caerwent, the only Romano-British town in Wales. The coin sequence of Caerwent will be discussed presently, but here we may mention that the sequence of coins from Caerleon tells a similar story in the first century to that of Segontium. The coins from the Prysg Field excavations of 1927–9 start with 8 Republican denarii, then come 2 of Augustus, an as of Tiberius, two of Claudius, 3 of Nero, 4 of Galba, 1 of Otho, 2 of Vitellius, then 48 of Vespasian.[43]

Roman Wales – The Second Century[44]

Coin and pottery evidence is of particular importance in studying the sequence of events in Wales after the Flavian conquest. This is because we have to rely entirely on archaeology and coins, the only literary aids being a few dated inscriptions found in excavations.

To rely on coins entirely for dating is very hazardous, as can be seen from two coins of Trajan found in the roadway of the altered west gate at Castell Collen in central Wales. From this find it was deduced that the fort was reduced in size in the time of Trajan, and this in turn led to quasi-historical deductions concerning the reasons. In reality both these coins were survivals, and more recent excavations have shown that the fort was reduced at a later date.

A very important case where a coin has led to a serious mistake in archaeological interpretation was at Caersws in central Wales, where a coin of Septimius Severus was found in the fort wall and used to date it. Subsequent investigation showed that the wall was badly disturbed by stone robbers, and that the coin probably had no connection with it. On the mistaken association of this coin, the stone defences of the fort were dated to the early third century, and the whole interpretation of events in third century Wales was affected by this wrong conclusion. As has recently been pointed out, the absence of Roman coins from a site can be very misleading.

The fort at Gellygaer yielded no coins later than the reign of Hadrian, and for this reason it was assumed that the fort was abandoned about 130. Subsequent excavation has shown, however, that the fort continued in use, as attested by samian and coarse pottery.

The Gellygaer story is a particularly interesting one because, on the basis of the absence of coin finds, everything, even the third and fourth century pottery, from the fort was dated to the early second century, and a theory that the Welsh forts were abandoned in the time of Hadrian grew up. This was simply because it was overlooked that the coins of the Flavians together with those of Trajan and Hadrian were in circulation for nearly a century after they were struck.[45]

A similar mistake was made at Caersws, though here the abandonment was set at a slightly later date, namely the time of Antoninus Pius (138–61). This was because the coins of the Antonines were rare in comparison with those of the period of 70–120/30. But again this is because the coins of the Antonines are generally much rarer in Britain than those of their predecessors.

On the basis of these sites and the lack of evidence one way or another from the other sites excavated before the First World War, an evacuation theory developed which died a slow death. It was believed that the province of Wales was so peaceful that the military

H

were withdrawn from the forts during the second century. The excavations of the forts at Segontium, Caer Llugwy and Caerhun following the War did little to alter the theory. Further coin evidence was brought in to substantiate it. It was suggested that on the evacuation of the forts *c.* 140 some people buried hoards because of the sudden loss of Roman protection, and that the six hoards from Wales which close with coins of Antoninus Pius or Hadrian must be associated with this evacuation.

Segontium, however, seems to have been largely rebuilt in stone at the time of the Antonines, and the theory that there is no Antonine occupation from the other forts is also rendered untenable on the evidence of the pottery, which can now be dated much more precisely. The hoards remain a puzzle, but it is possible that they are connected with the rebuilding of the forts *c.* 150 which is now known to have taken place.

If the forts were not abandoned, is it possible that they were maintained by a skeleton garrison? Certainly there is a marked lack of coins of the second century at Caernarvon, and at Caerhun there are no second century coins except for seven of Trajan. A similar story is told by Brecon Gaer. It is just possible that the forts were used as *mansiones* – rest houses for official travellers. This story is difficult to substantiate, though one Midland fort, that of Slack, seems to have been used in this way in the period under review.

Antonine Coins from Wales[46]

As we shall see later, although the coins of Trajan and Hadrian are common in Britain, and those of Antoninus Pius almost as numerous, those of the reigns of Marcus Aurelius and his son Commodus are rare. This phenomenon is not peculiar to Wales, or even to Britain, but is true for the Roman provinces as a whole. Although Aurelius and Commodus struck as many different types as their predecessors, there were probably fewer coins issued of each type. Broadly speaking, however, they are particularly rare in Britain. This may be connected with official policy, and the fact that there was an adequate number of coins circulating in Britain. It is notable that hoards closing with Aurelius are very common in Britain, especially in the Pennines, though they are rare in Wales. There are only two hoards of this date from Wales.

In the case of the finds from the Wroxeter Forum the percentage of coins of the period 161–93 compared with that of the period 96–161 is considerably less than even the customary discrepancy between the percentages of the two periods, for example the figures for Corbridge, Caistor or Richborough.[47] At Caerleon during the period, the settled base for Wales, we find, in contrast to the Welsh forts, an increase in the percentages during the second century. Segontium has only four coins struck between 142 and 193. This discrepancy is at first difficult to understand without bringing in some evacuation theory to explain it, as we have seen was done. If, however, the coin percentages for the whole of the first century are contrasted with those for the whole of the second century the figures are seen to be much less at variance. Thus at Segontium there are 54 first century coins and 41 of the second century, and the difference can be explained in terms of the survival of first century coins.

Agricola[48]

We may now turn back to the career of Agricola and consider his northern campaigns. In AD 79 he left his base of Chester and began his attack on the north. His route probably lay through Lancashire to Ribchester, where coins and pottery attest an early occupation,[49] then north along the valley between the Pennines and the Cumberland and Westmorland Fells to Carlisle. In this valley there are a large number of forts. On the east side Caristanius Fronto possibly advanced on a parallel line, using York as his base. Between Corbridge and Carlisle a series of forts was built, along the line of Dere Street. Corbridge itself, which later became the main supply base for Hadrian's Wall, began as a Flavian timber fort, and may in fact have been his base in the winter of 79–80. There are a few forts on the line of what became the Wall which have yielded evidence of Flavian occupation, and two of them have produced early coins. As yet the coin evidence is rather uncertain, but is nevertheless a clue to future finds. At Netherby was found an aureus of Nero, and at Jarrow at the extreme eastern end of the Wall, coin finds include an as of Nero and a denarius of Vitellius, which together with some first century bronzes might suggest an Agricolan occupation.[50]

The Agricolan advance into Scotland was along two routes, a western from Carlisle through Birrens to Castledykes led by the general himself and an eastern, from Corbridge through High Rochester to Newstead, led by Fronto. From here Fronto went on to Cramond on the Firth of Forth, while Agricola advanced to the neck of land between the Forth and the Clyde, and may have established a series of forts. There were possibly Flavian forts at Croy Hill, Bar Hill, Mumrills(?), Rough Castle(?), Castlecary, Cadder and Old Kilpatrick, some of which have produced pottery and coins of Flavian date. But the coin evidence is not very sound in most cases, as many of the early coins from the sites could have been lost in the Antonine Period.[51]

The coin sequence from Bar Hill, for example, begins with one legionary denarius of Antony, two coins of Vespasian, one of Domitian, one of Nerva and nine of Trajan. Nevertheless, excluding dubious coins, this consists of the majority of the coins from the fort, as Hadrian is only represented by three coins and there are none of Pius.[52]

Coins antedating Nero are very rare in Scotland, though a Claudian coin from Mumrills would suggest an Agricolan occupation. Coins of Antony, though seemingly an indicator of Flavian occupation, are in fact of little value due to their long circulation – his legionary denarii are represented at Mumrills, Rough Castle, Castlecary, Bar Hill and Balmuildy, but of these Balmuildy is most unlikely to have been occupied before the Antonine period.

Agricola did not stop at the Forth-Clyde line, but setting out probably from Camelon, another undoubtedly Flavian fort just to the north of what became the Antonine Wall, he went north into Perthshire, establishing again a series of forts, from Ardoch to Inchtuthil, with further forts at Cardean and Stracathro. Further north still, at Auchinhove in Banff an Agricolan temporary camp is known. A study of the first century coins from native sites in Scotland shows the extent of Roman influence – coins from Aberdeenshire and the Moray Firth are possibly the strays from Agricola's army and fleet.[53]

The coin sequence from Newstead, which is perhaps the richest site in the northern Empire in its yield of finds, gives us a good sequence of the kind of coins circulating in the army at the time of Agricola.[54]

Coinage and Currency, Nero-Trajan[55]

This is perhaps a convenient point at which to pause and review the general situation of coinage and currency in Britain during the first century AD. Under Nero there was a coinage debasement, which involved the reduction of silver in the denarius. This resulted in the amount of silver current in Britain enjoying a marked increase and, following Gresham's Law, the disappearance of older and better coins. The last years of the reign of Nero also witnessed an increase in the output of aes from the Senatorial mint, and in general terms the Flavian period was one of extensive coining.

For the first time in Britain in the Flavian period we see the marked increase in the volume of coinage in circulation, although the character of the currency remained fairly static. Bronze still continued to be hoarded, though not perhaps to the same extent, and the copying of official coins ended in the reign of Nero, whose coins were only rarely imitated.

An interesting hoard from Honley, near Huddersfield, reflects the gradual changes that were taking place in the composition of the Flavian currency. Here, in a hollow bone which contained a seal box, a brooch and two bronze rings, were found, together with twelve republican denarii, one denarius of Nero, five silverori Ctanian coins of VOLISIOS-CARTI type, and five aes of Nero and Vespasian. The hoard reflects the natural instinct among the British to use the old silver coins along with the new imported Roman bronze. It is also noteworthy that silver of pre-Neronian date is absent. Other hoards which close with Vespasian reflect a similar situation.

In Hampshire, Dorset and perhaps Somerset the native element remained strong much longer, and indeed we find the coining of native issues continuing for some time. The hoards of Flavian date from this area reflect the trend – one from Timsbury in Hampshire contained eighteen British 'Hod Hill' coins, along with forty-two Roman aes, and was buried about AD 90. Another native hoard, this time from Anglesey, buried about 87, gives a good idea of the nature of the currency soon after Agricola's conquest – there were eighteen Republican denarii with two denarii each of Augustus and Tiberius, then a series of silver and bronze coins from Nero to Domitian. Remarkable was the large percentage of silver coins in this hoard, which is perhaps not unconnected with the native familiarity with the metal, which was mined there by the Romans, at Parys Mountain.

Agricola's northern campaigns did not, perhaps strangely, have any affect on hoarding in the Midlands and the north, and there are few purely Roman hoards that can be connected with his army. As far as native hoards are concerned, it may be remembered that native coins do not seem to have been struck by any tribes further north than the territory of the Coritani, and did not circulate to any great extent beyond southern Yorkshire.

The relative rarity of first century coins both in hoards and site finds in the north emphasizes the transitory nature of Agricola's offensive. One hoard can possibly be associated with Agricola's Scottish campaigns, however. This is the Broomholm hoard of six aurei, the earliest gold hoard from Britain. Buried probably some time in Vespasian's reign it is noteworthy that there are more coins of Nero in it than those of Vespasian.

By the time of Trajan in Italy bronze coins struck before the time of Nero were passing out of currency, but in Britain they appear to have circulated more slowly, and Claudian pieces seem to have remained in use until c. 160. Trajan attempted a reform of the coinage, using to some extent 'Restitution' types of earlier emperors, and recalled old and worn coins. Like Nero before him he also debased the denarius.

The coin hoards which close with Trajan in Britain are almost entirely of denarii, although Trajanic denarii are relatively rare, suggesting that the new debased issues made the better, earlier ones worth hoarding. Occasionally one finds Antony's debased legionary denarii among them, presumably because of their abundance rather than because of their value. In the south the range covered by these hoards is considerable, even including denarii of the period Augustus-Claudius, though in the north, pre-Neronian coins are generally absent. Worn coins of Vespasian turn up in large numbers, apparently not hoarded until the new Trajanic coins came into circulation. With Trajan, Roman coins become very widely distributed in Britain, from what was to become the Wall to Somerset.

The towns in the east and south-east seem to show a drop in the volume of currency from the time of Trajan, possibly because of the growth of London and the emergence of York as the main military centre. The increase of currency can be observed at villa sites like Hambleden,[56] at a temple-market site like Woodeaton,[57] or in the main towns like Silchester[58] and Verulamium.[59]

The Growth of Towns[60]

Romano-British towns have many different origins – some seem to have been built where Belgic settlements were already in existence, like Leicester, Silchester, St Albans or Chichester. These were sometimes built on the site of their Iron Age predecessor, sometimes near it. Due to later rebuilding, Roman and Medieval, it is often difficult to be sure whether a town has a Belgic predecessor – even a few coins or sherds of Iron Age date do not constitute evidence, as coins could have been in circulation after the conquest, or the town could have swallowed up a small farmstead of Iron Age date. Thus at Irchester three or four coins of Cunobelin hardly constitute evidence for a Belgic predecessor.[61]

Some were military in their origins, either coloniae for veterans or simply shanty towns of traders and other camp followers (*canabae*) which grew into towns and continued to flourish after the fort fell out of use. Yet others grew round posting stations or spas. Some were deliberately laid out, with chess-board pattern streets, other developed more irregularly and only became towns when they were eventually enclosed by defences. The towns of the first century and even early second century were timber framed for the most part with only public buildings in stone, and may have been only occupied by many of the inhabitants for part of the year, the rest being spent in country villas. Only in the second century are there real town houses of a specialized sort.

Very few towns had defences in the first century, the building of a circumvallation of bank and ditch taking place in most towns towards the end of the second century at the time of their greatest prosperity. Later this was faced in stone.[62] At Silchester the street plan seems to have been laid out as late as the second century, on the evidence supplied by an as of Domitian and a trumpet brooch found underlying a street make-up.[63] Coins and pottery provide a dating for the earth defences and the subsequent town walls. At one time it was thought that the town walls were constructed soon after the earth defences. At Silchester for example a denarius of Septimius Severus and some Rhenish ware was taken as evidence that the wall was Severan,[64] and at Aldborough a similar date was proposed, where a coin of Julia Domna was found in the foundation trench. In both cases however these coins must have been quite old when the walls were built.[65]

The town walls must antedate the time of Carausius when the Saxon shore forts were built, but are probably not much earlier. Canterbury and Brough-on-Humber have yielded coins of about 270 from their ramparts. At Verulamium a gateway was built contemporary with the town wall, and from this gateway a hoard of five coins came, ending with one struck 227–9 which suggested that the gate (and therefore the wall) must have been built sometime before 250. Another coin hoard further substantiates this, for when one of the towers of the gateway collapsed due to weak foundations another coin hoard of 275–85 was buried by the ruins.[66] In the fourth century the walls were further defended by bastions for ballistae (field catapults). The date of these again has been partly established by coins – at Caerwent a coin of 330–35 was found under a bastion.[67]

Interpretations of Coin Finds from Towns

The potential value of comparative analyses of coin lists from town sites is great, but in reality is fraught with difficulties. Unless a town has been completely excavated the coin finds can at the best only be a random sample, and there is no completely excavated Roman town – even Silchester, which was extensively excavated, was far from completely explored. Different areas in a town may have different histories; one region may have been unoccupied in a period when elsewhere there was a flourishing settlement in the same town. Such random samples can be very misleading, and it has frequently happened that archaeologists have commented on the relative rarity of the coins of a certain period from a site, only to find that in the next season of excavation a large number of issues of that period come to light, greatly altering the picture. One site, for example, during four years of excavation produced no coins of Carausius, while in the fifth season more coins of that emperor turned up than of any other.

Hadrian

Agricola, having penetrated as far north as Banffshire and having won a victory at Mons Graupius, was recalled in 84, before he had completed his policy of subjugating the north. In the following period, during the reigns of Domitian and Trajan, there were further troubles in the north, one outbreak probably following the withdrawal of troops for Trajan's Dacian Wars in 101–2 and 105–6. Corbridge was one of the places attacked at this period, and a coin hoard in which the latest coin was dated AD 98 was found in the burnt debris of the fort, while a coin of 103 was found in the rampart of the fort that was built to replace it. A further war broke out at the time of Hadrian's accession in 117, presumably again in the north, but was put down in 118, as attested by an inscription from Jarrow. The first of the 'Britannia' issues of Hadrian described below were probably struck to commemorate this, in 119. Soon afterwards Hadrian came to Britain himself – he was noted for his assiduity in visiting the provinces – and he brought with him the VI Legion, Valeria Victrix. He probably came to Britain in 122, though the length of his visit is not known. The planning and building of the defences which we now know as Hadrian's Wall, following the line of the Agricolan forts from the Tyne to the Solway, took place in the following years, AD 122–38.[68] To commemorate the visit a number of coins were struck between AD 134 and 138.[69] A group of sestertii refer to the army in Britain. One shows the emperor on horseback addressing five soldiers, while another shows the emperor on a tribunal addressing three soldiers. The legend in the first case reads EXER BRITANNICVS, in the second EXERC BRITAN. A third sestertius shows the emperor facing a female figure sacrificing from a patera over an altar – the legend in this case refers to his visit, and reads ADVENTVI AVG BRITANNIAE.

Another group of coins is perhaps of even greater interest, as the reverses all depict Britannia seated, in some cases resting her foot on a pile of stones. This has sometimes been taken to represent Hadrian's Wall.

The first of this series was struck in the period AD 119–22 though the majority of the issues belong to the period 134–8. These coins, sestertii, dupondii and asses, are the precursors of a series of coins of Britannia type. The legend in each case includes or consists of the word BRITANNIA.

In this connection mention may be made of an interesting coin die found during the Verulamium excavations in 1930. It is a reverse die of hard bronze, and has the legend ADVENTVS AVG, depicting the emperor being greeted by Roma. The type has been dated to the period 134–8, thus it cannot be connected with Hadrian's visit to Britain. It was found in a late second century context, and cannot be readily explained as it seems to be an official die and not that of a forger[70] (Figure 43).

Coins and Hadrian's Wall[71]

The coin sequence from excavations on Hadrian's Wall is surprisingly weak, and with a few exceptions most of the sites on the Wall have produced only a few coins. Thus, if we group together all the

Fig. 43 Die of Hadrian from Verulamium (Verulamium Excavation Committee)

milecastles, turrets and miscellaneous Wall structures we find that they have only produced a total of 83 coins, lasting from the legionary denarii to the time of Valentinian or Valens. Of the 82 coins that can be deciphered 29 are pre-Hadrianic and 18 of the period from Hadrian to Commodus.

A more useful story is told by the coins from three hoards, all of which were deposited in the early years of Hadrian's reign. One is of the famous Thorngrafton Hoard, which was found in a bronze arm purse in 1837, the other two both come from Birdoswald and were found in 1930 and 1949. The contents of the hoards are tabulated below:

	Thorngrafton	Birdoswald I	Birdoswald II
Republican	9	8	18
Nero-Nerva	30	13	7
Trajan	17	6	3
Hadrian	4	1	2

These hoards may conveniently be compared with later hoards such as those from Greatchesters (1897) or Mallerstang, where Republican denarii are notably absent. This shows that Republican denarii fell out of circulation in the second half of Hadrian's reign, with the exception of the legionary denarii of Antony. The picture is further amplified by the Rudchester Hoard of 1766, which closed with Marcus Aurelius but which contained almost 70 per cent coins of pre-Hadrianic date, of which almost 50 per cent were pre-Trajanic.

Pius and the Antonine Wall[72]

Hadrian's Wall was not altogether satisfactory as a *limes*, and further troubles arose on the frontier. Accordingly, about AD 140, the construction of a new series of defences was undertaken. Along the line of the Flavian forts between the Forth and the Clyde a new wall was built, this time of turf rather than stone. The work was done between 139 and 142 under the direction of Lollius Urbicus. Hadrian's Wall was abandoned, though it was to be redefended again later. This operation was considered of sufficient importance to merit a commemorative series of coins being struck.[73]

There are two series of Britannia commemorative coins struck under Pius. The first, struck in AD 143–4 shows Britannia seated on a globe above waves, with the legend BRITAN beneath. The second was struck in 154–5 and shows Britannia seated on a pile of rocks in an attitude of dejection, and bears the legend BRITANNIA COS IIII. This second coinage followed further serious trouble in Britain between 154 and 158, during which the first Antonine occupation of the Antonine Wall was brought to a close with destruction – the coins suggest the revolt had been put down by 155 and were possibly admonitory. The second period of Antonine Occupation in the north covered the years *c.* 158–84 (Plate 18d). Yet another series of commemorative coins struck by Antoninus have Victory as a reverse type. These date from the first period of commemoratives. Many of the Britannia coins are of poor workmanship, and may have been struck in Britain, where they are more common than elsewhere in the Empire.[74] In the famous votive deposit from the Well of Coventina, at Carrawburgh on Hadrian's Wall, no fewer than 327 of the coins of Antoninus Pius were of this type. Die links suggest the mint was not far away.

As one might expect the coin finds from the forts of the Antonine Wall reflect the Antonine developments. In addition to the Flavian forts a number of new forts were built, so that there was one fort every two miles along the Wall. Most of these forts have yielded coins, usually starting with those of Trajan and Hadrian. The sequence ends with Commodus, suggesting that the Wall was abandoned early in his reign. One fort, Kirkintilloch, has produced a coin of his, and a coin of his wife Crispina has been found at Newstead. Some of the forts have yielded much later coins – of the third and fourth century – but these are not an indication of an occupation at that date but rather that squatters settled there and used Roman coins.

There are two sites, not on the Wall, which have coins of a later date than Commodus, but to these we shall return presently. Apart of course from the Roman forts in Scotland, other sites have produced coins of late first or second century date, but to the native sites we shall also return.

Marcus Aurelius[75]

Trouble does not seem to have been allayed for long, and the reign of Antoninus' successor, Marcus Aurelius, probably witnessed further skirmishes. Marcus and his co-emperor Lucius Verus did not strike any coins with direct references to Britain on them, but in a series of 'Restitution' coins using the types of Mark Antony's legionary denarii was included one which paid tribute to the VI Legion, Valeria Victrix, which was stationed in Britain. Like Antony's, these coins had a galley on the obverse, an aquila and two standards on the reverse. On the coins however dedicated to the Sixth instead of the eagle we find a figure of Victory, and this indicates that the legion honoured was the VI Victrix, not the VI Ferrata, which was stationed in the Middle East. The Victrix had been brought to Britain from Germany in the time of Hadrian and would have been engaged in northern campaigns.

Coinage and Currency, Hadrian-Aurelius (117-180)[76]

What was happening to the general currency in Britain during the period from Hadrian to Marcus Aurelius? First we find the native coinages disappearing completely, and a marked rise in the popularity of the denarius, which was widely hoarded. Republican denarii fall out of use, and gold becomes popular for the first time, though it seems to be confined to Hadrian's Wall and its neighbourhood. To this period belongs the famous hoard of gold coins from Corbridge, which consisted of 160 aurei from Nero to Antoninus Pius. Another type of hoard which also seems to be confined to the Wall consists of gold coins mixed with silver – the Thorngrafton Hoard falls into this category, as does another hoard from Corbridge.

In the time of Pius we find that Flavian coins are less common in hoards, and there is a large percentage of issues of Trajan and Hadrian. Mixed hoards of silver and aes also seem to be a feature of the north, and bronze hoarding becomes less popular in the south. This is probably due to the copious aes coinage of Pius.

There remained in Hampshire and Dorset a small enclave of users of native coins until the time of Hadrian. This is shown by the finds from Hengistbury Head and by the 'Southants' Hoard. The 'Southants' Hoard contained 630 British coins of 'Hengistbury Head' type, along with 13 Republican denarii and a mixture of Imperial coins, the latest being of Hadrian. The finds from Hengistbury ended with Pius, some of whose coins were stabbed, possibly because the natives took them to be gold from their shiny appearance.

The hoards ending with coins of Aurelius are extremely common, and certainly silver hoards of this date are commoner than those of any other period until 260. Possibly this is due to the troubles soon after his death when the Antonine wall was broken and a general killed. In the north, as one might expect, military activity in the period resulted in an increase in the amount of currency, as is clearly reflected in the coins from the Well of Coventina.

Elsewhere in Britain the coin level varied – some sites show an increase, others a marked decrease. Chester for example shows an increase, Wroxeter a decrease, and in the Midlands there is an almost universal increase. Some sites that were important in the Claudian period, like Richborough and Clausentum, show a decrease because of their lessened importance. But with Aurelius throughout Britain we see a marked drop in the numbers of coins in site finds.

The Bar Hill Copies[77]

A curious series of imitation coins have been found at Bar Hill which, it will be recollected, was an Agricolan predecessor of an Antonine Wall fort. In a well the excavator found imitations of denarii of Antony, Vespasian, Domitian, Hadrian and Marcus Aurelius, together with a large number of imitations of denarii of Trajan. They were all, save those of Antony and Vespasian, cast in moulds out of pure tin, except for one of copper-silver alloy. These seem to have been made as offerings for throwing into wells and holy springs on ceremonial occasions, just as imitation money is made in China as offerings to the dead. Similar coins, probably made for the same purpose, have been found in the Thames.

Third Century Counterfeiting[78]

We now come to the most complex period in the history of Roman Britain, and indeed in the Empire as a whole, the third and fourth centuries. Throughout the third century there were military, political, social and economic crises. It was the period of the Thirty Tyrants, which include the Gallic Emperors, Victorinus, Postumus and the Tetrici.

As far as coinage is concerned, it was a period of debasement of the silver coin. The debasement of the denarius had begun in 198 with Septimius Severus as we have seen. In 215 it was succeeded by the 'double denarius' or antoninianus, which by 238 had replaced the denarius altogether. The antoninianus rapidly sunk to the level of the old denarius, and indeed from the time of Trajan Decius antoniniani were sometimes even struck on old denarii. In the 260s there was further debasement in which the level of bullion in the official coin was regulated at about 5 per cent. During the next ten years most of the coins have less silver, and the antoninianus is little better than a copper coin. Aurelian, somewhere between 270 and 275, attempted a reform though his coins were still of poor alloy. The new coins of Aurelian, marked rather mysteriously xx i (possibly to indicate the alloy contained 5 per cent of silver, or alternatively that 20 sestertii was the value of one new antoninianus), were not favourably received in the west, especially in the area of the Gallic Empire (which flourished between 259 and 273), and indeed the mark of value was not applied to coins of the Lyons mint. Carausius, the infamous emperor of whom more will be said below, only put this mark of value on his coins between 290 and 292, when he was trying to establish cordial relationships with the central government. The reformed coins of Aurelian are very rare as site finds, in both Britain and France.

There were two major waves of counterfeiting in Britain and France in the third century. The first can be associated with the reign of Septimius Severus, starting in 198, when the debased denarius was the starting point for a series of even baser imitations. Alongside the copies of debased silver coins we have a lesser wave of imitations of senatorial aes.

Senatorial Aes[79]

As has been noted, the Antonine period was one when large numbers of coins seem to have come into Britain, with the result that fewer were hoarded. The sestertius became the most important coin, and the Antonine sestertii, though of less intrinsic value than the earlier sestertii, was balanced in the currency by the large numbers of Flavian, Trajanic and Hadrianic asses and dupondii in circulation. After 198 however it ceased to be an economic propostion to strike large numbers of aes, when the metal content of the denarius was so debased. The aes coins of the Severi are rare in Britain, and until the time of Alexander Severus and Gordian III and his successor Philip I, when again there was a considerable coinage of sestertii, the demand was met in Britain by cast copies.

There are a few cast copies of the Antonine period, and even earlier – there is one of Hadrian from Cirencester and others of Pius and Aurelius from Woodeaton, Gloucester, Cirencester and Chester. These, judging by the condition of the prototypes from which the moulds were made, were not in fact struck until the late second or early third century. The series seems to end with coins of Gordian III (one from Caerleon). The sites which seem to be the most prolific in Britain are Silchester and Caerleon.

Severan Silver[80]

Throughout Britain from the time of the Severi onwards cast imitations of silver coins were made, not as has sometimes been suggested semi-officially, but as forgeries. There are four main areas of forgery – Somerset, Lincolnshire, Yorkshire and Shropshire. The moulds for casting these coins have been found on no fewer than twenty-two sites in Britain, and extend down to Maximinus I (235–8). Antoniniani rarely seem to have been forged, the coins chosen for imitation being denarii. Although moulds of earlier coins exist, the copies seem to have first been made in the time of Severus and Caracalla.

The phenomenon is not confined to Britain – similar moulds for denarii have been found in France, Germany, Noricum and Africa, and although moulds for denarii are absent, moulds for senatorial aes occur in Pannonia. None however come from Italy or the east. The methods of production are attested from a number of sites on the Continent, notably Damery (Marne) and Epernay (also Marne) and from several sites in this country, the best known finds being the Lingwell Gate find of the early nineteenth century and the recent finds from Whitchurch, Somerset (Figure 5).

Whitchurch[81]

The finds from Whitchurch are particularly interesting as it is later than most of the forger's sites known, and must be dated between AD 265–70. Although the moulds include one for Hadrian, the majority of the coins forged on this site were the antoniniani of the Gallic Empire. Notable, however, is the fact that the counterfeiting seems to end early on in the reign of Tetricus I, at a time when the struck copies known as 'barbarous radiates' were becoming prevalent. Possibly the object of forging was to replace in the currency some of the many coins removed and melted down for their metal content.

In Gaul we find forgery of this sort continuing down to the Gallic Empire as well – at Damery and Bordeaux forgeries were being made until the time of Postumus.

It is interesting to observe that from Whitchurch comes a hoard of struck radiate copies dated to about 282, showing that the local inhabitants changed their technique of imitating coins about this time.

Commodus, Caracalla, Severus and the North

In the opening years of the reign of Commodus, Aurelius' son, (176–92) there were further uprisings beyond the Antonine Wall, resulting in its abandonment. The exact date of this disruption is uncertain, but we know that Commodus sent Ulpius Marcellus to Britain in 180, and that the raiders had to some extent been beaten back by 184, since in that year Commodus struck commemorative coins and assumed the title of Britannicus. Certainly the campaigns did not end in that year, since the coin issues continue in 185. There are several different types of these coins, the two main types showing Britannia standing holding a sword and wreath (or patera) and Victory about to inscribe a shield on her knee. In addition two large aes medallions were struck, one showing Britannia seated on a rock, the other showing Victory inscribing VICT BRIT on a shield. A hoard of silver coins terminating with an issue of 186–7 was found at Briglands (Kinross-shire) and may imply that campaigns were still continuing until that date, but it might just as easily be the hoard of a native or trader with access to contemporary currency.

A phase now follows in which the tribes of Lowland Scotland were granted their freedom with a certain amount of Roman influence,

in return for which they acted like the later foederati as buffers between the Caledonii of the North and Hadrian's Wall. The governor
who had been active during the campaigns of Commodus was later
followed by Pertinax in 185, who inherited a mutinous Roman army,
but who restored order rapidly if we can judge by his coin types of
186 with the legend CONCORDIA MILITUM. Commodus was
assassinated in 191, Pertinax in 193, having resigned the governorship
in 187 and having briefly been hailed Augustus by the praetorian
guard. There was a struggle for the purple; yet another governor of
Britain, Clodius Albinus, was involved – Albinus crossed to Gaul
with as large an army as possible in 196 to defend his claim. He left
the north wide open to insurrection, and insurrection followed. This
is what faced the emperor Septimius Severus when he finally dis-
posed of Clodius Albinus in 197. Septimius Severus himself took
part in British operations and died at York. Severus realized that in
the state of acute disruption with which he was faced decisive
military action was out of the question, and the northern raiders
were bought off to give him time to rebuild York and the devastated
forts south of Hadrian's Wall.

Chester seems to have been unaffected by this, but there was
nevertheless a feeling of unrest in Wales which led to a number of
hoards being buried, and the reoccupation in greater force of the
Welsh forts, including Segontium. The hoards from Wales which
close with Severus include one from Pentir, Caerns., with coins
ranging from 69 to 192, and another from the bed of a stream
near Llanfairfechan (also Caerns.) consisting entirely of denarii
covering a period of about 300 years, but mostly struck under
Severus.[82]

By 208 York was largely rebuilt along with the forts of Hadrian's
Wall and outpost forts beyond. In this year Severus came to Britain,
and along with his son Caracalla and his court made York his base
for the British War of 208–11. The object of this offensive was the
warlike Maeatae of Strathmore and Strathearn. The coins of
Caracalla, already joint emperor, struck in 207, herald British victories – possibly he had arrived in Britain in advance of his father –
as do the coins of Severus himself and his other son Geta, struck
during the period 208–13.[83] There are a great many varieties of these
coins, usually with Victory on the reverse and the legend
VICTORIAE BRIT or a variant thereof – Victory sometimes is
shown setting up a shield on a palm tree which she is inscribing,
presumably with the name of Britain, sometimes standing beside

a trophy at the foot of which cowers a captive, while a woman in a turreted crown stands facing alongside it. (Plate 18e) Most of these coins were struck in Rome, but one interesting example with Greek legends, is a billon tetradrachm of Alexandria. Corbridge was used as the supply base for the Scottish campaigns, and a naval base was established at Cramond, on the Forth. Here the coin sequence clearly reveals the Severan occupation, with coins extending down to this date.[84] Two issues of coins support the suggestion that the campaign was chiefly seaborne. One, an issue of Severus, shows a permanent bridge with towers at either end, the second, of Caracalla, shows a bridge of boats with the legend TRAIECTVS. Later coins of 209 also show Neptune and Oceanus. The bridges depicted probably are symbolic of the bridging of the Forth or Tay.

Further north another site has produced numismatic evidence of a Severan occupation. This is Carpow in Perthshire, where there seems to have been a legionary base in the early third century. Carpow seems to have been built after the first victory over the Caledonians in 209, and was probably chosen because it could be supplied by sea. The two coins which attest a Severan date for the building of the fort are of Caracalla (under Severus), and Plautilla, Septimius' wife. They suggest that the fort was built c. 209 with the intention of continued occupation, but abandoned c. 211 on the death of Severus as Caracalla did not intend pursuing his father's policy.[85]

Coinage and Currency – Commodus to Aurelian[86]

Under Commodus there is a sudden drop in the number of hoards buried. In Scotland there is, as one might expect, a slight revival under Severus, when a few silver hoards were concealed. In the south the drop could probably be associated with the more general circulation of coins. A few of Antony's denarii survive, but coins of Nero become rare, and the copious coinage of the Flavian emperors is also less predominant. There are likewise few hoards of Severus and his sons, except in the north where they are to be associated with his campaigns.

Caracalla introduced the antoninianus, which is named after him (his real name was Antoninus), but this was not well received in Britain until the time of Gordian III and Philip I. The hoards buried in the time of Severus Alexander (222–35), even in the 'civilized' south, contain relatively few antoniniani in comparison with denarii – one hoard from East Anglia contained 107 antoniniani but as many as 3,062 denarii, and many hoards contain nothing but denarii. Silver hoards predominated at this period, though there are one or two mixed hoards and one of aes extending in date from Claudius to Alexander Severus.

For the ensuing period, down to the middle of the century, hoards are relatively rare, and consist chiefly of silver, again mainly denarii. It might, however, be pointed out that the Dorchester Hoard of 20,000 silver coins consisted almost entirely of antoniniani and might for this reason be taken as proof that by the time it was buried in the reign of Gallienus (c. 260) the antoninianus had replaced the denarius. It might be stressed that this was not a savings hoard but probably a tax collection (Plates 18f; 24).

Broadly speaking, too, we find a sudden drop in the amount of currency circulating in Britain. Site finds show that this decline started with the Severi and reached its ebb about 235. This, coupled with the disappearance of hoards, points to the first half of the third century being a period of relative peace and poverty.

Gallienus to Diocletian[87]

The next period is one of great complexity from the point of view of the archaeologist and the numismatist. For literary evidence we have to depend upon the unreliable gossip of the *Historia Augusta*. This lack of reliable historical material means that in turn there is a lack of sound chronology for coins. Coupled to this is the fact that economically it was a period of collapse and politically one of anarchy – it has been pointed out that the Empire was in a considerably weaker state in the late third century than it was at the end of the fourth and beginning of the fifth – only the myth of Roman power kept the barbarians from flooding in across the frontiers.

In Britain and northern parts of the Empire generally the coins of the Gallic usurpers and slightly later the British usurpers Carausius and Allectus are much more abundant than the official issues of the emperors in Rome, and are of greater value to the archaeologist than the official pieces.

The start of the trouble came about 259 when Postumus seized the purple at Cologne, and Saloninus, the son of Gallienus, was killed. Gaul, Britain and possibly Spain as well broke away from the

Empire, and their history becomes veiled in darkness for about ten years. The coins of Postumus are very common, as are those of his successor, Victorinus (Plate 18g), but do not, rather surprisingly, seem to have come to Britain in as great numbers as the 'official' coins of Claudius II, or his predecessor Gallienus, whose reigns cover roughly the same period.

With the accession of Aurelian in Rome the coins of the Gallic Empire suddenly flood over, replacing the products of the Rome mint. Coins of the Tetrici are not infrequently a hundred times commoner than those of Aurelian. The coinage reforms of Aurelian cannot account for this phenomenon entirely, and we should probably interpret it in the light of the theory that Britain became isolated from the central authority of the Empire at this time. One large hoard, however, would suggest that some official issues were reaching these shores.

To consider the period more closely, we find that in the phase 259–68 the influx of the bad coins of Gallienus together with the 'silver' coins of Postumus led to a period of hoarding in which the coins struck prior to Gallienus' reign were concealed along with a fair percentage of the coins of Postumus, which were of tolerable standard in comparison with the antoniniani of Gallienus. A hoard from Ulnes Walton (Lancashire) consisted of 65 coins from the time of Valerian and afterwards – of these 53 were of Postumus and 6 of Gallienus. Another hoard contained only coins of Postumus and Valerian.

In the next phase, between 268 and 270, we find that the Gallic issues were of as poor a standard as those of Gallienus (being the issues of Victorinus, Claudius Gothicus, Marius and Quintillus) and the coins of Postumus were in even greater demand for hoarding. Alongside hoards of this sort we find other hoards which consist chiefly of coins of Victorinus. These were buried in the hope that they might be later redeemed in better money, rather than because they were of good quality.

In the final phase, that of the Tetrici, the influx of vast numbers of base coins drove out the few better coins of Postumus and the earlier third century emperors. Only six out of a group of fifty hoards closing with Tetricus contain coins earlier than Valerian, and in most cases the number of early coins is restricted to one or two. Wales and southern Britain seem to have been more severely afflicted with the coins of the Tetrici than the north.

The coinage reforms of Aurelian resulted in the demonetizaton of the coins of the Gallic Empire, which must have circulated as a sort of token coinage, but at first these new silver washed coins did not circulate widely, and hoards mainly consisted of older coins – a few hoards contain, rather surprisingly, hardly any coins of the Tetrici. The 'reformed' coins of Aurelian and his successors seem to have had a much higher value than the Gallic antoniniani. From 260 to the time of Carausius there was a marked rise in the amounts of coinage in circulation, though the coins from Aurelian to Numerian are relatively scarce.

'Barbarous Radiates'[88]

The coins of the Gallic Empire were widely copied in Britain, and these copies, scarcely more barbarous in many instances than their prototypes, circulated alongside them. Such copies exist in Gaul, but nowhere in as great numbers as in Britain. They turn up on most sites where there is a late third century occupation, and often out-number the official coins. Likewise they are well represented in hoards (Plates 18h; 18i; 20; 21).

The problem of 'barbarous radiates', their classification and dating, is a very thorny one indeed. Many numismatists have en-deavoured to make some kind of classification, and have so far failed. Attempts at classifying them according to their barbarity fail – good copies and bad circulated side by side. Most numismatists are agreed that the large size copies circulated alongside the coins they imitated, and were struck within the third century. Agreement, however, is not so readily reached on the question of the very tiny radiates or minims. There are two schools of thought concerning these. Members of the first, headed by C. H. V. Sutherland and P. V. Hill, are in-clined to think that although some of these may be dated to the third century, some at least must be ascribed to the later fourth century.[89] The grounds on which they base their conclusions are these: whereas official coins may have a long circulation it is unlikely that tiny, barbarous copies could survive a century of circulation, and indeed some are so small it is a miracle that they survive even a few years. Secondly they claim that mules are found in which radiate obverses (the term 'radiate' is derived from the radiate crown worn by the emperors on these coins) are combined with fourth century reverses of 'Fel Temp Rep' variety.

The second school of thought, headed by Dr J. P. C. Kent, believes that the occurrence of radiates in fourth century hoards is due to survival, and points out that all kinds of radiates, from the large to the tiny, are present in the Verulamium Theatre Hoard found in 1934 and dated to 300 on archaeological evidence. As a second defence they also point out that where radiate overstrikes occur it is always on coins of the third century.[90]

Arguments have been put forward to update the Verulamium Theatre find, but these have been advanced by numismatists rather than archaeologists, and hardly stand up to critical analysis.

The coins imitated are chiefly those of the Tetrici, with the coins of Victorinus and Postumus taking second place. Apart from these, one finds copies of coins of Claudius II struck after his death with an altar reverse, and occasionally the coins of Gallienus. Other emperors, such as Quintillus and Aurelian, are very rarely copied indeed.

All the arguments concerning radiates and their date cannot be advanced here, nor a stand taken in favour of either of the two schools. Probably, although a very late date (fifth century) for radiate minims is suspect, some at least continued to be struck in the fourth century (Plate 18i).

The Romano-British Empire[91]

During the third century no official coins were struck in Britain until the time of the usurpers Carausius and Allectus, in the period 287–96. Nor for that matter were any coins struck with types which relate to Britain, except for two aurei struck by Victorinus in his series of legionary issues paying tribute to the Twentieth Valeria Victrix and having as a reverse type the legion's standard, a boar. These coins were struck by Victorinus to pay tribute to the legions which were either under his control or of which he thought he might gain control.

At the beginning of the reign of Maximianus (286–305) the Channel was infested with Saxon and Frankish pirates, and the Classis Britannica, which had been in existence since the first century and which had as its bases Dover and Lympne, was strengthened to deal with them. The first appearance of Saxon pirates was on the east coast in the second century. There is a marked increase in the numbers of coin hoards of Marcus Aurelius and Commodus in East Anglia, Kent, and to some extent along the south coast. This was followed by a lull in hoarding, and presumably a lull in raiding, until the period 268–82. This can be seen in the following table:

Hoards AD 238–82

238–49	19 hoards	(1.7 per year)
253–68	24 hoards	(1.6 per year)
268–70	23 hoards	(11.5 per year)
270–75	128 hoards	(25.6 per year)
275–82	41 hoards	(5.9 per year)

Hoards closing with coins of the Tetrici are especially numerous in east England and the Bristol Channel regions. The admiral appointed by Diocletian to rid the Channel of pirates was Marcus Aurelius Carausius, who is usually described as a Menapian (i.e. coming from what is now Holland) but who may have been British.

Carausius came of a stock that was more suited to piracy than the prevention of it, and so mismanaged the operation to his own ends that Maximianus ordered his arrest. Unperturbed, Carausius won over the British forces, and set himself up as emperor. The details of how he did this are largely legendary, but he appears to have crushed a Roman army near York and marched on London, where he set up his court.

Once established, Carausius set up mints in London and Colchester, and possibly at two other places as well (Plate 18j), On the continent he established a mint at Rouen for a short period. He struck in gold, silver and copper. Some coins of the London mint bear the mint mark ML (Moneta Londiniensis), those of Colchester, C. This C mint mark has sometimes been interpreted as being indicative of Bitterne (Clausentum) rather than Colchester, but this is improbable. Two other problematic mints occur – one with the mint mark RSR, which may have been that of Richborough (Rutupiae) but is more probably London, and one with the mint mark BRI, which again is probably just London, though Wroxeter has been suggested (usually Viroconium, but in late Latin inscriptions V frequently becomes a B). Some of Carausius' coins also seem to have been struck at Boulogne.

Particularly interesting among the coins of Carausius are some with the RSR mint mark which have as a reverse type Britannia greeting the emperor and the legend EXPECTATE VENI – a tag from Virgil's Aeneid, that is Queen Dido's greeting to Aeneas. Carausius also issued coins with the reverse legend SAECVLARES AVG, which would imply that Carausius celebrated some games after the fashion of the Secular Games to herald a new Golden Age and ritually to purify past deeds. In theory this should have been held in

Rome, but in the case of Carausius must have been held in London, to herald a new age for Britain.

During the winter of 288–9 Maximianus sent a fleet against Carausius which was defeated, and the result was that Maximianus had to make a truce with Carausius, allowing him to assume the title of co-emperor. Coins were struck by Carausius to proclaim the fact, with the conjoined busts of Carausius, Maximianus and Diocletian, and the proud legend CARAVSIVS ET FRATRES SVI. Carausius also struck coins in the name of his 'colleagues' from British mints.

In 293 Carausius was murdered by his minister Allectus, who for a brief period (till 296) maintained the British Empire. His coins are of lesser interest than those of Carausius, but do include a new denomination, or rather an old denomination revived, the quinarius, which was about 60 per cent of the weight of the antoninianus, and had the mark of value Q. These coins had a galley as a reverse type. In 296 the so-called British Empire came to an end, when Constantius Chlorus, the young colleague and successor of Maximianus, landed in Hampshire and reconquered Britain. Allectus was killed in the struggle.

Among the treasure of Roman medallions found at Beaurains, near Arras, in 1922 was a very fine gold medallion of Constantius Chlorus. On the reverse it shows the emperor advancing on the gates of London and being welcomed by a personification of the City, with LON beneath her to identify her. Below his horse is a galley. The legend reads REDDITOR LUCIS AETERNAE – The Restorer of the Eternal Light. The medallion was struck at Trier (Plate 23).

Carausius is perhaps one of the most romantic figures of later Romano-British history, a precursor of Arthur. Apart from coins and a milestone there is little contemporary documentation of his career, and we have to depend on the Medieval Scottish historians, Fordun and Boethius, for an account of his reign.

The Forts of the 'Litus Saxonicum'[92]

One of the important acts of the reign of Carausius was probably the commencement of the building of the forts of the Saxon shore. These forts were intended as a defence against Saxon raids. They were built partly with the old type of earthworks, and partly with stone walls and bastions like the new town defences. They ran right round the coast from Norfolk to the Isle of Wight, and there were others on the west coast to act as a defence against Irish raids, notably at Cardiff, Lancaster and Caer Gybi on Holyhead. These are probably later than the time of Carausius, and possibly can be ascribed to Constantius Chlorus.

The coins from the forts of the Saxon shore give a clear picture of their history. Many of them, like Richborough, were earlier forts which were remodelled. Here the first fort was levelled between 270 and 285 (attested by finds of coins of Claudius II and Tetricus from the ditches), then rebuilt. At Reculver early coins are fairly common indicating an early fort. From 250 on however after a break in the sequence we find that coins are extremely common down to the mid fourth century. The coin sequence at Dover is continuous from the first to the fourth century, showing that it too must have been remodelled.

At Lympne there is only one second century coin, but 95 for the period 253–306, of which no fewer than 41 are of Carausius and Allectus. At Bradwell the sequence starts with Gallienus, but not until Carausius are the numbers for each reign high. Brancaster and Walton Castle tell a similar story. The coin sequence is less clear for Portchester and Burgh Castle, but they are also probably of late third century origin.

Pevensey was probably the work of Constans – a coin was found in the beam hole of a bastion, datable to 334–5.

Wales in the Third and Fourth Centuries[93]

Wales in the third century was afflicted with raids from Irish pirates, and the result of this was the burial of large numbers of hoards, chiefly in the coastal region. There are a large number of hoards which close with coins of the Tetrici, but probably these were buried much later, in the time of Diocletian's reform of the coinage in 296. It was the issue of the follis under Diocletian that resulted in the disappearance of the coins of the Gallic Empire from the currency. Proof of their continued use can be seen in the find from the strong room in the fort at Bewcastle in Northumberland, which consisted of 11 coins of the Tetrici, deposited at the time of its destruction in 296.

Almost half the coin hoards of Carausius and Allectus found in Britain have been found in Wales, and coins of Carausius are well represented in the Welsh forts (Map 12). Allectus, however, probably

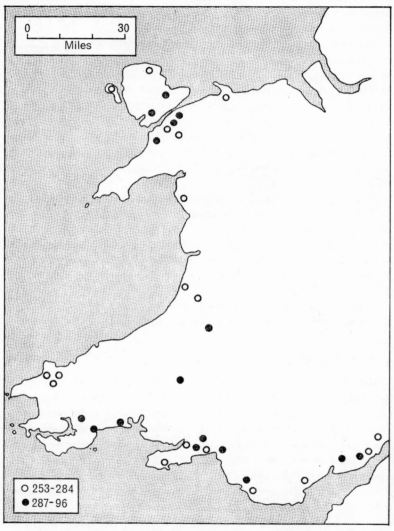

12.   Roman coin hoards in Wales, 253–96 AD (after Simpson, 1964)

withdrew the garrisons from the Welsh forts, as is attested by the absence of his coins at Caernarvon, Forden Gaer, and Brecon Gaer, an absence which is similarly reflected in other western forts like Ribchester and Templeborough. At this time many of the forts suffered damage from the natives, including those mentioned as well as Chester and York. The Wroxeter forum was also damaged, and at Kenchester, in Herefordshire, evidence of raids takes the form of the emergency burial of a woman in whose grave a coin of Carausius was found.

In the fourth century the Welsh forts seem to have been re-occupied – the coin sequence at Segontium continues from the mid fourth century, and Caer Gybi was built at this time. Elsewhere, eleven coins of the fourth century, ending with Gratian, have been recovered from Brecon Gaer. Gratian is likewise the last emperor represented at Caerhun, while at Caerleon the sequence ends with Valens.

The Tetrarchy[94]

To review the history of the period 284–306: in 284 Diocletian, chosen emperor by his troops, found the Roman administrative machinery in a state of anarchy. Throughout the third century the Empire had been torn by minor civil wars or the threat of civil wars, and between 211 and 285 there had been a succession of emperors, most of whom met with violent deaths at the end of a few years, sometimes in the case of usurpers after only a few months of rule. No emperor from Severus to Carinus ruled more than fifteen years.

Diocletian realized that in order to put an end to this, some definite arrangement should be made to determine the succession, and with this object in mind he devised a system known as the Tetrarchy. His plan was to divide the empire between two co-emperors, the one being responsible for the east, the other for the west. Each was to appoint an heir, given the title of Caesar (the emperors being Augusti) who was to look after the welfare of the state and prepare to take over the office of Augustus when at the end of twenty years the ruling emperors resigned. This fourfold administration, with two Augusti and two Caesars, was in theory admirable, but was not in fact practicable.

Diocletian appointed a general, Maximianus, as joint ruler. He himself took responsibility for the eastern empire and appointed

Galerius, an army officer, to the rank of Caesar. Maximianus appointed Constantius Chlorus as his Caesar, and made Milan his centre. Constantius had special responsibilities in Spain and Gaul, later adding Britain to his ambit, and made his headquarters at Trier, near the German *limes*.

In 305 Diocletian abdicated, and forced Maximianus to do likewise. Galerius and Constantius became the Augusti, and Maximinus Daza and Severus II were appointed Caesars. At this juncture the Tetrarchy broke down, for on the death of Constantius Chlorus in 306 at York his son Constantine assumed the title of Caesar and was later raised to the purple by the army. Galerius wanted peace, and this threat of civil war was overcome by his recognition of Constantine as Caesar jointly with Severus. Constantine, however, would not agree to this – it had to be Augustus or nothing. The matter was aggravated by the fact that Maximianus' son Maxentius had himself hailed Augustus, and Maximianus came out of retirement to join in the struggle for power. In 206, then, five instead of two men claimed the title of Augustus. The following year, at the end of further struggles, Severus was dead but two other contenders had appeared on the scene – Licinius and Maximinus Daza.

It is important to understand this, to unravel the sequence of coins struck by the London mint during the period. The output of the mint was quite considerable, though the subsidiary mints used by Carausius had now closed down, including that at Colchester. Coins were struck for all the main parties involved in the struggle – Diocletian, Maximianus, Constantius Chlorus, Galerius, Severus II, Maximinus Daza and Licinius I, as well as Constantine.

The only denomination struck at the London mint during this period was the follis, which was a large silver washed bronze coin introduced as part of Diocletian's monetary reform in *c.* 295.

We find that there is a short period in which coins were struck with the London mint mark, then a period of about ten years when coins were struck at London without any mint mark, then once again mint marks appear on the coins. It was for some time uncertain whether the unmarked folles were in fact struck at London, but a careful analysis of hoards of the period in Britain, France and Germany shows that the unmarked folles circulated in northern France and Britain primarily, and outside this region are only represented by small numbers of coins in hoards. There are remarkably high numbers of unmarked folles from hoards from Domquer (Somme) and Montouy (Loiret), but this does not necessarily prove that the coins were not struck at London, merely that the Channel was the key area for their circulation. Hoard evidence suggests that Trier supplied the military area of the Rhine frontier, while Lyons supplied southern Gaul and Spain, which did not have a mint of its own.

It is difficult to understand why the mint signature should disappear after Diocletian's earliest issues – it has been suggested that London fell into disgrace because she did not accord Constantius Chlorus the welcome he felt was deserved or because she had harboured so many usurpers. This theory, however, seems to be cancelled out by the fact that some early issues had the mint mark, and any punishment inflicted on London would have been inflicted from the start.

The coins of the Tetrarchy usually have as a reverse type the Genius of the Roman People and the legend GENIO POPVLI ROMANI or a variant, though, later, coins of 'Providentia' type were added (Plate 19a).

House of Constantine[95]

The London mint continued in operation under the House of Constantine, and struck a great variety of coins in the name of Constantine I, Constantine II, Crispus, Helena and Fausta. The mint seems to have closed down about 326 (Plate 19b).

Possibly the importance of London in the period under review, i.e. the Tetrarchy and the House of Constantine, should be seen in its historical setting. Severus had divided Britain up into two provinces, and under the Tetrarchy these had been increased to four, Britannia Prima, Britannia Secunda, Maxima Caesariensis, and Flavia Caesariensis. This took place at a time when the Empire was being divided up into twelve dioceses for the purposes of administration. Britain was one such diocese, and had at its head a vicarius. The vicarius seems to have been responsible not to the emperor but to the praetorian prefect in Gaul, who administered all Gaul, Spain and Britain from his centre at Trier. London seems to have been his capital, and was also the capital of one of the four provinces. We are not certain which this was, but Giraldus Cambrensis says that it was Flavia Caesariensis, which is very probably accurate since he tells us that Britannia Prima was in the west and an inscription from Cirencester seems to confirm this. It was not, however, the capital of Britain in the modern sense – the military capital was at York – and is better regarded as a major trading centre.

Coinage and Currency in the Early Fourth Century[96]

The first half of the fourth century was a period of peace and prosperity. It is well known that on sites with a long occupation early fourth century pottery is particularly abundant, and there seems to have been a period of rebuilding on many sites. To some extent, however, the economy of Britain as a whole was vitiated by the general economy of the Empire which was in a perilous state. Prices soared everywhere, as is shown by Diocletian's *De Maximis Pretiis* edict, and the inflation was accompanied by a series of complex debasements and 'reforms' of the coinage. Diocletian had introduced the follis, which was welcomed at first in Britain and widely hoarded. Some hoards consist of nothing except folles, though elsewhere mixed hoards containing pre-reform radiates show that the pre-reform coins were so abundant that, valueless as they were, they still formed a natural part of the currency. The majority of hoards of the time of the Tetrarchy, however, consist of the later reduced weight folles, which were little better than the old radiate antoniniani. The majority of the hoards of the early fourth century consist of the folles of Diocletian's reform together with some pre-reform Æ 3 and some post-reform issues. Coins of Carausius are very common in Welsh hoards of the period, such as the Llangarren hoard or the Little Orme's Head hoard, which closed with Constantine.

Hoards of precious metals are very rare, but there is a series in the west of England, starting with the Alcester hoard buried in the time of Constantine I, which may be connected with an effort to avoid taxation, since bronze was tariffed on the basis of gold, and silver coins were relatively scarce and seldom issued.

From the 330s a flood of small 'Urbs Roma' and 'Constantinopolis' coins were struck to commemorate the transfer of the Imperial capital to Constantinople, and these are extremely common in both site finds and in hoards (Plate 19d; e).

From 337 the large folles of the Tetrarchy seem to have disappeared, and hoards show that the coins in circulation were the Æ 3 of the House of Constantine. The Walford Hoard of 17,550 coins illustrates the content of the coinage at this time – apart from one coin each of Claudius II, Diocletian and Maximian there were 2,455 coins of Constantine I, 3,683 of Constantine II, 450 of Constans, 2,201 of Constantius II and 3,512 and 4,214 Constantinopolis and Urbs Roma commemoratives respectively. Thus it may be seen that almost a half of the hoard consisted of these little pieces.

Magnentius[97]

During the reign of Constans a barbarian soldier, Flavius Magnentius, became one of the foremost generals in the Empire. In 350 he rebelled, had himself proclaimed emperor, and was recognized in most of the west. He led an army against the successor of Constans, Constantius II, but was defeated and withdrew to Gaul in 352. He was defeated again in 353 and, deserted by his troops, committed suicide.

During his brief rule he issued a series of very large centionales from Trier, Lyons, Arles and Amiens which were welcomed in the western Empire (Plate 19f). They reached Britain almost immediately, and their popularity can be gauged by the fact that a hoard buried early in 351 at Croydon consisted of coins of Constans, Constantius II and Magnentius, the coins of Magnentius being 724 in number in comparison with the 1,311 of Constans and 738 of Constantius 11. One hoard of slightly later date consisted entirely of coins of Magnentius and was found at the market and temple site of Woodeaton, which has also produced a large number of his coins as site finds. Another hoard, from Balgreggan in Galloway, shows that his coins even reached southern Scotland – in this hoard, buried c. 354, there were more coins of Magnentius than of the House of Constantine.

Fel Temp Reparatio

Slightly earlier than Magnentius there had been a very large and important coinage struck by Constans and Constantius II reviving the old follis type of coin, this time under the new name of the centenionalis. These coins, slightly smaller than those of Magnentius were first struck in 348. They had the legend FEL TEMP REPARATIO (The Renewal of Happy Times) on the reverse, with a type showing a soldier spearing a fallen horseman. Other variants, with the same legend, showed a captive being dragged into a hut, the emperor in a galley with Victory, and a phoenix. These coins were quickly reduced in weight, but enjoyed an enormous popularity, and were extensively copied almost immediately after their introduction. The legend, it has been suggested, may be related to a celebration of the Secular Games in Rome (Plate 19g).

About 350 the amount of currency in circulation began to diminish.

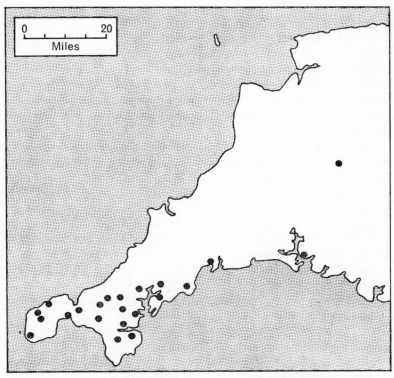

13.   Roman Coins in Cornwall, AD 251–423 (After Thomas, 1965)

Fourth Century Coins in Cornwall, and in Scotland

In the late third and early fourth centuries there is a marked up-
surge of coins in mid and west Cornwall. It seems that this is the
result of an increase in the tin working there. There are some quite
large hoards of the period, including one of 1,600 coins at Breague.
These coins were brought in from outside as a result of mining
profits, and turn up on small mining settlements such as Godrevy.
Until this time relatively little Roman currency had circulated in
the south-west except in Exeter[98](Map 13).

A very remarkable phenomenon is to be noted in Scotland in the
finds of coins of the late third and fourth centuries. As there was no
Roman source for these coins after the departure of Severus, it might
be thought at first that they were collectors' losses, many being stray

finds. However, that they entered Scotland in Roman times is borne out by the fact that large numbers of third and fourth century coins have been found on the native site of Traprain Law (East Lothian) and by the fairly large numbers of hoards of fourth century coins found generally in Scotland. These have been found even as far north as Fort Augustus (Inverness) though as one might expect the majority are in the south. Third and fourth century coins also turn up on Roman sites in Scotland, but in the absence of Romans we

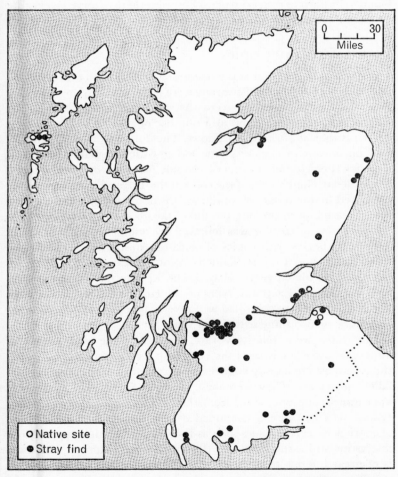

14.   Distribution of Fourth Century Roman Coins in Scotland (After Robertson, 1963)

I

must see this in terms of a squatter native occupation. Also at Birrens we find coins of Victorinus, Constantius Chlorus and Constantine I, that of Constantius being of gold.[99]

It may also be observed there is a large number of late coins in Dumfries and Galloway. This may be connected with the infiltration from Hadrian's Wall and in particular from Carlisle, but it is just possible that there was a partly Romanized community in Galloway in the fourth century, possibly of Christians, since St Ninian did not found Whithorn to convert pagans but went there to serve an existing Christian community (Map 14).

Fourth Century Copies

There was a short period at the beginning of the fourth century when cast copies of folles of the Tetrarchy were being made in the same way as the radiate antoniniani were cast at Whitchurch. Moulds for these folles have been found at a number of sites, of which the best known is that at Duston, Northants. These moulds were found in a well on a Roman cemetery site, along with a crucible fragment. Another site, Norton, produced moulds for coins of Constantine I and Helena. These copies of the coins of the Tetrarchy were probably prompted by the reduction of the weight of the follis, and may have been an attempt to prolong the life of the good-weight coins.[100]

This phase of casting was followed by one of struck imitations. This series begins with copies of coins of Constantine I, chiefly the Urbs Roma and Constantinopolis commemoratives, which as we have seen circulated very widely. Later the extremely common Æ 3 and Æ 4 'Gloria Exercitus' types of the House of Constantine were also imitated. These coins had as a reverse type two soldiers holding either one or two standards (Plate 19c).

Imitations were relatively rare, however. The real period of forgery followed the issue of the Fel Temp Reparatio coins, of which the type most commonly copied was that of the soldier spearing the fallen horseman. They were first imitated fairly soon after their appearance, and one hoard from the Nodens shrine site at Lydney (Glos.) dated to c. 364 contained a large number of them, some overstruck on earlier issues such as the Gloria Exercitus types. More interesting still is the small hoard from Covesea (Moray). This cave is of great interest to archaeologists because it has an occupation starting in the Late Bronze Age (one phase of the Bronze Age in Scotland is in fact named after it) carrying on until the late fourth century. The Covesea Hoard consisted of 9 orthodox coins along with 200 copies. In date it is more or less the same as Lydney, and it has been suggested that the orthodox coins were looted from some English source at the time of the Conspiratio Barbarica of 367, the copies being made in Scotland. This is perhaps slightly fanciful, and the copies as well as the prototypes should be regarded as English. Some were pierced for wearing, suggesting that they were not used for currency. Many of the Fel Temps were overstruck on issues only slightly earlier than those copied, and sometimes even on relatively unworn coins[101] (Plate 19h; i).

Fel Temps continued to be struck during the later fourth century, and alongside them were copies of a few later issues, including those of Magnentius, all of which are rare.

The Houses of Valentinian and Theodosius[102]

In 367 the combined forces of Irish, Picts and Saxons raided all parts of the country. Both the Count of the Saxon Shore and the Duke of Britain were killed, Hadrian's Wall was broken through and the north devastated.

Under Count Theodosius the defences of Britain were reorganized – the Wall was refortified, a chain of look-outs was built along the coast of Yorkshire and Corbridge was repaired, having been destroyed slightly earlier (c. 350) as three hoards attest. Prosperity returned to Britain for a short period, and some villas seem to have been rebuilt, at least in part. Ditchley (near Oxford) was certainly occupied in greater strength from the time of Valentinian 1 onwards (364–75) as the coin sequence shows, and even villas like Lullingstone in vulnerable Kent seem to have continued their life as before, as is attested by coins of Valens and Valentinian from the hot bath.[103] In other villas, however, such as King's Weston, coins end in 367.[104]

Strangely the Great Raids of 367 are not marked by large numbers of hoards of coins ending with Valentinian or Valens, but probably this is in part because their coins were slow to reach Britain, and coin hoards ending with the later issues of the House of Constantine can be related to this event. One coin hoard which can be related directly to the 367 raids was found at Wroxeter. Here, in a hypocaust, were found three skeletons with a small hoard of 132 coins ending with Valens. Clearly the people had crawled into the hypocaust for safety, but had suffocated.[105] Another skeleton was associated with the destruction of King's Weston villa probably later in the century again in the hypocaust. Here the man had been found in hiding and had died a violent death, as was attested by the sword cuts on his skull.[106]

About this time silver coins began to circulate more extensively in Britain, and were even imitated. These new siliquae which were being struck in reasonable numbers by Julian, Valens (Plate 19j) and Gratian circulated mainly in the south and south-west, but turn up as site finds even in Lincolnshire on relatively poor native sites like Dragonby. A few siliquae turn up in the Yorkshire signal stations, but here they are later than the majority of the southern finds, notably of Eugenius and Honorius.

The coin figures from the signal stations of Huntcliff, Goldsborough, Scarborough and Carr Naze give us some idea of the extent of the endeavours of Count Theodosius to fortify the east coast. Following, however, the usurpation of Magnus Maximus, troops were withdrawn from the forts and the coin figures decline. Goldsborough finds show that occupation must have ceased around 394, and the same story is told by Huntcliff. Scarborough seems to have been abandoned in the time of Gratian.[107]

The Abandonment of Hadrian's Wall[108]

A subject hotly contested in the first few decades of this century was that of the date of the abandonment of Hadrian's Wall. It was first suggested that the Wall forts were abandoned at the time of Magnus Maximus (AD 383–8), but this was contested and R. G. Collingwood, as a result of a survey of late fourth century coin finds from British sites, put forward the suggestion that the forts were in fact abandoned earlier, believing that the latest coins from the Wall were those of Gratian, with the exception of one notorious coin of Arcadius found near Heddon-on-the-Wall. A second school of thought, which turned to the literary evidence in the form of the Notitia Dignitatum, suggested that the Wall was held until 410.

Recent work on the coin finds shows that the old picture is, in fact, incomplete. Some sites such as Rudchester have no fourth century coins at all, other sites may end somewhere between Constans and Gratian. Some sites have produced evidence of later coins, some surface or instratified finds, as in the case of the Valentinian II from Chester or others from South Shields, Corbridge and Carlisle. There are, in addition, a few stratified coins including one of Valentinian II from Chesterholm, and further finds from the Wall forts of Birdoswald and Carrawburgh. In the case of the last named site the coins come from the Well of Coventina, and five are later than 383. In addition there is a small and very late barbarous hoard from Carrawburgh, which includes very worn coins of Valentinian and Valens.

The scarcity of late coins, notably the Theodosian issues, need not surprise us. Even on sites in the south like London, Verulamium, Pevensey, Brough or Leicester the numbers are small in comparison with those of the House of Constantine, and the majority from Verulamium came, not from the town itself, but from the abandoned theatre. This must be explained by the fact that since Theodosian coins were the first good issues to come to Britain since c. 345 they were extensively hoarded and the coins in circulation were the old Constantinian issues. Hoards which are made up of a random cross-section of the currency, such as those from Worle Camp or Redenhall, show clearly that pre-Theodosian coins predominate, with a fair number of both the Houses of Constantine and Valentinian. Constantinian coins seem to have been six times commoner than Theodosian issues, even in the south, and on Hadrian's Wall the proportion must have been much greater.

If the coin evidence points to occupation after 390, can the evidence of the Notitia support this? A recent reconsideration of this would seem to agree, and therefore we may now say that the Wall was not abandoned until after 385. This would rule out Gratian and also, it might be added, Magnus Maximus.

Fourth Century Inflation and Romano-British Coinage[109]

A complex type of analysis can be applied to a whole series of sites in order to study a particular numismatic problem. This has recently been brilliantly demonstrated by Dr Alison Ravetz in her study of fourth century inflation as shown by Romano-British coin finds.

Her analysis was based on the theory that certain types of fourth century coins are rarer than others, and when a series of a few dozen sites are studied a basic pattern emerges. Eight different periods were recognized, and instead of merely calculating percentages on the basis that each period is of equal value, the lifetime of the group is taken into consideration, and the formula for arriving at the final figure is, for each site, as follows:

$$\frac{\text{the number of coins in the group}}{\text{lifetime of the group} \times \text{total number of fourth century coins}}$$

From this it could be seen that all types seem to have penetrated British sites equally, and there was no uneven distribution of some groups due to regional variation. Where a group was absent it was because the site had a very small number of coins, too few to give a true picture. The second fact which becomes obvious is that two basic patterns emerge, an 'A' pattern and a 'B' pattern. In the 'A' pattern the most characteristic feature is the abundance of coins of period III (AD 330–46) whereas in the 'B' pattern the main period is period V (AD 364–78). Pattern 'A' is typical of old established sites and pattern 'B' is found on sites which were mainly fourth century foundations, but nevertheless occurs on some long established sites such as Woodeaton or Frilford Temple, and at Great Witcombe Villa the rise in percentages of coins in the Valentinianic period was even associated with the decline of the villa, and so it cannot be dismissed as being merely associated with the history of the sites concerned. A third pattern, with a peak in period VII (AD 388–402) is reflected in a small number of sites, such as Cirencester, Silchester, Bitterne, Brean Down or Bourton. Here fourth century structural developments cannot be associated with the increase in coin percentages.

What is the significance of such varying rises in coin percentages? The answer, for a rise in all coin percentages on a series of sites, is not a rise in trade but copper inflation. In a period of inflation more coins are in circulation, prices rise, and more coins are exchanged in transactions of no greater magnitude. This explains for example the rise in coin percentages in the mid third century.

Broadly speaking, new coinages very often meant in the fourth century devaluation of the coinage, and for a brief period a check on the number of losses. Bad coins change hands more rapidly, and are lost more frequently. The coinage patterns on fourth century sites reflect the contemporary inflation. Thus in 330 we find with the issue of Urbs Roma and Gloria Exercitus types of small, base coins there is a marked increase in losses, which is checked in 346 by the issue of a new coinage with 'Fel Temp Reparatio' reverses on a better module. In following the course of fourth century inflation it is important to remember that the value of base metal coins in the period was determined by their silver content to some extent, as in the copper coins there was a little silver. Throughout the fourth century, as analysis of the metal content of the coins has shown, there were alternate phases of better quality coins after coinage reforms and of debased issues low in silver content and small in size.

Within this pattern of inflation and debasement as reflected in the coin percentages certain anomalies occur, which are of interest in their own right. Very strangely in period III (330–46) we find that the poorest coins (those with the VICTORIAE DD AVGG Q NN legend) are actually quite rare, whereas one would expect them to be very common. Sometimes they are even outnumbered by the better coins of period IV. Possibly this could be explained by the fact that the coinage was accompanied by a devaluation, and by the presence of Constans himself in Britain in 343.

This comparative study of coin patterns on sites and their relationship to debasement and other factors is of greatest value in understanding what happened in the last days of Roman Britain.

The pattern on the 'A', 'B' and 'C' sites each tells a different story. Broadly speaking we find that between 375 and 378, although copper coins were still coming into the Rhineland and the Danube area, there was a dearth of them in Britain. There seems to have been something of a revival in the time of Theodosius. But strangely, in spite of their poor quality, they do not seem to have been often lost although on the other hand they are very common in hoards. Why should this be? The answer is not that the times were very troubled, as they no doubt were, for there is little evidence that silver coins were hoarded to the same extent, but more likely that coins were going out of use, and people were hoarding them in the hope that perhaps the latest pieces at any rate might some day be redeemed and coinage restored. Silver coins had a silver value, and were frequently clipped. Evidence suggests, in the light of hoards and site finds that coinage as a regular means of trading was extinct by about 410. Coins stopped being imported about 402.

This explains the general situation, but not that of class 'C' sites when late coins seem to increase in numbers. The pattern affects no one class of site, and is spread out evenly over the country. The pattern does not coincide with that of sites where there was a late continuity of town life either – the greatest number of Theodosian coins from St Albans came not from the area where rebuilding was being carried on into the fifth century but from the sector of the town which was decaying. Nor does it coincide with fortified sites – many Theodosian coins occur at undefended Langton, whereas few came from the fortified Malton. The explanation is that pattern 'C' is really what one would expect from the baseness of the coins, and that 'A' and 'B' are exceptional, the result of the great significance of current events. Mediums of exchange became not coins but commodities which were known to be of some fairly static value. With this we pass into the Dark Ages and the problems of coinage and currency in the subsequent period will be discussed in the next chapter.

Further Reading

The new standard work on Roman Britain is S. S. Frere's *Britannia* (1967), which now takes the place of Collingwood and Myres' *Roman Britain and the English Settlements* (1937). Valuable also for general background are the late Sir Ian Richmond's *Roman Britain* (1955) which is available as a Penguin book, and A. L. F. Rivet's *Town and Country in Roman Britain* (1958) which has splendid bibliographies.

The standard study of coinage and currency in Roman Britain is still C. H. V. Sutherland's *Coinage and Currency in Roman Britain* (1937) which, though written thirty years ago, is still broadly sound, though in detail has been modified by recent work. The standard account of the coins struck in Britain under the Romans and of the coins with types relating to Britain is Gilbert Askew's *Coinage of Roman Britain* (Reprinted 1967).

NOTES

1 For a full discussion of this see Frere, 1967, and Dudley & Webster, 1965.
2 Bushe-Fox, 1949.
3 Carson, 1959.
4 Suggested by Rivet, 1958.
5 Briscoe, 1964.
6 Askew, 1967.
7 Dudley & Webster, 1965.
8 Askew, 1967.
9 Main source Sutherland, 1937.
10 Robertson, 1956.
11 Main source Sutherland, 1935.
12 Boon, 1949.
13 Hawkes & Hull, 1947, report on the coins by C. H. V. Sutherland.
14 Dudley & Webster, 1965; Frere, 1967; Richmond, 1955 main sources.

15 Wheeler, 1943.
16 Publication by I. A. Richmond & J. W. Brailsford, 1968.
17 Pilmer, 1956.
18 Wedlake, 1958; Carson, 1951.
19 Hogg & Stevens, 1937.
20 Sutherland, 1937.
21 Fox, 1952; Fox, 1966.
22 Webster, 1966.
23 Oswald's various publications issued by Nottingham University are the main sources. The full coin list, however, has never been published, but the coins are in Nottingham University Museum. See also Webster, 1966.
24 Webster, 1966.
25 Kenyon, 1947.
26 *V.C.H. Worcs*, i, 205.
27 Webster, 1966.
28 Webster, 1966.
29 Mattingly, 1934c.
30 Pearce, 1929.
31 Mattingly, 1932b.
32 Sutherland, 1937.
33 Dudley & Webster, 1961.
34 Merrifield, 1965.
35 Wheeler, 1930.
36 Dunnett, 1966.
37 Dudley & Webster, 1965; Frere, 1967; Jarrett, 1965.
38 Jarrett, 1965.
39 Dudley & Webster, 1965.
40 Wheeler, 1923.
41 Watson, 1965.
42 Watson, 1965.
43 Nash-Williams, 1932.
44 General discussion in Simpson, 1963.
45 Ward, 1903.
46 Simpson, 1963.
47 Atkinson, 1942, for Wroxeter. For others, see Sutherland 1937.
48 Main sources Macdonald, 1936; Frere, 1967; Robertson, 1960.
49 Birley, 1961.
50 Birley, 1961.
51 Macdonald, 1936; Robertson, 1952, 1960a, 1960b.
52 Macdonald, 1906.
53 Robertson, 1960b.
54 Curle, 1911.
55 Sutherland, 1937.

I*

56 Cocks, 1927.
57 Milne, 1931.
58 Pearce, 1929.
59 Mattingly, 1932b.
60 Rivet, 1958; Frere, 1967; Richmond, 1955 etc. See also Wacher, (Ed.) 1966.
61 Rivet, 1958.
62 Wacher, 1962.
63 Boon, 1958.
64 Boon, 1958.
65 Frere, 1967.
66 Frere, 1967.
67 Rivet, 1958.
68 Birley, 1961.
69 Askew, 1967.
70 Wheeler, 1936. The possibility of a British mint reconsidered in Todd, 1967.
71 Birley, 1961.
72 Macdonald, 1936; Robertson, 1952, 1960, 1960a.
73 Askew, 1967.
74 Todd, 1967.
75 Askew, 1967.
76 Sutherland, 1937. For Southants, Hill, 1911.
77 Macdonald, 1906.
78 For external history of the coinage of the period, Mattingly, 1962.
79 Sutherland, 1937.
80 Akerman, 1844; Sutherland, 1937; Boon & Rahtz, 1966.
81 Boon & Rahtz, 1966.
82 Simpson, 1963; Watson, 1965.
83 Askew, 1967.
84 Robertson, 1960a.
85 Birley, 1965.
86 Sutherland, 1937.
87 Sutherland, 1937; Reece, 1961.
88 Hill, 1949, Hill, 1955 and in Askew, 1967; Kent, 1959; Sutherland, 1936, 1937; Mattingly, H. B., 1963.
89 Sutherland, 1936, 1937, 1956; Hill, 1949, 1955.
90 Kent, 1959, 1961.
91 Hill, 1911; Askew, 1967.
92 Bushe-Fox, 1932b.
93 Simpson, 1963; Sutherland, 1937.
94 Sutherland, 1937; Askew, 1967; Carson & Kent, 1957.
95 Askew, 1967; Carson Hill & Kent, *Late Roman Bronze Coinage*

(1960), for catalogue; Merrifield, 1965 for some general observations on the London mint.

 96 Sutherland, 1937.
 97 Sutherland, 1937.
 98 Fox, 1964; Thomas, 1966.
 99 Robertson, 1960b.
100 Sutherland, 1937.
101 Macdonald, 1931, in Benton.
102 Sutherland, 1937.
103 Meates, 1955.
104 Boon, 1950.
105 Frere, 1967.
106 Boon, 1950.
107 Mattingly, 1932a.
108 Kent, 1952.
109 Ravetz, 1965.

9 Coins and Medieval Britain

Medieval archaeology is a relatively new study in comparison with either prehistory or Classical archaeology. During the last thirty years scholars have been devoting more attention to this neglected field, and indeed during the last decade it has acquired considerable importance. Much of the basic groundwork nevertheless still remains to be done.

Rarity of Coins from Excavations

Coins are of less value in Medieval studies than in Classical archaeology. One reason for this is that coin finds are rare in excavations in comparison with the finds from Roman sites. While it is not uncommon for a Roman site which was occupied in the late third or fourth century AD to yield a dozen or more coins, and if it is a rich site possibly even hundreds, Medieval sites seldom produce more than one or two coins at the most. At the moment in Britain the record number of Saxon coins from a season's excavation is held by Winchester Cathedral, which in 1964 produced nine gold and silver Saxon coins. But Winchester is exceptional, and the excavations carried out in the city since 1963 by the Winchester Excavations Committee have probably produced more Saxon coins than had previously been found in all the excavations in England put together.[1]

There are many reasons why coins are rare on Medieval sites, the chief one being that the only denomination coined until the time of Edward 1 was the silver penny, a coin which had a high purchasing value and which was accordingly worth searching for when it was accidentally dropped, unlike some of the small, almost valueless, bronze coins of the late Roman Empire. Silver was scarce in the Middle Ages – fresh supplies were not being mined to the same extent as they had been in Roman times and the same silver was being reused. Coins in the Middle Ages were not subjected to the same vicissitudes of debasement that they suffered in the time of the inflation of the late Roman Empire. Coinage and the flow of currency remained relatively stable, though coins did not enjoy a very long circulation and were called in at regular intervals and completely reissued. In England this custom seems to have started with Eadgar in 973 and took place every six years until the time of Edward the Confessor, and thereafter every three years until the time of the Anarchy of Stephen. In the later Middle Ages such recoinages were less frequent, but the reliability of the standard of the old coins was greater after 1281 when Edward I instituted the Trial of the Pyx.[2] At this trial, held sometimes quarterly, sometimes after an inter-mission of a few years, sample coins were tested against a trial plate of fixed standard. It was in the interests of both the king and the merchants for the standard of the coinage to be maintained.

Coins for Dating Associated Material

Even when we do find coins associated with other Medieval material in excavations the evidence is not always very reliable. Thus in the excavations of the Dark Age and Saxon site at Mawgan Porth in Cornwall, a silver penny of Aethelred II of AD 990–95 was found to be of little value for dating due to confused stratigraphy, and in the past this has been true of a number of finds of Medieval coins.[3]

The most trustworthy of such finds are those found in pits or wells with large groups of material. Groups of pottery have been securely dated in this way at Old Sarum (Wilts.),[4] St John's College, Oxford[5] and at Windsor Court in the London Cripplegate.[6] In the last named case a major group of pottery was found in 1947 asso-ciated with a penny of Edward III, which provided a reliable fourteenth century date for that type of pottery.

The usual problems of coin survival of course apply, and we shall consider this again presently, but broadly speaking, it is true to say that the earlier a coin is (i.e. nearer Eadgar) the less time it is likely to have been in circulation. In the past in Medieval archaeology there has been, perhaps, too much reliance on coin finds for dating, in the absence of other evidence, and as a result some badly stratified coins have led to wrong dates being attributed to groups of pottery. One of the old Sarum pits is a case in point, where a coin find led to a whole class of pottery in Wessex, 'scratch marked' pottery, being dated to the late eleventh and early twelfth century. Thereafter contexts in which this pottery occurred were dated accordingly, setting up a whole series of equations. The dating had to be radically altered when the same pottery was found with late thirteenth century decorated jugs at Laverstock near Salisbury.[7] Similarly excavators have dated other classes of pottery to one limited period where, like 'scratch marked' pottery, they have in fact a very long life. One, the 'Selsey Common' type, was dated to about the middle of the thirteenth century on the grounds that it was first found with a coin dated to that period on the type site, and again with a coin of 1248–50 at Stratton St Margaret in Wiltshire.[8] Actually the same ware lasted into the fourteenth century, as has been established by later discoveries.[9]

Problems relating to the validity of coins as dating evidence arise at all periods in archaeology where coins are used for giving a limited dating, but in the case of Roman Britain for example the chronology of pottery is much more precise with plenty of cross-checks, from not only coins but other evidence. Coins do not merely serve to date pottery, but have also served in dating other material as well. Perhaps the most famous case of this is the Trewhiddle Hoard, which was found in Cornwall and consisted of a vast amount of metalwork including a number of coins.[10] The hoard is of major importance in Anglo-Saxon art, since the objects in the hoard were decorated in a distinctive way using chased silver inlaid with black niello and sometimes gold plate, often with tendril ornament. This style of ornament has been called the Trewhiddle Style, and the hoard has been dated by the coins to AD 875–95. The hoard must have been buried at the time of Danish threat during Alfred's reign.

Again a Saxon disc brooch from Sutton which appeared to be stylistically similar to a Viking brooch from Beeston Tor was dated to the late eleventh century by an associated coin of William I, and as a result it could be seen that the influence was due to Norwegian art of the period 1050–1100, rather than that of the Vikings of c. 875.[11]

A group of Medieval bronze tripod bowls found in Scotland have been dated by coin hoards contained in them which show they were current in the time of the Edwardian campaigns in Scotland. A hoard of Edwardian coins from Coventry and others from Ayr and Canonbie also provides us with a date for a class of ring brooches, common in Scotland[12] (Plate 27). It would be easy to extend the list.

Coin Hoards

Medieval coin hoards are of great importance in chronology and in Medieval studies as a whole, and much more will be said about them later in the chapter. But coin hoards as a means of dating the pots in which they were contained or with which they were associated is not always reliable.

In Scotland we have a series of fixed dates for pots from hoards found at Aberdeen, Ayr, Dunfermline, Penicuik and almost a dozen other places, but these few finds are hardly sufficient and only provide evidence that the types of vessel in question were in use at the time the hoards were buried. Rather more valuable is the hoard of Saxon and Norman pennies of 1067–70 from St Mary Hill Church in London which was associated with late Saxon crucible vessels. The dating of these pots was verified by another hoard from York.[13]

Occasionally stratigraphical deceits lead to unreliable associations between coins and pots, so that a coin hoard may be said to have been found with pots whereas in reality the association was fortuitous. One of the few well-excavated Medieval settlement sites in southern Scotland is at Glenluce Sands, in Wigtown, dug by Professor Jope in the 1950s. Here a hoard of coins was found, datable to about 1495, apparently buried in a building. But the excavation showed that the building was actually occupied in the early fifteenth century, and the hoard was buried, not while the building was occupied or even at the time of its destruction, but at a time when it had already become covered with the heath. Had the dating of the pottery not been known, the latest pottery from the site might have been dated to the end, not the beginning, of the century.[14]

Value of Medieval Coin Types and Legends

On the whole Medieval coins are of little value to the archaeologist or the historian from the point of view of their types or legends, though sometimes they can help the historian in an indirect way. At first sight English and Scottish Medieval coins display a monotony in their types, and an English short-cross penny to the untrained observer could have been struck in the reigns of Henry II, John, Richard I or even Henry III, while an English long-cross penny is often difficult to attribute to a particular one of the first three Edwards, even by someone who is relatively familiar with numismatics.

Early in this century numismatists made a very detailed study of varieties of Medieval British coinage, and as a result have been able to work out a complex classification based on such details as variations in the forms of letters, initial marks or the treatment of the king's crown.[15] Unlike the other aspects of Medieval archaeology the study of English coinage has been developing over a long period of time, to the credit of British numismatists. Except in a few special series, work on Medieval coinage on the Continent tends to lag behind.

Coins and Dark Age Britain

An important problem which has troubled British numismatists and archaeologists this century is the question of what happened in Britain in the fifth and sixth centuries AD. It is not strictly true to say that we do not have any historical records for the period, but unfortunately the accounts that do relate to the phase are often mythical and were written long after the events that they describe, and for this reason it is extremely difficult to separate truth from legend. Archaeology, however, has shed a great deal of light on the period as a whole, and terms such as 'The Lost Century' can no longer be applied – the Dark Ages are not as dark as they seemed to scholars earlier this century. In some ways we know more about the period than we do about some other aspects of the later Middle Ages.[16]

One important question that affects our thinking about the Dark Ages is whether or not some kind of coinage was still being struck in Britain. If this was in fact the case, then it would point to the survival of a central authority or authorities responsible for such a coinage, and would also tell us that trade continued to flourish internally in Britain. Archaeology has shown that in the period under consideration there was certainly a continental trade that even brought amphorae from the east Mediterranean, and other products from France and the Rhineland to British shores.[17]

It is perhaps important to realize that at the end of the fourth century and the beginning of the fifth we do not find complete social disintegration in Britain as was once believed. In spite of the threats of barbarian raids in the fourth century Britain was perhaps richer than it had been throughout the Roman occupation, a fact attested by the considerable quantities of fourth century pottery and evidence of Constantinian and even Valentinianic rebuilding on numerous sites. Even into the fifth century there was some continuity of town occupation – it seems that at St Albans not only was there some occupation but even civic building which included the construction of a water supply system and the laying of mosaics. There is similar evidence for the continuity of towns from other sites, most notably Carlisle, York, Leicester, Chester, Winchester, Silchester and Cirencester, together with Canterbury and less certainly Exeter.[18] We find, too, even after 367 the villa system seems to have continued, and Longton (East Yorks.) after being damaged in the raids of that year was repaired. At East Denton (Lincs.) a new villa was built. Another Lincolnshire villa, that of Great Casterton, had a mosaic pavement laid there at the end of the century. What is important, then, to remember, is that by the late fourth century *Romanitas* was deeply rooted, and we shall see it as an undercurrent re-emerging after the barbarian raids.

Britain, however, had started experiencing the troubles that afflicted Romania as early as the third century or even the end of the second when the building of town walls commenced. After a period of recovery at the time of the House of Constantine there was a period of prosperity until the great raids of 367, when in a Conspiratio Barbarica Irish, Picts and Saxons made devastating raids in all parts of the country. This was followed by another period of recovery under Theodosius, but the period of Roman control in Britain was coming to an end. The date of 410 can no longer be accepted as one at which the final collapse of Roman organization took place in Britain. A date nearer 415 seems more likely for the final abandonment of Roman Britain to its own devices.

The Coin Situation in the Early Fifth Century

In order to understand the problem of Dark Age coinage we must establish the point at which Roman coins ceased being imported to Britain from the Continent. In this connection mention has already been made of Ravetz' study of the percentages of coins on fourth century sites (p. 245–7) which has clearly demonstrated that coinage as a regular means of trading was extinct by 410. After 400 coins do not seem to have been imported to Britain in any numbers.

The last Roman silver to turn up in Britain are the Milan 'Virtus Romanorum' siliquae, which were struck in AD 402, though we do find some silver coins of Constantine III, and three Trier mint siliquae of Honorius from Telering, Coleraine and St Pancras. The last bronze coins are the 'Victoria' and 'Salus' types of 396 and 402, with the exception of three coins struck between 404 and 417. This does not mean that the coins went out of circulation immediately, but they were probably out of circulation by *c.* 430.

The next date we have for coinage in England is that for the early Saxon gold coinages and the subsequent coinage of silver sceattas. The date of the start of these coinages is in dispute, but as we shall see a date of *c.* 670 seems the most probable. Can we then fit any coins into the intervening period between 430 and 670?[19]

Very possibly there were some barbarous copies, imitating Roman coins. At one time it was thought that the barbarous radiates and later the Fel Temp Reparatio imitations were struck over a long period, continuing into the Dark Ages. It is now known, however, that extreme barbarism is not necessarily an indication of late date, and as far as the 'radiates' are concerned there is no evidence to suggest that they were struck later than the pieces which they were copying. The majority, if not all, belong to the third century.[20] From this some people have argued that the minims and other imitations of fourth century diademed bust coins are also contemporary with their prototypes, and do not outlive the fourth century.

Three sites are important in this respect, Bourton-on-the-Water, Lydney and Richborough. The stratigraphical evidence for fifth century barbarous minims from Bourton (Glos.) is unreliable, but the evidence from Lydney is more difficult to interpret. Here in 1928–9 Wheeler excavated a temple of Nodens with an associated guest house, which seems to have been built at the end of the fourth century. The coins in question consist of a hoard of 'minimissimi' seemingly deposited in the bath house of the hostelry on top of a broken tesselated pavement. The room in which these coins were found was dated by a coin of Gratian to 367–83 or later.[21] But the dating for the coin hoard is inferential, and based on the assumption that if the pavement was new in *c.* 370 and was badly damaged when the hoard was deposited then the hoard could not have been earlier than the end of the fourth century or the beginning of the fifth. The third important find is the Richborough Hoard, which is important because many of the minims look like Saxon sceattas – so similar in fact that it was even suggested by one authority that they were 'the coinage of Hengist and Horsa with their Jutes'.[22] If we can rely on stratigraphy the hoard should date to the third century, which is difficult to accept since some of the coins seem to have radiate obverses coupled with reverses derived from Fel Temp Reparatio coins of the fourth century. This in itself would suggest that copies were not invariably contemporary with the coins that they are copying. Perhaps the question of whether the minims were being struck in the fifth century or not should be left unanswered, for it is unwise to argue that, because we do not have any coins that were undoubtedly struck in the fifth or early sixth century, none were in fact struck.[23]

To try to find parallels on the continent is an unwise procedure. Gaul, for example, retained its Roman ways much longer than Britain, even in the teeth of Visigothic invasion, as we can see from the letters of Sidonius Apollinaris. Certainly we find elsewhere in Europe little evidence of copper coinage, except perhaps in urban areas of North Africa and in Italy, where one might expect coinage to continue, and there seems to have been a coinage struck at Lyons in the period under review. Gold coins, on the other hand, were being struck, mostly copies of Roman solidi. The Visigoths in southern Gaul struck coins of this sort from c. AD 440 on. But not until the second half of the sixth century do we find the barbarians striking coins in their own names, the earliest issues being the Visigothic tremisses of France and Spain. Solidi until the time of Heraclius (610–41) imitated the Byzantine. One early attempt to introduce solidi and tremisses in the name of a barbarian ruler, the Merovingian Theodebert, about 535, ended in failure. The majority of the gold coins of barbarian Europe stemmed from the solidi stellati of the eighth century Lombards in Italy.[24]

Sutton Hoo and Crondall

If we are forced to admit that there is no evidence, either positive or negative, for a Dark Age coinage in Britain, when were the first Anglo-Saxon coins struck? There are two important hoards which require to be studied in this connection. The first of these comes from Sutton Hoo in East Anglia, perhaps the most famous site in British archaeology apart from Stonehenge. Here in 1939 was found a royal Saxon ship burial containing a unique collection of treasures, including gold jewellery inlaid with garnets, silver bowls, and elaborate arms and armour. Its importance was inestimable. It shows that there was flourishing in seventh century East Anglia a rich kingdom with contacts extending as far afield as the Byzantine Empire, Scandinavia, the Frankish kingdom and Coptic Alexandria. Hanging bowls from the ship show that native British products were in use in areas settled by the Saxons, and the ship itself gives us information about the kind of vessels used by the pagan Anglo-Saxons. From the richness and artistry of the objects we have learned much about the final flowering of pagan Saxon art, in part derived from that of Kent but in which other elements of a more exotic nature are combined to produce a distinctive style. East Anglia was not the richest of the early Saxon kingdoms, and we can infer that equal, or even greater splendours were to be found in the courts of Northumbria, Wessex or Kent. [25]

Although the burial's date depends on a number of factors the most important of these is a hoard of gold coins found in a fine purse decorated with a gold frame and fittings, with garnet and glass inlay. This purse contained thirty-seven gold coins, three unstruck blanks, and two small ingots. All the coins were struck by the Merovingian Franks, but only one can be attributed to a particular king, and was issued under Theodebert I (AD 595–612). Our knowledge of Merovingian coinage is very imperfect, largely due to the fact that over 2,000 mints appear to have been issuing coins. Thirty per cent of the legends on the coins are illegible or dubious, and nearly all of those that can be identified are the names of mints and moneyers, not kings. Most of the work so far carried out on the series has been concerned with identifying these mints and moneyers, not with chronology, and due to the large numbers of mints in operation at one time and the blundered copying and recopying of types, dating according to style is more or less useless, and the other badly needed chronological indicators such as hoard sequences or die links are largely lacking.

Until 1960 it was generally held that the coins dated from the period 650–70,[26] but in that year Lafaurie of the Bibliothèque Nationale's Cabinet des Médailles in Paris, where most of the Merovingian gold coins are kept, set forth a chronology based on a hoard found at Escharen near Nijmegen. On the basis of this, he suggested the date for the Sutton Hoo coins should be c. 625. Lafaurie's date has met with the approval of Dr Kent of the British Museum, on other grounds, but there are still adherents of the later date for the hoard. One interesting feature of the Sutton Hoo hoard is that all the coins are different, no two coins of the same mint being present. This is remarkable, and suggests that the coins represent an artificial selection, for a normal mercantile hoard would show concentrations of coins of one or two mints. The mints represented at Sutton Hoo are scattered all over the territory of the Merovingian Franks, and it seems very likely that they represent a diplomatic present, selected in Merovingian France (and presumably then including one of the latest issues) as a gift for an East Anglian king. It does not follow from this that the date of the ship burial is necessarily as early, for the 'hoard' could have been kept as treasure for some time before it was deposited in the ship. The fact that it was contained in a purse is not sufficient evidence to assume that the coins were currency, for other valuables were kept in purses. The presence of blanks at first suggests that provision was made for striking coins, but the blanks are underweight and would probably have been rejected for coins, though quite easily could have been used as a means of exchange on the basis of their metal content. If it were a diplomatic present from France one need not be surprised it contained no native coins, even if they were being struck. If it represents currency in East Anglia *c*. 625–30 or slightly later, then the absence of local issues might argue that there was no Anglo-Saxon coinage before that date. In further defence of this it has been claimed that down to the mid seventh century Roman, Byzantine and Merovingian coins were used as jewellery in gold and garnet mounts, but no Saxon coins have been found so used. Sutton Hoo then offers negative rather than postive evidence for the date of the earliest Saxon coinages. It is nevertheless important to remember that the earliest Saxon gold coins were struck in eastern Kent with strays along the Thames valley. East Anglia, apart from two irregular pieces of solidus size, has produced no Anglo-Saxon gold coins at all. On the other hand it has yielded a scatter of Merovingian coins, and the obvious continental contacts that the kingdom enjoyed would lead one to expect Merovingian, rather than Saxon, coins from the burial.[27]

The other important find is the Crondall Hoard, which was discovered in 1828 and which consisted of a hundred gold coins, two jewelled ornaments and chains, an ancient forgery of a coin and three blank flans.[28] Among the surviving coins in the hoard are

  Fig. 44 Anglo-Saxon gold coin from the Crondall Hoard

twenty-one Merovingian and continental gold coins, but none of these can be dated very precisely, though one coin, at one time believed to have been a copy of a coin of Leo (451–74) is now known to be a Lombard copy of a tremissis of Phocas (602–10).

This coin, unlike the others in the hoard, was quite worn, suggesting that the hoard could not have been earlier than AD 650–70. Some scholars, including Dr Kent, believe that the hoard cannot be earlier than AD 675 or could even be later (Figure 44).[29]

This does not essentially imply that Anglo-Saxon gold coins were not being struck before this date. On the basis of a study of the finds of Merovingian gold coins in Britain it has been suggested that between 550 and 575 large numbers of Merovingian coins were being absorbed by southern England, and towards the end of the century coins were being struck here imitating these prototypes and sometimes executed by Merovingian craftsmen. These pieces, along with imitations of Roman models, lasted till c. 675 when it is generally accepted that the silver sceattas were struck. If one dates the gold coinage to about 670 then it would mean that there were only a few years between the first gold coins and the change over to silver, which seems strange in view of the number of gold coins struck.

A coin also exists with the legend CIOLH and this name has been identified with that of Ceol of Wessex. If this is so, the coin would therefore have been struck between AD 591 and 597. A medallet ound at St Martins, Canterbury with the name of Bishop Liuhardus is datable to the mid sixth century, but it is not a coin in the strictest sense.[30]

The earliest Franco-Saxon coins are the outcome of a period of trade between the Continent and Britain, most notably north-east Kent. Here we find, from 575, Kentish style jewellery which had Frankish as well as native (Romano-Celtic enamel work) elements in it. Other evidence for the trade takes the form of Gallic and Rhenish glass, Byzantine, quasi-Byzantine and Merovingian coins, bronze bowls and amethyst beads of Egyptian origin. Nearly all the gold imported coins come from east Kent. Although there is no tangible proof that this coinage started flowing in a steady trickle from 525, the date of the earliest coins, there is good reason to suppose that from 575 there was a growing import trade.[31]

Apart from a commercial contact between Kent and the Frankish kingdom, we have evidence of diplomatic relations, too, at this period. Charibert i, who ruled in Paris between 561 and 567, allowed his daughter to marry Ethelbert of Kent who came to the throne just after 561. Therefore it seems fairly reasonable to suppose that the earliest Saxon gold coins are derived from the imports of this period, and are only a little later than them, even though the Crondall Hoard is not earlier than 670.[32]

The Earliest Silver Coinage of England

The earliest silver coinage of England must begin *c*. 695, and the transition from the gold tremissis to the silver sceatta must have been very rapid. This is clearly demonstrated by a series of coins imitating the Victoria Augg solidi of the late fourth century which, though similar in types, vary in metal from good gold to silver. It is also demonstrated by the 'Pada' series which was obviously not struck over a long period but which was coined in a variety of electrum alloys and then in silver. There is an identical transition from gold to silver among the Franks slightly earlier, i.e. *c*. 680, which was an equally brief process.[33]

There is a valuable chronological equation between these early sceattas and the Kentish school of disc brooches, as one series of sceattas, the 'Celtic Cross' type, is in fact stylistically related to the step pattern cruciform brooches, and indeed one coin is identical in type to the design on the famous Kingston brooch. A very interesting point about these early sceattas is their dependence on Roman prototypes, suggesting that Roman coin hoards were being unearthed and the types imitated, in preference to the types of contemporary Merovingian or Byzantine coins. This says much for the continuity of tradition in Britain through from the Roman period. The problem of the Richborough Hoard again arises in this context, since some of the coins were almost identical in type to early Anglo-Saxon sceattas, so much so that Derek Allen suggested a date of *c*. 600 for the hoard, though this would even so be too early for the first sceattas.

The Significance of Sceatta Distributions

The distribution of sceattas is interesting archaeologically.[34] As one might expect the main concentration lies to the south of the Fosse, with densities of coins round London and the Thames estuary, Cambridge and its environs, and Southampton (Plate 28a). There is one remarkable group of finds from Whitby, suggesting an Anglo-Saxon nucleus in the area at the end of the seventh century or the beginning of the eighth. The 'London' type of sceattas are very common round Southampton, suggesting that these coins travelled to France rather than the Low Countries. One interesting group is Frisian, and is not often found in Britain. The occurrence of Frisian coins in Britain, and conversely purely Anglo-Saxon types on the

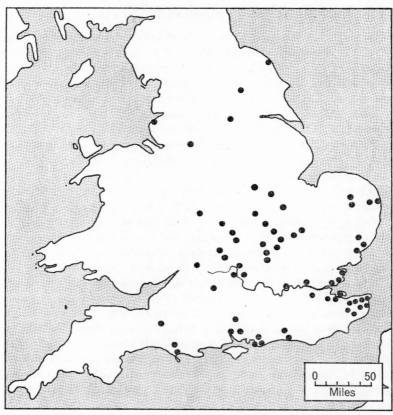

15.   Distribution of Early Anglo-Saxon Sceattas in England (After Hill, 1952)

Continent, sheds interesting light on Frisian trade at this period. Already it seems possible that they were building up an important cloth trade, and coin distributions tell us a lot about their markets. They had depots round the coasts of the Channel, Atlantic, North Sea and even the Baltic, and their main trading centre was Duurstede, where there was a meeting point for three important trade routes. Here the Frisian sceattas were coined. From Duurstede come several important sceatta hoards.

Recently a metrical analysis of 'Porcupine' sceattas was made, and has shown that although isolated 'porcupines' are found in England, they do not turn up in hoards and were in fact struck on the continent between c. 720 and 740, except for a few special types (namely type D, the 'VOIC' series and 'plumed bird' types) which appear to be English derivatives. Probably English silver was exported to Frisia, and among the products imported to Britain from there was Rhenish pottery and wine.[35]

In passing, it is interesting to see that there was a marked increase in the hoarding of sceattas in the eighth century, nearly all hoards being concentrated in the south-east.[36]

Byzantine Coins in Britain

We may now turn to the interesting question of Byzantine influence in English coinage, and the problem of Byzantine coin finds from Britain.[37] Historical sources show us that there was a great deal of Byzantine cultural influence in Britain from the end of the seventh century, probably transmitted from Italy and the west. The influence took many forms, but is particularly marked in the sphere of art. In Anglo-Saxon coinage, too, there is some borrowing from Byzantine models, though of course it is not necessary to have a widespread influx of a certain series of coins for them to be imitated.

In Britain the imitation of Byzantine coins seems to have been an irregular process, and it is evident that Byzantine coins were not reaching Britain in large numbers. There are about ninety finds, nearly all of them, like the Greek coins described in an earlier chapter (p. 116f), strays. Only two hoards actually include Byzantine coins, one a very dubious and late hoard from London consisting of nine coins covering a period of seven hundred years, the other being the famous Viking hoard from Cuerdale in Lancashire. Of the other finds only two coins from Ilchester are undoubtedly ancient losses. The distribution pattern, and the wide range of dates from Anastasius (491–518) to Andronicus II (1282–95) tell us little. Nearly all these coins are of silver or bronze, though there are a few gold, the majority of these dating from the late sixth century, and consisting of coins of Justinian I (527–65) to Heraclius (610–13). In addition there is one eighth century solidus of Leo III from Westerham, Kent.

One series of coins in the Crondall Hoard seems to have been derived from Byzantine models, through a Merovingian intermediary stage. These are derived from the 'Cross on Steps' coins of Heraclius or Constans II. Another small group of coins of this period is derived from a reverse type of a solidus of Valentinian II, and the same type was borrowed later by Ceolwulf of Mercia and Alfred of Wessex.

On the whole, however, Byzantine coin influence is rare in Anglo-

Saxon coinage, and this is hardly surprising in view of their rarity in northern Europe as a whole. They do not turn up in Norway and Sweden before the mid tenth century, except in the Norwegian Hon hoard, where they were made into ornaments. On the other hand there are 36,000 Moslem coins in Sweden alone. During the period 950–1070 we have about four hundred Byzantine coins from Scandinavia, but these probably relate to the Viking trade route to Constantinople. Even the Byzantine revival under the Macedonians had little effect on coinage in Scandinavia.

Offa's Dinar[38]

Offa is perhaps the first great name in Anglo-Saxon history, a man who became so important that Charlemagne even felt him a worthy contemporary. Offa is important to the numismatist because he was the first king to issue a major series of pennies instead of the earlier sceattas, though the change-over is not due to him but to Heaberht and Ecgberht, two contemporary kings of Kent who followed the example of the Frankish king Pippin and went over to a larger, thinner coin. The change in France took place about 755, in Kent some twenty years later. Offa took over the Canterbury mint and put his own name on the coins about 784, having subjected Heaberht and Ecgberht (Plate 28b).

It is not without significance that Charlemagne imitated some of the coins of Offa, and conversely that Offa, later in his reign, changed the weight of his coins to conform with that of the coins of Charlemagne. Stylistically the coins of Offa are remarkable, and attempts have been made to see parallels in them with the Carolingian. But Carolingian coins are singularly uninspired artistically, even though Charlemagne and his successors were responsible for an artistic renaissance in France. Many of the elements in the style of Offa's coins are reminiscent of the Classical, just as earlier Saxon coins had borrowed from Roman coins more directly. There are elements of the Lindisfarne Gospel style of Northumbria, or again of the Mercian stonecarvers' art. Coins of Offa travelled far and wide. Two reached Russia, and others have been found in Rome, or in hoards from Norway.

The most remarkable coin of Offa, however, is a gold piece, imitating a dinar of the Caliph Al Mansur struck in AD 774. This unique coin was found in Italy, and its significance has puzzled numismatists and historians. Why should Offa wish to issue a gold coin imitating an Arab piece? Presumably for foreign trade, unless it means that the kind of gold coins that were then circulating in Britain were in fact Arab dinars. One suggestion has been that it was a 'mancus' or gold piece equivalent to thirty pennies sent to the Pope as a tribute 'in gratitude for the victories of the Kingdom which he held by the support of St Peter'.

Viking Coin Hoards in Britain[39]

An extremely interesting story is told by coin finds which relate to to the period of the Vikings, and it is perhaps not out of place if we consider these in some detail here.

In Britain in the early ninth century we find two distinct coinages, one based on the silver penny, used in the south, and the other based on the small copper styca which was in use in Northumbria and the north[40] (Plate 28c). No pennies are found in hoards of stycas, such as those from Kirkoswald, Hexham or York, and very few stycas in the hoards of pennies, though strays sometimes have turned up in London. The group of Northumbrian styca hoards relates to the troubles which culminated in Northumbria being overrun by the Vikings, and Aella and Osberht are the last kings whose coins appear in the hoards. After this the stycas are replaced by the series of Viking pennies struck in York (Plate 28d).

At first the threat of the Vikings did not seem unduly to trouble the south, at least not to the extent of precipitating widespread hoarding. The few hoards that do date from this time are interesting, since they contain deniers of Charlemagne and even sometimes papal issues, showing British contacts overseas.

From the 870s hoards increase in number, most of these being found in northern England with some from Ireland and the Isle of Man. There are a few such hoards from northern Scotland, such as one notable find from Iona, and others from the Northern Isles. Wessex, standing alone against the Viking raids, needless to say did not have an unwavering faith in Alfred. As a result hoarding was fairly widespread. Some of the hoards, like the Trewhiddle Hoard already mentioned or the Gravesend Hoard, are associated with contemporary objects.

Apart from these 'domestic' hoards in Britain we have another series which represent Viking loot hoards. The most famous of these is the Cuerdale Hoard from Lancashire, which consisted of more than seven thousand coins and nearly a thousand ounces of silver. Other important hoards of this category include those from Harkirke, also Lancashire, Goldsborough in Yorkshire and Bangor in Caernarvonshire. All these hoards contained Viking coins along with Mercian and Wessex pennies, Frankish deniers and a few Arabic silver coins, not to mention silver bullion in ingot form. The presence of southern pennies indicates commerce between the Saxons and the Danes in the peaceful southern half of the Danelaw.

Viking Hoards in Scandinavia and Russia

The pattern of Viking hoards outside Britain is much more interesting, and tells us a great deal about the Vikings' thirst for silver, which was indeed one of the main motives behind their voyages and travels, whether as raiders, traders or mercenaries. During the period of Viking activity they seem to have accumulated a remarkable amount, and well over a thousand hoards of gold and silver have been found.[41] From Gottland alone come 93,500 coins and 16,000 coin fragments, and one hoard from Stora Velinge, found in 1936, contained 2,673 Arabic coins and a silver arm ring. The Vikings themselves had no native supply of silver, and all of it was obtained from outside.

The composition of the hoards taken as a whole from Scandinavia gives us a good idea of the source of this wealth, and of the relative importance of different currencies in Europe. About 85,000 of the coins were those struck in the Moslem world, and were imported in the ninth and tenth centuries. In addition there are some 70,000 from German mints, and 40,000 from England.

This picture is further expanded by a study of the coin hoards from Russia, where some of the hoards are enormous. In 1868 on the River Oka at Murom no fewer than 11,077 Kufic coins of the ninth and early tenth centuries were found, together with about 12 lb. of coin fragments, and it seems that much of the silver was imported into Scandinavia from Islamic territory south and east of the Caucasus and the Caspian.

The distribution of Kufic Coins

The presence of Kufic (i.e. Moslem) coins in the Viking hoards raises the question of the distribution of Kufic coins themselves in Europe. Although the Kufic coins in the Scandinavian hoards seem to have come from the east by way of Russia, it is true to say that Kufic coins had a very wide distribution in Europe.

From the ninth century on, gold from the Arab world poured into the west in exchange for slaves, and some went back again to the Arab lands in exchange for spices. Some, too, flowed into Byzantium.

In Britain Anglo-Saxon monetary policy tried to prevent the flow of Kufic coins and their circulation, and those that did reach this country were usually recoined. This was due to Eadgar's policy of banning the circulation of foreign silver as part of his reforms. It is a mark of his success that foreign coins, and in particular Kufic coins, usually only turn up in areas outside the control of the English kings. Until recently it was believed that all the Kufic coins that reached Wessex were restruck by the English kings, but in 1964 on the Assize Courts site at Winchester a Kufic dirhem of Ismail ibn Ahmad (dated AD 898) was found stratified on the cobbled surface of a late Saxon street.[42]

Apart from the Viking hoards already referred to, Kufic coins have turned up elsewhere in Britain, associated with Viking material, most notably in the Northern Isles. The date of these Kufic coins in the British Isles lies between 870 and 950, and it has been argued very convincingly that they were exported from the Baltic from about 890 (Plate 25).

English Coins in Viking Hoards

It is one of the ironies of archaeology that there are more Anglo-Saxon coins of the tenth century in Copenhagen than there are in the British Museum, and the Stockholm Cabinet is vastly more important than the British Museum collection for the period. Even an 1881 catalogue was able to describe 8,000 different pennies of Ethelred II and Cnut (Plate 28e). This is because so many Anglo-Saxon coins have been found in Viking hoards.[43]

Before the time of Ethelred II some English coins turn up in Viking hoards – one mid tenth century hoard from Terslev in Denmark which consisted of 1,751 coins contained ten English coins. The majority of the Anglo-Saxon coins from the Scandinavian hoards, however, date from the end of the century, the time of the intensified Viking raids on this country. Quite probably one of the reasons for these attacks was the fact that Kufic silver was dwindling away to a trickle, and another supply of the metal had to be sought. The earliest Anglo-Saxon coins are in fact tribute money paid by the English, but after the time of Cnut's accession Anglo-Saxon coins still came to Scandinavia as payment to the soldiers employed by Cnut and his successors. After 1051 there is a sudden drop in the number of English coins in Scandinavia, and in that year, so we are told by the Anglo-Saxon Chronicle, Edward the Confessor disbanded the last remaining Scandinavian soldiers.

The reason why the supply of Kufic silver dried up probably lies in the crisis in the silver supply in the Islamic world about 970 and, though there was a revival for a short while, the Islamic metal resources had run out permanently by 1012. The problem had been further complicated by the fact that the Volga-Baltic route had been blocked by Kiev princes, and during the short period of the recovery the route that the coins took was a different one, through Poland, with a correspondingly different series of mints indicating a different centre for the supply.

British Hoards in the Tenth and Eleventh Centuries

In Britain in the tenth century we find that a period of peace in the south under the rule of Alfred, Edward the Elder and Aethelstan meant few hoards were being buried, or rather more hoards were being recovered. An exception to this is a group of four hoards of tenth century date from Chester, which suggests that it was an important centre and was acting as a clearing house for the Viking kings of Dublin. Similarly there are a number of hoards from the neighbourhood of the Danish settlements round Dublin.

Although Kufic coins were not in circulation to any great extent in Wessex, Alfred was certainly influenced by the design of these pieces when he struck pennies without his portrait. The reason for this lies again with the Viking fondness for these coins, and the Anglo-Saxon pieces were struck with an eye for the foreign market. Under Edward the Elder there was a marked revival of coin art, which can be paralleled with a contemporary artistic revival in other fields. From this period on until the Norman Conquest there are fewer hoards in Britain, except for some in the peripheral regions such as Iona, which may be connected with Viking activity.

Burghs and Mints in Late Saxon England[44]

In late Saxon England it was first the custom and then a necessity to put the mint name and the moneyer's name on coins. This fact is very important, as it sheds a great deal of light on the burghs in late Saxon England. By comparing the relative outputs of different burghs it is possible to determine which had thriving markets and trade and which had not. Similarly by tracing the relative output of mints over a long period it is possible to trace the fluctuation of the trade of individual burghs. Thus we can see how at one time Chester was important, while at another Exeter was particularly thriving. On the other hand, the picture is not always an accurate one due to the chance survival of coins, and though documentary evidence clearly shows that Norwich, Thetford, Lincoln and Hereford were very important burghs in the period, there is no confirmation of this from coin evidence. Another important facet of this study emerges when we remember that one of the essential qualifications of a burgh was the possession of a mint, and indeed the opening of a mint in a town would elevate it to burgh status. This is perhaps a rather generalized statement, as of course there are many subtle variations in the meaning of the term 'burgh' which originally meant a fortified place which also had a market, but broadly speaking the possession of a mint is a more convenient way of recognizing a burgh than the characteristics of fortifications, special legal procedures, royal administration or special tax liabilities. It is difficult, for example, to regard as a burgh in the strictest sense South Cadbury hillfort which was an emergency mint during the time of the Danish raids on account of its security and replaced the regular mints of Bruton, Crewkerne and Ilchester.

Trade was undoubtedly important not only between the Continent and Britain but within the country itself. Such trade, not necessarily carried on only by traders for commodities like metal, but also by farmers for livestock or seed, often involved quite distant regions, and this is attested by the finds of coins of remote mints in hoards. One hoard from Shaftesbury contained only coins that had been struck in the Danelaw.

In the period under consideration we find that London was far more important than any other centre producing coins. It seems to have supplied about a quarter of the country's coinage. After it in importance came York, which supplied about a tenth, then Lincoln and Winchester. Thereafter, with variations in importance at different periods, come Exeter, Chester, Thetford and Norwich.

Anglo-Saxon coins are useful in many other ways. In the *Anglo-Saxon Chronicle* there is an entry which tells us that the Danish army burnt Wilton and 'came to' Salisbury. The coins of the Wilton mint stop abruptly just at that time and the Salisbury mint replaced it, the Wilton moneyers signing the Salisbury coins. This attests the abandonment of the badly defended valley site in favour of Old Sarum, which was of course the predecessor in turn of Salisbury. Anyone who has stood on the defences of Old Sarum or attempted to climb the banks of the fortifications will understand the motives behind the transfer of the mint.[45]

Again we often have interesting proof in the form of coins of historical statements sometimes considered dubious by historians. In the twelfth century monks at Peterborough claimed that Eadgar had allowed the monastery to strike coins. This was long doubted until recently some unique coins of Aethelred II and Cnut struck at Peterborough were rediscovered in museums on the continent. Admittedly as yet no coins of Peterborough of Eadgar have come to light, but as Eadgar was responsible for opening large numbers of mints at the time of his reform to which few mints were added later (some by Edward the Confessor), it seems reasonable to suppose that such coins were in fact struck but are now lost [46]

Anglo-Saxon Coins and Philology

Although not strictly speaking archaeology, valuable information can be derived in the fields of epigraphy and philology from the legends on Anglo-Saxon coins. Thus an Anglo-Saxon coin has proved that the name of Ipswich is actually derived from a personal name, Gip. Similarly we can gain clues about pronunciation from the spelling on Anglo-Saxon coins – for example Alfred's name can appear as Aelbred or Aelfred, and Sigered can appear as Sired. Again. there have been disputes concerning the authenticity of a copy of an eleventh century charter, because some names use a Aegal- form rather than Aethel-. This however can be seen in a correct light by studying the forms of moneyers' names on the coins of Ethelred II, which employ both forms. Hints as to dialect, too, may be obtained from name forms – at Chester, names seem to begin Ele- rather than Aethel-.

At a later date we can trace the survival of certain Saxon letter forms, such as Wen (Þ) which is always used on the coins of William the Conqueror, whose name reads PILLELM, and which continues in use until the time of Stephen, though the W form is also used.[47] (Plate 28f).

A parallel story is told by the moneyers' names in the Norman period. At first we find they have Saxon and Scandinavian names (like Brand, Godwine or Colblanc), and this situation seems to last until the time of the Anarchy of Stephen, but with Henry I we begin to see foreign names appearing, like Germane, Gilpatric, Rodbert or Willelm. Jewish names seem to start appearing later. They are very common on the coins of Henry III, and to a lesser extent under John and Richard I. The earliest occurrence of Jewish names seems to be under Henry II, one Sawul striking coins for him at the Gloucester mint. Also worthy of mention in this context is the fact that until the end of the eleventh century christian names only were used, but from then on we find the initial of the surname appearing sporadically.

Coin Hoards and the Norman Conquest[48]

As might be expected the Norman Conquest produced an outbreak of hoarding. About thirty hoards are associated with William I, and the pattern is especially interesting since the area of hoarding shifted further north and east as the Norman advance affected these areas. Within the general pattern certain regional groups can be distinguished. There is one group in Sussex which must be associated with the time of the invasion and which is very valuable to the numismatist, as it produces a good cross-section of late Saxon coinage. Another group from York and the north is probably connected with William's devastation of the northern Earldoms in the period 1069–75. Yet another group of hoards from the Midlands and Isle of Ely possibly has some connection with the Saxon rebellion of 1071 which is associated with Hereward the Wake.

Norman coinage did not replace the Anglo-Saxon immediately, but the process was fairly rapid, and hoard evidence shows us that by 1080 the pennies of William had generally replaced the Anglo-Saxon issues. During the eleventh century English coins travelled fairly extensively, even turning up in a hoard of *c.* 1100 from Piep in the Ukraine, and reciprocally we find evidence of trade with Germany, Flanders, France and Italy in the form of imported coins.

Medieval English Trade with the Low Countries[49]

In this and the following section it is proposed to examine two interesting facets of Medieval trade as reflected in coinage. English trade with the Low Countries at the time of the 'Hanseatic League' is attested by finds of English coins abroad and by the way in which English coin types were imitated there. The second section describes

K

a reverse situation – the significance of foreign coins found in late Medieval England.

In an earlier section the origin of trade between Britain and the Low Countries was discussed. This trade, once established, continued to a greater or lesser extent until 1053, when the Baltic and the north of Europe was severed from contacts with Britain. During the period of the Norman kings British trade was directed towards France, and only a few English coins reached lands further north.

During this period in north Germany new trading cities were founded which were intended from the start to conduct trade and take commercial enterprise out of the hands of the Flemish and Scandinavian traders. Out of these towns grew the Hanseatic League.

English trade with the Hanse began again in the early thirteenth century, following negotiations with Cologne merchants which had taken place in the reigns of Henry II, Richard I and John.

From 1207 until the end of his reign John entered many trans-actions with merchants in the Rhineland and in the Netherlands. From this date we find that the English short-cross penny appears in a hoard from Ladenburg and from elsewhere in the Rhineland, and is used as money of account at Utrecht. About this time (between 1209 and 1218) Otto IV, the nephew of John the King of the Romans, began striking short-cross sterlings at Cologne, Dortmund and Duisburg. It is noteworthy that John had helped Otto in 1209 against a French supported rival. About the same time Otto's rival Frederick II began striking English-type sterlings from the Rhenish mints.

The first interesting phase of intensive imitation comes in the period 1228–40, when the short-cross pennies are imitated in Westphalia, and large numbers of the pennies themselves turn up in hoards, as at Hesseln (1235), Lechtingen (1238) or Brummerlohe (1240) all of which are rich in English coins. The majority of these copies are struck by clerics, though there is another group struck by regional counts and the Lord of Lippe, Bernhard III. The explanation for this phase probably lies in Henry III's period of negotiations with the Empire, which was symbolized by exchange visits of clerics and the betrothal of Henry's sister to Frederick II in 1235.

Along with these diplomatic moves came various economic treaties, including an English declaration of liberties to the merchants of Cologne. But there were misgivings in England that negotiations should be continued with the Easterlings, in view of their excommunication and the way in which the trade was affecting the London merchants' privileges, and in 1240 Henry III withdrew his previous support for the trade. Just at this time the export of English pennies ceases. The coins were probably concentrated in Westphalia rather than being spread out evenly through Germany, because it was in Westphalia that English wool was made into cloth.

This lull in trade was only brief, and by 1250 English long-cross pennies (the type may have been partly introduced to prevent export) were once again reaching the continent, where they were copied though not very extensively. At this time we find the centre of attention shifting from Germany to the Baltic on the one hand and Frisia on the other.

Meanwhile, in the Netherlands, most notably Brabant, the long-cross penny provides a prototype for a long series of coins, which start about 1273. Apart from some early issues the first main series seems to have been struck about 1293, following a prototype first struck in Brabant substituting a garland of roses for the crown in Edward's bust. For this reason they are called 'rosarii'.

These rosarii are for the most part confined to the Netherlands, and were imported to Britain in large numbers, mixing with the Edwardian pennies and turning up in hoards. They are specially common in Scotland and appear in the Melendean and Galston hoards. Within Scotland they enjoyed special currency in Galloway; indeed, most of the finds come from there, and it is not insignificant that Galloway was itself an important exporter of wool. In England the problem was less acute and the coins less popular, but as a result Edward in 1299 banned 'Leonines' (i.e. pieces from Brabant) and 'pollards and crockards' (bare headed imitations and rosarii) on the grounds that they were plated and not of pure silver. This was only an excuse, as they were struck on the English standard. This may have affected their production on the Continent, as they do not seem to have been struck after 1304-6.

The coins that replaced them were an even bigger problem to the English monarch. These did not trouble to alter the types in any way from the original but employed exactly the same designs, altering only the legends. That they came across to Britain and passed as currency can easily be seen by the Boyton hoard from Wiltshire, which contained a representative selection of the types that had been struck abroad till the date of the hoard, 1324. The series of crowned head copies seem to begin about 1310. The problem became even more acute, when some princes started issuing coins which copied the legends, blundering them slightly, but not unduly. Robert of

Béthune at Ghent even copied a Scottish sterling, and another imitation of a Scottish coin was struck in Lorraine.

The vicissitudes of the imitative sterlings follow closely the political intrigues of the time. The initial impetus came as a result of Edward I advising English merchants to trade with Brabant and along the Schelde, rather than the Rhine. This happened in 1293, and was followed by an alliance with Gui of Flanders which took the form of English financial and military aid. At the same time merchants were encouraged to trade in wool. Numismatically, the British side of the story is reflected in the refounding of Kingston-upon-Hull for the conducting of this trade, and the opening of a mint there about 1300. This lasts for about forty years when interest in Flanders was withdrawn. The period is that of the imitative sterlings in Flanders. Holland comes into the story for a short while, and then ceases to be important, as the imitative sterlings there were struck on an earlier, light, standard.

At the time of the death of Alexander III of Scotland, when the 'Maid of Norway' was heir to the Scottish throne it is not surprising to find that in Norway Haakon was striking coins imitating those of Alexander III. At the same time some English coins were also reaching Norway.

The subsequent story of the Easterlings continues under Edward III with a further series of imitative sterlings struck in the Netherlands, most notably by John the Blind of Luxembourg whose coins were blatant forgeries. They caused much trouble in England, and in 1350 Edward passed an act making the importing of 'Lushbournes' an offence punishable by death.

To sum up, the shifting pattern of imitative sterlings reflects accurately the story of the English wool trade in the early Middle Ages, where the wool was being exported and when. It emphasizes too the importance of the river systems and the Schleswig isthmus at this period, and the way in which English coins seem to be closely associated with the Netherlands and Lower Saxony apart from the times when political ties with France or Germany closed the Channel, namely in the Norman period and, if we had space here to trace the story further, the period 1365–1400.

By the last quarter of the fourteenth century Edward III, through his extensive coinage of groats and nobles and his legislation against imitative sterlings, managed to free English coinage of a large number of these, though they occur in hoards until about 1435, and died a slow death.

The establishment of the wool staple at Calais in 1361 can be seen as connected with the opening of a mint there soon afterwards, showing the maintenance of the old association between silver and wool. No doubt the silver gained through the buying and selling of wool was subjected to various and fraudulent negotiations at the Staple itself.

Galeyhalpens and Venetian Trade[50]

English trade in the fifteenth century was founded on wool and cloth. The export to a large extent was regulated by the Company of the Staple at Calais, as we have seen, though the Hansard also continued to export wool from the London Steelyard, and the Venetian and other Italian merchants built up a wool trade with Italy through the ports of London, Sandwich and Southampton.

The Venetians used to set sail in May, some going to Flanders, the rest to England, meeting up again at Sandwich in the late summer. These fleets of galleys brought large numbers of base metal coins called soldini, which, because they had been brought by the Venetian ships, were called galeyhalpens, that is, Galley Halfpence. These enjoyed great popularity in England on account of the shortage of small change, a shortage which seems to have affected currency in England at several other periods, most notably in the later seventeenth century and the last two decades of the eighteenth century, when the deficiency was met on both occasions by a considerable output of tradesman's tokens. In early fifteenth century England the lowest denominations struck were the silver halfpenny and the farthing, both of which were scarce, in spite of the mint regulations which demanded that a large percentage of the silver coined should be in the low denominations. At this time prices could involve sums like half a farthing.

Their popularity is attested by the number in the Highbury Hoard which was deposited early in the reign of Henry v. Even in the period 1959–63 stray finds of galeyhalpens were made at Northampton, Newport (Isle of Wight), Eye, Hethersett (near Norwich) and in Somerset. They are fairly common as stray finds in England.

They were first imported in 1400, and were used by the Venetians as payment for wool. Attempts to put an end to the circulation of these coins were made constantly, and in 1402 the king even ordered that a third of all silver was to be coined in halfpence and farthings, following a lull when none had been struck. But galeyhalpens remained an integral part of the currency for about fifteen years. Regular seizures did little to prevent the black market, and the accounts of 'raids' in docks at the time sounds strangely reminiscent of contemporary raids on drug traffickers. In 1416 pressure on the Venetian Senate resulted in the export of soldini being prevented at source, as they forbade the transport of Venetian halfpence to London in the London galleys. Even so they managed to reach Britain, and the action of the government against these and other imported coins, 'Zeskins' and 'Duitkins' (the quarter groat of Flanders and the denier of Holland), became more and more violent. Although they seem to have been stamped out by about 1423–4 they came back again at the beginning of the sixteenth century – one turns up in the Maidstone hoard of 1538, and there are a number of stray finds of about the same date.

Coinage and Currency in England Before Edward I

We may now turn back again in time to review some other aspects of Medieval coinage.

From the time of the Norman Conquest an attempt was made to reduce the number of mints in operation. William I discontinued the custom of striking coins in many mints and endeavoured to centralize to a greater extent. In Somerset, for example, the mints of Cadbury Castle, Bruton and Langport were all closed, and under William Rufus, Maldon and Malmesbury were also closed. In the early Norman period the most important mints, that is, those with the most moneyers, were London, Norwich, Winchester, Lincoln and York, which shows that these were the most important towns in the period. After these comes Thetford, which seems to have been as important as Ipswich or Norwich. This would seem to prove that in the Norman period trade was extremely active in the eastern counties. Under Henry I yet another dozen mints were closed.

In the north there were no mints which operated very regularly, and in the reign of Henry II, Richard Fitz Nigel tells us that from the time of Henry I the counties of Northumberland and Cumberland were not expected to pay their dues to the king in pennies from any particular mints, but could pay them in any kind of coin provided it was of good weight. There was one mint, however, in Cumberland which had a rather varied history – this was the mint of Carlisle, which flourished on silver supplied by the mines at Alston. It was supplying Carlisle with silver before 1133, but fell into the hands of

David I of Scotland for a while who used the silver for his own coins, before Henry II recaptured it and put it into his service again.

Another series of mints seem to have operated mainly because they were near silver mines, and this was a good way of putting the silver into circulation. The Derby mines supplied the Peverel family with silver until the time of Henry II, and then the silver was channelled into the Midland mints of Derby, Nottingham, Lincoln and York. Similarly the mints of Bristol, Gloucester, Exeter, Devizes, Sherbourne, and Wivelscombe were all in operation under Matilda because of the supplies of silver that were available in the Mendips. For the twelfth century we have valuable information about which mines supplied which mints from the Pipe Rolls.

During the thirteenth century the main mints remained London and Canterbury, and indeed it was London and Canterbury that supplied the largest percentage of England's coinage in the fourteenth century too. This is reflected in the Colchester Hoard, which was buried about 1260 and contained 10,000 coins, of which 9,000 were of London or Canterbury.

The historian learns from literary sources that Henry I wished to establish towns and settle traders in South Wales, and this is proved by the coins of the Pembroke mint of the period. A very important hoard was found at Llantrithyd in Glamorgan in 1962 which sheds light on this.[51] The hoard is of great importance because it contained Henry I pennies of Shaftesbury, Wilton, Bristol and Cardiff, all new mints for the class of coins represented, Class XI.

Until 1962 only fifteen coins of the class were known and, though there were only seven coins in the hoard in all, it means that the hoard constitutes a third of the coins known. Its economic significance is, however, even greater, for it means that the economic historian will need to reconsider the economic situation in the south west of England and South Wales during this period. The hoard, it might be added, was found on a domestic site during excavations by a local archaeological society.

Under the Angevins the old connection between boroughs and mints ceased to be valid due to the closure of mints. By the beginning of Henry II's reign the sheriff of Norfolk and Suffolk was allowed £6 off his payment to the crown because there were fewer moneyers at Ipswich and Thetford. Henry II struck coins at thirty places. Some only had one moneyer, but Northampton had no less than seven.

Under John there were even fewer mints operating – only twenty-one. A remarkable story is, however, reflected in the mint of Lynn, which had three moneyers. This town was newly enfranchised, and for a time was drawing trade away from Norwich. The mint belonged to the Bishop of Norwich, and flourished because of John's friendship with the Bishop — he intended to make him Archbishop of Canterbury. Needless to say the mint did not outlast the friendship![52]

By the time of Henry III the mints were reduced in number to six, and we can witness the emergence of Bury St Edmunds, which was to remain an important mint under Edward I. For a time in Henry III's reign only London, Canterbury and Bury were operating. However, the output of these mints was not sufficient, and with the introduction of the long-cross coinage some sixteen other mints were opened again. The king's brother met some of the crown's expenses, and in return was allowed to share the profits. For this reason it is not surprising to find one of the new mints opened was at Wallingford, which had strong connections with him. A hoard from Beddgelert, in Caernarvonshire, dating from the time of Henry, may reflect his campaigns in Wales.

The Scottish Wars of Independence

During the period 1280 to 1377 large numbers of hoards were buried, more perhaps than at any other period. A large number of these can be associated with the Scottish Wars of Independence, waged against Edward I and Edward II (Map 16).

The majority of this group of hoards is, as one might expect, concentrated in Scotland, and is divided in two areas following the two main lines of Edwardian advance. One group in the east is centred round Berwick-on-Tweed and Roxburgh, and is represented in finds like those from Coldingham, Cleuch Head and Mellendean, with an outlier at Newminster in England. The other group is to be found in the western Lowlands, opposite Carlisle and in the path of Edward I's Solway advance. Hoards that fall into this category include those from Dumfries, Blackhills, Borscar and Ayr.

The second stage of the war is documented by a group of hoards dated to 1330–5 round Edinburgh, Stirling and Fife, with outliers in Perth and Aberdeen – it may be remembered that Edward I constructed extensive fortifications at Kildrummy Castle in Aberdeenshire.

Associated with this phase of wars was the opening of a number of mints in the north to supply the soldiers. The most important of these was Berwick, which only operated for a short period but which

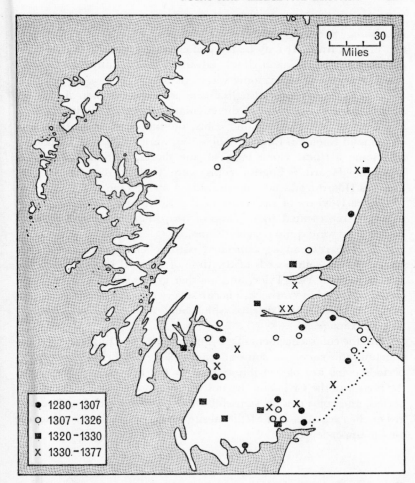

16.   Distribution of Edwardian Coin Hoards in Scotland (After Thompson, 1956)

struck large numbers of coins at this time. Other northern mints which supplied the English armies during the wars were Newcastle, York, Lincoln and Durham.

The Later Middle Ages

Coins and coin hoards do not add a great deal to our knowledge of Medieval England from the mid fourteenth century, and at the most only provide a corroborative comment on history.

K*

Between 1280 and 1350 the mint at Chester seems to have been flourishing, and this reflects the importance of the town in the context of Irish trade. It may be remembered that it had a similar importance in Anglo-Saxon times. Edward I had a mint there about 1290, when the Irish economy was at its best.

In the fifteenth century English coins are fairly common abroad in hoards, largely as a result of the circulation there of English nobles struck at Calais. Anglo-Gallic coins, on the other hand, did not circulate in England. English nobles, too, were imitated in Flanders, and some of these came back to our shores, turning up in the Westbury Hoard.[53] English coins were well represented in the Pozières Hoard from the Somme, buried about 1430.

The early years of the Wars of the Roses are not, rather surprisingly, represented by a phase of hoarding. Probably for most people they were quite peaceful times.

A few hoards can be associated with rebellions, including one group of gold coin hoards of the time of Edward III which can be associated with Wat Tyler, and another group which can be associated with Perkin Warbeck. There is a very remarkable medallion of Perkin Warbeck's in existence which may or may not have been a pattern coinage.

With the commencement of the Tudor dynasty in England we may conclude this survey of coins and archaeology in Britain. For later periods coins are of less importance to the archaeologist, though the hoards of the Civil War are not without interest in a study of the period, and coins can prove useful even to the industrial archaeologist or the excavator of a Medieval site who requires dating evidence for the upper levels.

Further Reading

The main study of English coins is G. C. Brooke's *English Coins* (1951). A recent and very important study of Anglo-Saxon coins is the Stenton Festschrift, *Anglo-Saxon Coins* (1961) edited by Michael Dolley. For a brief introduction to Saxon pennies the British Museum publication *Anglo-Saxon Pennies* (1964) also by Dolley will be found very useful. The standard reference for English hammered coinage as a whole is North's *English Hammered Coinage*, 2 vols. (1960-3) and for Scottish coins is I. H. Stewart's *The Scottish Coinage* (1955). Although there are good recent works on aspects of Irish coinage, chiefly by O'Sullivan, there is no recent work covering the whole of Medieval Irish Coinage.

Hoard evidence is discussed in Thompson's *Inventory of British Coin Hoards, AD 600–1500* (1956) which also discusses the general character of the currency at different periods. This work is now out of date, especially in some points of interpretation, and a new edition is awaited.

For Viking hoards the most useful study is in P. Sawyer's *The Age of the Vikings* (1962).

NOTES

1　Biddle, 1964; Biddle, 1965.
2　Accounts of Trial of the Pyx to be found in Stride, 1959, and Whitting, 1966.
3　Bruce Mitford, 1956.
4　Stone & Charlton, 1935.
5　Jope & Rigold, 1950.
6　Grimes, 1956.
7　Hurst, 1959.
8　Dunning, 1949.
9　Barton, 1960; Rahtz, 1960.
10　Wilson & Blunt, 1961.
11　Reference to this in the Introduction to Thompson, 1956.
12　Thompson, 1956, Introduction. A revision of Thompson's survey of Scottish Medieval coin hoards is due to appear soon which may alter the dating of some hoards and associated finds. A survey, partly based on coin hoards, is being made at present of bronze tripod bowls, in order to classify and date them.
13　Thompson, 1956.
14　Jope & Stewart, 1959.
15　The typology of English pence was initiallyou tlined by Earle-Fox and L. A. Lawrence in the earlier part of this century, short-cross coins being discussed in Vol. XI (1915), long-cross in Vol. IX (1913) and Edwardian pence in Vols. VI to X (1910–14) of *British Numismatic Journal*. Recent material in North, 1960, and to some extent Seaby, 1948.
16　Useful background summaries in Chadwick, 1962, and Frere, 1967. Also useful is the summary in Thomas, 1964.
17　Thomas, 1959.
18　Discussion of town evidence in Frere, 1967.
19　The literature on Dark Age coinage is extensive, the main case for the 'pro' school being given in Sutherland, 1956, that of the

'anti' in Kent, 1961. Other key articles in the dispute are Hill, 1952, Kent, 1954, Kent, 1959, and Sutherland, 1936.

20 Hill, 1955a; Hill, 1950; Kent, 1959.

21 Wheeler, 1932.

22 Mattingly and Stebbing, 1939; Hill, 1948; Bushe-Fox, 1949.

23 Kent, 1961.

24 Rigold, 1954, le Gentilhomme, 1946.

25 Articles on this famous discovery have been many, but Bruce Mitford, 1968 is the best and also the most up-to-date. The coin discussion here is based on the longer study in that work. See also Philips, 1956 and Glass, 1962.

26 Grierson, 1952. Grierson still supports this dating.

27 Kent, 1961.

28 Main discussion of Crondall, Sutherland, 1948.

29 Kent, 1961.

30 Grierson, 1955.

31 Sutherland, 1948.

32 Whitting, 1961.

33 The literature on early sceattas is also extensive, but the most valuable study is Rigold, 1962. Earlier important articles are Sutherland, 1942, and Hill, 1948; Hill, 1954a, Hill 1954b and Hill, 1955b. Grierson's Ford lectures for 1954 were on this, but are still unpublished.

34 Useful discussion in Sutherland, 1942. The subject is also dealt with in Rigold, 1952.

35 Metcalf, 1967.

36 Thompson, 1956, Introduction. This important work is now in need of slight revision, especially in interpretation.

37 Key article in this connection is Whitting, 1961. Some discussion of Byzantine coin finds in Britain is given in G. C. Boon's note on the Byzantine coin finds at Caerwent, published in *The Bulletin of the Board of Celtic Studies* (1959), but Boon tends to be over-sceptical. Byzantine art influence discussed briefly in Talbot Rice, 1952.

38 Blunt, 1961.

39 Thompson, 1956. For Irish material, refer to Dolley & Ingold, 1961a; Dolley 1966a, Dolley 1966b. The Viking coinages of York have recently been discussed by C. S. Lyon and B. H. I. H. Stewart in Dolley (Ed.), *Anglo-Saxon Coins* (1961). For the Cuerdale Hoard see Banks, M., *The Problem of Cuerdale* (1967) and the same writer's paper in *Numismatic Gazette* (1966), 258–63. Special aspects of Cuerdale in Seaby, 1967.

40 Classic study of styca series in Lyon, 1956. Earlier but still useful is Creeke, 1904. For a short, recent, summary, see Kay, 1966.

41 Sawyer, 1962 for key discussion. Less useful are Arbman, 1961, and Brondsted, 1965. Sawyer based his discussion, which perhaps shows too great a faith in Viking hoard material, on a partly unpublished study by S. Bolin, *Studier over mynt och mynt-fynd i ostra och norra Europa under vikingatiden*. He stressed the Kufic element in the hoards and neglects the English and German coins.

42 Biddle, 1965.

43 Hildebrand's *Anglosachsiska Mynt* (1881).

44 Loyn, 1961.

45 Dolley, 1964.

46 Dolley, 1964.

47 Dolley, 1964.

48 Dolley, 1966a.

49 Rigold 1952 is the main study. This supersedes a number of earlier works, of which the classic is Chautard, 1875. A recent study is to be found in Meert, 1960. Useful historical material on earlier Frisian trade in Levison, 1946.

50 Spufford, 1963. Later imports are discussed by Spufford in a paper in *B.N.J.* 1964, 110–17, on Burgundian double-patards. The story of continental imitations of Edward IV's rose nobles is given in Thompson, 1951.

51 Dolley, 1962.

52 Useful material in Stenton, 1952.

53 Thompson, 1951.

Descriptive Notes on the Plates

1   Belgic coin flan mould from Bluehouse Hill, St Albans, found in 1957, the most complete so far found in Britain.

2a   A bronze coin die of Hadrian, found at St Albans in 1936.
& b   It is for a reverse of an aureus or denarius showing Roma greeting the emperor, with the legend ADVENTVS AVG. The type can be dated to AD 134–8.

3   Iron trussel or reverse die of David II of Scotland, 1329–71, from King Malcolm's Castle, Pittencrieff, Dunfermline, Fife. It appears to be unused. How it reached the castle is unknown, as there was no mint there.

4   Sterling (penny) of David II, First Coinage, struck before 1357. This is similar to the type of coin that would have been struck from a die like 3.

5   Coins Illustrating Coin Production Methods

a   Reverse of a siglos of Arses of Persia, 338–337 BC showing a punchmark. Although late in date it conforms to the earliest punchmarked coins of Asia Minor.

b   Silver stater of Thasos, 550–465 BC. *Obv.* Nymph being carried off by a satyr. *Rev.* Square punchmark of evolved form.

c   Silver diobol of Miletos, in Ionia. Fifth century BC. This reverse shows a square punchmark elaborated into ornamental star design.

d   Bronze coin of Syracuse, Sicily, 412–345 BC. Struck on a flan cast in a bivalve mould. The *rev.* shown here is a quadrupartite incuse square with a star in the centre.

e   Silver hemidrachm of Argos, 228–146 BC. The *rev.* here shown retains the incuse square as a decorative feature. The A is for Argos. A symbol (eagle) and a magistrate's name ($IPE\Omega NO\Sigma$) appear in the field.

f   Silver stater of Corinth, 400–338 BC. *Obv.* Pegasos, koppa (ϙ) beneath. *Rev.* Athene, symbol (rose) behind. The reverse type is in an incuse, as a result of being engraved on the punch die, even though it is the 'head' type. The main type on coins of Corinth was the city badge, Pegasos.

g Silver stater of Caulonia, southern Italy, 530–510 BC *Obv.* and *Rev.* show Apollo advancing with a deer in front. The smaller figure on his arm and the legend is missing on the reverse, which is incuse.

h Bronze serrate coin of Antiochus VI of Syria. (145–142 BC). *Obv.* Head of king. *Rev.* Elephant holding torch.

i Silver stater of Pergamum in Mysia, struck under the Romans, 133–27 BC. The types refer to Dionysiac rites, and the coin belongs to a large series known as cistophoric tetradrachms on account of the *cista mystica* on the obverse. They are struck on large, flat flans.

Denarius of Titus Carisius, 49–44 BC. The reverse shows a moneyer's anvil, tongs and hammer (the last off the flan of this coin) surmounted by the Cap of Vulcan.

k Denarius of Lucius Scribonius Libo, *c.* 55 BC showing the *puteal Scriboniarum*, a well-head in the Forum Romanum, decorated with lyres, festoons and moneyer's hammer. Other coins in the same series shows moneyer's tongs or anvil.

l Bronze scyphate of Alexius III, AD 1195–1203. *Obv.* Facing head of Christ. *Rev.* Alexius and St Constantine facing.

m Medieval bracteate, the reverse similar to the obverse but incuse and in reverse.

6 Coins Illustrating Chronology

a Silver tetradrachm of Ptolemy XI of Egypt, 114–88 BC struck at Paphos in Cyprus. *Rev.* Eagle on a thunderbolt L Θ (i.e. Year 8) to L., mint letters Π A to r.

b Billon Imperial tetradrachm of Alexandria, struck under Maximianus, AD 286–305. *Rev.* date L Γ (Year 3).

c Judaea, bronze lepton of Marcus Ambibulus. The reverse shows a palm tree, date L Λ Θ (Year 39), being the regnal year of Augustus.

d Silver shekel of the Second Jewish Revolt, AD 132–5. *Obv.* Screen of the Tabernacle with the ark of the Covenant. *Rev.* bundle of twigs and citron. Hebrew legend 'Second year of the Deliverance of Jerusalem'.

e Gold 'Bonnet piece' of James V of Scotland, 1513–42. Dated 1540.

f Silver tetradrachm of Athens, 'Old style', 403–365 BC. For comparison with *g*.

g Silver 'New Style' tetradrachm of Athens, 117–116 BC. *Rev.* owl on amphora, symbol (Isis) in field with magistrates' names. Control mark Δ I below amphora. Date letter A. The date is in fact wrong.

h Stater of Corinth, *c.* 600 BC. Pegasus on the obverse of this coin can be compared with Figure 10 p. 45. Compare it also with Plate 4, *f*.

i   Denarius of Publius Crepusius, *c.* 82–81 BC. *Obv.* Apollo, sceptre over shoulder, control mark X in front. *Rev.* Galloping horseman, sequence mark XXVI behind.

j   Denarius of Caius Piso, *c.* 71–58 BC. *Obv.* Apollo, symbol (shell) behind, sequence number VII. *Rev.* Galloping rider, sequence mark VII above, legend and monogram below.

k   Denarius of Brutus, with reverse type of Cap of Liberty between two daggers, legend EID MAR below. The type refers to the murder of Caesar.

l   Denarius of Augustus, showing Apollo of Actium between IMP X. ACT(ium) appears in the exergue. The type is commemorative of the battle of Actium.

7   Coins being unearthed at Masada in Israel, dating from the time of the First Jewish Revolt. The Masada coins have been invaluable to students of the coinage of Palestine.

8   Classical Coins and the Prehistorian

a   Silver tetradrachm of Philip II of Macedon, 359–336 BC. *Obv.* Head of Zeus. *Rev.* Horseman. The prototype for some of the coins of the East European Celts.

b   Silver stater of the Celts of the Danube, imitating 8*a*. The legend is omitted on the reverse, and a head appears under the horseman.

c   Gold stater of Philip II of Macedon, 359–336 BC. *Obv.* Head of Apollo. *Rev.* Charioteer. This stater was widely copied by the Celts: Compare Plate 9*b* or 10*a*.

d   Silver tetrobol of Massalia, after 200 BC. The latest of a long series of similar coins. *Obv.* Head of Artemis. *Rev.* Lion.

e   Silver coin of the League against Ariovistus and the Helvetii. Struck in the Rhône Valley, it is modelled on Republican denarii. *Obv.* Head modelled on Roma, DVRNACOS in front. *Rev.* Horseman, AVSCRO(cos) below.

f   Silver coin of the Celts of Central Europe, of 'Biatec' type. *Obv.* Conjoined heads, BIA in front. *Rev.* Horseman, BIATEC in panel beneath. In style it is influenced by Roman denarii.

g   Silver coin of the Volcae Tectosages. *Obv.* Female (sic) head. *Rev.* Rose design. This is modelled on the drachms of Rhoda (see Figure 19).

h   Denarius of Lucius Consconius, *c.* 112–109 BC. *Obv.* Roma. *Rev.* Naked Gaul (Bituitos) in a chariot with a sheld and carnyx. The representation is not strictly accurate – he should have a charioteer.

i   Denarius of Hostilius Sarsena, *c.* 49–44 BC. *Obv.* Head of a Gaul (usually taken to be Vercingetorix) with lime-washed hair, Celtic shield behind. *Rev.* Naked Gaul in chariot, with charioteer. The types refer to Caesar's campaigns in Gaul.

j Denarius of Albinus Bruti filius. *c.* 49–48 BC. *Obv.* Head of Mars. *Rev.* Crossed carnyxes, with two types of Celtic shield in angles. The types again refer to Caesar's campaigns.

k Denarius of Augustus, struck probably in Asia Minor. *Obv.* Head of the emperor. *Rev.* Romano-Celtic temple, with architrave inscribed IMP CAESAR. The type is difficult to explain unless it alludes to Caesar.

9 Celtic Coins and the Prehistorian 1

a Obverse of a silver coin of the Carnutes, showing a moustached head.

b Obverse of a gold coin of the Osismii, with unusual crest.

c Reverse of a silver stater of the Baiocasses. The charioteer of the prototype is here represented by one horse, with a severed head beneath and wheel symbol in front.

d Obverse of a stater of the Mediomatrici showing a janiform head (bearded) within a torc.

e Bronze coin of the Remi, struck about the time of Caesar. *Obv.* Three jugate heads, REMO in front. *Rev.* Charioteer in a Celtic chariot, REMO beneath. Although showing Roman influence, the chariot is of Celtic type.

f Reverse of a silver coin of the Pictones, inscribed VIIPOTAL, with a warrior in chain (or scale) armour holding a Celtic shield, spear and boar standard.

g Reverse of a gold stater of the Baiocasses, with a bird on a horse's back and a scorpion-like creature beneath.

h Reverse of a gold coin of the Unelli, showing a horseman with starched hair brandishing a severed head and a shield. From the horse's mouth comes a 'streamer'.

i Reverse of an early gold stater of the Veneti showing a human-headed horse and a charioteer with a blossoming branch; rectilinear 'comet' in front. Beneath is a winged human figure. The obverse of this coin appears enlarged as Plate 12*a*.

j Reverse of a gold coin of the Unelli, with a horse and charioteer. Above is a ship with dragonesque prow and stern and a mast. Stylized anthropomorphic sword beneath.

k Reverse of a bronze coin of the Petrocorii, showing a wolf beneath a tree; symbol (bull's head) in field. The obverse is a head with the legend of Coututos.

l Obverse of a silver coin of the Ambiani, showing a bearded head in front of which is a vessel like a pedestal urn (see Figure 39).

m Potin coin of the Continental Catuvellauni. *Obv.* Squatting facing figure holding a torc. *Rev.* Boar, serpent (?) above.

n Celts of Central Europe, silver stater reverse, showing a helmeted 'Harpy'.

10 Celtic Coins and the Prehistorian II.

a Gallo-Belgic A stater, *c.* 125 BC. *Obv.* 'Apollo'. *Rev.* Horse. One of the first coins to circulate in Britain.

b British speculum coin, with types derived from bronze coins of Marseilles. *Obv.* 'Apollo'. *Rev.* 'Bull'. Derived from Celtic copies found in Central and East Gaul, in Britain found in the South-East. Mainly first century BC.

c Gallo-Belgic E stater reverse, showing horse. The obverse is without a type. Mid first century BC.

d British Q uninscribed stater of 'triple tailed horse' type. From these prototypes (QA) which are found in the Middle Thames Valley stem the coins of the Dobunni in the Cotswolds and those of Commius of the Atrebates. In type it is derived from Gallo-Belgic F of *c.* 52 BC.

e Gold stater of Verica, *c.* AD 10–40. *Obv.* Vine leaf. *Rev.* Horseman with shield. The coin shows Roman influence. Verica ruled over the reduced territory of the Atrebates, probably from Selsey.

f Silver coin of Tincommius (*c.* 20 BC – AD 5) of the Atrebates. *Obv.* Beardless male head. *Rev.* Bull. Tincommius was one of the sons of Commius, and his coins show Roman influence.

g Gold stater of Tasciovanus of the Catuvellauni (*c.* 20 BC – AD 10). *Obv.* Ornamental design ultimately derived from the obverse of 'Wonersh' staters. *Rev.* Horseman brandishing carnyx. TASC and wheel symbols in field.

h Silver coin of Eppillus of the Atrebates. (*c.* AD 5–10). *Obv.* EPP. Eagle with expanded wings. *Rev.* REX CALLE and crescent between two stars of pellets. Struck at Silchester (Calleva) and showing Roman influence.

i Silver coin of Verica (see *e* above). *Obv.* [VERI]CA. Partly draped seated figure. *Rev.* Sceptre between two cornucopiae. double-handled vase beneath. The type is derived from one of Mark Antony, where a globe appears instead of a vase.

j Billon stater of the Coriosolites from the Le Catillon Hoard, buried 56–51 BC in Jersey. *Obv.* Head of 'Apollo'. *Rev.* Horse, boar beneath.

11 Celtic Coins and the Prehistorian III

a Bronze coin of Tasciovanus of the Catuvellauni (see *g* above). *Obv.* Two jugate heads, one bearded. *Rev.* Ram. TASC.

b Tasciovanus of the Catuvellauni, bronze coin. *Obv.* Beardless male head. *Rev.* Seated figure, VER in exergue. In front is an object on a pole. Verulamium mint.

c   Bronze coin of Cunobelin (*c.* AD 10–40). *Obv.* Head modelled on that of Augustus. CUNOBELINI. *Rev.* Centaur blowing a horn. TASCIOVANI F.

d   Cunobelin, bronze coin. *Obv.* Beardless, winged male head. CVNOBELIN. *Rev.* Figure beating a metal vessel. TASCIO behind.

e   Silver coin of Cunobelin. *Obv.* CVN on a tablet. *Rev.* Figure carrying a club over his shoulder. CVN.

f   Bronze coin of Cunobelin. *Obv.* Sphynx, CVNO beneath. *Rev.* Naked figure with (?) apron, holding severed head. Altar behind. CAM. Colchester mint.

g   Gold stater of Eppillus, when king in Kent. *Obv.* Winged Victory holding wreath. *Rev.* Horseman carrying a carnyx.

h   Durotriges, cast bronze coin of 'Hengistbury Head' type, which were current until the second century AD. The types stem from earlier Durotrigan coins, and represent the ultimate degeneration of the types of the gold stater of Philip of Macedon.

i   Uninscribed silver coin of the Dobunni, Type F, ultimately derived from the 'Triple Tailed Horse' coins like Plate 10*d*.

j   Silver coin of the Coritani, Early type. *Obv.* Boar. *Rev.* Horse.

12 Enlargements of Celtic Coins

a   Obverse of an early gold stater of the Veneti, showing a head with subsidiary heads attached to it from cords. The head is crowned with a 'hippocamp'. The *Rev.* is illustrated on Plate 9*j*.

b   Gold coin of Vercingetorix. *Obv.* Head of Apollo. VERCINGE-TORIX. *Rev.* Horse, amphora beneath.

13 Pendant made out of a denarius of Augustus. Found in the chieftain's burial at Lexden, Colchester, along with continental imports. It has sometimes been suggested that the burial was that of Cunobelin himself.

14 Reconstruction model of the chariot from the votive deposit at Llyn Cerrig Bach, Anglesey. Compare it with Plate 9*f*.

15 Gold ring-headed terminal of a torc, from Shaw Hill, Peebles-shire similar in type to one from Snettisham dated *c.* 25 BC, along with two surviving 'bullet' shaped coins, from the Marne-Aisne area of France, dating from the first half of the first century BC. The hoard also included two other gold torcs and thirty-eight other coins, the latter now lost.

16 Buffer ended torc, from Kelton, Kirkcudbright, in bronze. It has a movable section, a common feature of Continental torcs, and may in fact be an import. First century BC.

17   Mouthpiece of a bronze carnyx or boar-headed trumpet, from Deskford, Banffshire. Probably second century AD.

18   Coins and Roman Britain I

a   Base silver denarius of Mark Antony. *Obv.* ANT AVG III VIR R P C round galley. *Rev.* Aquila between standards, LEG XI beneath. These legionary denarii enjoyed a long currency in Britain.

b   British imitation of a 'Ceres Augusta' dupondius of Claudius I (AD 41–54). Found at Dragonby, Lincolnshire.

c   Gold aureus of Claudius. *Obv.* Bust and titles. *Rev.* Triumphal arch inscribed DE BRITANN, surmounted by equestrian statue and trophies. Struck in AD 46–7 to commemorate the British campaigns.

d   As of Antoninus Pius. *Obv.* Bust and titles. *Rev.* BRITANNIA COS IIII, Britannia seated in attitude of dejection on a pile of stones. Struck in AD 154–5, to commemorate British campaigns, possibly in a British mint.

e   Denarius of Septimius Severus. *Obv.* Bust and titles. *Rev.* Victory inscribing a shield on a palm tree. P M TR P XV COS III P P. Struck in AD 207–8 it is similar to a series struck 206–10 with legends relating the type to British campaigns.

f   Antoninianus of Philip I from the Dorchester Hoard (see Plate 24). *Obv.* Bust and titles. *Rev.* ADVENTVS AVG, emperor on horseback. AD 244–49.

g   Antoninianus of Victorinus, AD 268–70. *Obv.* Bust and titles. *Rev.* Sol. INVICTVS. 'Radiates' like these of the Gallic emperors came to Britain in large numbers, and were widely copied.

h   'Barbarous radiate'. Imitation in barbarous style of an 'Invictus' coin like g above.

i   'Radiate minim'. Very tiny copy of the same coin, probably late third century. From Dragonby, Lincs.

j   Antoninianus of Carausius, AD 287–93. *Obv.* Bust and titles. *Rev.* Peace. PAX AVG. London mint. From the Little Orme's Head Hoard.

19   Coins and Roman Britain II

a   Follis of Constantius Chlorus, retaining some silver wash, Struck c. 295–305. *Obv.* Bust and titles. *Rev.* Genius of the Roman People sacrificing at an altar.

b   Follis of reduced weight of Constantine I, AD 303–37. London mint. *Obv.* Bust and titles. *Rev.* Sol.

c   Small bronze coin of Constantine I. *Obv.* Bust and titles. *Rev.* GLORIA EXERCITVS. Two soldiers with two standards. These small coins (sometimes with one standard) are extremely common in fourth century contexts in Roman Britain.

d   Small bronze coin of the period 330–46, struck to commemorate the renaming of Constantinople and the transference of the capital from Rome. This, the 'Urbs Roma' commemorative, honours Rome, *e* (below) Constantinople. *Obv.* Head of Roma. URBS ROMA. *Rev.* Romulus and Remus with the wolf.

e   'Constantinopolis' commemorative. *Obv.* Head of Constantinople. *Rev.* Victory on a prow. This, along with *d* above, is among the most common types of coin in early fourth century contexts in Britain.

f   Centionalis of Magnentius, AD 350–3. *Obv.* Bust and titles, A behind head. *Rev.* Victories holding a wreath inscribed VOT V MVLT X on a pillar. Found at Woodeaton, Glos.

g   'Fel Temp Reparatio' coin of 'Soldier Spearing Fallen Horseman' type. This one, struck under Constantius Gallus AD 351–4, is of the same type as those introduced in 348, but of much reduced weight. They were widely copied in Britain.

h   British copy of a 'Fel Temp Reparatio' coin like *g* above. Found at Dragonby, Lincs.

i   Minim, fourth century AD. This is another, smaller imitation of the 'Soldier Spearing Fallen Horseman' coins. The type is still just recognizable. The obverse of this coin (not illustrated) is blank.

j   Silver siliqua of Valens, AD 364–78. *Obv.* Bust and titles. *Rev.* Roma seated holding Victory and sceptre.

20   Hoard of Barbarous Radiates of the third century AD from Newgate Street, London, before cleaning.

21   The same hoard; a selection of the coins after cleaning.

22   Coin of Trajan in the mast-step of a Roman boat from Blackfriars, London. The coin was put there for luck, a custom which continues till the present. It was invaluable for dating the boat.

23   Electrotype copy of a gold medallion of Constantius Chlorus found at Beaurains, near Arras, in 1922, along with other medallions and jewellery. The reverse shows the emperor's triumphal entry into London, as the 'Restorer of Eternal Light', being welcomed by a kneeling personification of the city at the gate. Beneath is a galley, and the Trier mint mark.

24   The Dorchester (Dorset) Hoard, as found in 1936. It consisted of 22,000 coins, ranging from Caracalla to Gallienus, and was buried in the mid third century. It was probably a treasury in the charge of an official – possibly the tax collection of Durnovaria. The jug was an antique and dates from *c.* AD 100.

25   The Skaill Hoard, Orkney. A selection of silver ornaments and coins from a late tenth century Viking plunder hoard discovered in 1858. The ornaments are probably ring money. The coins

consist of an Anglo-Saxon penny of Aethelstan (top right), a Danish 'St Peter of York' penny (second bottom row, middle), and dirhems and fragmentary dirhems of the Samanid and Abbasid Dynasties.

26   Brooches and ornaments associated with coins in the Canonbie (Dumfriesshire) Hoard, *c.* 1295 The hoard was found in 1863, and consisted of 77 English, Scottish and Irish pennies of Edward I–II, Alexander III and John Baliol

27   Sixteenth century money box (Pirlie Pig) from Perth, with two of the coins found in it. That on the far right is of Ferdinand and Isabella of Spain (1479–1504).

28   Coins and Medieval Britain

a   Anglo-Saxon sceatta, *c.* AD 700–50. *Obv.* Fantastic animal. *Rev.* Ornamental (floral) swirl.

b   Penny of Offa (757–96) of Group II (787–92). *Obv.* Bust and moneyer's name, IBBϽ *Rev.* ◇ERY. Quatrefoil with panel in centre with cross.

c   Bronze sceatta of Northumbria (sometimes called a styca), Eanred (810–41). *Obv.* Title round cross *Rev.* Moneyer's name ENDVIH round cross.

d   Vikings of York, Cnut (early tenth century). Silver penny. *Obv.* CNVT REX round cross. *Rev.* CVNNETI round cross in circle.

e   Aethelred II of All England, 978–1016, silver penny. *Obv.* ÆDELRED REX ꓕNGLᴼ round bust *Rev.* GODPINE M O LVND. Long cross. Moneyer Godwin, London mint.

f   Penny of William I, 1086–7. 'Paxs' type. *Obv.* Title round facing bust. *Rev.* SEPINE ON IEXIC. Exeter mint. Cross with PAXS in circles in angles.

g   Silver penny of John, 1199–1216. Short-cross type, with the name of Henry. *Obv.* Title round facing bust holding sceptre. *Rev.* Moneyer and mint name round short cross with quartefoils in angles. London mint.

h   Silver penny of Henry III, 1216–72. Long-cross type, after 1247. Canterbury mint. *Obv.* Title round facing bust. *Rev.* Moneyer and mint name round angles of long cross, pellets in intersections.

i   Silver penny of Edward II, 1307–27. London mint.

j   Silver groat of Edward III, 1327–77. Pre-Treaty Period C (1351–2).

k   Gold noble of Edward III, Fourth coinage, Post-Treaty period (1369–77).

Glossary

AES (Æ)	A term and symbol used to indicate that a coin is of copper or bronze.
ARGENTEUS (AR)	A term and symbol used to indicate that a coin is of silver. Also a denomination struck in the Roman Empire between the times of Diocletian and Julian the Apostate.
AUREUS (A/)	A term and symbol used to indicate that a coin is of gold. Also a Roman gold coin worth 25 denarii.
AUTONOMOUS	Coins are described as 'autonomous issues' when they have been struck by cities and states rather than in the name of an individual ruler.
BILLON	An alloy of silver and copper, in which copper predominates.
BLANK	A synonym for 'flan' (see below).
BRACTEATE	A coin which has been struck on a thin flan with a die which has the type in relief as opposed to incuse, with the result that it appears in incuse on the obverse and in relief on the reverse. This process of coining is akin to repoussé work.
BROCKAGE	An error in coining which results in damage to the coin. Normally this means that a coin has had another wedged under it in striking with the result that one type is in reverse and incuse.
DIE	The punch engraved with the type that is used to strike the coin. There are two dies involved in coining, an obverse and a reverse.
DIE SINKER	A die engraver.

DIE VARIETIES — A coin is referred to as a die variety when the types vary slightly while still conforming to standard pattern.

EXERGUE (Ex.) — The segment of the coin field which is divided from the rest of the type by a line. On modern coins the date appears in the exergue in some cases, on late Roman coins the mint mark was sometimes put there.

FIELD — The area of the coin which is not taken up by the type or legend.

FLAN — The blank piece of metal on which a coin is struck.

HYBRID — An expression sometimes used to describe a mule (see below).

INCUSE — In intaglio.

JETTON — A reckoning counter.

LEGEND — The inscription.

MILLING — The process of striking a coin by machinery as opposed to manually (which is termed hammering). It originates in the early days of mechanical striking when the coining presses were operated by a water mill. The term is wrongly used to describe the grooving on the edge of many modern coins, which is not 'milling' but 'reeding'.

MINT MARK — Letters or symbols put on a coin to denote the mint. The term is also applied to 'privy marks', symbols used to distinguish the pieces struck by individual moneyers and to prevent forgery. It can also mean the symbol (usually a cross) which indicates the start of the legend. In England in later times they have a chronological value as they were changed annually.

MODULE — The size of the flan on which the coin is struck.

MONEYER — The person responsible for the mint shop, whose name sometimes appeared with that of the mint on the coin.

MULE — A coin which combines a current type with an earlier one. Also used to describe a coin struck from dies not usually found in combination.

OBVERSE (Obv.)   The 'head' side of a coin.

PATTERN   A trial piece.

PILE   A term used in Medieval numismatics to described the anvil into which the obverse die was set.

RETARIFFING   The alteration of the face value of a coin due to inflation.

REVERSE (Rev., R_x)   The 'tail' side of a coin.

SIGNATURE   The name or initials of the engraver or artist who designed the coin type.

SYMBOL   A secondary type, letters or monogram that appears in the field.

TRUSSEL   The reverse die in Medieval numismatics.

TYPE   The principal design on either obverse or reverse.

Abbreviations

A.J.A.	*American Journal of Archaeology.*	*J.H.S.*	*Journal of Hellenic Studies.*
Ant.	*Antiquity.*	*J.I.M.*	*Journal of the Institute of Metallurgy.*
Ant.J.	*Antiquaries Journal.*		
Arch.	*Archaeologia.*	*J.R.S.*	*Journal of Roman Studies.*
Arch. Ael.	*Archaeologia Aeliana.*		
Archaeom.	*Archaeometry.*	*Med. Arch.*	*Medieval Archaeology.*
Arch.J.	*Archaeological Journal.*	*Museum Notes*	*American Numismatic Society Museum Notes.*
Arch.N.L.	*Archaeological Newsletter.*		
B.B.C.S.	*Bulletin of the Board of Celtic Studies.*	*N.A.J.N.*	*North American Journal of Numismatics.*
B.M.Q.	*British Museum Quarterly.*	*N.C.*	*Numismatic Chronicle.*
		N.Circ.	*Numismatic Circular.*
B.N.J.	*British Numismatic Journal.*	*N.N.M.*	*Numismatic Notes and Monographs.*
B.S.F.N.	*Bulletin de la Societé Française de Numismatique.*	*Oxon.*	*Oxoniensia.*
		P.P.S.	*Proceedings of the Prehistoric Society.*
C.I.N.	*Congresso Internazionale di Numismatica, Roma.*	*P.R.I.A.*	*Proceedings of the Royal Irish Academy.*
C. & M.	*Coins and Medals.*	*P.S.A.S.*	*Proceedings of the Society of Antiquaries of Scotland.*
C.A.S.	*Proceedings of the Cambridgeshire Antiquarian Society.*	*R.A.*	*Revue Archéologique.*
		R.N.	*Revue Numismatique.*
E.C.	*Études Celtiques.*	*Rev. Num. Belge*	*Revue Numismatique de Belge.*
H.M.G.B.	*Historical Metallurgy Group Bulletin.*	*S.A.C.*	*Sussex Archaeological Collections.*
J.N.G.	*Jarbüch fur Numismatik und Glageschichte.*	*S.M.*	*Schweizer Münzblätter.*
		S.C.M.B.	*Seaby's Coin & Medal Bulletin.*

Trans. B.&G. A.S.   *Transactions of the Bristol and Gloucestershire Archaeological Society.*

Trans. C.&W. A.A.S.   *Transactions of the Cumberland and Westmorland Antiquarian and Archaeological Society.*

Select Bibliography

1 *Techniques of Coin Production*

Akerman, J. Y.	1844	*Coins of the Romans Relating to Britain* (1844).
Balog, P.	1955	'Notes on Ancient and Medieval Minting Technique', *N.C.* 6th Ser., XV (1955), 195–202.
Boon, G. C. & Rhatz, P.	1965	'Third Century Counterfeiting at Whitchurch, Somerset', *Arch.J.* CXXII (1965), 13–52.
Dolley, R. H. M.	1952	'The Significance of Die Axis in the Content of later Anglo-Saxon Coinage', *B.N.J.* XXVII (1952), 167–74.
Grierson, P.	1965	'Medieval Die Cutting and Minting', in *History of Technology* II (1965), 485–92.
Hill, G. F.	1922	'Ancient Methods of Coining', *N.C.* 5th Ser., II (1922), 1–43.
Keller, F.	1862	'Notice of a Die for Striking Helvetian or Gaulish Coins', *Arch.J.* XIX (1862), 252–8.
Knobloch, F.	1965	'A Note on Coin Moulds', *N.A.J.N.* IV, (1965), 115–22.
MacDonald, G.	1916	*Evolution of Coinage* (1916).
Milne, J. G.	1922	'Two Notes on Greek Dies', *N.C.* 5th Ser., II (1922), 43–9.
Smith, E. A.	1939	'The Composition and Production Techniques of Some Roman Silver Coins of the Third Century AD', *J.I.M.* 65 (1939), 271–5.
Selwood, D.	1963a	'Some Experiments in Greek Minting Technique', *N.C.* 7th Ser., III (1963), 217–31.

Selwood, D.	1963b	'Medieval Minting Techniques', *B.N.J.* XXXI (1963), 57–65.
Svoronos, N.	1967	'A Die of an Athenian Tetradrachm', *N.A.J.N.* IV (1967), 115–22.
Tylecote, R. F.	1962a	*Archaeology and Metallurgy* (1962).
Tylecote, R. F.	1962b	'The Method of Use of Early Iron Age Coin Moulds', *N.C.* 7th Ser., II (1962), 101–9.
Vermeule, C. C.	1954	*Ancient Methods of Coining* (1954).
Von Wedel, E.	1960	'The History of Die Forming', *Metal Treatment and Drop Forging* XXVII (1960), 401–8.
Wheeler, R. E. M.	1936	*Verulamium, a Belgic and Two Roman Cities* (1936).
Wooton, A.	1960	'Brass, a Roman Coining Metal', *S.C.M.B.* June 1960, 223–5.

2 *Chronology*

Baldwin-Brett, A.	1947	'Dated Coins of Ptolemy v', *Museum Notes* II (1947), 1–12.
Earle-Fox, H. B. & Shirley Fox, J.	1909–14	'The Pennies of Edward i, ii and iii', *B.N.J.* VI–X (1909–14), *passim*.
Grant, M.	1950	*Roman Anniversary Issues* (1950).
Hartmann, J.	1966	'Greek Numismatic Epigraphy', *N.A.J.N.* V (1966), 9–12.
Head, B. V.	1910	*Historia Numorum* (1910).
Hersh, C. A.	1952	'Sequence Marks on the Denarii of P. Crepusius', *N.C.* 6th Ser., XII (1952), 52–66.
Hill, G. F.	1906	*Historical Greek Coins* (1906).
Jacob, K. A.	1949	'Pennies of Edward i & ii', in Seaby (Ed.) *Notes on English Coinage*, I (1949), 19–28.
Jacobsthal, P.	1951	'Date of the Ephesian Foundation Deposit', *J.H.S.* LXXI (1951), 85–96.

| Jones, J. R. | 1963 | 'Revised Datings for the Earliest Greek Coins', *S.C.M.B.* May (1963), 147–8. |

Kraay, C. M.   1956   'The Behaviour of Early Imperial Countermarks', in Carson (Ed.), *Roman Coinage* (1956), 113–6.

Kraay, C. M.   1964   'Hoards, Small Change and the Origins of Coinage', *J.H.S.* LXXXIV (1964), 76–92.

Koumanides, S.   1965   'The Lion of Astias', *N.A.J.N.* IV (1965), 101–3.

Laing, L. R.   1962   'The Historical Significance of Coins Illustrated by the Coinage of Augustus', *S.C.M.B.* (1962), March-August, *passim*.

MacDonald, G.   1916   *The Evolution of Coinage* (1916).

Mattingly, H.   1922   'Some Historical Coins of the Roman Republic', *J.R.S.* XII (1922), 130–40.

Mattingly, H.   1952   'The Different Styles of Roman Republican Coinage', *N.C.* 6th Ser., XII (1952), 67–71.

Mattingly, H.   1963   *Roman Coins* (1963), 2nd Ed.

Mattingly, H. & Sydenham, E. A.   1923   *Roman Imperial Coinage* I (1923).

Noe, S. P.   1952   'A Group of Die Sequences at Poseidonia', *Museum Notes* V (1952), 9–19.

Robinson, E. S. G.   1956   'The Date of the Earliest Coins', *N.C.* 6th Ser., XVI (1956), 1–9.

Sear, D. R.   1962   'Dating Roman Imperial Coins', *S.C.M.B.* (1962), October–December.

Seltman, C.   1921   *Temple Coins of Olympia* (1921).

Seltman, C.   1924   *Athens, History and Coinage* (1924).

Seltman, C.   1955   *Greek Coins* (1955), 2nd Ed.

Sydenham, E. A.   1942   'Ornamental Detail as a Guide to the Classification of Republican Denarii', *N.C.* 6th Ser., I (1942), 117–27.

Sydenham, E. A.   1952   *The Roman Republican Coinage* (1952).

Thompson, M. 1952 'The Beginnings of the Athenian New Style Coinage', *Museum Notes* V (1952), 25–33.

Thompson, M. 1961 *The New Style Coinage of Athens* (1961).

Williams, R. T. 1967 'The Owls and Hippias', *N.C.* 7th Ser., VI (1967), 9–13.

5 *Coins and the Scientist*

Aitken, M. J. 1961 *Physics and Archaeology* (1961).

Allin, E. J. & Wallace, W. P. 1954 'Impurities in Euboean Monetary Silver', *Museum Notes* VI (1954), 35–69.

Biek, L. 1963 *Archaeology and the Microscope* (1963).

Brunetti, L. 1963 *Aspetti statistici della numismatica* (1963).

Bluysen, H. & Smith, P. B. 1962 'Determination of the Silver Content of Greek Coins by Neutron Activation', *Archaeom.* 5 (1962), 114 f.

Caley, E. R. 1964 *Analysis of Ancient Metals* (1964).

Carter, G. F. 1964a 'Preparation of Ancient Coins for Accurate X-Ray Analysis', *Archaeom.* 7 (1964), 106–13.

Carter, G. F. 1964b 'X-Ray Fluorescence Analysis of Roman Coins', *Analytical Chemistry* 36 (1964), 1264–8.

Carter, G. F. 1966a 'Ancient Coins as Records of the Past', *Chemistry* 39 (1966), 14–19.

Carter, G. F. 1966b 'Analysis of Copper and Brass Coins of the Early Roman Empire', *Science* 151 (1966), 196–7.

Carter, G. F. 1966 'How Accurate are X-Ray Fluorescence Analyses of Copper Coins?', *N.A.J.N.* V (1966), 181–87.

Condamin, J. & Picob, M. 1964 'Etudes de quelques problèmes analytiques propres aux monnaies antiques', *R.N.* (1964), 69–89.

Cope, L. H. &
Billingham, H. N.
1967
'Composition of 35 Roman Coins of the Period AD 284–363', *H.M.G.B.* **1** (9) (1967), 1–6.

Das, H. A. & Zonderhus, J.
1964
'The Analysis of Electrum Coins', *Archaeom.* **7** (1964), 9 f.

Forbes, J. S. & Dalladay, D. B.
1962
'The Composition of English Silver Coinage', *B.N.J.* XXX (1962), 82–7.

Grierser, D.
1966
'A Graphical Description of Coin Weights during the Roman Empire', *N.A.J.N.* V (1966), 115–7.

Hall, E. T.
1963
'Physical Methods of Chemical Analysis', in Pyddoke (Ed.), *The Scientist and Archaeology* (1963), 168–92.

Harris, E. J.
1961
'The Stuff of Coins', *S.C.M.B.* (1961), 389–90.

Hawkes, S. C., Merrick, J. M. & Metcalf, D. M.
1966
'X-Ray Analysis of some Dark Age Coins and Jewelry', *Archaeom.* **9** (1966), 99–138.

Hemmy, A. S.
1938
'Weight Standards of Ancient Greece and Persia', *Iraq* V, (1938), 65–81.

Hemmy, A. S.
1942
'A Summary of the Application of Statistical Methods to the Determination of Weight Standards of Roman Coins', *N.C.* 6th Ser., II (1942), 86–101.

Kraay, C. M.
1958a
'Gold and Copper Traces in Early Greek Silver, I', *Archaeom.* **1** (1958), 5–6.

Kraay, C. M.
1958b
'Composition of Electrum Coinage', *Archaeom.* **1** (1958), 21–2.

Kraay, C. M.
1959
'Gold and Copper Traces in Early Greek Silver, II' *Archaeom.* **2** (1959), 11.

Kraay, C. M.
1963
'On the Weight of Ancient Coins', *N.Circ.* **71** (1963), 116.

Kraay, C. M. & Emeleus, V.
1962
The Composition of Greek Silver Coins (1962).

Kosambi, D. D.
1965
'Scientific Numismatics', *Scientific American* (1965), 102–11.

Organ, R. M.   1963   'Analysis and Microscopic Study of Metals', in Pyddoke (Ed.). *The Scientist and Archaeology* (1963), 141–67.

Ravetz, A.   1963   'Neutron Activation Analysis of Silver in some Late Roman Copper Coins', *Archaeom.* **6** (1963), 46–56.

Reece, R.   1963   'Some Analyses of Late Roman Silver Coins', *N.C.* 7th Ser., III (1963), 241–2.

Sutherland, C. H. V. & Harold, M. R.   1961   'The Silver Content of Diocletian's Post-Reform Coins', *Archaeom.* **4** (1961), 56–62.

Tylecote, R. F.   1962a   'The Methods of Use of Early Iron Age Coin Moulds', *N.C.* 7th Ser., II 101–9.

Tylecote, R. F.   1962b   *Archaeology and Metallurgy* (1962).

Windler, R. J.   1965   'A Proposed Weight Classification of Fourth Century Roman Coins', *N.A.J.N.* IV (1965), 59–61.

Yao, T. C. & Stross, F. H.   1965   'The Use of Analysis by X-Ray Fluorescence in the Study of Coins', *A.J.A.* **69** (1965), 154–5.

6 *Classical Coins and the Prehistorian* & 7 *Celtic Coins and the Prehistorian*

Allen, D. F.   1944   'The Belgic Dynasties of Britain and their Coins', *Arch.* XC (1944), 1–47.

Allen, D. F.   1958   'Celtic Coins as Illustrations of Life in Late Pre-Roman Iron Age Britain', *P.P.S.* XXIV (1958), 43–63.

Allen, D. F.   1961a   'The Paul (Penzance) Hoard of Imitation Massalia Drachms', *N.C.* 7th Ser., I (1961), 91–106.

Allen, D. F.   1961b   'The Origins of Coinage in Britain: A Reappraisal', in Frere (Ed.), *Problems of the Iron Age in Southern Britain* (n.d. but 1961), 97–308.

L

Allen, D. F.   1961c   'The Coins of the Dobunni', in Clifford, E. M., *Bagendon, a Belgic Oppidum* (1961), 75–148.

Allen, D. F.   1961d   'A Hoard of Cisalpine Coins from Britain', *Atti Congresso Internazionale di Numismatica* Roma, (1961), 195–98.

Allen, D. F.   1962   'Celtic Coins', in *O.S. Map of Southern Britain in the Iron Age* (1962), 19–32.

Allen, D. F.   1963   *The Coins of the Coritani* (1963).

Allen, D. F.   1964   'Celtic Coins from the Romano-British Temple at Harlow', *B.N.J.* XXXIII (1964), 1–7.

Allen, D. F.   1967   'Iron Currency Bars in Britain', *P.P.S.* XXXIII (1967), 307–36.

Anon   1962   'A Mint and a Roman Road Found at Rochester', *N.Circ.* **70** (1962), 158.

Anon   1968   'Harlow Roman Temple', *Current Archaeology*, I (1968), 287–90.

Babelon, E.   1902–32   *Traité de monnaies grecques et romaines* (1902–32).

La Baume, P.   1960   *Keltische Münzen* (1960).

Brailsford, J.   1958   'Early Iron Age "C" in Wessex', *P.P.S.* XXIV (1958), 101–20.

Biddle, M.   1966   'Excavations at Winchester, 1965', *Ant.J.* XLVI (1966), 308–32.

Birchall, A.   1964   'Aylesford Revisited', *B.M.Q.* XXVIII (1964), 21–9.

Birchall, A.   1965   'The Swarling-Aylesford Culture: The Problem of the Belgae Reconsidered', *P.P.S.* XXXI (1965), 241–368.

Blanchet, A.   1902   'Récherches sur les monnaies celtiques de l'Europe Centrale', *R.N.* (1902), 36–51; 157–73.

Blanchet, A.   1905   *Traité des monnaies gauloises* (1905).

Blanchet, A. 1913 'Récherches sur l'influence commerciales de Massilia, en Gaule et dans l'Italie septentrionale', *R.N. Belge*, (1913), 291–328.

Blanchet, A. 1951 'Réflexions sur les monnaies gauloises', *R.N.* (1951), 21–34.

Blanchet, A. & Dieudonné, A. 1913 *Manuel de numismatique francaise*, I *Monnaies frappées en Gaule depuis les origines jusqu'à Hugues Capet* (1913).

Bonnet, E. 1937 'Les influence helléniques sur les monnaies de la Gaule Narbonnaise', *Bull. Arch. du Com. de Trav. Hist.* (1936–7), 77 ff.

Boardman, J. 1964 *The Greeks Overseas* (1964).

Bolin, S. 1930 Summary of *Fyndan av romerska mynt i det frie Germanien* in *Bericht des Deutches Arch. Inst.* 1929 (1930).

Boon, G. C. 1954 'A Greek Vase from the Thames', *J.H.S.* LXXIV (1954), 198.

Boon, G. C. 1958 *Roman Silchester* (1958).

Briscoe, G. 1964 'An Icenian Find from Lakenheath', *C.A.S.* LVIII (1964), 123.

Brooke, G. C. 1933 'The Philippus in the West and the Belgic Invasions of Britain', *N.C.* 6th Ser., XIII (1933), 88–138.

Brooke, G. C. 1933b 'The Distribution of Gaulish and British Coins in Britain', *Ant.* VII (1933), 268–89.

Cary, M. 1924 'The Greeks and Ancient Trade with the Atlantic', *J.H.S.* XLIV (1924), 166–79.

Callender, M. 1965 *Roman Amphorae* (1965).

Castelin, K. 1956 'Drobne Keltiske mince typu Alkis', *Num. Listy* XI (1956), 130–9.

Castelin, K. 1960 'Keltische Münzformen aus Bohmen', *Germania* (1960), 32–42.

Castelin, K. 1962 'Zur Chronologie des keltischen Münzwesers in mitteleuropa', *J.N.G.* XII (1963), 199–207.

Castelin, K. & Kellner, H. J. 1963 'Die glatten Regenbogenschüsselchen', *J.N.G.* XIII (1963), 105–30.

Chadwick, N. & Dillon, M. 1967 *The Celtic Realms* (1967).

Christ, K. 1957 'Ergebnisse und Probleme der Keltischen Numismatik und Geldeschichte', *Historia* VI (1957), 215–53.

Clayton, J. 1880 'A Description of Roman Remains near Procolita', *Arch.Ael.* VII (1880), 1–49.

Clifford, E. M. 1961 *Bagendon, a Belgic Oppidum* (1960).

Colbert de Beaulieu, J. B. 1950 'L'Attribution controuvée d'un monnayage gaulois aux Abrincatui', *Rev. Num. Belge* XCVI (1950), 27–33.

Colbert de Beaulieu, J. B. 1951 'Le monnayage de Coriosolite', *N. Circ.* **59** (1951), 321–4.

Colbert de Beaulieu, J. B. 1953a 'La numismatique celtique de la Gaule', *Ogam* V (1953), 67–106.

Colbert de Beaulieu, J. B. 1953b 'Une enigme de la numismatique armoricaine: les monnaies celtiques des Vénètes', *Mem. de la Soc. d'Hist. et d'Arch. de Bretagne* XXXIII (1953), 5–52.

Colbert de Beaulieu, J. B. 1954 'La contremarqué dans la monnayage d'or gaulois', *Gallia* XII (1954), 55–73.

Colbert de Beaulieu, J. B. 1955a 'Peut-on dater par la numismatique l'occupation gauloise d'un oppidum?' *R.A.* VI fas 3. (1955), 260–70.

Colbert de Beaulieu, J. B. 1955b 'Numismatique celtique d'Alesia', *Rev. Num. Belge* **101** (1955), 55–83.

Colbert de Beaulieu, J. B. 1958 'Armorican Coin Hoards in the Channel Islands', *P.P.S.* XXIV (1958), 201–10.

Colbert de Beaulieu, J. B.   1962a 'Les monnaies gauloises au nom des chefs mentionés dans les Commentaires de César', *Collections Latomus* LVIII (1962), 419–46.

Colbert de Beaulieu, J. B.   1962b 'Chronique de numismatique celtique', *E.C.* X (1962), 186–209.

Colbert de Beaulieu, J. B.   1963 'Les monnaies de Vercingetorix', *Gallia* XXI (1963), 11–75.

Colbert de Beaulieu, J. B.   1964 'La numismatique d'Alesia', *B.S.F.N.* June, 1964, 365–6.

Cunliffe, B.   1965 *Excavations at Winchester 1949–60* I (1965).

Déchelette, J.   1911 'Les origines de la drachme et de l'obole', *R.N.* XV (1911), 1–59.

Déchelette, J.   1927 *Manuel d'Archéologie* ... IV (1927).

Decker, K. V. & Scollar, I.   1962 'Iron Age Square Enclosures in the Rhineland', *Ant.* XXXVI (1962), 175–8.

De Gaudan, A. M.   1954 'Algunos problemas fundamentales de las amonedaciones de plata de Emporion y Rode', *Numisma* **4** (1954), 9–47.

De Navarro, J. M.   1928 'Massilia and Early Celtic Culture', *Ant.* II (1928), 423–42.

Eggers, H. J.   1951 *Der Romische Import im freien Germanien* (Atlas der Urgeschichte I), (1951).

Eggers, H. J.   1955 *Jarbuch des Rom-Germ. Zentramuseum* (1955).

Evans, J.   1964 *The Coins of the Ancient Britons* (1864) with Supplement (1890).

Feachem, R. W.   1960 'The "Cairnmuir" Hoard from Netherurd, Peeblesshire', *P.S.A.S.* XCI (1960), 112–16.

Filip, J.   1962 *Celtic Civilization and Its Heritage* (1962).

Forrer, R.   1908 *Keltische Numismatik der Rhein- und-Donauland* (1908).

Forrer, R. 1923 'Les statères et quarts de statères helvètes en or trouvés à La Tène', in Vouga, *La Tène* (1923).

Forrer, R. 1925 *Les monnaies gauloises ou celtiques trouvées en Alsace* (1925).

Fox, A. 1956 'Teignmouth', *Proc. Devon Assoc.* (1956), 216–17.

Fox, A. 1964 *South-West England* (1964).

Fox, C. 1946 *A Find of the Early Iron Age from Llyn Cerrig Bach, Anglesey* (1946).

Fox, C. 1958 *Pattern and Purpose, Early Celtic Art in Britain* (1958).

Frere, S. S. 1941 'A Claudian Site at Needham', *Ant. J.* XXI (1941), 50–1.

Frere, S. S. 1957 'Excavations at Verulamium, Second Interim Report', *Ant. J.* XXVII (1957), 1–16.

Frere, S. S. 1958 'Excavations at Verulamium, Third Interim Report, *Ant. J.* XXVIII (1958), 1–15.

Frere, S. S. 1961 'Some Problems of the Later Iron Age', in Frere (Ed.) *Problems of the Iron Age in S. Britain* (1961), 84–92.

Gimbutas, M. 1965 *The Prehistory of Eastern Europe* II (1965).

Giot, P. R. 1960 *Brittany* (1960).

Goodchild, R. 1937 'The Greek Coins from Exeter Reconsidered', *N.C.* 5th Ser., XVII (1937), 124–8.

Grant, M. 1958 *Roman History from Coins* (1958).

Harden, D. B. 1950 'Italic and Etruscan Finds from Britain', *Atti del 1º Congresso Preistorica et Protohist. Mediterranea* (1950), 215–24.

Haverfield, F. & MacDonald, G. 1907 'Greek Coins at Exeter', *N.C.* 4th Ser., VII (1907), 145–55.

Hawkes, C. F. C. & Dunning, G. C. 1930 'The Belgae of Gaul and Britain', *Arch. J.* LXXXVII (1930), 150–335.

Hawkes, C. F. C. & Hull, M. R. 1947 *Camulodunum, First Report on the Excavations at Colchester* (1947).

Hawkes, C. F. C.   1968   'New Thoughts on the Belgae', *Ant.* XLII (1968), 6–16.

Head, B. V.   1911   *Historia Numorum* (1911).

Head, B. V.   1959   *A Guide to the Principal Coins of the Greeks* (1959).

Hiess, A.   1870   *Description générale des monnaies antiques de l'Espagne* (1870).

Hencken, H.   1932   *The Archaeology of Cornwall & Scilly* (1932).

Hencken, H.   1955   *Indo-European Languages and Archaeology,* (*Am. Anth. Ass. Mem.*) **84** (1955).

Hill, G. F.   1906   *Historical Greek Coins* (1906).

Hill, G. F.   1931   'Notes on the Ancient Coinage of Hispania Citerior', *N.N.M.* **50** (1931).

Jackson, K. H.   1961   *The Oldest Irish Tradition, a Window on the Early Iron Age* (1961).

Jazdzewski, K.   1964   *Poland* (1964).

Joffroy, R.   1954   *Le Trésor de Vix* (1954).

Joffroy, R. & Brezt-Mahler, D.   1959   'Les Tombes à Char de la Tène dans l'Est de la France', *Gallia* XVII (1959), 5–35.

Klindt-Jensen, O.   1958   *Denmark* (1958).

Klindt-Jensen, O.   1961a   *Gundestrup Kedelen* (1961).

Klindt-Jensen, O.   1961b   'Gundestrup, a Reassessment', *Ant.* XXXIII (1961), 161–70.

Koenig, M. E. P.   1966   'Celtic Coins, A New Interpretation', *Archaeology* **19** (1966), 24–30.

Laing, L. R.   1961   'Belgic Flan Moulds from Britain', *S.C.M.B.* Oct. 1961, 383–7.

Laing, L. R.   1966a   'Roman Republican Coins in Britain', *S.C.M.B.* (1966), 56–7.

Laing, L. R.   1966b   'Greeks and Barbarians: The Numismatic Evidence for Greek Contact with Barbarian Europe', *N.A.J.N.* V (1966), *passim.*

Laing, L. R.   1967   'Western Europe's Oldest Coinage', *C. & M.* IV (1967), 214–39.

Lambrechts, P.   1954   'L'exaltation de la tête dans la pensée et dans l'art des Celtes', *Diss. Archeol. Gand.* II, (1954), 50 ff.

Laver, J.   1927   'Excavation of a Tumulus at Lexden, Colchester', *Arch.* LXXVI (1927), 214–54.

Lengyel, L.   1954   *L'art gaulois dans les médailles* (1954).

Mack, R. P.   1964   *The Coinage of Ancient Britain* (1964), 2nd Ed.

Mattingly, H.   1932   'Coins from a site Found in British East Africa', *N.C.* 5th Ser., XII (1932), 175–7.

Mattingly, H.   1962   *Roman Coins* (1962), 2nd Ed.

May, J.   1966   'Note on Greek Coins from Ancaster', *East Midlands Arch. Bull.* 7 (1966), 9.

Milne, J. G.   1940   'The "Philippus" Coin at Rome', *J.R.S.* XXX (1940), 11–15.

Milne, J. G.   1948   *Finds of Greek Coins from the British Isles* (1948).

Moberg, C. A.   1952   'Om Gundestrup kitteln och de keltiska mynten', *Några synpunkter* (1952), 362–71.

Mongait, A. L.   1961   *Archaeology in the U.S.S.R.* (1961).

Muret, E. & Chailbouillet, A.   1889   *Catalogue des monnaies gauloises de la Bibliothèque Nationale* (1889).

Neustupný, E. & J.   1961   *Czechoslovakia* (1961).

Noe, S. P.   1937   'A Bibliography of Greek Coin Hoards,' *N.N.M.* **78**, (1937).

Ondrovich, V.   1958   *Keltiske Mince Typu Biatec* (1958).

Paulsen, R.   1933   *Die Münzprägungen der Boier* (1933).

Piggott, S.   1950   'Swords and Scabbards of the British Early Iron Age', *P.P.S.* XVI (1950), 1–28.

Piggott, S.   1953   'Three Metalwork Hoards of the Roman Period from Southern Scotland', *P.S.A.S.* LXXXVII (1953), 1–50.

Piggott, S.	1959	'The Carnyx in Iron Age Britain', *Ant. J.* XXIX (1959), 19–32.
Piggott, S.	1965	*Ancient Europe* (1965).
Piggott, S. & Clark, G.	1965	*Prehistoric Societies* (1965).
Pick, B.	1898	*Die Antiken Münzen von Dacien und Moesien*, I (1898).
Pick, B. & Regling, K.	1908	*Die Antiken Münzen von Dacien und Moesien*, II (1908).
Pink, K.	1936	'Die Goldprägung der Ostkelten', *Wien. Prahist. Zschr.* XXIII (1936), 8–41.
Pink, K.	1939	*Die Münzprägung der Ostkelten und iherr Nachbarn* (1939).
Pink, K.	1960	*Einfuhrung in die keltische Münzkunde mit hesonderer Beruchsichtigung des osterreichischen Raumes* (1960).
Powell, T. G. E.	1958	*The Celts* (1958).
Raftery, J.	1964	*The Celts* (1964).
Reece, R.	1967	A Numismatic 'Tour de France', *S.C.M.B.* (1967), *passim*.
Robertson, A. S.	1956	'Romano-British Coin Hoards', in *Essays Presented to Harold Mattingly* (1956), 262–85.
Rolland, H.	1935	'Sur les drachmes lourdes de Marseille', *Provincia* XV (1935), 238–46.
Rolland, H.	1936	'Fouilles d'un habitat preromain à Saint-Remy de Provence', *Provincia* XVI (1936), 193–243.
Rolland, H.	1949	'L'expansion du monnayage de Marseille dans le pays Celto-Ligure', *Rev. Et. Ligures* XV (1949), 139–48.
Rolland, H.	1961	'Monnaies Gallo-Grecques', *C.I.N.* I (1961), 111–19.
Ross, A.	1959a	'The Human Head in Pagan Celtic Religion', *P.S.A.S.* XCI (1959), 10–43.
Ross, A.	1959b	'Chain Symbolism in Pagan Celtic Religion', *Speculum* XXXIV (1959), 39–59.

Ross, A.   1967   *Pagan Celtic Britain* (1967).
Roth, B.   1913   'Ancient Gaulish Coins, In-
                                          cluding those of the Channel
                                          Islands', *B.N.J.* IX (1913),
                                          1–80.

Seltman, C.   1955   *Greek Coins* (1955).
Shortt, W.   1841   *Sylva Antiqua Iscanea* (1841).
Sjoenstedt-Jonval, M-L.   1936   'Légendes épiques Irlandaises
                                          et monnaies gauloises, Ré-
                                          cherches sur la constitution de
                                          la légende du Cuchulainn',
                                          Études Celtiques I (1936), 1–77.

Stead, I. M.   1967   'A La Tène III Burial at
                                          Welwyn Garden City', *Arch.*
                                          CI (1967), 1–62.

Stenberger, M.   1963   *Sweden* (1963).
Stevens, C. E.   1951   'Britain Between the Invasions',
                                          in Grimes (Ed.), *Aspects of
                                          Archaeology* (1951), 332–43.

Stevenson, R. B. K.   1967   'Metalwork and Some other
                                          Objects in Scotland and their
                                          Cultural Affinities', in Rivet
                                          (Ed.), *The Iron Age in North
                                          Britain* (1967), 17–44.

Sutherland, C. H. V.   1937   *Coinage and Currency in Roman
                                          Britain* (1937).

Sydenham, A. E.   1944   'The White Horse and Ancient
                                          British Coin-Types', *N.C.* 6th
                                          Ser., IV (1944), 65–76.

Sydenham, A. E.   1952   *The Coinage of the Roman Re-
                                          public* (1952).

Tierney, J. J.   1960   'The Celtic Ethnography of
                                          Posidonius', *P.R.I.A.* LX(C)
                                          (1960), 189–275.

Tierney, J. J.   1964   'The Celts and the Classical
                                          Authors', in Raftery (Ed.),
                                          The Celts (1964), 23–35.

Thompson, F. C.   1962   'A Note on the Composition of
                                          British pre-Roman Tin Money',
                                          N.C. (1962), 7th Ser., II, 111–2.

Todd, M.   1965   'Germanus Indutilli L – Remi
                                          ou Treveri? *S.M.* Heft 57, 3–7.

De la Tour, H.   1892   *Atlas de monnaies gauloises* (1892).
Toynbee, J. M. C.   1962   *Art in Roman Britain* (1962).

Toynbee, J. M. C.   1964   *Art in Britain Under the Romans* (1964).

Tylecote, R. F.   1962a   'The Method of Use of Early Iron Age Coin Moulds', *N.C.* 7th Ser., II (1962), 101–9.

Tylecote, R. F.   1962b   *Metallurgy in Archaeology* (1962).

Uenze, O.   1958   *Frürömische Amphoren als Zeitmarken im Spätlatène* (1958).

Villard, F.   1960   *La Ceramique grecque de Marseille* (1960).

Vouga, P.   1923   *La Tène* (1923).

Wainwright, F. T.   1955   *The Problem of the Picts* (1955).

Wheeler, R. E. M.   1936   *Verulamium, a Belgic and Two Roman Cities* (1936).

Wheeler, R. E. M.   1943   *Maiden Castle, Dorset* (1943).

Wheeler, R. E. M.   1955   *Rome Beyond the Imperial Frontiers* (1955).

Wheeler, R. E. M. & Richardson, K. M.   1957   *Hillforts of Northern France* (1957).

Wild, J. P.   1966   'Papyrus in Pre-Roman Britain', *Ant.* XL (1966), 139–41.

Würtrich, G.   1945   'Celtic Numismatics in Switzerland', *N.C.* 6th Ser., V (1945), 1–33.

8 *Coins and the Archaeology of Roman Britain*

Akerman, J. Y.   1844   *Coins of the Romans Relating to Britain* (1844).

Askew, G.   1967   *The Coinage of Roman Britain* (1967).

Atkinson, D.   1942   *Excavations at Wroxeter, 1923–7* (1942).

Birley, E.   1961   *Research on Hadrian's Wall* (1961).

Birley, R. E.   1965   'Excavation of the Roman Fortress at Carpow, Perthshire', *P.S.A.S.* XCVI (1965), 184–208.

Boon, G. C.   1949   'A Claudian Origin for Sea Mills', *Trans. B. & G.A.S.* LXVIII (1949), 184–88.

Boon, G. C.   1950   'Excavations at King's Weston Park', *Trans. B. & G.A.S.* LXIX (1950), 5–58.

Boon, G. C.   1958   *Roman Silchester* (1958).

Boon, G. C.   1966   'Third Century Counterfeiting at Whitchurch, Somerset', *Arch. J.* CXXII (1966) 13–52.

Briscoe, G.   1964   'Icenian Coin Find from Lakenheath', *C.A.S.* LVII (1954), 123.

Bushe-Fox, J. P.   1915   *Excavations at Hengistbury Head* (1915).

Bushe-Fox, J. P.   1926   *Excavations at Richborough, I* (1926).

Bushe-Fox, J. P.   1928   *Excavations at Richborough, II* (1928).

Bushe-Fox, J. P.   1932a   *Excavations at Richborough, III* (1932).

Bushe-Fox, J. P.   1932b   'Notes on Roman Coastal Defences', *J.R.S.* XXII (1932), 60–72.

Bushe-Fox, J. P.   1949   *Excavations at Richborough, IV* (1949).

Carson, R. A. G.   1951   'Roman Coins from the Excavations at Camerton, Bath', *N.C.* 6th Ser., XI (1951), 130–1.

Carson, R. A. G.   1959   'The Bredgar Treasure of Roman Coins', *N.C.* 6th Ser., XIX (1959), 17–22.

Clarke, R. R.   1960   *East Anglia* (1960).

Cocks, A. K.   1921   'A Romano-British Housestead at Hambleden Valley, Bucks', *Arch.* LXXI (1921), 141–98.

Collingwood, R. G.   1930   *The Archaeology of Roman Britain* (1930).

Collingwood, R. G. & Myres, J. N. L.   1937   *Roman Britain and the English Settlements* (1937).

Corder, P.   1930   *The Defences of the Roman Fort at Malton* (1930).

Corder, P.   1939   *Excavations at the Roman Fort at Brough* (1939), Hull Mus. Pub., **189**.

Corder, P.   1961   *Third Report on the Roman Town Town and Villa at Great Casterton, Rutland* (1961).

Cotton, M. & Gathercole, P.   1958   *Excavations at Clausentum* (1958).

Curle, J.   1911   *Newstead, a Roman Frontier Post and its People* (1911).

Donovan, H.   1935   'Roman Finds from Bourton', *Trans. B. & G.A.S.* LVII (1935), 234.

Dudley, D. & Webster, G.   1962   *The Rebellion of Boudicca* (1962).

Dudley, D. & Webster, G.   1965   *The Roman Conquest of Britain* (1965).

Dunnett, B. R. K.   1967   'Excavations on North Hill, Colchester', *Arch. J.* CXXIII (1967), 27–62.

Frere, S. S.   1967   *Britannia* (1967).

Fox, A.   1952   *Roman Exeter* (1952).

Fox, A.   1966   'Roman Exeter', in Wacher (Ed.), *Civitas Capitals of Roman Britain* (1966), 31–46.

Gould, J.   1964   *Excavations at Wall, 1961–3* (1964). (Lichfield and S. Staffs. Arch. & Hist. Soc. Pub.)

Hartley, B.   1966   'Dating Town Buildings and Structures', in Wacher (Ed.), *Civitas Capitals of Roman Britain* (1966), 52–60.

Hawkes, C. F. C.   1927   'Excavations at Alchester, 1926', *Ant. J.* VII (1927), 155–233.

Hawkes, C. F. C. & Hull, M. R.   1947   *Camulodunum* (1947).

Hill, G. F.   1911   'A Hoard of Roman and British Coins from Southants', *N.C.* 4th Ser., XI (1911), 42–56.

Hill, P. V.   1949   *Barbarous Radiates, N.N.M.* **112** (1949).

Hill, P. V.   1952   'Coinage of Britain in the Dark Age', *B.N.J.* XXIV (1952), 1–27.

Hill, P. V.   1950   'Barbarous Imitations of Fourth Century Roman Coins', *N.C.* 6th Ser., X (1950), 233–76.

Hill, P. V.   1955   'Barbarous Roman Coins', *N.C.* 6th Ser., XV (1955), 233–76.

Hogg, A. H. & Stevens, C. E.   1937   'Dorchester Defences', *Oxon.* II (1937), 41–73.

Hull, M. R.   1958   *Roman Colchester* (1958).

Iliffe, J. H.   1927   'Excavations at Alchester, 1927', *Ant. J.* VII (1927), 105–36.

Jarrett, M. G.   1965   'Early Roman Campaigns in Wales', *Arch. J.* CXXI (1965), 23–39.

Kent, J. P. C.   1952   'Coins and the Evacuation of Hadrian's Wall', *T.C. & W. & A.A.S.* LI (1952), 4–16.

Kent, J. P. C.   1959   'Barbarous Copies of Roman Coins', *Limes-Studien* (Proc. 3rd Internat. Cong. on Limes) (1959), 66 f.

Kenyon, K. M.   1947   *The Jewry Wall Site, Leicester* (1947).

Laver, J.   1927   'Excavations at a Tumulus at Lexden, Colchester', *Arch.* LXXVI (1927), 241–54.

Macdonald, G.   1905   *The Roman Forts on the Bar Hill* (1906).

Macdonald, G.   1931   'The Coins', in Benton, S. 'The Excavation of the Sculptor's Cave, Covesea', *P.S.A.S.* LXV (1931), 177–217.

Macdonald, G.   1934   *The Roman Wall in Scotland* (1934).

Mattingly, H.   1932a   'Hoards of Roman Coins Found in Britain and a Coin Survey of the Roman Province', *J.R.S.* XXII (1932), 88–95.

Mattingly, H.   1932b   'St Albans Site Finds', *N.C.* 5th Ser., XII (1932), 239–42.

Mattingly, H.   1934a   'Clausentum, Site Finds', *N.C.* 5th Ser., XIV (1934), 223.

Mattingly, H.   1934b   'Site Finds from Duston, Northants', *N.C.* 5th Ser., XIV (1934), 221–4.

Mattingly, H.   1934c   'Finds from Great Chesterford', *N.C.* 5th Ser., XIV (1934), 225–6.

Mattingly, H.   1962   *Roman Coins* (1962), 2nd Ed.

Mattingly, H. & Pearce, I.   1938   'The Amlwych Hoard', *B.B.C.S.* IX (1938), 168–83.

Mattingly, H. B.   1963   'The Lightwood Hoard and the Coinage of "Barbarous Radiates" ', *N. Staffs. J. of Field Studies*, III (1963), 19–36.

Meates, G. W.   1955   *Lullingstone Roman Villa* (1955).

Merrifield, R.   1965   *The Roman City of London* (1965).

Milne, J. G.   1931   'Woodeaton Coins', *J.R.S.* XXII (1932), 88–95.

Nash-Williams, V.   1932   'The Roman Fortress at Caerleon', *Arch. Camb.* LXXXVII (1932), 48–105.

Nash-Williams, V.   1954   *The Roman Frontier in Wales* (1954).

O'Neil, B. H.   1935   'Coins and Archaeology', *Arch. J.* XCII (1935) 64–80.

O'Neil, B. H.   1945   'Excavations at Park Street', *Arch. J.* CII (1945), 21–111.

Pearce, I. W.   1929   'Coins Found at Silchester', *N.C.* 5th Ser., IX (1929), 328–33.

Pilmer, J. G.   1956   'Analysis of Early Roman Pottery', *S.A.C.* XCIX (1956), 111–39.

Radford, C. A. R.   1935   'Excavations at Ditchley', *Oxon.* I (1935), 24–69.

Ravetz, A.   1965   'Fourth Century Inflation and Romano-British Coin Finds', *N.C.* 7th Ser., IV (1965), 201–35.

Reece, R.   1961   'Coins and Archaeology', *S.C.M.B.* May-December, 1961.

Richmond, I. A.   1955   *Roman Britain* (1955).

Richmond, I. A. (Ed.)   1958   *Roman and Native in North Britain* (1958).

Rivet, A. L. F.   1958   *Town and Country in Roman Britain* (1958).

Robertson, A. S.   1952   'Roman Coins found in Scotland', *P.S.A.S.* LXXXIV (1952), 137–69.

Robertson, A. S.   1956   'Romano-British Coin Hoards', in Carson (Ed.), *Roman Coinage* (1956), 262–85.

Robertson, A. S.   1960a   *The Antonine Wall* (1960.)

Robertson, A. S.   1960b 'Roman Coins Found in Scotland', *P.S.A.S.* XLIV (1960), 137–69.

Simpson, G.   1964 *Britons and the Roman Army* (1964).

Sutherland, C. H. V.   1935 'Romano-British Imitations of Coins of Claudius I', *N.N.M.* 65 (1935).

Sutherland, C. H. V.   1936 'Minimi, Radiate and Diademed', *Trans. Inter. Num. Cong.* (1936), 252–65.

Sutherland, C. H. V.   1937 *Coinage and Currency in Roman Britain* (1937).

Thomas, A. C. (Ed.)   1966 *Rural Settlement in Roman Britain*, (1966).

Todd, M.   1967 'Romano-British Mintages of Antoninus Pius', *N.C.* 7th Ser., VI (1967), 147–53.

Toynbee, J. M. C.   1964 *Art in Britain Under the Romans* (1964).

Wacher, J. (Ed.)   1966 *Civitas Capitals of Roman Britain* (1966).

Wade, W. V.   1953 'Coins from Aldborough', *N.C.* 6th Ser., XIII (1953), 132–4.

Ward, J.   1903 *Gellygaer* (1903).

Watson, K.   1965 *North Wales* (1965).

Webb, P. H.   1907 'Reign and Coinage of Carausuis', *N.C.* 4th Ser., VII (1907), 1–107.

Webster, G.   1959 'Cirencester – Dyer Court Excavations 1957', *Trans. B. & G.A.S.* LXXVIII (1959), 44–85.

Webster, G.   1958 'Roman Military Advance Under Ostorius Scapula', *Arch. J.* CXV (1958), 49–99.

Webster, G.   1966 'Fort and Town in Early Roman Britain', in Wacher (Ed.), *Civitas Capitals of Roman Britain* (1966), 31–46.

Wedlake, W. J.   1958 *Excavations at Camerton* (1958).

Wheeler, R. E. M.   1923 'Segontium and the Roman Occupation of Wales', *Y Cymmrodor* XXXIII (1923).

Wheeler, R. E. M.   1930 *London in Roman Times* (1930).

Wheeler, R. E. M.   1936   *Verulamium, a Belgic and Two Roman Cities* (1936).

Wheeler, R. E. M.   1943   *Maiden Castle, Dorset* (1943).

9 *Coins and Medieval Britain*

Arbman, H.   1961   *The Vikings* (1961).

Barton, K. J.   1960   'Excavations at Back Hall, Bristol, 1958', *Trans. B. & Glos. A. S.* LXXXIX (1960), 251–87.

Biddle, M.   1964   'Excavations at Winchester 1962–3', *Ant. J.* XLIV (1964), 188–220.

Biddle, M.   1965   'Excavations at Winchester 1964', *Ant. J.* XLV (1965), 230–64.

Blunt, C. E.   1961   'The Coinage of Offa', in Dolley (Ed.), *Anglo-Saxon Coins* (1961), 1–23.

Brooke, G. C.   1951   *English Coins* (1951).

Brondsted, J.   1965   *The Vikings* (1965).

Bruce Mitford, R.   1956   'A Dark Age Settlement at Mawgan Porth, Cornwall', in Bruce Mitford (Ed.), *Recent Archaeological Excavations in the British Isles* (1956), 167–97.

Bruce Mitford, R.   1968   *The Sutton Hoo Ship Burial: A Handbook*, (1968).

Bushe-Fox, J. P.   1949   *Fourth Report on the Excavation of the Roman Fort at Richborough, Kent* (1949).

Chadwick, N.   1963   *Celtic Britain* (1963).

Chautard, J.   1875   *Imitations des monnaies au type Esterlin* (1875).

Creeke, A. B.   1904   'The Regal Sceatta and Styca Series of Northumbria', *B.N.J.* I (1904), 65–96.

Dolley, M. & Ingold, J.   1961a   'Viking Age Coin Hoards from Ireland and their Relevance to Anglo-Saxon Studies', in Dolley (Ed.), *Anglo-Saxon Coins* (1961), 136–69.

Dolley, M. & Metcalf, D.   1961b   'The Reform of the English Coinage Under Eadgar', in Dolley (Ed.), *Anglo-Saxon Coins* (1961), 136–69.

Dolley, M.   1962   'The 1962 Llantrithyd Hoard
                                      and Some Thoughts on the First
                                      Norman Coinage in Wales',
                                      B.N.J. XXXI (1962), 74–9.
Dolley, M.   1964   *Anglo-Saxon Pennies* (1964).
Dolley, M.   1966a   *The Norman Conquest and the
                                      English Coinage* (1966).
Dolley, M.   1966b   *Viking Coins of the Danelaw and
                                      Dublin* (1966).
Dolley, M.   1966c   *Sylloge of Coins of the British Isles:
                                      The Hiberno-Norse Coins on the
                                      British Museum* (1966).
Dunning, G. C.   1949   'Report on Medieval Pottery
                                      from Selsey Common, nr.
                                      Stroud', *Trans.B. & G.A.S.*
                                      LXVIII (1949), 22–44.
Frere, S. S.   1966   'The End of Towns in Roman
                                      Britain', in Wacher (Ed.),
                                      Civitas Capitals of Roman Britain
                                      (1966), 87–100.
Frere, S. S.   1967   *Britannia* (1967).
Le Gentilhomme, P.   1946   *Le monnayage et la circulation
                                      monetaire dans les royaumes bar-
                                      bares en occident (V^e – VIIIe
                                      siècle)* (1946).
Glass, S.   1962   'The Sutton Hoo Ship Burial',
                                      Ant. XXXVI (1962), 179–83.
Grierson, P.   1952   'The Dating of the Sutton Hoo
                                      Coins', *Ant.* XXVI (1952),
                                      83–6.
Grierson, P.   1955   'The Canterbury (St Martins)
                                      Hoard of Frankish and Anglo-
                                      Saxon Coin-Ornaments',
                                      B.N.J. XXVII (1955), 39–52.
Grimes, W. F.   1956   'Excavations in the City of
                                      London', in Bruce Mitford
                                      (Ed.), *Recent Archaeological Ex-
                                      cavations* . . . (1956), 167–97.
Hill, P. V.   1948   'Sceatta like Barbarous Imita-
                                      tions', *N.C.* 6th Ser., VIII
                                      (1948), 142–57.
Hill, P. V.   1950   'Barbarous Imitations of Fourth
                                      Century Roman Coins', *N.C.*
                                      6th Ser., X (1950), 233–76.

Hill, P. V.   1952a   'Coinage of Britain in the Dark
                                                   Age', *B.N.J.* XXVI (1952),
                                                   1–27.

Hill, P. V.   1952b   'Saxon Sceattas and Their
                                                   Problems', *B.N.J.* XXVI
                                                   (1952), 129–155.

Hill, P. V.   1952c   'The Standard and the London
                                                   Series of Anglo-Saxon Sceattas',
                                                   B.N.J. XXVI (1952), 251–80.

Hill, P. V.   1955a   'Barbarous Roman Coins', *N.C.*
                                                   6th Ser., XV (1955), 233–76.

Hill, P. V.   1955b   'Animal, Anglo-Merovingian
                                                   and Miscellaneous Series of
                                                   Saxon Sceattas', *B.N.J.* XXVII
                                                   (1955), 1–39.

Hurst, J. G.   1959   'White Castle and the Dating
                                                   of Medieval Pottery', *Med.
                                                   Arch.* III (1959), 13–31.

Jope, E. M. & Rigold, S. E.   1950   'Pottery from a late Twelfth
                                                   Century Well and other Medi-
                                                   eval Finds at St John's College,
                                                   Oxford', *Oxon.* XV (1950).
                                                   44–62.

Jope, E. M. & Stewart, B. H.   1959   'A Hoard of Fifteenth Century
                                                   Coins From Glenluce and their
                                                   Context', *Med. Arch.* III
                                                   (1959), 259–79.

Kay, L.   1966   'Northumbrian Sceats as a
                                                   Challenge to Numismatists',
                                                   N.A.J.N. V (1966), 109–15.

Kendrick, T. D.   1938   *Anglo-Saxon Art* (1938).

Kent, J. P. C.   1952   'Coins and the Evacuation of
                                                   Hadrian's Wall', *Trans.C. &
                                                   W.A. & A.S.* LI (1952), 4–16.

Kent, J. P. C.   1954   'The Search for Fifth Century
                                                   Coins in Britain', *Arch. N.L.*
                                                   (1954), 115–19.

Kent, J. P. C.   1959   'Barbarous Copies of Roman
                                                   Coins' in *Limes-Studien* (Proc.
                                                   3rd Int. Cong. on *Limes*),
                                                   (1959), 66 f.

Kent, J. P. C.   1961   'From Roman Britain to Saxon
                                                   England', in Dolley (Ed.),
                                                   Anglo-Saxon Coins (1961), 1–23.

Leeds, E. T.   1936   *Anglo-Saxon Art and Archaeology*
                                        (1936).
Levison, W.   1946   *England and the Continent in the*
                                        Eighth Century (1946).
Loyn, H. R.   1961   'Boroughs and Mints, AD 900–
                                        1066', in Dolley (Ed.), *Anglo-*
                                        Saxon Coins, (1961). 122–35
Loyn, H. R.   1962   *Anglo-Saxon England and the*
                                        Norman Conquest (1962).
Mattingly, H. &   1939   'The Richborough Hoard of
    Stebbing, W. P. D.   Radiates', *N.N.M.* **80** (1939).
Meert, C.   1960   'European Sterlings of Edwar-
                                        dian Type', *S.C.M.B.* April,
                                        1960, 134–6.
Metcalf, D. M.   1967   'A Stylistic Analysis of the
                                        "Porcupine" Sceattas', *N.C.*
                                        7th Ser., VI (1967), 179–205.
North, J. J.   1960   *English Hammered Coinage, II*
                                        (1960).
North, J. J.   1963   *English Hammered Coinage, I*
                                        (1963).
Philips, C. W.   1956   'Excavation of the Sutton Hoo
                                        Ship Burial', in Bruce Mitford
                                        (Ed.), *Recent Archaeological Ex-*
                                        cavations . . . (1956), 145–67.
Rahtz, P. A.   1960   'Excavations by the Town Wall
                                        Baldwin Street, Bristol', *Trans.*
                                        B. & G. A. S. LXXIX (1960),
                                        221–51.
Ravetz, A.   1965   'Fourth Century Inflation and
                                        Romano-British Coin Finds',
                                        N.C. 7th Ser., IV (1965),
                                        201–35.
Rigold, S. E.   1952   'The Trail of the Easterlings',
                                        B.N.J. VI (1952), 31–56.
Rigold, S. E.   1954   'An Imperial Coinage in
                                        Southern Gaul in the 6th and
                                        7th centuries?' *N.C.* 6th Ser.,
                                        XIV (1954), 93–140.
Rigold, S. E.   1962   'The Two Primary Series of
                                        Sceattas', *B.N.J.* XXX (1962),
                                        6–54.
Sawyer, P.   1962   *The Age of the Vikings* (1962).
Seaby, H. A.   1948   *Notes on English Silver Coins,*
                                        1066–1648 (1948).

Seaby, P. J.   1967   'Some Cuerdale Queries', *S.C.M.B.* June-Sept. 1967.

Spufford, P.   1963   'Continental Coins in Late Medieval England', *B.N.J.* XXXII (1962), 74–9.

Stenton, D. M.   1952   *English Society in the Early Middle Ages* (1952).

Stewart, I. H.   1955   *The Scottish Coinage* (1955).

Stone, J. F. S. & Charlton, J.   1935   'Trial Excavations in the East Suburb of Old Sarum', *Arch. J.* XV (1935), 174–248.

Stride, H. G.   1959   'The Trial of the Pyx', *S.C.M.B.* Aug.–Oct. 1959.

Sutherland, C. H. V.   1936   'Minimi, Radiate and Diademed', *Trans. Inter. Num. Cong.* (1936), 252–65.

Sutherland, C. H. V.   1937   *Coinage and Currency in Roman Britain* (1937).

Sutherland, C. H. V.   1942   'Anglo-Saxon Sceattas in England, Their Origin, Chronology and Distribution', *N.C.* 6th Ser., II (1942), 42–76.

Sutherland, C. H. V.   1948   *Anglo-Saxon Gold Coinage in the Light of the Crondall Hoard* (1948).

Sutherland, C. H. V.   1956   'Coinage in Britain in the Fifth and Sixth Centuries', in Harden (Ed.), *Dark Age Britain* (1956), 1–10.

Talbot Rice, D.   1952   *English Art, 871–1100* (1952).

Thomas, A. C.   1959   'Imported Dark Age Pottery in Western Britain', *Med. Arch.* III (1959), 89–111.

Thomas, A. C.   1964   'The Coveted Isles', in Talbot Rice (Ed.), *The Dark Ages* (1964), 241–68.

Thompson, E.   1951   'Continental Imitations of the Rose Noble of Edward IV', *B.N.J.* XXV (1951), 185–209.

Thompson, J. D. A.   1956   *Inventory of British Coin Hoards, AD 600–1500* (1956).

Wheeler, R. E. M.   1932   *Excavations at Lydney Park, Gloucestershire* (1932).

Whitelock, D.   1952   *The Beginnings of English Society*, (1952).

Whitting, P. D.   1961   'The Byzantine Empire and the
                                            Coinage of the Anglo-Saxons',
                                            in Dolley (Ed.). *Anglo-Saxon
                                            Coins* (1961), 23–9.
Whitting, P. D.   1966   *British Coinage and the Pyx Trial*,
                                            (1966).
Wilson, D. M.   1960   *The Anglo-Saxons* (1960).
Wilson, D. M. & Blunt, C. E.   1961   'The Trewhiddle Hoard', *Arch.*
                                            XCIX (1961), 75–123.

Index